THE COLOR OF THE LAND

THE COLOR OF THE LAN

■ ■ ■ ■ ■ ■ ■ ■ ■

THE UNIVERSITY OF NORTH CAROLINA PRESS *Chapel Hill*

Race, Nation, and the Politics of

Landownership in Oklahoma, 1832–1929

DAVID A. CHANG

Library of Congress Cataloging-in-Publication Data
Chang, David A.
The color of the land : race, nation, and the politics of landownership in Oklahoma, 1832–1929 / David A. Chang.   p. cm.
Includes bibliographical references and index.
ISBN 978-0-8078-3365-0 (cloth : alk. paper) — ISBN 978-0-8078-7106-5 (pbk. : alk. paper)
1. Creek Indians—Land tenure—Oklahoma—History. 2. Creek Indians—Oklahoma—Ethnic identity. 3. Allotment of land—Oklahoma—History. 4. Land tenure—Social aspects—Oklahoma—History. 5. African Americans—Land tenure—Oklahoma—History. 6. Whites—Land tenure—Oklahoma—History. 7. Oklahoma—Race relations—History.
I. Title.   E99.C9C428 2010   305.8009766—dc22   2009027708

cloth   14 13 12 11 10   5 4 3 2 1
paper   14 13 12 11 10   5 4 3 2 1

Contents

Illustrations, Maps, and Tables

ILLUSTRATIONS

MAPS

TABLES

Acknowledgments

It astonishes me how fortunate I have been to benefit from the help of so many talented people at every stage of the development of this book. At the University of Wisconsin–Madison, Linda Gordon was a model of rigorous scholarship and political commitment. I will always remain grateful for her generosity to me in time and advice. I am thankful to William Cronon, whose intellectual vigor and breadth made this a better project. Thanks to Ned Blackhawk for helping me begin to understand the place of my work in American Indian history. Tim Tyson's unbelievably rapid and insightful readings of my work were a gift I will not forget. Thanks to Jess Gilbert for his close reading of this work and his excellent suggestions for ways to improve it. At Madison, friends provided warm camaraderie and intellectual challenge, and I am grateful to Reid Paul, Monica Najar, Sarah Fatherly, Eric Morser, Louise Pubols, Shelby Balik, T. J. Mertz, Ellen Baker, Dorothea Browder, Sarah Marcus, and Marsha Weisiger, my first guide to Oklahoma. Thanks to Joe Hall and William Philpott for crucial early critiques of my ideas and writing.

Teachers and guides in Oklahoma provided invaluable help. Danney Goble, Don Pisani, and Circe Sturm in Norman gave a warm welcome, much needed encouragement, and very useful suggestions for research. Brad Raley provided a much appreciated helping hand. Rufus Cox generously shared his remarkable knowledge of and insight into Creek history with a newcomer. Robert Guess and his family took the time to share their memories and their insights into the history of their family, and while few of their words are here, they helped me greatly. Napoleon Davis shared his wealth of historical knowledge and inspired me with his dedication to the history of his people. Thanks to Joe Long for his kindness and *mahalo nui loa* to Doobie Potter for an unexpected Hawaiian welcome on the prairie.

I am grateful to professionals at research institutions around the country who skillfully guided me toward the treasures in their keeping. I am grateful to the extraordinary Pete Daniel and Rayna Green at the Smithsonian for their guidance and inspiration. Thanks to Bill Welge and Phyllis Adams and the rest of the wonderful people at the Oklahoma Historical Society, John Lovett and Kristina Southwell at the Western History Collections at the University of Oklahoma Library, Joyce Bear and Emman Spain at the Cultural Preservation Office of the Muscogee (Creek) Nation, Kent Carter and others at National Archives and Records Administration (NARA)–Fort Worth, and the helpful staffs at the Oklahoma State Archives, the Creek Council House Museum, the Muskogee Public Library, the National Archives, the Library of Congress, the Mary McLeod Bethune Archives, and the extraordinary Wisconsin Historical Society Library.

At the University of Minnesota, I have the privilege to work with scholars of high caliber and people of character who have challenged and encouraged me and made this work far better than it would otherwise have been. Jean O'Brien-Kehoe was a true mentor, and I am grateful for her encouragement and honesty. Many thanks to her and to Mary Jo Maynes and Erika Lee for their generous and helpful reading of an early version of this manuscript and to Michael Lower and Lianna Farber for their invaluable reading of it in its final stages. Thanks to Kay Reyerson for her early guidance at Minnesota and to Ann Waltner, Barbara Welke, Brenda Child, and Gary Cohen for their support and helpful conversations. I am grateful to the Markets in Time reading group and its members Tracey Deutsch, Karen Ho, George Henderson, Jeff Crump, and Eric Sheppard for helping me think through central issues in this book. Thanks also to Keith Mayes, Karen-Sue Taussig, Malinda Lindquist, and Kevin Murphy for crucial help in the process of creating a book. Wonderful friends like Kristin Sziarto, Ryan Holifield, Debra Farkas, Moira McDonald, and Ann Wilner sustained me through that process with their kindness.

This work benefited immeasurably from the painstaking labor of Jenny Tone-Pah-Hote, Chantal Norrgard, Andrea Robertson, Robert Gilmer, Kate Rainey, and Georgia Noyan. Thank you so much for your help. Many thanks to Mark Lindberg and Mike Foster of the University of Minnesota Cartography Laboratory for their stellar and generous work on the maps.

I am grateful to Chuck Grench at the University of North Carolina Press for ushering this book through the publication process, to Paula Wald and Katy O'Brien for their much needed guidance, and to the anonymous readers of the manuscript for their excellent and careful suggestions. Grace Carino's expert copyediting greatly improved the clarity and style of this book.

I benefited from helpful input and words of support from many scholars along the way. Thanks to Claudio Saunt, Tiya Miles, Celia Naylor, Circe Sturm, Barbara Krauthamer, Phil Deloria, Ray Fogelson, Fred Hoxie, Bonnie Lynn-Sherow, J. Kēhaulani Kauanui, Noenoe Silva, Tol Foster, William Hart, and Laura Edwards for their kind encouragement and insightful guidance.

For their generous support in terms of funding and time away from teaching, I am grateful to the University of Wisconsin Department of History, the University of Wisconsin College of Arts and Sciences, the Wisconsin Alumni Research Fund, the Lincoln Institute for Land Policy, the Western History Association, the Smithsonian Institution, the University of Minnesota Department of History, the University of Minnesota College of Liberal Arts, and the Institute for Advanced Study at the University of Minnesota.

This book is a tribute to my parents, Anne Therese Craig and Joseph S. M. J. Chang. I thank my father. His pride in his Hawaiian ancestry and his love for all things Hawaiian were the seeds of my dedication to indigenous studies. My mother taught me the elements of writing. If this book contains any passages graced by a felicity of style, they should be heard in her voice. I thank my parents for their love and support, which sustained me in the writing of this book. My brothers and sisters are all heroes to me in their own ways. Each one of them inspires me, and I thank Aileen, Sarah, Joe, and John and their families for this inspiration and their love. Al and Sharon Deutsch have been unstintingly generous in their confidence in me.

Most of all, I am thankful to Tracey Deutsch, whose love and encouragement and intellectual fellowship have meant more to me than I can ever say. She has constantly challenged me to see the meaning and power in what might seem the most prosaic of words or the most mundane of actions. Without her insights I would never have arrived at the ideas in this book. Without her help, I'm quite sure I never would have finished. Tracey has made every day of the years I spent with this book better. For all of this, for her humor and her commitment to justice and most of all for her love, I am grateful.

This book is dedicated to my sons, Gabriel and Nathaniel. I am so thankful you have come into our lives. You fill me with joy and hope. "He hiʻi alo ua milimili ʻia i ke alo, ua haʻawe ʻia ma ke kua, ua lei ʻia ma ka ʻāʻī."[1]

THE COLOR OF THE LAND

████████ ████████████ ██ ████████ ██████████ ████

Oklahoma as America

"Oklahoma" means "red man" in the Choctaw language, is run though by a "Black Belt," and has been claimed by some as "white man's country." It has been termed an Indian homeland, a black promised land, and a white heartland.[1] All these competing racial claims to one place seem extraordinary. This book suggests, however, that Oklahoma is really exceptional only because it encapsulates so much American history within its borders, revealing much about how the struggle over land has given shape to the way Americans—indigenous, black, and white—created and gave meaning to races and nations.

Phrases like the ones above mark Oklahoma with a race and tie that race to the land. Of course, land itself cannot have a race. Race is a way that we imagine differences between people and make hierarchies among them seem right and natural. So racializing a land (marking it with a race) really means tying it to a particular people, whether they be Creek Indians, African Americans, white Americans, or some other group that we believe can be identified racially in some way. After all, speaking of "a land" is also a way of speaking of a country or a nation. The title of this book is an attempt to evoke this relationship between land, race, and nationhood. This book considers both the symbolic power people give land in such terms as "homeland," "Black Belt," or "white man's country" and the economic power that land possesses. Oklahoma, like the rest of America, was until recently a largely rural and agricultural society. Land was a foundational form of wealth, a source of power, and an object of contention in that society. To understand the differences of wealth and power between people of different races, we must understand the place of land in their histories. *The Color of the Land* tells part of this story through the history of the Creek Nation and its lands, which now constitute much of east-central Oklahoma. This is a place that straddles the South and the West. Here, just as cotton fields abutted ranchlands, southern history collides with western history. The past of east-central Oklahoma brings together the histories of American Indians, African Americans, and white Americans.

The nature of this story is suggested by two iconic images that the words "Oklahoma history" might call up for many Americans. In the first, a covered wagon rumbles westward across the prairie. A white settler family makes its way to a fine patch of virgin grassland that the father has already claimed when he, along with thousands of other white men on horseback, made a mad dash at the signal of a starting gun to stake a homestead in the Oklahoma Land Run of 1889. The second image that might come to mind is an overburdened jalopy chugging down Route 66. In it, the Joads in John Steinbeck's *The Grapes of Wrath* (1939) head westward out of Oklahoma, leaving the desolation of the Dust Bowl behind. This pair of images is telling. The covered wagon heading in is paired with the broken-down car heading out. Together, the images frame the story of white settlement with movement: the arrival of white settlers in 1889 and the departure of their children only forty years later. If one looks a little more closely, they also frame that story with the issue of landownership. The settlers of 1889 came in search of farmland. The Joads left, Steinbeck tells us, because as landless tenant farmers, they could be blown off the land like so much dust by the whim of the cotton market and the order of a bank.[2] For all the short-comings of these images (where are the Indians? the blacks? the oil? the Oklahomans who *stayed* in the state in the 1930s?), they capture a certain truth. The history of Oklahoma is a history of movement, possession, and dispossession. It is American history told in fast-forward. It captures the dynamics of global history in the middle of a continent.

In east-central Oklahoma, peoples who traced their ancestry to indigenous America, Europe, and Africa came, worked the land, and then to a large extent either had it taken from them or left it behind. The history of this region is not only, or even primarily, the story of white settlers, although movies and novels have often told it that way. It is the story of the coming of the Creeks, who made their living and society on that land and saw it mostly wrested from them. It is also the story of black people, both

Creek and African American, who worked the land of Oklahoma in slavery and freedom and made a claim for it. This book tells the story of three peoples in one place. It traces how those peoples came to understand themselves as nations and as races in their struggles over that land and especially the ownership of it.

By the 1870s, white Americans had filled Arkansas and Missouri to the east, Texas to the south, and Kansas to the north with their plantations, ranches, and farms. In the center lay Indian Territory, present-day Oklahoma, the home of more than two dozen sovereign indigenous nations. Whites wanted the lands of those nations for their homesteads. The demand grew only more strident when the federal government unleashed the Land Run of 1889, in which whites staked claims in the "Unassigned Territories," former Creek and Seminole lands west of the Creek Nation. More land runs followed. Instead of relieving the pressures on Indian lands, each intensified the demands by whites for the lands of the Five Tribes in Indian Territory—the Cherokees, Chickasaws, Choctaws, Creeks, and Seminoles. Soon after Oklahoma had become a state in 1907, most Indians had been stripped of their land. But instead of becoming farm owners, most white Americans in the region became farm tenants. Poverty brutalized the tenant farmers, and the farmers brutalized the delicate soils of the prairie. East-central Oklahoma was located hundreds of miles east of the true Dust Bowl but was nonetheless devastated by soil exhaustion, erosion, and drought. The farm depression of the 1920s was followed by a general depression in the 1930s. When drought hit at the same time, the brief history of the cotton fields of Oklahoma began to come to an end.

A decades-long exodus from rural eastern Oklahoma began in the 1930s.[3] The most famous of the migrants were the white "Okies" who headed west. Many remained agricultural proletarians: like the Joads, Oklahoma sharecroppers became California migrant fruit pickers or Arizona cotton laborers. The migration was most famously white, but to accept this image is to misunderstand profoundly Oklahoma and the nation that sometimes calls it its "heartland." Some black farmers left rural eastern Oklahoma for the same western locations to which their white neighbors were headed, but others joined the stream of African American migrants to the great cities of the industrial Midwest. Creek Indians had particularly powerful ties to the region and reasons not to leave, but many of them, too, joined the emigrant streams. Creek names—Fixico and Harjo and Grayson and Perryman and others—can now be found in the phone books of metropoli-

MAP 1. Oklahoma and Indian Territories, 1886–1889. (Adapted from John W. Morris, Charles R. Goins, and Edwin C. McReynolds, *Historical Atlas of Oklahoma*, 3rd ed. [Norman: University of Oklahoma Press, 1986], 55.)

tan areas across the United States. Most Creeks remained in the region, but by the 1930s they owned only scraps of a landscape that had been almost unrecognizably altered by a forty-year experience of intensive commercial agriculture.

THE COLOR OF THE LAND, a history of landownership in the Creek Nation and eastern Oklahoma, uses a regionally focused study of rural land tenure to consider major issues in the history of American society and politics: southern slavery, western conquest, Indian resistance, the making of black and white and Indian peoples, the making of rich and poor, radical social movements and their suppression. It places emphasis on the Creek people and the lands that constituted its national domain until Oklahoma statehood in 1907. This people and this region are of particular interest because they were racially heterogeneous and the land was farmed in ways that depended on hierarchies of power between people. Studying the politics of race among Creeks therefore sheds light on the complexities of American Indian identities and polities. It suggests the ways that race and racial politics in this Indian society compare to more familiar histories of race and racial politics in the United States. Native Americans, African Americans, and whites in eastern Oklahoma all engaged in agriculture, and relations between these groups frequently centered on who owned the land, who rented it, who farmed it or pastured cattle on it or mined it, and who would profit from its use. These struggles over access and control of the crucial

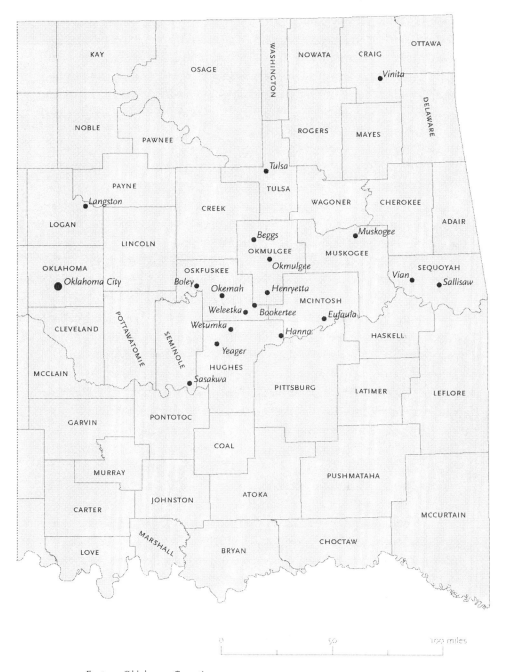

MAP 2. Eastern Oklahoma Counties, 1910

form of capital in this rural society therefore also hinged upon relations of class, both between and within racial groups. And although this region was in some ways exceptional, it encapsulates in its history central issues in American history: chattel slavery; the enclosure of the commons for private profit; conflicts between ranchers and farmers; the dispossession of Native peoples; and struggles between landlords and tenants. Finally, this region concentrates many of these issues not only in space but also in time. In most of the nation, the transition from Native American semicommunal ownership to the beginnings of agribusiness took at least a century and a half. In Oklahoma, it took only about forty years. This rapid, violent transformation of Oklahoma throws into stark relief patterns of Native American land loss, black landlessness, and white class divisions that are emblematic of the history of landownership across the United States.

As much as *The Color of the Land* is a book about land, it is also a book about ideas. I investigate how the meanings of nation and race have changed over time for three of America's historically foundational "races": Indians (specifically Creek Indians), whites, and blacks. Yet this is not the kind of history of ideas that spends most of its time looking at intellectuals or even highly educated individuals. More often, I look for ideas in the actions and words of Creek town *miccos* (often translated as "kings") or black farm tenants or white small-town politicians. I look to their actions and voices because I suspect they are expressing ideas that others felt but did not put so plainly or that were never recorded. This is a history, then, about political ideas of inclusion and exclusion, of belonging and not belonging, of equality and inequality. It is a history of race and nation, and it demonstrates the ways that these ideas sometimes coincided and sometimes did not. The story of Creek notions of nationhood and struggles among black and white people over nationhood help us to understand that there are multiple kinds of nation in American history. This book suggests that ideas of race and nation exist in dynamic relation to property, land, and the means of production. It argues that excluding or appropriating wealth goes with excluding people, and it demonstrates how that exclusion has proceeded along the lines of race and nation.

Land is not, of course, just any form of wealth, and many Creek people in this book contended that it was inappropriate to treat it as private wealth at all. *The Color of the Land* argues that land has been central to the ways people in the Creek Nation and the United States have defined their races, nations, and classes. Historians and theorists writing on American nationalism and the making and remaking of American races (or racial formation, as it is sometimes called) have dedicated much attention to immigration, slavery, law, labor, and other issues but surprisingly little to land.[4] Even historians of the West, where land played a central issue in national and racial self-definition, have dedicated relatively little attention to this issue.[5] For the people in this study, land loomed large in the way they understood themselves and their relations to others. For most Creeks in Indian Territory in the nineteenth century, land was homeland, inseparable from the polity of the nation. It was a means of defending the autonomy of Creek farmers and the sovereignty of the people as a whole. For African American settlers from the South, it represented the hope to establish themselves as a truly free and politically empowered race within the American nation. For poor white settlers from the South and Midwest, Oklahoma lands represented the hope to fulfill a birthright denied, to take on the yeoman status to which they believed their whiteness entitled them. Land was thus the physical manifestation of the nation, the earth in which races took root, and the capital over which the landless and the landed struggled. Nation, race, and class converged in land.

To understand this intersection of nation, racial construction, and class conflict, we must look at the ideas and practices of nonwhite and nonelite people as well as those of white elites, who have traditionally dominated American cultural and intellectual history. Although the recently reinvigorated research on American nationalism is invaluable, the national identities and nationalisms it studies are overwhelmingly those of white people.[6] This tendency is not new. Indeed, one of the most important precursors to contemporary studies of American national identity is Edmund Morgan's *American Slavery, American Freedom* (1975). In this study of colonial Virginia, which has deservedly influenced generations of scholars including myself, Morgan demonstrates that white American freedom depended upon African American slavery. The ideas of freedom and nationhood that he studies, however, are those of whites, not blacks.[7] Similarly, scholarship on racial construction has tended to consider the ways that more powerful people elaborated ideologies of difference that legitimated their authority over less powerful peoples. Much of the energy behind this literature has come from scholars of white racial formation who, though hardly focused on the white elite, have centered their work on the ideas of those people who drew the wages of whiteness—whites themselves.[8] Again, the tendency is well established. The title of George Frederickson's *The Black Image in the White Mind* captures the essential concern of a large body of works that investigate white racial ideologies about people of African, Asian, indigenous American, and Latin American descent.[9] The ways that these "non-white" racialized peoples have understood racial difference, however, have received less attention. Innovative works such as Mia Bay's *The White Image in the Black Mind* (2000) and Nancy Shoemaker's investigation of Indian racial ideology have begun to explore how African Americans and Native Americans have perceived white people and other people against whom they have defined themselves.[10] Nonetheless, much work remains to be done in considering how whites' "others"—such as Native Americans, African Americans, Asian Americans, Chicanos and Latinos, and Hawaiians—have imagined their own races, their own nations.

It is important to note that creating a national state is not synonymous with creating a nation, and neither is synonymous with nationalism. Both the national state and the nation are ideas that rose to dominance in Europe and the areas of European colonialism in the eighteenth century—in fact, the period when they came to prominence among Creek people. To my mind, a national state is an administrative structure that rules a nation and asserts that it has the right to rule that nation because it emerges from it. A nation, in contrast, is a group of people that has a sense of itself as set apart from all others by some combination of factors. These might include history, language, religion, artistic tradition, ancestry, homeland, or other factors. I would emphasize, however, that people who believe they are part of a nation commonly believe they have a shared future. It is here that a sense of national identity can become *nationalism*, which I use to describe a kind of political program that is built around the nation. One of the most powerful claims nationalism makes on members of the nation is that, because they have a shared future, they must act as one to achieve a better future. In other words, the claim that the nation *is* one unified group becomes a demand that all members *act* as one unified group. In addition to demanding this sort of allegiance to a national program and enforcing it by means of the national state, nationalists have often shored up their claim to the internal unity of the nation by removing those people whom they consider outsiders.

There is much to be gained from examining American Indian "tribalism" in the context of the rich historical literature on nationalism. Decades of efforts by indigenous people to revindicate their national sovereignty should direct historians' attention to the national dimension in the Native American past. American Indians have had recourse to a wide variety of concepts of tribe and nation, and their racial self-constructions have evolved in dynamic relation to their ideas about tribe and nation. Fundamental to understanding Native American history is the realization that, as David Wilkins puts it simply, "Indian peoples are nations, not minorities."[11] Historical studies of tribalism (understood in contemporary studies as an ideology or movement that emphasizes the particularity of a tribe in order to pursue the goals of at least some of its members) generally situate themselves in opposition to essentialist ethnographic literature on identity.[12] Since 1980, historical literature has emphasized the dynamic relation between federal policy and American Indian tribal identities, exploring in differing ways how federal policy has enforced tribal boundaries both spatially, in the making of reservations, and socially, in the process of enrolling tribal members.[13] The federal government has reinforced nationalism (in the guise of tribalism) by giving it power in policy, but the idea of nations in American Indian identity does not spring just from relations with colonial powers and spreads far beyond relations with Washington. Pan-Indianism, for example, asserts the fundamental unity of all Native American peoples, which would seem to contradict the idea of multiple Native American nations. By maintaining, however, that American Indian peoples share a history that mandates a common program to achieve a better future for all, pan-Indianism gives American Indian identity a national shape and throws light on the central place of nationalism in Native American politics and identity.[14]

Indigenous scholars have brought nationalism to the center of American Indian studies through their work on American Indian literary nationalism. None has been more important to this effort than Craig Womack, a Creek scholar and critic. Womack explores the Creek literary tradition, tracing the ways that it (like other Native American literatures) expresses and transmits "a people's idea of themselves, their imaginings of who they are." My subject in this book is not literary, but I proceed from the same insistence as Womack's that we seek "a tribal voice" that "gives sovereignty a meaning that is defined within the tribe rather than by external sources."[15] Indeed, I argue that listening to multiple tribal voices on Creek sovereignty reveals that different Creeks, though equally dedicated to sovereignty, gave different meanings to their nationhood.

The discourse of nationhood has similarly had a long and rich history in African American life, yet it has not received the attention that it deserves in the rapidly growing literature on relations between black and Indian peoples. Different African Americans at different times have pursued their goals as citizens of the American nation, or as citizens of a nation within a nation, or via the internationalist nationalism of pan-Africanism. In all these political identities, they have continually defined and redefined the national meaning of being African American. Before there was a United States, people from different African ethnic groups had created an African American identity with both racial and national dimensions. Enslaved Africans turned their ethnic heterogeneity into a more unified identity in the struggle to survive the trials of slavery.[16] This process was, however, an ongoing project. The complexity of African American life—cultural variety, regional differences, class divisions, Caribbean and African immigration— guaranteed that this process would continue on through the nineteenth and twentieth centuries and into the twenty-first. From at least the early nineteenth century, African Americans of various ideological stripes have engaged nationalism in their efforts to understand their past and unity as a people, their efforts to obtain rights within the American nation, or their pursuit of cultural, religious, economic, and political self-determination and self-sufficiency. Scholars of twentieth-century immigration have considered the complex relations of race and nation that both united and separated twentieth-century Afro-Caribbean immigrants and U.S.-born African Americans.[17] The study of Native American peoples of African descent has developed rapidly in recent years, but it has mostly emphasized the place that people of African descent occupied in Native American societies.[18] While this focus is essential to understanding the experience of black members of Native American polities and those polities themselves, it makes it difficult to place their history in the context of African American history. This book contends that considering the history of relations between Indian citizens of African descent and other African American people helps us better understand the ways racialized peoples have made and remade races and nations in American history.

This study demonstrates how complex ideas of nationhood evolved in relation to the racial self-constructions of Creek Indians and African Americans as well as white Americans. It further argues that in this rural context class conflict over landownership gave added impetus to the already potent politics of race and nation. At the turn of the twentieth century, when the federal government forcibly divided Creek common lands into privately owned plots, some Creeks came increasingly to identify their nation as a group of people with indigenous Creek ancestry and possibly some European ancestry as well, but no black ancestry. For some Creeks, race came to define the nation, although this idea always existed in tension with the older and still vital notion that "Creek" is fundamentally a political status independent of race. For African Americans, the process was almost the inverse: discourses of nationhood helped to establish racial unity, in large part around the goal of black landownership. The defense of African Americans' rights as U.S. citizens and a nationalist effort to build autonomous, affluent, and landed black towns gave power to the idea of a unified black race.

This understanding of the construction of Creek, African American, and white American racial and national identities makes two fundamental contributions. First, it emphasizes that Americans have constructed race and nation, these two quintessentially modern ways of forming and mobilizing identities, in relation to each other. Second, it brings together the study of discourses of race and nation with the material consideration of class conflict over land. This book emphasizes that these modes of analysis are not only compatible but also necessary to each other. The study of class conflict has much to offer the study of racial and national identity, and vice versa.

Chapter Summary

This book is organized into three parts, with the first dedicated to the ways that Creek nationhood and Creek systems of property were made and contested from the eighteenth century through the post–Civil War period, the second considering the racial politics of the debate over the American imposition of private land title (allotment), and the third tracing the working out of a politics of race and land under the order of property that allotment created. Part I (Chapters 1 and 2), on the period prior to allotment, explores how in the Creek Nation the struggle to create, take, and retain possession of property in land was inseparable from questions of nationhood, race, and the control of labor. In Chapter 1, I trace the ways that events in the Creek Nation's homeland in Alabama and Georgia set the stage for an intensification of the practice of private land use after removal to what is now Oklahoma. In the years stretching from the 1780s to the beginning of the Civil War, a powerful and wealthy minority of Creeks adopted Euro-American ideas and practices of race, chattel slavery, and nationalism. These ideas served the interests and the power of this elite minority but divided the nation into factions that faced off in a number of conflicts, including the U.S. Civil War. Chapter 2 explores contending visions of Creek nationhood. I turn my sights to the small-scale farmers who made up the majority of the Creek Nation—a nation that included, in the wake of emancipation, a sizable black citizenry. This small-farmer majority, both black and Indian, had a common stake in defending Creek national lands. That shared interest underlay the construction of a remarkable political alliance that resisted the effort by the elite to consolidate wealth and power and impose a form of racial nationalism on the Creek Nation.

Part II, which consists of Chapter 3, explores the racial politics of the privatization of landownership (a process known as allotment). White agrarianism, white racial nationalism, and even a desire to remake Indians into American yeomen and liberal individuals drove the push to force the unwilling Creeks to accept allotment and the dissolution of their governmental authority. The chapter shows how allotment, a colonial imposition, propelled a politics that undermined the sense of a Creek nationhood that transcended racial lines.

Part III (Chapters 4, 5, and 6) describes the aftermath of allotment, with a chapter each focusing on Creeks, African Americans, and whites. Chapter 4 traces how public policy was crucial to the making of a capitalist order in Oklahoma after statehood in 1907. Along with taxation and credit, a critical policy in the making of a landlord elite and a landless tenantry was the principle that race was fixed and unchanging. In a context of rapid land loss, Creeks engaged in a combination of explicitly political action, politically charged cultural and spiritual practices, and day-to-day resistance to challenge the denial of their national autonomy, the loss of their lands, and the cultural transformations that allotment was intended to bring about. Chapter 5 considers how, in a context of Jim Crow, disenfranchisement, and deepening economic inequality, African Americans and Creeks of African descent, who had long been suspicious of each other, redrew the lines of race and nation to defend the racial community. Chapter 6 traces the ways that poor whites challenged the emerging economic order that denied them the place in society to which they felt entitled by dint of their race. It argues that the white elite called upon a racialized sense of white American national unity to undercut working-class insurgency in the state. Land remained an important part of this effort, despite an economic and political environment that was hostile to poor whites' retaining it.

In the Epilogue, I draw on the history and changing fortunes of one Creek family, the Haynes-Lerblance-Cox lineage, to argue that the issues of property, race, and nationhood that ran through political and class conflict in the region in the late nineteenth century and early twentieth are not relegated to the past or to Oklahoma. They continue to animate American life today. Considering the history of the Creek Nation and east-central Oklahoma can compel us to rethink the categories of race and nation, their relation to each other, and their relation to class and economic conflict.

A Note on Usage

The complexities of the terminology of identity merit discussion. "Full-blood," "mixed blood," and "blood quantum" were frequently used terms in Indian Territory in the period under consideration. Scholars and activists today correctly denounce these terms as racist, nonindigenous in derivation, and part of a political project that limits Indianness and tribal membership to biological categories instead of recognizing that they are political categories. Explaining the evolution of the racial schema that these terms describe is part of my larger project in this book. That racial schema was and remains powerful. The current Creek constitution, adopted in 1974, follows federal enrollments from the early twentieth century when it declares that Creek citizenship is reserved for individuals who are "Muscogee (Creek) Indian by blood."[19] Given the power of this terminology, I refer to and sometimes use the terminology of "blood," but only in the context of a larger argument that emphasizes the role that federal policy and struggles among Indian people played in giving power to notions of "blood." Similarly, this study emphasizes that the Creek Nation is a polity born of the modern era that was created by the confederation of different peoples. For that reason, I use the term "Creek" to describe members of that society no matter what the proportion of their indigenous, African, and European ancestries, while nonetheless describing how Creeks and others created and gave power to the divisions of race and ancestry that existed among them.

I use the words "Native," "American Indian," "Indian," and "indigenous" somewhat interchangeably to refer to people identified by ancestry and political affiliation with the original peoples of North America. I use the term "Creek" rather than "Muskogee" because the latter originally referred to just one of the language groups in the nation. I generally reserve the term "African American" for people of African descent from the United States (and thus not those from the Creek Nation) until Chapter 5, when I describe the racial coalescence of these two groups. Drawing on the postemancipation Indian Territory phrase "colored Creek," I term people of African descent who were socially or politically part of the Creek Nation "black Creeks." In this book, the problematic term "black" signals situations in which racialized status is becoming or has become determinative. For more on terminology and the use of the word "conservative" as it refers to a Creek cultural and (I argue) political and economic orientation, please see Chapter 2, note 4.

PART I

Before Allotment

LAND AND THE MAKING OF CREEK NATIONHOODS

*From the 1700s to the late 1800s, questions of owning
(land, objects, people, and crops) and belonging (to families,
towns, races, and nations) were at the center of Creek history.
Established Creek practices of communal ownership confronted
new ways of using land for private gain. Long-held means
of social inclusion butted up against new ways of defining
Creeks in opposition to racial and national outsiders. Chapter 1 traces how conflict over property and power, and related
notions of race, slavery, and nationhood, divided Creeks from
the 1760s forward. Those divisions ultimately led them to
take opposing sides in the American Civil War. As Chapter 2
recounts, in its aftermath, Creeks faced off over who was Creek
and would enjoy the use of the lands of the Creek Nation.*

Owning and Being Owned

PROPERTY, SLAVERY, AND CREEK NATIONHOOD TO 1865

On January 18, 1802, an American man named Benjamin Hawkins walked through Tuskegee, a Creek town perched on a bluff above the point where the Coosa and Tallapoosa rivers meet in present-day Alabama. In his account of the visit, he made particular note of where the people of Tuskegee raised their crops. He remarked on the large fields across the Tallapoosa and admired the "small patches well formed in the fork of the rivers, in the rich flat land below the bluff."[1] It was January, so no one was working in those fields. But if Hawkins had come back in the spring, he would have seen the fields full of Creek women, perhaps assisted by Creek men and children, sowing corn, beans, squash, melon, and other crops. They planted the fields together, allowing them to grow along the contours of the terrain, curving to follow the rich bottomland. As spring turned to summer, the women and children returned, again working together to tend their crops. In late summer, the women harvested the crops, with some of the produce going to each household and some to the town granary. These stores, along with gathered foods and game, would feed the people of Tuskegee until the next year.[2]

Six decades later, just before the Civil War, when travelers came to the Moses Perryman plantation on the Arkansas River in present-day Oklahoma, they took in a very different sight. For one thing, the terrain was different—thirty years earlier, the United States had forced the Creeks, including Perryman, to move to this new land. But more striking differences emerged if one looked at the people working. Now men did much of the work in the fields rather than women. Women and children still worked, of course. Sometimes they planted and hoed and harvested in the fields, but other times they labored in a large home where they cleaned, cooked, spun yarn, knitted, and washed clothes. Other differences emerged when one looked at the crops: rather than corn and beans to eat, the focus now was on cotton to sell. Not only did the fields and crops and work differ from those in Tuskegee six decades before, so did the people who did the work on the Perryman plantation. They were enslaved, and while some undoubtedly had indigenous or European ancestors, it was their African ancestry that made them subject to enslavement. Their master was free and wealthy and had indigenous Creek and European ancestry. Even if, following Creek law, he did not own the land, he owned the slaves and all that they made with their labor.[3]

Among the most striking contrasts between a Creek town field in 1802 and a Creek plantation just six decades later is the contrast between communal property in the first and private property in the second. How had some Creeks come to own black men, women, and children, the fields they worked, and the product of their labor? How did private plantations arise in a society long fed by communal farming? Why did fields dedicated to the private profit of one person appear among fields dedicated to feeding many? In other words, the differences between the Tuskegee town field in 1802 and the Perryman plantation in 1860 raise the question of change. This change can be overstated because in 1802 some Creeks already owned enslaved people, in 1860 some Creeks still farmed communal town fields, and in both periods the land itself was considered communal property. Nonetheless, the rise of plantation slavery among a mostly communal farming people amounted to a profound shift. It was visible and palpable to Creeks, and it was controversial among them. And property in land lay at the center of that shift.

In the eighteenth century, the communal ownership of lands and the inclusion of people of African descent were established facts among the loose confederacy of *talwas* (towns) that the English knew as the Creeks. After about 1760, however, a small minority of Creek people came to embrace not only property in general but property in land and black chattel slaves in particular. They accumulated wealth and wanted the power that would secure it. With the encouragement of the American authorities, they built the beginnings of a national state: a national council and a police force to protect the new order of property.[4] But the majority of Creeks rejected the

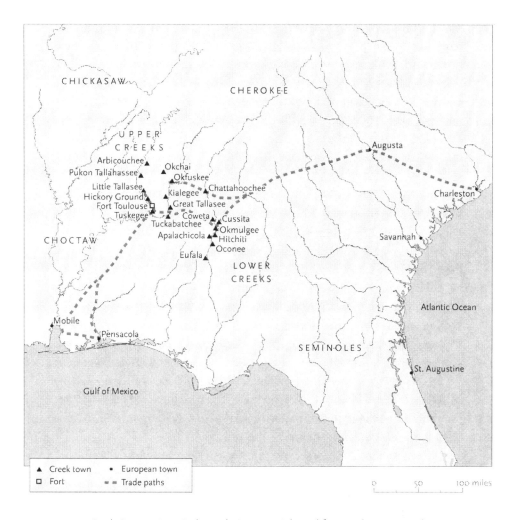

MAP 3. Creek Country, Late Eighteenth Century. (Adapted from Joshua Aaron Piker, *Okfuskee: A Creek Indian Town in Colonial America* [Cambridge, Mass.: Harvard University Press, 2004], opposite page 1, and Kathryn E. Holland Braund, *Deerskins and Duffels: The Creek Indian Trade with Anglo-America, 1685–1815* [Lincoln: University of Nebraska Press, 1993], 10.)

accumulation of private wealth, racial slavery, and the creation of a coercive state. They favored instead communal town agriculture, the dispersal of wealth, and town and clan governance. Bitter divisions between those who embraced and those who resisted the innovations of wealth, racial slavery, and centralized power escalated into war among Creeks in 1813. They were exacerbated by American demands for land cessions, demands that forced the Creeks to surrender their homelands and move west in the 1830s.

These rifts survived the Creeks' forced move to Indian Territory (present-day Oklahoma). In the west, the practices of slavery and property in land intensified. What is more, the bond between them, the consolidation of political authority, and the idea that the Creeks were a racially defined people became ever clearer in the mid-nineteenth century. Ultimately, the differences between a Tuskegee town field and the Perryman plantation point to the enormous tensions that property in land, people, and goods introduced to Creek society, tensions that would ultimately split it in two in the Civil War.

Prior to the late eighteenth century, Creeks lands belonged to Creek towns, and Creek people tied ownership closely to their system of communal agriculture directed by women. Each town had one or more large communal fields upon which it practiced swidden (or "slash and burn") agriculture. The fields, which sometimes encompassed thirty acres or more, could produce prodigious amounts of corn and other crops. The town fields were divided by strips of grass and shrubbery into sections. The produce of each section went to one matrilineage (the extended family of people related through the maternal line), with a portion of the harvest going to a town granary. In addition to the communal fields, women tended small gardens, working and harvesting them individually. The produce of these gardens belonged to the women who worked them, but the land itself did not.[5] This system countered the accumulation of wealth, to which Creeks were hostile until the late eighteenth century.

The eighteenth-century Creeks did have a land property system, but their concept of property was quite distinct from what Americans today call property. In legal thinking, property is not a thing that one owns but a bundle of rights. In American landownership practice today (called "fee-simple property" in legal terminology), the rights in that bundle include the right to buy and sell land through the instrument of a title. Ownership generally (though not always) applies to the soil and the buildings on it. The rights in the bundle are not limited in terms of time: one retains property until one sells or otherwise transfers it. The Creek bundle differed substantially. Creeks emphasized that all of the lands belonged to the town. Families had the right to clear and plant a garden on town lands that others were not using. Their matrilineage would then own the produce of the plot and would even own the garden, but it would not own the ground in which the garden was planted. This is akin to owning a building but not owning the lot it is built upon, which was also Creek practice. One owned some rights but not all. The Creek use-rights land property system was a species of what the legal and anthropological literature calls "usufruct rights." This system was common among farming and gardening peoples of North America. In such a system, one can own the control of fields that one clears and tends, and one can own the crops grown on these fields, but one cannot own the land itself. One who owns control of the fields one works and the crops grown on them can be said to own use-rights property in land. Although the system allowed Creeks to take use-rights property in land, few Creeks accumulated much property at this time. None of the principal Creek economic activities for most of the eighteenth century—farming town fields, gardening small individual plots, and hunting and preparing hides for the deerskin trade—depended on extensive private land use.[6]

The Creek towns that owned these lands incorporated people of indigenous, European, and African descent through a variety of practices. Over the seventeenth and eighteenth centuries, about seventy-five villages in what is today Alabama and Georgia formed a loose confederacy that became known as the Creeks or the Muscogee Confederacy. With a total population of 15,000 to 20,000, it was heterogeneous and inclusive to new arrivals. Indigenous villages added linguistic and cultural diversity to the nation when they and their inhabitants joined the confederacy and became Creek.[7] So too did many African and African American individuals. Some black people fled to the Creek country from the southern English colonies to escape slavery. Many were initially subject to a Creek form of slavery. It was certainly a form of domination, but it seems to have been permissive in comparison with Anglo-American slavery of the period and was neither heritable nor permanent.[8] In fact, prior to the end of the eighteenth century, most enslaved people regained their freedom. They often married Creeks and became integrated into Creek towns and clans.[9] British (particularly Scottish) men also came to live among the Creeks, especially after about 1760, when white settlement in Georgia and Florida accelerated. As was the case throughout eastern North America, European traders often intermarried with indigenous women. They thereby gained access not only to their labor and skills of interpretation but also to their kinship networks and clan memberships. These facilitated the men's business success and especially the social inclusion of their children because the Creeks delineated kinship and clan lines through their mothers.[10] Europeans and people of African descent entered Creek society by marrying into Creek families and thus Creek clans or by being otherwise adopted into Creek clans and towns. Their integration into Creek society illustrates the Creeks' practice of classifying people by clan and loyalty, not by what we today call "race." That is to say that Creeks did not have an entrenched belief that the bodies and characters of Africans and Europeans were fundamentally and irreducibly different from their own.[11] The Creeks were a self-consciously heterogeneous society and one hostile to property accumulation.

Trade, Slavery, and Power

The Creeks' way of life began to change over the last four decades of the eighteenth century. Some of the European traders and the children they fathered with indigenous wives began to introduce a new system of property in farms and in slaves. They began to farm for profit on private fields. This practice marked an important though incremental shift in the use-rights system: the land itself still belonged to the town, but these farmers used the fields for profit in a way that was novel to Creek society. The new scale at which they farmed required labor, and to secure it, this small minority of Creeks embraced human property—specifically the racial, chattel slavery of people of African descent.[12] By the 1790s, traders and planters in Creek towns held at least three hundred such people as slaves. Whites felt that most Creeks were far too lenient toward enslaved people and required far too little labor from them. Often slaves farmed independently and gave their master tribute in a system quite unlike that practiced by white Americans.[13] But this period was a turning point, and some enslaved people worked on plantations that bore a striking resemblance to those of white planters. Alexander McGillivray, the son of a Creek mother and a Scottish father, had established a plantation named Old Tallassee just above present-day Montgomery, Alabama. Old Tallassee featured a large log home with dormers, orchards, hogs, horses, cattle, fields, and the crucial property that provided labor: about sixty enslaved people of African descent. And just as McGillivray hired white drovers to drive his animals, he hired a white overseer to command his slaves.[14] Free nonblacks commanded; enslaved blacks labored.

This racial division of labor demonstrates the historical connection between property in land and ideas of race in Creek history. By about 1790, Old Tallassee depended on chattel slavery, and chattel slavery depended in turn on the idea that race was the defining characteristic of a people. To the small but politically assertive minority of plantation- and ranch-operating Creeks, blackness became the mark of slavery and nonblackness the mark of freedom.[15] Furthermore, for this minority of Creeks, race (non-blackness) became a constituent part of Creekness—that is, their sense of what made them distinctive as an autonomous people. There was no need for this concept to be a conscious creation; it was, rather, a logical result of making blackness the mark of slavery. The trajectory bore the mark of British and American colonialism and resembled the way that the American racialization of slavery came to define a heterogeneous European-derived population as white and free and "American."[16] In the same way, binding chattel slavery to blackness implicitly defined Creeks of mixed European-indigenous ancestry and "full-blood" Creeks as one people. By racializing slavery and freedom, the minority of Creeks who held men, women, and children as slaves racialized what it meant to be Creek.

Not all Creek people—not even most—embraced this idea, however. Some people of African descent lived as free and full members of Creek towns. Their numbers are unknown, but their presence was noted at the time and has been emphasized by historians. Ninnywageechee was a "trader among the Lower Creeks." Philatouche was a leader in the town of Chiaja, a center of free black life in the Lower Towns. Nothing expresses the inclusion of Africans into Creek society better than the name of Cudjomicco, a prominent man in Chiaja, or perhaps in Usiche. In the manner of West African speakers of Akan languages, "Cudjo" marked him as a male born on a Monday. In the manner of the Creeks, "micco" marked him as a political leader.[17] Imperialism, trade, and economic transformation had introduced a number of crucial and divisive changes to Creek society, shaping a world where some Africans were called "slave" and others "micco."

The imported ideas and practices of property, slavery, and race gained the most ground in the Lower Towns (Coweta, Cussetah, Hitchitee, and other towns in the Chattahoochee River basin on the southern branch of the trade path from Charleston), where there was a greater presence of Britons and their descendants.[18] The Upper Towns (Tuckabatchee, Tuskegee, Okfuskee, and other towns on the Coosa and Tallapoosa rivers on the northern branch of the path) were slower to be influenced by these ideas and practices, though the innovations were present there also.

At the end of the eighteenth century, wealthy Creek men began to assert their authority not only in their own towns but over the other Creek towns, as well. From 1795 forward, the U.S. agent Benjamin Hawkins urged the centralization of Creek power in a national council.[19] For the Americans, the council was an authority they could turn to in their efforts to wrest lands from Creek hands and penalize Creeks who clashed with or raided white settlements. For their part, profit-seeking and property-oriented Creeks sought to control this new state power as a tool to protect their own interests, which included the security of property and peaceful relations with the United States and its people.[20]

These impositions of property and power were rejected by most Creeks, and the effort at centralization only increased divisions among them.[21] Most of the conflict over property took place in actions that reveal the terms of this "debate." When impoverished Creeks took goods from wealthier neighbors, they called it "borrowing," but the wealthy called it "theft." When they raided white settlements, Creek hunters considered it a bold and brave act that ensured that humbled Europeans would make proper gifts to Creeks in the future, but wealthy Creeks called raids a crime and a threat to good relations with the United States. When wealthy Creeks bought locks for their doors and built fences for their fields, they redefined sharing as stealing and movement as trespass.[22] As Robbie Ethridge notes, building a fence was a symbolic act as well as a means to keep cattle and hogs out of the corn.[23] By older standards, the acquisitiveness of the would-be leaders of this nation marked them as antisocial. Many Creeks bristled at the pretensions to power that the creation of a national council and police force represented. And Creeks with black ancestry—people who had escaped slavery and their descendants—had reason to fear the rise of the slave order that the council portended. After all, to defend the rights of the owners of property was to protect the rights of the owners of people.

In 1813, conflict over property and authority drove Creeks to civil war. Dissidents known as Redsticks (including many Upper Town Creeks, Seminoles, and black Creeks) took up arms against wealthy and accommodationist Lower Town leaders, the concentrating of power by the council, and American militias. The intervention of U.S. forces under the command of Andrew Jackson ensured the defeat of the Redsticks. Nearly three thousand Upper Town members died in the war, which concluded with the disastrous Treaty of Fort Jackson in 1814. The Creeks surrendered 23 million acres— half of their remaining lands.[24] In such a context, no Creek side can be said to have won, but the Lower Town forces and advocates of private property and centralized authority did prevail.

The Redstick War demonstrates how conflicts over property, slavery, and power brought to the fore another conflict by the second decade of the 1800s: What was the nature of the population of Creek country? Was it a nation? If so, was it a unitary nation that could rightly be ruled by a unitary power? Or was it a loose confederation of towns? In effect, it was both. From the point of view of their relations with the American government and neighboring Indians, the Creeks were a sovereign nation. The

U.S. recognized them as such in the first treaty it signed with the "Kings, Chiefs, and Warriors of the Creek Nation" in 1790.[25] However, in terms of describing the internal relations among Creeks in the nineteenth century, the term "nation" can overstate their cohesiveness. The political, social, and even linguistic independence of the towns was significant, and Creeks' actions suggest they identified more strongly as members of a town—Hitchitee or Coweta or Tuskegee and so forth—than as Creeks.[26] Furthermore, the two major regional groupings, the Lower Towns and the Upper Towns, existed before the creation of a central council and often overshadowed it. It is conventional to call these splits of class, of region, and of politics "factionalism," but that term incorrectly implies that they were factions of some settled, unitary whole. Although the Creeks were a sovereign nation, precisely what that meant for relations among Creeks long remained in question.

Land Cessions and Removal

The United States did recognize Creek national sovereignty, but it also coveted Creek land. From 1790 to 1827, U.S. authorities succeeded in using manipulation and intimidation to secure a series of treaties in which the Creek Nation (or individuals claiming to represent the Creek Nation) ceded the bulk of its lands. Territory was surrendered from east to west—most of eastern Georgia in 1790, 1802, and 1805; southern Georgia and the bulk of Alabama in 1814 after the Redstick War; western Georgia in 1818, 1821, 1826, and 1827. By 1827, all that remained was a fraction of their original lands—and that was claimed by the state of Alabama.[27] Starvation and smallpox struck the now crowded and impoverished Creeks.

Americans were not done taking Creek lands, however. At the urging of President Andrew Jackson, Congress passed the Removal Act of 1830. Forcing all Indians east of the Mississippi off their treaty-protected lands became official federal policy. The law provided for moving all eastern Indians to an "Indian Territory" west of the Mississippi. But agreements had to be put in place with each tribe. In 1832, the representatives of the Creek council were induced to sign a compromise treaty relinquishing all the national lands east of the Mississippi in exchange for national lands in Indian Territory. Although the treaty's stated purpose was to move the Creeks to those western lands, it did arrange for the distribution of some lands in Alabama to individuals. By the provisions of the treaty, ninety "principal Chiefs" (*miccos*) would take ownership of individual plots (allotments) of five square miles each of Alabama land, and "every other head of a family" would receive one square mile each. The *miccos* believed that their larger allotments would preserve the continuity of their towns and their leadership thereof, as well as put wealth in their own hands.[28] The treaty had promised protection of the Creeks' individual allotments in Alabama. Unsurprisingly, federal officials quickly reneged on this pledge. Thousands of square miles changed hands as Creeks were tricked out of their lands by land speculators assisted by hostile American courts and complicit officials. Just three years after allotment began, Creeks held only a few scraps of Alabama land.[29]

At this point, the United States forced the Creeks west with a brutality that was shocking even given the history of American policy toward them. A first party of about 630 Lower Creeks had already left for the west in 1834. In 1836 and 1837, the War Department forced nearly 23,000 Creeks—free and enslaved—to follow.[30] In the words of Angie Debo, some were set "literally naked, without weapons or cooking utensils . . . down on their bare new land to live or die." Debo concludes that no more than half the total removed population survived.[31]

Talwas (towns) and the conflicts among them did survive the move. Creeks carried with them the ritual and sacred items that embodied the life of their towns. On the Canadian River, six hundred miles from his homeland, Hotulke Emarthla, the *micco* of Okchiye, planted the ashes of his town fire in the earth. On them, he rekindled the town fire. The location may have changed, but the place remained Okchiye.[32] Even when *talwas* dispersed to the point where "town" served as a poor translation, they continued to function as a primary form of social and political organization. The Lower Towns, often referred to as the McIntosh faction, settled in the valley of the Arkansas River (soon dubbed the Arkansas District), where their elite established plantations in bottomlands. The Upper Towns made their new homes in the Canadian District, in the valleys of the Canadian, North Canadian, Deep Fork, and Little rivers. The two divisions maintained separate councils for several years after they moved west. Although they began to meet again as a national council around 1840, the Upper Towns and Lower Towns still functioned as social and political blocs and recognized different chiefs.[33]

The Indian Territory to which the Creeks were sent never became a territory of the United States in the sense in which that word is normally used. It never had the administrative and legal structures that the Northwest Ordinance of 1787 provided for territories. It was not Washington's intention to set Indian Territory on the path to statehood in the manner that

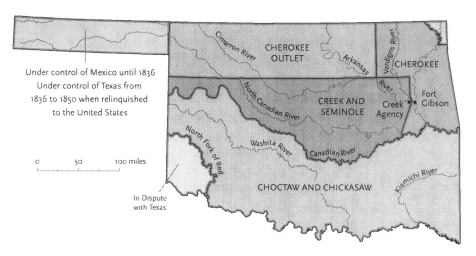

MAP 4. Indian Territory, 1830–1855. (Adapted from John W. Morris, Charles R. Goins, and Edwin C. McReynolds, *Historical Atlas of Oklahoma*, 3rd ed. [Norman: University of Oklahoma Press, 1986], 23.)

the ordinance prescribed. Nor did the federal government allow the nations of Indian Territory to function as fully sovereign powers. Rather, just as the federal government had forced the Creeks, Cherokees, Chickasaws, Choctaws, Seminoles, and other peoples to move to Indian Territory in the 1830s, it forced them into the position of "domestic dependent nations." This American legal doctrine, which is fundamental to Native American history, law, and politics, needs to be understood as part of the history of removal. U.S. Supreme Court chief justice John Marshall formulated it in the context of the effort to remove Cherokees from Georgia in the 1830s. In practice, the federal government considered the Creeks (like other American Indian nations) to be a self-governing entity outside the jurisdiction of any state but subject to the authority of the federal union. The Creek Nation exercised authority over lands it had acquired by treaty with the United States. The border between the Creeks and Seminoles in the west would not be fixed until 1856.

Land and Slavery in the West

The move west brought a shift toward private land use and an intensification of slavery—two interrelated developments. In Indian Territory between the 1830s and the 1860s, both the elite slave-owning minority and the modest majority increased the practice of private farming and owning use-rights property in land. For the latter, much larger group of people who did not own slaves, the expansion of use-rights property in land coexisted with a continuation of the kind of collective farming they had practiced in the East. A federal Indian agent reported in 1842, "Many of the Creeks have separate fields, but their ancient custom of working a town field is still to a great extent observed. They raise large quantities of corn, melons, pumpkins, beans, and lately are cultivating rice to some extent."[34] In 1843, a number of towns in the Upper Creek district together farmed a cornfield that reportedly stretched three miles wide by eight miles long—twenty-four square miles of Canadian River bottomland.[35] In good years, such common fields were capable of producing large surpluses of corn that could be sold.[36] Working in the town fields and on the fences that surrounded them was obligatory for all able-bodied members of the community.[37]

Even farmers such as these, however, took part in the increasing practice of private land use in Indian Territory. In addition to the town fields, many families also farmed and harvested their own private plots. Family farming created use-rights property in land. Any Creek citizen could make property in land by clearing and planting it, that is, by using labor to transform land into what was called an "improved" field. To retain their use-rights property to a field, Creeks had to keep it cultivated. If it was abandoned, a field reverted to the status of simple and "unimproved" land, and the family that had planted it lost its use-rights property to it.[38] The same legal principle obtained in Indian Territory as before removal, and indeed the change was incipient in the conflicts over property in the East. In Alabama, however, a shift toward private farming may have been restrained by the fact that Creeks lived among fields they had long planted together. When they were forced westward to Indian Territory, Creeks left the old communal fields behind. Although they planted new ones in the west, they also planted family fields that bore a greater resemblance to American-style property.

Despite this resemblance, these modest farmers may have drawn on two sources internal, rather than external, to Creek society when they took up the practice of property in land. First, communal town fields had long been divided into family sections, with each matrilineage gathering the harvest from its section. These divisions may have served as part of the inspiration and justification for the creation of private fields once the Creeks moved west.[39] Second, the private fields that Creeks established in Indian Territory resembled the garden plots that women had planted prior to removal.[40] Creek women had owned use-rights property in those gardens, which may have expanded in scale to become the small family farms of

Indian Territory. Of course, small Creek private farms in the west differed from these models in important ways. Unlike the town farms, they were neither worked collectively nor concentrated spatially. Unlike the gardens in the East, private fields were worked by Creek men as well as women. This interpretation must be speculative, but the modest farmers' proximity to the established forms of communal farming and family gardening make it plausible that they followed a different trajectory to property than the wealthy, who emulated the American plantation model.

For wealthy Creek families, removal facilitated a more dramatic expansion of the private ownership of land-use rights, and this change depended on intensifying the demands they placed on the men, women, and children they held in slavery. As soon as the Creeks arrived in their new territory in the 1830s, the Creek elite began to establish farms and plantations. The number and proportion of enslaved people increased accordingly, owing to the birth of children to enslaved women, the purchase of enslaved people from outside the nation, and a decline in the free Creek population caused by the brutality and disruptions of removal. Before removal, in 1832, there were 914 enslaved people living among 21,780 free Creeks—4 percent of the population.[41] In Indian Territory by 1860, the number of enslaved people had almost doubled to 1,800, while the free population had fallen to 13,537. Slaves had become 11.7 percent of the population.[42] The slave population was centered in the Arkansas District, home of the Lower Town faction and its plantations. The slaves of Roley McIntosh, Ben Marshall and his cousin Lafayette Marshall, John Lewis and his brother Kendle, Moses Perryman, and others all farmed new plantations in the area between the Arkansas and Verdigris river valleys. Some Upper Town leaders in the Canadian District, such as Opothleyahola of Tuckabatchee town, also owned considerable numbers of slaves.[43] As enslaved men and women transformed the bottomlands, the plantations grew and planters imported more slaves from the southern states.[44]

The intensity of slavery seems to have corresponded to the size of the farm or plantation, although the information on these topics permits only tentative hypotheses. On the larger plantations, the heavy labor of enslaved people transformed unimproved land into ownable fields for their owners. Enslaved people cleared trees, drained swamps, and removed fieldstone from the red clay. The work was equally unremitting once the plantations were established. Phoebe Banks, who had belonged to planter and rancher Moses Perryman as a girl, later remembered, "The slave men work in the fields, chopping cotton, raising corn, cutting rails for the fences, building log cabins and fireplaces." Phoebe's mother, Eldee, was "the house girl—cooking, waiting on the table, cleaning the house, spinning the yarn, knitting some of the winter clothes, taking care of the mistress girl, washing the clothes." Banks remembered that enslaved people did all the labor in the home and farm.[45] When owners found their slaves' labor lacking, the penalties could be brutal. Alex Haynes recalled that when his father could not pick cotton quickly enough to satisfy his owner, he "was whipped until the blood came. . . . My father has said that he came through the slave days with much whipping and blood shed."[46]

The chattel and dehumanizing nature of Creek plantation slavery in the west is clear in one term for "slave": *este-vpuekv*. It translates directly as "livestock person" and complicates the sense in much of the writing on slavery among American Indians in Indian Territory that it was less taxing and more humane than the slavery practiced by white Americans.[47] It is unclear when and where the term *este-vpuekv* came into usage, but it conveys the position of the enslaved men, women, and children who worked the plantations of elite Creek families in the 1840s and 1850s.[48] As in the American South, chattel slaves were fungible, and slave owners could bring an *este-vpuekv* with them to the market towns of Fort Smith, Arkansas, or Paris, Texas, and exchange him or her for plows, bridles, seeds, wagons, or other goods.[49] As in the American South, Creeks bought and sold people as part of the larger cash economy.[50] Moses Perryman sold his *este-vpuekv* Harry Harrison to a slave buyer just before the Civil War. More than six decades later, in the 1930s, Harrison's son John recalled that he and his mother never heard from his father again.[51]

In contrast, other Creek slave owners in antebellum Indian Territory practiced a different and less restrictive form of slavery that corresponded to a less intense and less concentrated accumulation of use rights to land. Most Creeks were what U.S. agents and traders termed "traditionalists" who herded cattle or farmed smaller fields. Some of these, including some important *miccos*, owned people and their labor. The experiences of their slaves differed substantially from those of slaves who worked on the plantations. Lucinda Davis's parents belonged to two different masters but lived together in one home some distance from both. They farmed independently, directing their own labors on a small plot of land, and rendered part of their harvest to their masters. Their position was akin to that of people whom Orlando Patterson, a scholar of comparative slavery, calls "enslaved tenant farmers." The life of these people was hardly idyllic—as the fact that

Davis's parents chose to escape to freedom demonstrates. It was, however, substantially less restrictive than that of people enslaved on plantations.[52] The smaller farms and their less intensive concentration of the ownership of land-use rights corresponded to a less intensive use of slave labor.

Labor, Slavery, Race, and Citizenship

The interrelated stories of the owning of people and the owning of use-rights property in land reveal that what made the Creek property system distinctive was the place that labor played in it. Whether Creeks lived in the Southeast in the 1750s or in Indian Territory in the 1850s, the Creek property system emphasized the *making* of property. The right to land was created and retained by labor. In contrast, Anglo-American land law emphasized *having* property—possessing title to land. Ideally, that title was a document, but even if one lacked the document, in the Anglo-American system one could prove that the property was one's own by demonstrating that one had obtained the rights to land from the previous owner. Unlike in Creek society, labor might transform land, but it did not create the right to own it. In some ways, mid-nineteenth-century Creeks practiced a very egalitarian property system. Owning use rights to land was more feasible in Creek society than owning land title was in American society. All Creeks who labored had access to owning use rights to land. In coming decades, this fact would become something Creeks would point to with pride.

There were two very important limits, however, to who could own the product of his or her labor in land. They indicate how the Creek property system had changed from the Southeast in the 1750s to Indian Territory in the 1850s. The first limit was slavery, which had increased in scale and intensity since the 1750s. A person had to own his or her own body to own the product of its labor. If he or she did, and cleared and planted a field, that person therefore owned the improvements on that land and had use rights to it. Thus a Creek woman owned her garden in both the 1750s and the 1850s. But the new form of chattel slavery, well established by the 1850s, meant that an enslaved person did not own her own body. Her labor was not her own, and so when she labored and made a field, that field belonged to the person who owned her. No amount of work would transform it into her property. There were very likely some exceptions to this: antebellum Creek slaves did own small chattel property, and some accumulated savings.[53] Nonetheless, the foundations of wealth in the changing Creek society in the antebellum west were enslaved people and land, and enslaved people did not own land. This situation is not unique to Creek society, of course. Anglo-American slavery also denied slaves the right to the product of their labor, and the spread of chattel slavery among Creeks was in part a strategic accommodation to Anglo-American society.

The relationship between labor and property in the Creek Nation, however, throws a particular light on the nature of land tenure and slavery. In a situation in which land was held in common but labor created property rights to it, the ownership of labor—that is, the ownership of slaves— powerfully determined land tenure. Owning people meant owning labor, and owning labor meant owning property rights to land. And the crucial concept that created the link between owning people, owning labor, and owning property was race, since race determined who could be enslaved and who could be a slave owner.

The second limit on the owning of the product of one's labor was citizenship: only Creek citizens could make and own property in land. A racialized national citizenship created the linkage between race and property in Creek law. Moreover, the formalization of citizenship corresponded to a centralization of power in Creek society. This point raises the difficult question of how Creeks understood national citizenship—a complex issue that cannot be explored in depth here. While historians have no detailed history of this development, it seems that a formal sense of national citizenship was a novelty and that it evolved in concert with the centralization of authority and the practices of chattel slavery and race. The first time the term "citizens" of the "Creek nation" appeared in a treaty with the United States was 1796, but the document gives little sense of what that meant.[54] One *can* say that national citizenship did not exist in the 1750s but did in the 1850s. In the mid-eighteenth century, escaped slaves and white traders had become Creeks indirectly: by being adopted into clans and towns. This form of belonging corresponded to one kind of political organization—the loose confederation of towns linked by clan ties that the Creeks were for most of the eighteenth century. Town and clan membership, not the nation, was primary. A different kind of belonging emerged with the rise of the Creek council—a governmental body that was conceived to centralize authority and assert the interests of propertied Creeks. This new kind of belonging was national citizenship, and laws passed by the council in the 1850s created racial boundaries around such citizenship. It extended citizenship to all people who had been born free and had been regarded as Creeks—unless they were of African descent. This law immediately excluded enslaved people from citizenship. As for freeborn blacks, special limits applied. They could be admitted as citizens only if their mothers were Creek and if they were not more than half African by ancestry. Together, the freeborn, matrilineal, and ancestry rules excluded the great bulk of black Creeks from citizenship.[55] Significantly, no such rules were established for people of partial European descent.

Liberal political theory emphasizes how citizenship formalizes rights, but the story of Creek citizenship, slavery, and property in land in this period serves as a reminder that making some people citizens with rights means making others noncitizens without rights.[56] Using national citizenship to grant rights to some while denying them to others is hardly unique to the Creek Nation. Rather, creating citizens always creates noncitizens, no matter how much this process is justified in the rhetoric of liberalism. Creek history simply throws this fact into vivid relief and points up the place of race in this process of exclusion. Much remains unclear about Creek citizenship in the mid-nineteenth century, including just who enjoyed its rights, precisely what those rights were, and to what extent the rights of female and male citizens differed. What is clear, however, is that formalizing citizenship reinforced changes in Creek society that were consolidating a Creek nation and intensifying practices of chattel slavery, race, and private use-rights ownership of land.

A series of pairings points to the way that practices of citizenship, race, slavery, and property in land worked together. The pairing of citizens and noncitizens, people who did not descend from Africans and people who did, people who could be enslaved and people who could not, people who could own use-rights property in land and people who could not—all of these binaries structured mid-nineteenth-century Creek politics, economy, and experience. The maintenance of the lines between them was of structural importance to the society.

By their nature, free people of African descent confused those lines and therefore constituted a particular challenge to racial notions of Creekness. The citizenship law of 1859 was just one of a series of laws that the council passed between the 1840s and 1860 that encoded the differences between Creek and black, enslaved and free. The laws mimicked slave codes in the southern states, protected owners' property interest in their chattel, mandated a fine or whipping to punish anyone who assisted a person escaping slavery, and tried to force enslaved people to remain on their owners' premises.[57] It is unclear whether these laws were effectively enforced, but they do demonstrate the intent of the council members who passed them. Prohibitions on slaves' owning property were particularly revealing because they made it difficult for enslaved people to save up to buy themselves and thus to buy their freedom. Some enslaved people had done just this. For example, in recompense for skilled work—such as translating for his owners between English and Creek languages with horse traders at Kansas City—an enslaved person might receive "a colt or calf or maybe money" for his efforts. Siegel McIntosh recalled that the slave would "save the money and . . . the animals to sell for more money. In that way, he would finally get enough to buy himself."[58] The law barring enslaved people from owning property discouraged this saving, this self-purchase, and the growth of the free black population. Toward the same end, the council declared that any Creek who would manumit his human property must remove them from the nation. The council, moreover, made intermarriage between people of African descent and other Creeks punishable by whipping, and it imposed poll and property taxes on "freed men and women who had not been adopted as Creek citizens."[59] In these laws differentiating free black people from other Creeks we can see another step in the effort to define the Creek Nation racially.

What is important to recognize is that these laws, like dominant elements in the council itself, represented one particular group of Creeks and their political project of nationhood (and especially racial nationhood). What it meant to be a Creek nation was no more decided in the 1850s than it had been in 1813, at the time of the Redstick War. It is noteworthy that historians who have looked at the antebellum Creek Nation and at the laws discussed above have come to very different conclusions. Some see a rigid racism; others see a tolerant and inclusive society. Some emphasize the passage of the laws; others point out that it is uncertain whether they were ever enforced with any regularity.[60] These conflicting conclusions reflect the fact that the meaning of Creek nationhood was still under debate. The Lower Creeks and Upper Creeks had, after all, maintained separate councils for some time after removal. The towns still maintained significant autonomy. And the actions of free and enslaved black Creeks tell us as much about Creek beliefs regarding race and nationhood as does the Creek council's legislation. By saving to buy their freedom, by making farms as other Creeks did, and in all the other actions that the council was seeking to outlaw, free and enslaved black people suggested a different future for Creeks than leading elements on the council envisaged.

These divisions go far toward explaining the Creek experience of the American Civil War. The Civil War reshaped property, nationhood, and citizenship in the region. It did so, however, in the context of existing class and factional divisions. Sarah Aklin Odom's memories of the events of 1861 suggest how those divisions shaped the way that Creeks engaged the war. At the time, Odom was a girl, about ten or eleven, who lived with her family in North Fork Town. She later recalled that most Creeks initially paid scant attention to the trouble brewing far to the east and "said it was a white man's trouble and not theirs." Class and cultural divisions, however, gave some families a stake in the outcome. On the one hand, she noted: "Some of the wealthier Creeks owned slaves and they believed in slavery." On the other hand, Odom recalled, Christian preachers largely opposed slavery. The result was that "the Creeks who were just poor, old plain Indian farmers" had to listen to the opposing sides and decide how to approach the difficult question of what, if anything, to do about this war. The issue came to a head in 1861 when Albert Pike, the Confederate commissioner of Indian Affairs, came to North Fork Town to try to seal an alliance with the Creeks. Odom remembered that "the whole village talked of nothing for days except to discuss what must they do."[61]

Both the Creek Nation and its neighbors, the Seminole and Cherokee nations, divided over the Civil War. The division roughly followed lines of ancestry. John Jumper, principal chief of the Seminoles, reported that "all the full blood element" favored the Union. U.S. Indian agent E. H. Carruth claimed that despite some exceptions, the mixed-race people of the Five Tribes (Cherokees, Choctaws, Chickasaws, Creeks, and Seminoles) were more sympathetic to the Confederacy.[62] Jumper and Carruth made it clear that intermarried and mixed-race families tended to side with the Confederacy while those with fewer cultural or kinship ties to Anglo-American culture ("the full blood element") sided with the Union. As Sarah Aklin Odom's recollections remind us, however, these racial characterizations need to be placed in the context of Creeks' different economic positions. Given the wealth in lands, homes, slaves, and other property they had amassed, the defeat of the Confederacy would have marked a distinct threat to wealthy planter families. Most of these were of mixed ancestry, but the Confederacy also won plantation-owning supporters who had no European ancestry. Most prominent among these, perhaps, was Samuel Checote. Commonly referred to as a "full-blood," Checote was an important planter and slave owner in the Creek Nation who went on to lead the pro-Confederate faction of the Creeks in the Civil War.[63] Nonetheless, it is undeniable that some prominent Creeks gave their support to the Confederacy in order to defend the class and race hierarchy embodied in slavery.

That was not the whole story, however. Creek nationalism also played a role in the making of a Creek-Confederate alliance. Specifically, the alliance with the southern states was part of the defense of Creek national sovereignty and Creek lands. Creeks had every reason to share with Confederates a strong distrust of federal power, which had forced the Creek Nation away from its homeland and imposed itself on Creek sovereignty.[64] In 1860, in fact, the federal agent to the Creeks had given them an additional reason to distrust the U.S. government. He proposed that all of the Creeks', Cherokees', and Choctaws' national lands be "allotted"—that is, divided into private parcels and distributed among their respective citizenries. Having already suffered through one disastrous experiment with allotment in Alabama, the Creek council declared its "unqualified and absolute refusal." It reasoned that owing to the Creeks' lack of experience with Anglo-American land titles, Creek allottees would rapidly lose their land. In fact, in 1861 the Confederate commissioner of Indian Affairs seized upon this federal misstep when he made the defense of Indian lands his first argument to the Creeks for why they should support the Confederacy. This suggests that he suspected that federal proposals of allotment had prepared the Creeks to align with his government.[65]

So was the Creek council's alliance with the South a racist defense of slavery and its class privileges, or was it a nationalist defense of Creek lands and sovereignty? The answer has to be "both." Race, slavery, property, and privilege were constitutive elements of the Creek Nation as leading figures in the council understood it. They had made this much plain in the laws and policies they had encoded in the decades before the war. Citizenship and property laws built racial boundaries around the nation, as did the slave code. As noted above, there is nothing particularly surprising or unusual about this: throughout the modern world, race is deeply embedded in nationalism, and vice versa. There was nothing inconsistent between the proslavery and nationalist elements of pro-Confederate Creek politics in the early 1860s. They had built each other.

The Creek council did not, however, have a monopoly on the defense of Creek sovereignty. Upper Town faction leaders put their weight behind the North in an effort to secure the best future for their nation in a difficult situation not of Creek making. In the end, the members of the various towns seem to have followed the dominant factions of each. In the Creek Nation, this meant that most of the Lower Towns supported the Confederacy, and the Creek council signed a treaty with the Confederate States in 1861. In contrast, most of what had been termed the Upper Creek towns prior to removal went with the Union. Slaves of Lower Town owners largely threw their weight behind the Union cause. Many of these slaves freed themselves by heading north to Kansas. There, they and other "Loyal Creeks" (as the Union considered them) sought refuge among and offered their support to Union forces. The family of Phoebe Banks, for example, "slipped away" from the Moses Perryman plantation and joined up with pro-Union Creeks, who were led by Opothleyahola. Banks later recalled, "There was lots of Creek Indians and slaves in the outfit when they made a break for the North. The runaways was riding ponies stolen from their masters." Once in Kansas, they joined a similarly multiracial group from the Seminole Nation in struggling to survive and fight on the side of the Union. Some 1,575 Creeks enlisted in the Union forces, while 1,675 fought for the Confederacy. Meanwhile, many pro-Confederate Creeks, fearing that their slaves would escape or be seized, moved themselves and their human property south into the Red River region, where the Chickasaw Nation bordered Texas.[66] Some, like Ben Marshall, tried to use enslaved labor to reestablish themselves as planters there.[67] Still, the desire for liberation was strong, and enslaved people continued to escape Creek owners to find freedom and join the ranks of the Union forces. Creeks fought each other as Union and Confederate soldiers in a number of engagements, the most notable of which was the Battle of Honey Springs in July 1863. There, black Creeks in the First Kansas Colored Infantry and other Creeks in the Indian Home Guards fought alongside whites from Wisconsin to rout Confederate Creeks, Cherokees, Choctaws, and whites from Texas. This remarkable combination of nations, states, loyalties, and racial categories encapsulated the complexity of the war in Indian Territory and the deep divisions in Creek society.[68]

Of course, this was not the first time that Creeks faced each other on the battlefield. A half century earlier, divisions between Creeks had erupted into the Redstick War. There were resemblances between the sides at the Battle of Horseshoe Bend in 1814 and those at the Battle of Honey Springs in 1863. In both conflicts, Lower Creeks dominated one faction and Upper Creeks and people of African descent the other. And in both the Redstick War and the Battle of Honey Creek, victory for one faction cannot be understood without reference to the intervention of the American military. The most telling continuity between the two conflicts, however, is the central place that property—in objects, in enslaved people, in usufruct rights to land—played in defining the sides. This is not to say that the struggles between Creeks, in 1814 or 1863, were simply battles over property, or even a property system. The issues at stake were much larger than that because in the course of the eighteenth and nineteenth centuries property played a large role in transforming the ways that Creeks came to define the boundaries between peoples. Race and nation, the categories that separated the free from the enslaved and the Creek from the noncitizen, were deeply enmeshed with and to an important degree defined by property and its pursuit. Citizenship and slavery, especially, figured prominently in this transformation and largely determined who could own land. And because of the defeat of the Confederacy and its Indian allies, slavery would be abolished and citizenship radically refigured after the Civil War. In the aftermath of war, the lines of battle among Creeks would shift. The politics of race and property would bring the question of the nation increasingly to the fore.

■ ■ ■ ■ ■ ■ ■ ■ ▪ ■ ■ ■ ■ ■ ▪ ■ ■ ■ ▪ ■ ■ ▪ ■ ■ ▪ ■ ■ ■ ■ ▪ ■ ■ ▪ ■ ■ ▪ ■ ▪ ■ ■ ▪ ■ ■

An Equal Interest in the Soil

SMALL-SCALE FARMING AND THE WORK OF

NATIONHOOD, 1866–1889

One day in 1866, the members of the McIntosh family learned that they were free. Prior to that day, Jackson and Hagar McIntosh and their eight children had labored for their owner, Roley McIntosh. He was the *micco* of Coweta, one of the leading Lower Creek towns. Roley McIntosh, like many of the wealthiest Creeks, had taken up arms for the Creek faction that had allied itself with the Confederacy. When McIntosh's side had lost and a treaty of peace with the United States emancipated Creek slaves, he sent word that Jackson and Hagar McIntosh, their children, and his other slaves were freed. The good news did not stop there, however. More than six decades later, one of the McIntosh daughters, Nellie, would still recall hearing the momentous news that "we . . . can take up some land for our own selves." After the war, the McIntoshes stayed on the same land they had once farmed for their master. The land they farmed now became their own because of the nature of Creek citizenship and land tenure.[1] The 1866 treaty of peace between the federal government and the Creek Nation declared that freed slaves were full Creek citizens. In the eyes of Creek law, they were "colored Creeks." Moreover, the treaty explicitly stated that black Creeks would enjoy "an equal interest in the soil."[2] This was revolutionary. Before emancipation, enslaved people did not own their own labor and were not citizens. Thus, any fields they cleared and tilled and planted belonged to their owners. After emancipation and the 1866 treaty recognized their freedom and their citizenship, black Creeks—more than 1,850 people, 13 percent of the nation of 14,300 people—were able to use their labor to make property in land for themselves, just as other Creeks did.[3]

The Creek property system gave black Creek citizens the opportunity to minimize their dependency and maximize their autonomy in a way that was strikingly similar to the way other, nonblack Creeks did. A close look at the daily life of farmers in the Creek Nation reveals that, like other Creeks, black Creeks largely followed a small-farm strategy that emphasized home production, allowed for limited trade, and provided for a level of autonomy. This situation was quite unlike the one that African Americans in the South faced. The states of the former Confederacy denied emancipated slaves' equal citizenship rights, blocked their hopes for "forty acres and a mule," and reduced many landless sharecroppers to the position of debt peonage. In the Creek Nation, in contrast, a different form of land tenure and equal citizenship provided black Creeks like Nellie McIntosh with the opportunity to make property in land for themselves and preserve some level of independence. Conflict over land continued, however, and it would keep the meaning of nationhood at the center of Creek politics in the postwar decades. In the twenty years after the Civil War, wealthy Creeks who had allied with the Confederacy forwarded a racialized Creek nationalism and amassed vast expanses of land as privately owned pastures. In response, black Creeks and conservatives joined forces to defend their access to the common lands,[4] and that defense was tied to a broad vision of Creek nationhood.

The alliance between black Creeks and conservative Creeks upheld two fundamental notions: that being Creek meant belonging to a polity, not a race, and that the lands were to be defended as national property available to all who were part of the nation. For this Creek alliance, the nation had a dual nature. It was both a sovereign polity and land. To defend one was to defend the other. Furthermore, for this alliance, the Creek Nation was composite, made up of different kinds of people with different racial and cultural backgrounds. This sense of nationhood was sanctioned by Creek history as preserved in the oral tradition and built into the structure of Creek government.

There is a paradox here. Factional, racial, and class struggles expressed the very real *divisions* among Creeks, but those conflicts encouraged Creeks to define what *united* them as a nation—not just in terms of the external relations of the Creek state but also in terms of the internal workings of the Creek society and polity. Moreover, in conflicts that expressed the real divisions among them, Creeks may have come to think of themselves increasingly as members of one nation. Thus, while the Confederate Creeks' racial nationalism suggests the way that the struggle against American colonialism introduced a reductive sense of racialized political identity into Creek life (traceable back to several decades before the war), the story of the black-conservative alliance suggests that other forms of national identification, also deeply rooted in Creek history, emerged from the conflict with American colonialism. Seen in this light, the political conflict in the Creek Nation in the decades following the Civil War expressed fundamental disagreement over the nature of the Creek Nation but encouraged a mutual emphasis on the centrality of Creek nationhood to the Creek future.

From War to Peace: Citizenship, Land, and the Roots of the Alliance

As a little girl playing in the creek bottoms around 1900, Cora Smith would come across patches that struck her as odd. Here and there in the normally dense timber were spots where the trees were sparse and the trunks small. Stone chimneys stood alone, with no houses to warm. And, she later remembered, "always strawberries were growing wild." Though she was the daughter of a Creek father and a Cherokee mother, Cora did not understand that these patches were almost certainly farms left abandoned by Creek refugees from the Civil War.[5] The ruins in which she played and the strawberries she picked testified to the destruction and dislocation of the war. Almost three decades of the labor of free and enslaved people had gone into making a home in the west, and now homes and fields were burned. The plantations of the wealthy and the cabins of the poor stood empty as their owners sought refuge outside the nation or protection near a fort. At the end of the war, Creeks returned to burned homes and barns, overgrown fields, and the task of rebuilding. As the abandoned farm sites suggest, many moved on to new places, daunted, perhaps, by the idea of rebuilding their burned homes.

Perhaps just as daunting was the question of how to rebuild politically after the Civil War. Only five decades after the Redstick War of 1813–14, a second war had torn the Creeks apart. How could Creek society be rebuilt? What shape should it take? Something called the Creek Nation could sign a treaty with the United States, but what might Creek nationhood mean internally for Creek people? Answers to this question emerged from the factional politics of the postwar period. The postwar coalition of Union-allied "Northern" Creeks and black Creeks, and its clash with "Southern" Creeks, took root during the war and gained strength in its aftermath. During the war, the Union-allied faction and enslaved people fought their way to Kansas together, suffered deprivation in Kansas together, and fought to defeat the Confederate Creeks together. In August 1865, the "loyal Creeks" extended citizenship to former slaves.[6] The experiences of war laid the foundation of their alliance. It had also invigorated the rift with the Confederate-allied faction, which was intent on excluding blacks from the nation after the war.

The most powerful force in shaping the postwar Creek Nation and its politics was the 1866 treaty of peace between Creeks and the United States. In the treaty, the colonial power punished the entire nation for the alliance of one faction with the Confederacy. It seized half of the Creeks' territory at confiscatory prices, imposed federal courts, and granted a right of way for a railroad through the nation. The punitive infringement on Creek sovereignty was profound.

Freed slaves and Union-allied Creeks did, however, play a part in negotiations in 1865 and 1866 that laid the basis of their postwar alliance and guaranteed black Creeks' land rights. In 1865 five black Creeks acted as representatives of their population, and one black Creek acted as interpreter, at negotiations to work out a preliminary postwar agreement between Indian Territory tribes and the federal government.[7] The next year, both the Confederate-allied Creeks and the Union-affiliated Creeks took part in the treaty negotiations in Washington. Confederate officer Daniel N. McIntosh spoke for his faction when he wrote, "We can never recognize [freed slaves] as our equals," a notion he termed "contrary to nature and nature's laws."[8] McIntosh sounded very much like a southern white Confederate, but at the negotiations in Washington he and his allies confronted a Creek opposition that insisted that the Creek Nation take a very different path than the South. The commissioner of Indian Affairs reported that representatives of the Union-allied faction "held out firmly" for the citizenship rights of former slaves, considering it a "sacred pledge."[9] Rumors circulated long after the negotiations that black Creek interpreters such as Harry Island merely tricked gullible and non-English-speaking Creeks into recognizing the full citizenship of former slaves and other black people in the Creek Nation. This hardly seems likely. Negotiations included explicit debate of black citizenship rights, and false translations would have soon been discovered because a number of Creek representatives were conversant in English. Daniel N. McIntosh was fluent in it.[10] Still, black Creeks were present to look after their own interests and, along with their Union-affiliated allies, helped to secure the essential mandate that black Creeks "have and enjoy all the rights and privileges of native citizens, including an equal interest in the soil."

The meaning of this "equal interest in the soil" depended on well-established Creek land tenure law and practice. The principle that citizens owned the "improvements" on land they had tilled, fenced, planted, or built on was so fundamental to Creek law and practice that the council only defined it indirectly as it elaborated a legal code after the Civil War. In 1867, when the newly reconstituted council passed its very first civil law, it declared that owners of improvements who had not adequately fenced the land could not claim damages against the owners of livestock that entered their fields. The notion of use rights to improvements was so well established that it went unexplained in the law.[11]

A Heterogeneous and Complex Creek Nationhood

As was true in the Reconstruction-era United States, the nature of the Creek Nation was at stake in Creek debates over the rights of citizenship and who possessed them.[12] Claudio Saunt has recounted the postwar effort of Confederate Creeks (and some allies who had sided with the Union) to uphold a racial hierarchy that placed black Creeks at the bottom.[13] The motivation to suppress or even exclude black Creeks was certainly in part material. After the war, for example, former Confederate Creeks attempted to deprive black Creeks of their per capita shares of a federal payment for ceded lands.[14] But the goal was more far-reaching. The Creeks faced an expansionist United States and strident demands that their government be dissolved and their lands cut up into private parcels. Wealthy and educated nationalists such as George Washington Grayson were painfully familiar with American notions of racial hierarchy, which had so often been used against Creeks as individuals and as a people.[15] In the defense of Creek sovereignty and also of their own power, wealthy and educated Creeks (who were often of mixed European-Native ancestry) asserted that the Creeks were a racially distinct nation that was free of the taint of African "blood." Former Confederate Creeks encountered significant resistance not only from black Creeks, however, but also from other Creeks, especially those termed "full-bloods" or "conservatives" (which functioned as loose synonyms in this context). Together, conservatives and black Creeks built an alliance in opposition to the "Southern" Creeks. Conservative leader Ispar-hecher spoke for this alliance in 1883 when he affirmed a commitment to the rights "of every Muskogee [Creek] citizen, whether his skin be red, white or black."[16]

Isparhecher's affirmation is so striking, so different from the racial nationalism prevalent among his Creek political opponents and indeed in the United States of the time, that it deserves close attention. To better understand these ideas, their origins, and their repercussions, we would do well to turn away from the pronouncements of political leaders and look at the small-scale farmers who dedicated their votes and energies to and sometimes took up arms for the interracial alliance in Creek politics.

As the previous chapter emphasizes, Creek plantation and ranch owners forwarded a kind of racial nationalism that defined Creekness in ways that included people of exclusively indigenous ancestry and people of mixed indigenous-white ancestry but excluded people of African descent. A look at daily life in the Creek Nation in the three decades after the Civil War—how people farmed, what they ate, how they engaged spirits, the lan-guages they spoke, the clothing they wore, the medicines they made, and so forth—reveals a much more heterogeneous society than that envisaged by Creek nationalists of the faction that had allied with the Confederacy. Racial and cultural lines were far from clear in a nation inhabited by Creeks of differing degrees of indigenous, African, and European ancestry (and increasingly by settlers who entered illegally into the nation after 1870).

Creek heterogeneity and cosmopolitanism are documented in life histo-ries of Creek people that were collected in the 1930s as part of the Indian Pioneer History project, sponsored by the Works Progress Administra-tion (WPA). The source, much like the narratives of former slaves that WPA workers collected in the 1930s, richly documents daily life in the second half of the nineteenth century and is a particularly important source in American Indian history. But like the WPA narratives, the Indian Pioneer History papers must be read with care. The interviewers, some of whom were Indian and some of whom were white, seem to have had differing levels of familiarity with Creek people and history. The interviewers were particularly interested in the romantic, the heroic, and the exotic. The texts themselves, moreover, are not transcripts of interviews. Rather, the interviewers apparently wrote their notes as first-person narratives, pur-portedly in the voice of the individuals they interviewed. The process both reinforced and obscured the power of the interviewer to shape the narra-tive, raising difficulties for research. Nonetheless, the interviewers clearly pursued information about topics relevant to the present study—especially home production and market trading, foods, and the development of the cattle industry. Read against other sources, the narratives provide detailed insight into daily life in the various regions of the Creek Nation.[17]

These narratives portray a complex and cosmopolitan Creek society in each of the nation's three principal regions: the Arkansas River valley in the north, the Canadian River valley in the south, and the valleys and hills of the Deep Fork district in the west. In the north lay the Choska Bottoms, a densely settled region in the Arkansas River area in the vicinity of the old Perryman plantation. These valley lands, or "bottoms," were home to many former Perryman slaves and other black Creek citizens. This was a place where the cultures and bloodlines of Africa, indigenous America, and Europe flowed together. In the Choska Bottoms, some people spoke English, but others spoke American Indian languages: Muskogee (the principal Creek language), Seminole (closely related to Muskogee), and probably Cherokee, too.[18] The variety of languages spoken there attests to the residents' diverse origins. The clothing and the medical and spiritual practices of black residents of the Choska Bottoms also attest to their engagement with a number of cultures. Celia Naylor, drawing on the Indian Pioneer History narratives, demonstrates that enslaved people in Indian Territory acculturated to Indian practices and believed those practices marked them as belonging to Indian communities.[19] Such practices endured after emancipation. In the Choska Bottoms, in the manner of white Americans and many nonblack Creeks, they wore shoes and boots, but they also wore moccasins. They knew that to avoid getting sick after a funeral, one had to wash with *mekko-hoyvnēcv*, also known locally as "king root" and "red root." Creeks regarded this species of willow as a powerful curative and one of the greatest of medicines used at the Green Corn *poskita*, the great summer rite of renewal.[20] In fact, the residents of the bottoms followed many of the ways of Creek medicine, with its plant-based remedies and ritual practices. They also, however, were likely to worship at a Christian church, but a Christian church that brought together strands of Euro-American, African, and indigenous heritage. The spread of Christianity in the Creek Nation was strongly influenced by people of African descent. Black people were often among the first to preach Christianity and embrace it—winning missionaries the enmity of slave owners before the war.[21] But Christianity in the nation also took on a distinctly Creek cast: many Creek churches were laid out in the same format as Creek stomp grounds, with four seating areas arrayed around a central ritual space.[22] When they went

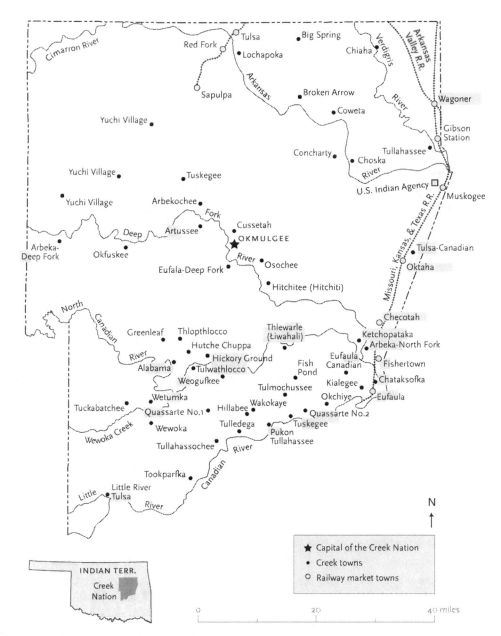

MAP 5. Creek Nation, Late Nineteenth Century. (Modified from John W. Morris, Charles R. Goins, and Edwin C. McReynolds, *Historical Atlas of Oklahoma*, 3rd ed. [Norman: University of Oklahoma Press, 1986], 41.)

to church, residents of the Choska Bottoms might listen to a preacher like Compsah Dinah.[23] The preacher's very name, Compsah (a common name in Creek country, though usually spelled "Cumsey"), spoke to the indigenous heritage alive in Creek Christianity. It derived from Tecumseh, the great Shawnee resistance leader (whose mother had Creek origins). The racial, linguistic, cultural, and religious complexity of the Choska Bottoms was tremendous.

One could find an equally impressive mix of cultures in the western hills of the nation and the towns of the Deep Fork River valley. Here lived people that many Creeks considered the most traditionalist in the nation — residents of towns like Wewoka, which was so dedicated to tradition that Duane Champagne terms it "fundamentalist."[24] After the Civil War, many conservative Creeks moved to the western sections of the nation. They were generally referred to as "full-bloods" in English (a term that described a dedication to tradition more than actual ancestry, which was frequently mixed). Anyone familiar with this reputation would not be surprised to encounter men and women who spoke only Creek, kept a small herd and corn patch, and participated in the annual cycle of ritual "stomp dances" that culminated in the Green Corn *poskita*. But more surprising might be the presence in this region of such individuals as Caledonia Perryman Morey, who was born into the same Perryman family that had farmed the Choska Bottoms with slaves before the Civil War. From her wealthy family came such dignitaries as her brother Legus C. Perryman, who was principal chief from 1887 to 1895. Yet her life was characterized by the intense heterogeneity and cosmopolitanism of the Creek Nation. Although she was a mixed-ancestry woman, married a white man, and taught Sunday school in her community, Caledonia Perryman Morey maintained deep connections to Creek "full-bloods" and traditional practices. She also practiced Creek medicine and midwifery among white settlers. Some Creeks attended church, and others took part in the annual cycle of ritual stomp dances. Still others participated at both the church and the stomp ground because the social and cultural lines were not always sharp. Whether one engaged in rituals of purification at the stomp ground or prayed for redemption at the church, life was sustained by corn, nurtured by Creek medicine, and enlivened by matches of the Creek ball game, a particularly rough cousin of lacrosse. Even the music adopted by Creeks for entertainments — fiddle dances — demonstrated their willingness to merge traditions: Native hands played British reels adapted by Creeks for their own social occasions.[25]

That same complexity was apparent in the south of the nation, in the Canadian River valley, where Creeks had differing relations to American commerce, commercial culture, and gender conventions. The Canadian River valley was a center of life for wealthy and commercially oriented Creeks but was also home to small farmers who grew their own food. There one found male-led trading houses but also female-led farming. The railway town of Eufaula was a center of life for Creeks displaced from their plantations by the Civil War. Its frame homes and stone commercial buildings were the residences and trading houses of such Creek men as former planter George Washington Stidham and his son-in-law (and a future principal chief) George Washington Grayson. Heads of families and heads of businesses, these men found authority in engaging American commerce and American gender conventions. But not far from the trading towns farmed people like Lida Davis Aklin and her children. When Aklin's husband, a Kentucky-born white man, did not return from fighting on the side of Union-allied Creeks in the war, Aklin and her children farmed without him. In that sense, Aklin's farm was not the norm: most Creek farms at this time were organized around a family that included men, women, and children. Still, her work demonstrates that the much older Creek practice of female-directed agriculture remained vital in the late nineteenth century on small farms. And while the family's one-room log home was quite different from the houses of town-based traders, it exemplified the dwellings of most small-scale Creek farmers. So did the basis of their diet: the corn that the Aklins grew and processed themselves in traditional ways, pounding it and soaking it with ashes to make *sofky*, roasting it and pounding it to make *puskee*, mixing it with beans and boiling it to make blue dumplings, and so on. Commercial development coexisted with traditional lifeways in the heterogeneity of the Creek Nation.[26]

Small-Scale Farming

This was the world in which the Creek majority lived, and this world was sustained in the same way that the bulk of the Creek Nation's population was sustained: through agriculture supplemented by hunting, gathering, and trade. When Joe Grayson, a Creek of mixed indigenous and European ancestry, described the life of Creek farmers in the years after the war, he recalled that the basis of the Creek diet in the second half of the nineteenth century was "corn and meat" that families had grown, raised, and hunted for themselves. Grayson's family was more affluent than other

Creek farmers, but most families, he said, farmed one or two acres of corn and ran a few hogs on the open range, and many owned several cattle. Other crops were grown, too. A few farmers grew rice, but only wealthier people could afford to plant wheat, which required costly, store-bought seed. More common were the beans, pumpkins, and sweet potatoes that Creek women had long cultivated in the fields and gardens. They preserved almost all these foods in various ways to make them last through the winter. Women picked beans after they were dry, dried ears of corn and strips of pumpkin after picking them, and, for winter storage, buried potatoes in the earthen floors of homes to keep them from vermin. Beef cattle were slaughtered in July. Some Creeks ate only fresh meat.[27] Joe Grayson recalled that others sliced beef thin, salted it, and let it stand overnight before drying it on the wood shingles of their roofs. Peaches were smoked, stored in barrels, and later reconstituted in water. Grayson recalled that "they tasted like pre-serves."[28]

The livelihood that the Aklins experienced and Grayson described was the norm for the small-scale Creek farming majority. With certain variations, that norm crossed racial boundaries. The family of Isaac and Hannah Smith belonged to Canadian Colored Town, yet the livelihood of these black Creeks bore a strong resemblance to that of the "mixed-blood" Aklins family. They, too, dedicated the bulk of their energies to producing goods for their own sustenance and engaged selectively in market activity in order to obtain goods they could not produce themselves. The Smiths farmed about an acre of corn per year in the Canadian River valley. The family subsisted mostly on this corn, along with its few cattle and hogs, which fed on the open range. The Smiths supplemented these foods with the prairie chicken (a large grouse) and other game they hunted and the wild grapes, berries, pecans, hickory nuts, and walnuts they gathered. These foods accompanied the *sofky* and *puskee* and other Creek staple dishes they made from the corn they grew, dried, ground, and parched.[29] Home production provided the basis of survival, and trade only the surplus, for this black Creek family, as for the "mixed-blood" Aklins.

The same was true for people known as "full-bloods," such as the family of Sam and Sulwee Taylor. Sulwee and her children were members of Okfuskee town, one of a cluster of three towns in the far western portion that had the reputation as centers of "full-blood" and traditionalist life. The residents of the area farmed and raised cattle, pigs, and horses on the common range. Game animals persisted on the commons in sufficient quantity that some families found little motivation to raise livestock for meat in the nineteenth

Unidentified black Creek family in
front of their home, late nineteenth
century. (Western History Collections,
University of Oklahoma Libraries)

century. Creeks hunted prairie chicken, deer, raccoon, beaver, otter, skunk, opossum, and other animals. Much of this game was consumed by hunters and their families as meat. But much game was also traded or sold. Prairie chickens were traded for their meat, whereas deer, opossum, skunks, raccoon, and beaver were largely valued for their skins. Women probably did the cleaning and preparation of hides for trading, as they had in the deerskin trade prior to removal.[30] Trading the animal products—steers on the hoof, dressed pig and deer carcasses, the hides and furs of game animals—meant a long trip to a trading post, perhaps twenty-five miles for the Taylors. One of the Taylor sons, named Sunday, recalled that Creeks like his family traded mostly for manufactured items and foodstuffs they could not produce themselves. Because their goods fetched low prices—as late as the 1890s, only $3.00 for "the best and fattest of any steer," $1.50 for a deer hide, and 25¢ for a skunk hide—they purchased only simple goods. Trading supplemented, rather than supplanted, the homegrown basis of life for most Creeks, whether "mixed-bloods" like the Aklins, black Creeks like the Smiths, or "full-bloods" like the Taylors. This was as true of clothing as it was of food. The Taylors traded for cloth, buttons, and thread to sew their clothes. "There was ready made clothing," Taylor remembered, "but the prices were too high."[31]

Bluestem Bustles and Strategies for Sovereignty

Indeed, clothing reveals much about the intertwined economic, cultural, and even political lives of small Creek farmers. This is particularly true in the case of the dresses and undergarments that Lida Aklin's daughter, Sarah, remembered women making and wearing. The link between bustles and land tenure may seem obscure, but it emerges if we place clothing in the context of Creek women's labor and choices. Sarah Aklin Odom recalled that sometimes "a woman was all dressed up in her homespun dress and shawl of bright colors, leggings and moccasins." But at other times, Creek women wore "hoops and bustles and hip pads" under American-style dresses to achieve the exaggerated figure favored for women in Victorian fashions. American-style ready-made bustles were undoubtedly available for purchase in the Creek Nation—the Graysons' trading house in Eufaula and Fred Severs's dry goods store in Okmulgee were known for their wide range of merchandise. But ready-made was beyond the means of most Creeks, and so Creek women made the bustles themselves, framing them with split hickory saplings, shaping the forms with plaited bluestem, filling them with dried grass, and strapping them to the body with strips of cloth.[32]

These garments challenge conventional boundaries between the traditional and the modern in American Indian life. Although white Americans at the turn of the twentieth century conceived of the Indian and the modern as two categories in opposition to each other, many American Indians were embracing a distinctively Indian form of modernity, as Phil Deloria argues.[33] Creek farmers (these women, their brothers, sons, and fathers) were familiar not only with the most basic goods available on the local market, like flour and sugar. They were also in touch with the fashions that dominated the American scene and could be bought by wealthier people in Indian Territory. Furthermore, at least some Creek small-scale farmers wanted to wear them at times, but they literally made the styles their own, and on their own terms. Creek women dedicated old skills—such as the plaiting of bluestem grass—to new ends, like shaping the curve of a bustle. In the process, they maintained control of the production of goods and kept a careful distance from the market—all the while selectively embracing its styles.

Creek women's hickory and bluestem bustles vividly illustrate the way that Creek farmers had crafted, in centuries of engagement with the market, a strategy to avoid dependency by simultaneously engaging trade and commercial culture while maintaining some distance from it. This strategy was both economic and political in nature and aimed at defending autonomy. This is not to deny that these farmers engaged that market and sought to benefit from it. Many grew cotton for sale as well as spinning, some grew wheat for sale, others engaged in occasional wage labor or small trading ventures. In fact, Sarah Aklin Odom's grandmother operated a "stage stand" in Eufaula, selling refreshments and perhaps offering lodging to travelers.[34] Nor could one deny that Creek farmers made their own bustles and hip pads because they could ill afford those that were for sale in town. After all, Sunday Taylor says that his family members made their clothes because store-bought was too expensive.[35] Yet Creek home production limited their need to buy, sell, and trade.

What bluestem bustles (or other items of Creek home production) ultimately reveal about the politics of land emerges when they are placed in the larger context of small-scale Creek farmers' economic strategies. The Creek land system was essential to small-scale Creek farmers like the Aklins, Smiths, and Taylors because they eked the bulk of their livelihood out of the land directly, through farming, raising livestock, and hunting. When farming, stock raising, or hunting provided a marketable surplus, it could be sold or, more likely, traded in kind. When times were relatively good, then, Creek small-scale farmers produced both a sustenance base and a market-derived surplus.

But, of course, times were not always good, and to understand small-scale Creek farmers' strategic approach to commerce, we need to understand that fact. As the U.S. Indian agent noted, droughts (such as a terrible stretch from 1879 though 1881) were a natural disaster and "great calamity" Creeks could do little to control.[36] They endeavored, however, to minimize their vulnerability to disasters that were human in origin—specifically, dependence on market forces. When Americans today think of small farmers' vulnerabilities, they are likely to think of the prices that crops fetch and the price farmers pay for loans. Yet in the late 1800s, small-scale Creek farmers ensured that their survival depended less on these prices than did commercial farmers of their time or of today. The food they ate was mostly their own produce, livestock, and game, and their farms were less dependent on credit. Obviously, Creek farmers did engage market forces. Yet most of the items small-scale Creek farmers traded for were not the foundations of their livelihood. Though it would involve sacrifice, they were generally items farm families could do without for some time, like sugar, or substitute with homemade articles, like women's homespun and woven cloth and hickory and bluestem bustles. By the 1870s, Creeks had centuries of experience in commercial trade with non-Indians, dating from the slave and deerskin trades of the late 1600s.[37] The fact that they continued to limit their engagement with the market demonstrates a shrewd familiarity with the vagaries of the commercial economy and the dangers of dependency.

Land Tenure, Race, and the Defense of Autonomy

In this strategy of small-scale farming and avoidance of dependency, no element was more essential than the Creek land system: communally owned land and privately owned use rights to fields. Reliance on that land system, moreover, was a fact that transcended race for the small-scale farming majority. For all the heterogeneity of the nation, this was something that small-scale farmers shared. Whatever their race, small Creek farmers could make fields to support themselves. This fact freed them from having to secure large amounts of cash income. The existence of undeveloped land was equally important to small farmers' way of life. Running livestock on the open range freed farmers from the labor and expense of raising and storing feed for cattle, hogs, and other livestock.[38] Similarly, the undeveloped commons was the source of the game that Creeks used for their meat and trade value.[39] In all likelihood, the commons were a particularly important resource in times of environmental distress, such as drought. The Creek land system made it possible for small-scale Creek farmers—whatever their race—to sustain themselves, their families, and their diverse and complex communities. It was an economic reality that sustained their culturally and racially complex social world.

In the 1870s and after, that land system would come under attack from forces within and outside the Creek Nation. The new politics of race in the Creek Nation emerged as soon as the 1866 treaty granted citizenship to the freed slaves. The former slaves were now Creek voters. They would hold the electoral balance between groups coming to be known as the Southern Creeks (also known as the McIntosh faction or Checote faction) and the Northern Creeks (also known as the Loyal Creeks, the conservatives, or the Sands faction). A new constitution created a bicameral legislature, known as the National Council, which consisted of the House of Kings and the House of Warriors. The machinery of state was retooled with a superficial resemblance to the U.S. government, but as Craig Womack argues, it adhered to a very old Creek principle: the *talwa*, or town, would remain central to governance. Just as they had always been, towns were represented in council. Each had one representative in the House of Kings, which was analogous to the U.S. Senate. In the House of Warriors, which was analogous to the U.S. House of Representatives, representation was proportionate to population, a town having one representative for every two hundred members.[40] The freed slaves (and soon, new black migrants from elsewhere) entered the Creek Nation as *talwas*. By at least 1869 and perhaps earlier, they became members of three new tribal towns: Canadian Colored, Arkansas Colored, and North Fork Colored.[41]

The creation of these towns had a variety of meanings and repercussions. At one level, it kept the bulk of black Creeks outside the other Creek towns.[42] This segregation would not have occurred if blacks had become members, for example, of their former owners' towns or the nearest "stomp ground" (as the central ritual space of a *talwa* was known). On another level, creating new towns was a long-established way of incorporating new peoples into the nation, following the practice and logic of the old Muskogee confederacy. Thus when new towns were created for freed slaves, they entered in the same way that Hitchitees and Yuchis and other peoples had come into the Creek confederacy: as new towns. Finally, creating three new towns gave black Creeks seats in both houses of the National Coun-

Creek National Council members, late nineteenth century. (Western History Collections, University of Oklahoma Libraries)

cil.[43] They thus came to have considerable weight in Creek government, especially given that the black towns were among the largest in the nation. They might have only three seats in the House of Kings, but because of representation based on town size, black town representatives occupied sixteen of the ninety-seven seats in the House of Warriors in 1878. One black judge was elected to the five-member supreme court.[44] Finally, black towns commanded about 15 percent of the popular vote, which directly elected constitutional officers such as the principal and assistant chief. Not surprisingly, black Creeks were loath to give their support to the Southern faction, led by former Confederate officer Sam Checote. Instead, they generally sided with the Northern faction, which was led by Oktarharsars Harjo (also known as Sands). There can be no doubt that Oktarharsars Harjo and his faction needed the votes of former slaves—both their popular votes and the seats they held in the National Council.

Black electoral power grew as the black towns grew. African Americans from the states contributed to some of the population increase (it is difficult to say how much). Like white American immigrants, many black immigrants came illegally into the Creek Nation and failed to obtain permits to stay. Unlike white American immigrants, many were taken in by Creek towns in the 1870s and 1880s and perhaps afterward. By becoming the members of a town, they effectively became citizens of the nation with which the town was federated.[45] The benefits for the newcomers were significant: they joined a community, adult men gained the franchise, and all received the right to use the national land. By the mid-1880s, some Checote-faction Creek legislators such as George Washington Stidham were complaining that the number of African American settlers had made it impossible to determine who was truly entitled to Creek citizenship. In 1884, Stidham (a former Confederate, wealthy merchant, and representative of the Lower Creek Hitchitee town in the National Council) predicted that if such immigration was not halted, in ten years, black Creeks would "control the whole country."[46] Stidham's alarm, voiced in terms of the racial nationalism of the Checote faction, reflected the growing electoral power of the black towns and the power the Northern faction drew from its alliance with the black towns.

Cattle, Pastures, and the Enclosure of Common Lands

This alliance gained strength as Creek ranchers and pasture holders began to threaten other citizens' access to "an equal interest in the soil." After emancipation, Creek planters had no sizable labor supply. Some black Creeks had briefly labored for their former owners in the immediate aftermath of the war, but by the 1870s black Creeks were largely farming for themselves. Similarly, other Creeks had little incentive to work on plantations, as they could make farms for themselves out of national lands.[47] In response, a number of displaced plantation owners turned to the growing western cattle trade for income. Ranching required much less labor than planting, and the demand for cattle was strong. In the late 1860s, Texas cattlemen began to drive their stock north through the Creek Nation and its neighbors, grazing their cattle on the nations' grasslands. They rarely paid for the privilege, as Creek law required.[48]

The turn toward ranching skyrocketed when the Missouri, Kansas, and Texas ("Katy") rail line was built, reaching the Arkansas River by 1872.[49] Thanks to the Katy, which linked Texas with Kansas, calves could be shipped up to the Creek Nation from Texas in April, fattened on the Creek grasslands, and then sent north to market in September.[50] The cattle trade represented an economic opportunity that the former planters were quick to exploit. They began to fence vast stretches of the undeveloped commons in the Creek Nation. In doing so, they transformed communal property that could have supported many small-scale farmers into pastures that they could claim as their own property. These entrepreneurial Creek families and white newcomers proceeded to operate ranches themselves and rent out pastures to non-Creek cattlemen.[51] As Angie Debo wrote, "The Creek Nation had all at once become a ranch country."[52]

The Fisher family made just this shift from plantation farming to cattle ranching. Samuel Fisher was a Creek of mixed European and indigenous ancestry. When he came to Indian Territory, his granddaughter Annie Noble later remembered, Samuel Fisher "brought many slaves with him and engaged in farming on a large scale." He died shortly before the Civil War. Creek families who made their fortunes in commerce, plantations, and ranching had largely adopted Anglo-American patrilineal inheritance patterns, so the plantation would normally then be operated by William, his son. But, as Annie Noble noted, "the slaves were made free." With no slave labor, William instead established a cattle ranch and traded cattle. By 1891, William Fisher was a wealthy man. His ranch boasted 1,600 head of cattle worth a total of $19,200, a cotton gin, a mill, and horses valued at $1,200. Although he had 50 acres under cultivation, his cattle accounted for the bulk of his land use. Fisher had a pasture one mile square (640 acres) fenced with five strands of barbed wire.[53] His ranch was larger than most ranches owned by Creeks. Lewis Bruner's ranch between Muskogee and Tulsa handled about 1,000 head per year, Una McIntosh near Eufaula put out about 600, and Roley McIntosh, also near Eufaula, fattened up about 400 or 500.[54] All these ranchers came from families that had operated plantations prior to emancipation.

These Creek-owned ranches were dwarfed by the largest cattle operations in the Creek Nation, most of which were operated by whites from outside the nation who leased land from Creeks. Principal Chief Legus Perryman and his brothers George, Tom, and Siah (or Josiah) were in the foremost ranks of Creeks who profited by helping outsiders to use huge amounts of land. They were in a good place to do so. Since removal four decades earlier, their family had been based in the eastern part of the nation, north of the Arkansas River, with ready access to the Katy rail line that facilitated shipping cattle. While Legus Perryman was chief, his brother George went before the council to secure a claim to a broad belt of land running from the Verdigris River to the Arkansas River—about 20 miles.[55] This first vast parcel—perhaps 120 square miles—formed the basis of a profitable business subleasing land to a number of noncitizens, including James Daugherty. Daugherty was a white Texan who was part of the inception of the postwar cattle trade and had been driving cattle through the Creek Nation for years. He was already a wealthy and well-connected man when he entered into a deal in 1885 to lease land from the Perrymans. Daugherty began a ranch that took up the bulk of the Perrymans' lands. On this land in 1894, Daugherty handled 60,000 cattle (some his, some belonging to other non-Creeks).[56] In 1890, the Perrymans leased some 120 square miles to D. H. Middleton, another cattleman from Texas. He later moved on to another large, leased parcel alongside the rail line near Muskogee, where he fattened 8,000–10,000 head of cattle per year.[57] These were hardly the only massive pastures that Creeks rented out to noncitizens or used for their own cattle in the 1880s and 1890s. Ranches of 10,000–20,000 acres were common enough in the nation. Frederick Severs, a white man who had been adopted into the nation, held a 20,000-acre ranch.[58] George Washington Grayson had 64,000 acres—100 square miles—under fence.[59] In 1887, the U.S. commissioner of Indian Affairs estimated that 61 Creek citizens controlled 1,072,251 acres, almost one-third of the Creek lands.[60]

The source and timing of these statistics raise a cautionary flag, reminding us of the pitfalls of discussing the politics of land concentration in Indian Territory in this period. That same year, 1887, the U.S. Congress passed the Dawes General Allotment Act, which provided for dividing up reservations into private parcels and doing away with tribal land tenure. The law culminated years of effort to wrest land from tribal hands, and it began a process that would be disastrous for tribal nations and Native individuals. The Creeks and the other nations of Indian Territory succeeded in ensuring that the act would not apply to them, but the pressure to force them to accept separate allotment agreements was already intense and growing. The commissioner of Indian Affairs was, then, hardly making a neutral observation when he claimed that a tiny minority of Creeks controlled a third of the nation's land. This statement was part of an effort to paint Creek leaders' opposition to allotment as merely a landed elite standing in the way of the interests of the broad mass of Creeks. The charge of land concentration was as patently self-interested as it was self-righteous. One hesitates to appear to endorse these colonialist attacks on Creek sovereignty. But, as Alexandra Harmon has shown, the concentration of land among the Creeks and neighboring tribal nations was a political issue raised not only by whites but by Indian citizens as well.[61] It became—along with the resistance to allotment—one of the central issues in Creek politics in the last decades of the nineteenth century. It must, therefore, occupy a central place in the analysis of Creek life and politics. Similar concerns about the political biases of sources apply to the use of Indian Pioneer History narratives that refer to Creeks taking hold of massive pastures. These heavily redacted accounts, written by project staff and not by the people interviewed, can be seen as shifting blame for the dispossession of Indians from whites to the Creeks themselves. But the controversies over land tenure that the narratives point to were real and were a divisive force in the Creek Nation.

The effects of large-scale ranching on the small-scale farming majority were significant, but they hit certain Creeks—poor people, blacks, and conservative "full-blood" towns—especially hard. Most directly affected were those who found their farms and homes literally fenced in as cattlemen enclosed pastures. Black Creeks tended to live in the old plantation regions in the east of the nation on lands close to the Katy and thus desirable to cattlemen. As Claudio Saunt argues, their very presence made "the appropriation of lands all the easier." Black Creeks like Vicey, Mollie, and Nanny Grayson found their farms and homes fenced in.[62] But the large pastures were a blow to other Creek districts and other small-scale farmers as well. In 1890, for example, a ranching company operating under the name Pussy, Tiger, and Company began building an 80-mile fence to ring a pasture of 256,000 acres. The pasture would have occupied much of the westernmost district of the nation. The principals in the firm were a Cherokee citizen and a white trader, but it did attract a hundred Creek partners, promising them $100 each per year. In accordance with the law, the company secured a vote of local citizens authorizing the pasture—though there were accusations that it bought the votes.[63] Creeks in this stronghold of the conservative and "full-blood" faction ran small herds of cattle on the open range. The fencing off of such a large and prime parcel would greatly interrupt the grazing of cattle and the free movement of people.[64] The growth of commercial ranching and the seizure of large pastures made the lives of Creeks, especially those who were poor, black, or conservative, more difficult.

This enclosure of the commons did not go uncontested. In the eastern part of the nation, the black Creek Graysons who had seen their lands enclosed wrote letters to Creek officials to protest this infringement on the spirit and law of Creek land tenure.[65] In the west, about seventy-five Creeks responded more directly. They destroyed the fence of Pussy, Tiger, and Company after sixty miles had been completed at considerable expense.[66]

These two cases — black Creek women writing letters to try to save their families' farms and conservative Creeks from the western reaches of the nation tearing down an offending fence — point to the way that large-scale enclosure of the common lands reinforced the alliance between black Creeks and conservative Creeks from "full-blood" towns. When we understand that small-scale farmers of different races faced the same threat from land enclosure, we can see that this alliance was born not only of wartime experience and electoral convenience but also of shared relationship to the land. The livelihoods of small-scale Creek farmers, whatever their race, depended on the Creek land tenure system. The large pastures were an assault on that land system and the way they made their living from the land.

These two cases also suggest why the enclosure of large pastures would encourage Creeks to take a national approach in their response and look to the National Council for action. Responding in this manner was a novelty among Creeks, for whom collective lands had historically been under the control of the individual towns of the confederacy. Admittedly, an 1818 law had shifted control of collective lands to the National Council. This law was, however, part of an effort to keep individuals or towns from ceding territory to the United States and was enforced in that sense. It is not clear that the law was intended to regulate the use of land internally — that is, within the Creek Nation — or that it was ever used in that way.[67] In the late nineteenth century, local community identities and politics remained powerful, and one might expect local political action in response to a conflict over land use such as the one the large pastures were precipitating. But a company like Pussy, Tiger, and Company was outside the control of town action. This company was based elsewhere, was largely capitalized by white Americans and Cherokees, had lined up a lessee promising $27,000 annually for the use of the pasture, and operated with the approval of the Creek Nation, and its fence was protected by a federal injunction.[68] Neither it nor its officers were under the control of town authorities. Similarly, it is certainly possible that the black Grayson women complained about the enclosure of their lands to their town officers, but no town *micco* (let alone a black town *micco*) would have been able to rein in such large players as the ranchers and cattlemen. By the time the pastures had grown to this scale, the issue was effectively beyond the scope of the individual towns. It is not surprising, then, that the response to the concentration of land took a decidedly national form. The small-scale Creek farmers' livelihood depended on the Creek land system, and protecting it required a national response.

The economic dimension of this alliance is essential, but it does not capture the way that this alliance was embedded in culture, in community, and most of all in a sense of interracial nationhood. In other words, small-scale producers—whether black or members of "full-blood" towns—had a similar relationship to the land, but that relationship cannot be understood in economic terms alone. First, it was not only individuals and their families but also their *communities* that depended on the commons. Complex and diverse small-scale farming communities like the Choska Bottoms and the "full-blood" towns of the western hills and the North Canadian River valley depended on the ready farmland availability and open range that the Creek land system provided. The heterogeneity of these communities, and of the larger Creek national community, was enmeshed with the Creek land tenure system and the Creek lands. The land these people were defending their access to was, moreover, not just any land. It was the land of the Creek Nation. When black Creeks and conservatives from "full-blood" towns asserted that they could not be denied access to that land, they asserted that this was their nation.

More important, when they made this claim *together*, they gave new power to the idea that theirs was a nation composed of a number of peoples. Historian Tanis Thorne puts succinctly an essential point in Creek history: "Pluralism was a defining characteristic of the Creek, an aggregation of diverse peoples fused into one nation."[69] What is more, Creeks in the late nineteenth century were *conscious* that pluralism was one of the defining characteristics of their nationhood. Although the narrow nationalism of George Washington Grayson and his allies might exclude black Creeks, the composite nature of Creek society was apparent and recognized in the oral tradition and the structure of Creek government. Creeks could draw on this idea to argue that they were a nation that could incorporate different peoples of different races.

Telling and teaching the oral tradition of the nation reaffirmed its composite nature. Oral traditions that were written down in the nineteenth and twentieth centuries shed light on how different peoples came together to form the Creeks in the seventeenth and eighteenth centuries. Yet those stories were not just of historical importance at the time ethnographers recorded them. Creeks told them in the context of ongoing struggles to defend Creek lands and sovereignty.[70] Indeed, the stories tell us much about how the Creek people who told them in 1890 or 1900 or 1910 conceived of their nation in their own time. They express, among other things, a Creek political theory of nationhood. Creek literary scholar Craig Womack has argued that, "to exist as a nation, the community needs a perception of nationhood." He contends that stories provide this perception. Stories help a community "imagine who they are as a people, how they came to be, and what cultural values they wish to preserve." In telling or listening to the stories, "the people are reconstituted as a nation."[71] As Womack argues, not all ideas of nationhood and sovereignty follow a European model. and "Creeks had their version of such notions."[72] The issue, then, is to tease those notions out of Creek stories. For the Creeks in the late nineteenth century, the oral tradition could demonstrate not only that they were a nation but also that they were a particular kind of nation: one composed of many peoples.

In the late nineteenth century and beyond, Creek oral tradition passed on the memory that different peoples came together to form the Creeks. and those stories were collected by ethnographers. The 1890s conservative political leader Isparhecher, a Kasihta, told how the Kasihtas and Cowetas had been on the brink of war when the Kasihta warriors whipped the Cowetas with switches but did not attack them with weapons. To "obtain revenge . . . Coweta challenged Kasihta to a game of ball." Following these somewhat mediated conflicts, Kasihtas and Cowetas together became the leading towns of the Creek white (peace) and red (war) moieties, respectively, maintaining the balance that preserved the alliance.[73] Zachariah Cook's stories extended the story of alliance. He recounted (in a story he had learned from Judge Nokosi, who had learned it from Napoleon Yahola, demonstrating the durability of the oral tradition) how Cowetas had allied with their former rival people, the Tukabahchees (Tuckabatchees), in a moment marked by mixing the Cowetas' medicine of *pasa* with the Tukabahchees' medicine of *mekko-hoyvnēcv*.[74] Napoleon Yahola, a Kasihta, further extended the story of alliance, explaining that the Tukabahchees and the Łiwahalis "were once in a fog or vapor which prevented them from seeing each other" but the Łiwahalis "wanted to see the Tukabahchee very much." Eventually, "the fog was blown away so that they could do so," At first, the Tukabahchees remained aloof, refusing to talk to the Łiwahalis. But once they finally began speaking and identified themselves, the Tukabahchees declared the Łiwahalis to be their "younger brothers."[75] This extensive body of oral traditions also explained how peoples such as the Yuchis and Hitchitis. who had substantially different languages and histories than the Muskogee-speaking towns like Coweta and Cusseta (Kasihta). became part of the Creek confederacy and ultimately the Creek Nation.[76] For example, around 1910 Jackson Lewis explained to ethnologist John Swanton how it was that the Hitchitis, whose language is not comprehensible to speakers of other Muskogee dialects, became allied with founding towns of the confederacy. The Hitchitis were living in Florida when Creek people arrived there. As the newcomers "were very warlike," Lewis reported, "the Hitchiti concluded it would be best to make friends with them and become a part of them. Ever since they have been together as one people."[77] It is important to note that the "one people" they became part of was not the Creek towns themselves but rather the Creek confederacy of towns. In the stories and in Creek political practice, towns maintained their distinctiveness (some were even be labeled "foreign") although they became parts of one nation.

The political structure of the nation, as mandated by the 1867 constitution and practiced in governance, also bore witness to this reality. As Womack emphasizes, although the Creek constitution reproduced the bicameral structure of the U.S. government and many of its features, it preserved the town-centered nature of Creek political life.[78] Both houses of the legislature were composed of representatives, not of the nation as a whole, but of towns, including the three black towns. Despite the centralizing efforts of some wealthy and powerful Creeks in the early nineteenth century, and despite the racially exclusive nationalism that was still associated with them, the composite nature of the nation remained apparent.

Defending their interests in land and nationhood despite their differences required Creek conservatives and black Creeks to do the work of nationhood rather than simply assert nationalism. Ill will often separated black Creeks from other Creeks, including conservatives. Black Creeks had reason to be wary. After all, a number of their conservative allies, including the conservative leader Isparhecher himself, had fought on the side of the Confederate States before changing sides and joining the Union forces.[79] Similarly, nonblack Creeks who feared black political domination were not wrong to charge that the black towns made themselves more powerful (by increasing their electoral clout) when they treated black newcomers from the states as Creek citizens. Divisions between the groups were longstanding and real. Indeed, in the decades after the war settlement patterns and churches became more segregated.[80] Tension could flare up dangerously. In November 1881, for example, newspapers warned of an impending "race war between full-blood Creeks and negroes" in one section of the nation. Reports circulated that drunken Lighthorsemen (national police officers) had shot and killed a black suspect named Culley while taking him into custody on an unnamed charge. Although "sober reflection" averted the predicted "war," the events illustrate that black Creeks were suspicious of authorities and willing to challenge "full-bloods," political alliance or no.[81] The tension that existed between the black Creeks and other Creeks (including conservatives) should not be denied or minimized. Rather, it makes even more significant the fact that some embraced an idea of nationhood that included difference.

The extraordinary nature of the alliance between black Creeks and conservatives comes into sharper focus when events in the Creek Nation are compared with those in the Chickasaw, Choctaw, and Cherokee nations. As work by Barbara Krauthamer and Tiya Miles demonstrates, like the Creeks, the Chickasaw, Choctaw, and Cherokee nations had populations of former slaves. As in the Creek Nation, entrenched, wealthy, and powerful interests in these nations denied that blacks were entitled to equal citizenship rights—or even to citizenship. And as in the Creek Nation, blacks in these nations asserted their citizenship rights. But unlike in the Creek Nation, conservatives and blacks in the Chickasaw, Choctaw, and Cherokee nations did not form an alliance that came to the political fore, let alone build a movement that asserted that their nationhood was of a composite and multiracial nature. Though it is only a partial explanation, it may be that interracial alliances found less fertile ground in these nations because their political traditions and structures emphasized a unitary rather than composite nationhood.[82] By admitting former slaves as separate towns, nonblack Creeks could include blacks in the nation but maintain distance from them.

The Alliance in Politics and Law

The black-conservative alliance is apparent in the politics of the 1870s and 1880s. As early as 1871, the alliance of those black towns with conservative Creeks, led by Oktarharsars Harjo (Sands), was apparent. That year, Canadian Colored Town, Arkansas Colored Town, and North Fork Colored Town unanimously voted for the "Sands party" candidate, Cotchoche, over Checote for principal chief. In doing so, they joined strongly conservative towns such as Nuyaka. The black and conservative votes might have won had it not been for the conservatives' refusal to use the new paper balloting method—part of ongoing resistance to the new, U.S.-derived practices of constitutional government. When they insisted instead on the older Creek form of voting (literally standing in a group for one's candidate), their votes were thrown out and Checote won. On other occasions black and conservative votes were not thrown out. In the next election, in 1875, the conservative candidate, Lochar Harjo, won the principal chieftaincy when the black towns, like the conservative town of Arbeka, gave him all their votes. Lochar Harjo repaid this loyalty when he tried to resolve the citizenship claims of a number of blacks and worked to give black Creeks and "full-bloods" more equal access to the form of schooling that had been previously mostly reserved for "mixed-blood" Indians—the local boarding schools. The House of Kings soon removed Lochar Harjo from office, however, because of financial improprieties and his unwillingness to do as the council wished. The political fact of the alliance is apparent in the council's vote on whether to remove Lochar Harjo from office, in which he received support only from "full-bloods" and black Creeks. In the 1878 elections for principal chief, black towns again voted in a bloc with the bulk of the "full-bloods." When the votes of the three black towns were thrown out, however, Checote again won the election.[83] By this time, all parties sought the votes of black Creeks because it was clear to everyone that black Creeks held the balance of power in the highly divided nation. Black towns continued, however, to support conservative politicians.

Factional rivalry in the Creek Nation reached a climax in July 1882, when a group of Creeks initiated an insurrection that is remembered as the Green Peach War, after the season in which it broke out. On the grounds that he would not enforce the law, the Checote government removed Isparhecher, a leader of the conservative Loyal Party, from his position of judge. It then attempted to arrest him on charges of sedition. Soon, the dissident movement was operating as a parallel and rival government. When Creeks who were loyal to Isparhecher met in council, only to be confronted by government Lighthorsemen who wanted to disarm them, the conflict escalated. Isparhecher had the support of the black and conservative alliance that opposed the Checote faction. Black Creeks such as Morris Rentie and Scott McIntosh joined conservatives in what Rentie called the "Spieche [Isparhecher] army."[84] This "army" was no match, however, for the militia assembled by the Checote government. The militia disbanded the resistance, forcing Isparhecher and a number of other conservatives westward into the Sac and Fox Nation. The conflict came to a negotiated end in August 1883, with Checote's government maintaining its authority. Accounts suggest that only a handful of men were killed, but several dozen were convicted of treason and received the heavy sentence of one hundred lashes. Checote pardoned almost all, however—except twelve blacks who received their whipping after they attempted to escape.[85]

This fact suggests that race may have played a larger (though indirect) part in the underlying tensions behind the Green Peach War than historians have recognized. Most historians see the war as a lashing out by conservatives against a more progressive and business-oriented Checote faction.[86] Historian J. Leitch Wright, however, argues that the internal diversity of the nation played itself out in the brief war. Wright suggests, indeed, that the internal dynamic of Creek history was shaped by a long-term conflict between the Muskogee towns and non-Muskogee towns. While his argument is too sweeping, he rightly emphasizes that the ethnic diversity of the Creeks was fundamental to their politics.[87] Unfortunately, he never incorporates black Creeks into his analysis. After all, three new non-Muskogee towns had just entered the nation—the black towns, which accounted for a sixth of the national population. If we extend Wright's insight to include black Creeks, we see that when they took part in the Green Peach War, they demonstrated that they had become part of the internal political dynamic of the diverse Creek Nation.

Isparhecher and his interracial group of allies were defeated in the Green Peach War, but they went on to reassert the principles of common nationhood and common national lands across racial boundaries. On August 20, 1883, only days after the Green Peach conflict was resolved, the Loyal Party issued its platform for the fall election. In addition to nominating Isparhecher to the principal chieftaincy, the platform affirmed the party's dedication to "nationality" and "lands in common." In a move that spoke to the uncertain position of blacks from the South who had settled among the Creeks, the party declared its intention to enfranchise noncitizens who had married citizens, regardless of race.[88] Just as they had helped give form to the 1866 treaty that affirmed their citizenship and their "equal interest in the land," black Creeks helped determine the course of the politics that aimed to protect that order. A black Creek named Robert Grayson chaired the committee that drafted the platform. In the 1883 election, Isparhecher defeated Joseph Perryman and Sam Checote.[89]

For Isparhecher, the election sealed the Creek notion of interracial nationhood to class politics. The new chief told the council that Creeks could learn a "useful lesson" from these events: "Every Muskogee citizen, whether his skin be red, white or black, has equal rights and privileges in this nation, and the most abject, poor and ignorant is entitled to equal consideration with the most distinguished, rich and learned at the hands of our officers."[90] Note that racial, class, and national politics are interwoven in this statement: citizens of the nation have "equal rights and privileges" whatever their race and also whatever their class.

Befitting this politics of race, class, and nation, the interracial alliance focused its energies on keeping landlords and pasture owners from concentrating landownership further. Isparhecher led a push to rid the Creek Nation of "intruders" (a group that included the prospective tenants of Creek landlords). The alliance also ultimately secured the passage of a law that made any Creek who employed a noncitizen subject to fines or whippings.[91] Working together in the Creek council, this same group secured passage of statutes limiting the size of pastures and regulating the introduction of cattle into the nation.[92] Laws forbade noncitizens who had a license to trade in the nation from keeping ranches or "permanent stocks of cattle"; banned the practice of renting out pastureland to U.S. citizens or hiring them as laborers or herders; and barred Creeks from renting land within three miles of the Katy train tracks (highly sought after by cattlemen) to noncitizens.[93] The laws were often ignored or skirted, and in response, the council repeatedly refined them. In 1881, for example, the statute forbidding noncitizens from maintaining cattle was made more explicit by the passage of a law barring any noncitizen from holding more animals than needed to do their labor.[94] This law would keep hired noncitizen farm managers, for example, from operating ranches for themselves. In 1884 and 1885, laws were passed to ban the practice of Creek citizens claiming to own cattle that they were really only pasturing for noncitizens.[95]

As these last statutes suggest, Creek citizens themselves played a large part in the concentration of land for grazing purposes. To counter the enclosure of common lands, laws could not just focus on noncitizens. It was to rectify this problem that the council passed a new pasture law in 1889. The law limited citizens to one square mile of fenced pasture lands, so long as they did not impinge on other citizens' lands. The law promised to sharply reduce the practice of leasing large tracts to noncitizens, although it made exceptions for pastures on the borders of the nation.[96] The passage of the law testifies to how the alliance of black and conservative towns succeeded in placing the defense of the national commons—which was also the defense of the interests of small producers and their communities—at the center of the Creek political agenda in the 1870s and 1880s. The passage of this law is one measure of the success of that alliance.

But the creation of an interracial alliance that asserted a nonracial sense of a composite Creek nationhood was a still more remarkable feat. It proceeded from the presumption that Creeks had the right to define their nation in their own terms. Faced with American colonialism, Creek nationalists from the rival faction had taken the opposite tack. Under the unrelenting pressure of colonialist racism, Creek nationalists of this kind tried to conform to its standards to defend their national sovereignty. They thus sought to legislate and demonstrate their nation's civilizing degree of European ancestry and its reassuring lack of African ancestry. In contrast, the alliance between conservatives and black Creeks defined their nation in a way that defied American standards.

This assertion of composite nationhood, rooted in the oral tradition, Creek political structure, and the shared small-farmer orientation of the Creek majority, helped black and conservative Creeks make significant gains in defending their access to the national lands. To focus on the ways that land, political structure, and the oral tradition provided the material from which Creek conservatives and black Creeks forged an alliance is not to deny the racial divisions that exist within Creek history, let alone indigenous history more broadly. Rather, it is to demonstrate that it was possible for an interracial nationhood to draw its sustenance from indigenous soil. But as the nineteenth century came to a close, the already unrelenting American pressures on the Creek Nation would reach a new intensity. Not only the black and conservative alliance but all Creeks faced a colonial power that wanted to take away the thing they had in common—the nation as land and the nation as sovereign polity.

PART II

Allotment

DIVIDING LANDS, NATIONS, AND RACES

At stake in allotment was the meaning of nations and the fate of races. From the point of view of a middle-class white reformer in the 1880s who was dedicated to the notion that America marched forward, what could Indian land tenure represent but a brake on the progress of the nation? For a working-class white agrarian, what could Indian farmers, landlords, and governments mean but impediments on the path to white American landownership and white American democracy? For white reformers and agrarians alike, for America to be America, Indian lands had to be allotted. But for Creeks, their nation and the land were equally indivisible. Cutting up the land threatened to dismember the people. The struggle over drawing new boundaries on that land brought new focus to the bound- aries between, and within, the American and Creek nations.

Raw Country and Jeffersonian Dreams

THE RACIAL POLITICS OF ALLOTMENT

"At first this was just raw country," Joe Grayson told his interviewer. In 1937, the elderly white man sat in his rural home northwest of Henryetta, Oklahoma, and recounted a classic pioneer story of which he was the hero. "I came to the Indian Territory when I was fourteen years old with my parents," in 1887. "We had two wagons with ox teams." On those wagons they hauled the possessions they needed to make a home. The family, he remembered, crossed into the territory "on the Goodlands in the Kiamichi Mountains. We crossed several rivers, forded the Mountain Fork, crossed the Kiamichi River on a ferry." The family went on and "passed through Talihina, Stringtown, Atoka and went on to Allen." What was his family looking for? Grayson explained simply, "You found a place that looked as if it would make good crops. Then you built a house and barns and fences to suit your requirements." Grayson's story is a familiar one. It resembles that of Laura Ingalls, whose memories of her family's little house on the prairie 150 miles northeast of the Graysons' have fired the pioneer fantasies of millions of American children. But a discordant note disrupts Grayson's idyll. He remembered that at first "you" (presumably a white man) could just find a fertile patch of land and build but "later you had to lease the land from the Indians. Sometimes they took money and sometimes the rent was paid by a portion of the crops." He found himself obliged to give his listener a short lesson on Indian land law: one could sell "improvements" or crops but not

...self. The indigenous presence erupts into the pioneer narrative ...indigenous law imposed itself on the Grayson family—and just as ...ge men strode into the Ingalls cabin, making it clear that this was not, ...n fact, their home.[1]

Just two years before Grayson and his family trespassed across Indian Territory nations to squat on Indian land, Senator Henry Dawes narrated another interrupted idyll in an address to a group of white eastern reformers. To the Board of Indian Commissioners he recounted his recent travels to the Cherokee Nation, where "the head chief" (presumably Cherokee chief Dennis Bushyhead) had informed him that "there was not a family in that whole nation that had not a home of its own. There was not a pauper in that nation, and the nation did not owe a dollar." Yet indigenous land use erupts into Dawes's tale, also. Despite the solvency of the nation and its people, to Dawes, "the defect of the system was apparent." Dawes believed in something he called progress, and he believed that, for Cherokees and other Indians as well, progress was halted "because they own their land in common." This meant "there is no selfishness, which is at the bottom of civilization." Dawes said that only one change could remedy this problem: "Until this people consent to give up their lands and divide them among their citizens so that each can own the land he cultivates, they will not make much progress."[2] This process, known as "allotment in severalty" (or simply "allotment"), was Dawes's primary cause. It consisted of taking the lands of an Indian nation and turning them into private plots, each plot assigned to one individual. Dawes and like-minded reformers believed that the individualization of property would individualize Indians and unleash the progress for which he hoped. He exhorted his colleagues to transform Indian lands into private property and Indian people into property seekers.

Class, region, education, and experience separated Grayson from Dawes, but much linked them as well. Both spoke as white American men. For both Grayson (a western farmer, cowhand, and oilfield worker) and Dawes (a wealthy senator from the East), that meant certain expectations about themselves, racial others, and land. For Grayson, white American manhood entailed the right to own land and even the right to take it from Indians. For Dawes, white American manhood entailed the right to decide how to transform racial others, which included changing their way of using land. Grayson talks of mountain ranges the family traversed and rivers they forded, but he fails to mention that his family was passing without permission from Arkansas into the Choctaw Nation, then on to the Chickasaw Nation.

He would later move north, into the Creek Nation. Grayson obscured all of that indigenous geography, polity, and presence with a simple statement: "At first this was just raw country." For his part, Dawes talks of Indians as if they were so much clay awaiting the hands of an American sculptor, white hands wielding the tool of land policy to shape Indian clay into proper Americans.

These stories enrich our understanding of the way that property in land—both the land itself and stories about the land and what one could do with it—built a foundation for white American racial nationalism and colonialism. National identity was as deeply tied to land tenure for white Americans as it was for Creeks. White Americans thought about land and ownership, and their relationship to race and nationhood, in very different ways than did most black Creeks, their conservative allies, and even their "progressive" Creek rivals. White Americans—especially the reformers and federal officials and would-be farmers who played such a large role in the transformation of the Creek Nation in the 1880s and 1890s—saw America as a republic of white landowning men. This conception of what it meant to be American and white gave many Americans a sense that they were entitled to impose their land tenure system and their political authority on the Creek Nation and other tribal nations. For white Americans, allotment and the dissolution (in American eyes) of tribal authority constituted the setting aright of hierarchies of race and gender. To such men, allotment and tribal dissolution were part of the inevitable expansion of a racialized nation that had taken a continent and was building an island empire. Two very different sets of white Americans brought these ideas to the Creek Nation. The first consisted of whites like Grayson who wished to settle there and own lands there and who believed they had a right to do so by dint of their race and nationality. The second consisted of reformers like Dawes who had no intention of moving to Indian Territory but who wished to do away with Creek government and land tenure and make Creeks and their nation culturally, economically, and politically part of the United States.

This chapter tracks the politics of allotment in the Creek Nation from the 1880s to 1906. To emphasize how that politics transformed the nation, this chapter stands alone as one of the three parts of this book. In its narrowest sense, "allotment" means the brief bureaucratic act of recording a name in a ledger book and assigning a deed to that name. If that were all allotment was, this book would have two parts instead of three, with the discussion of allotment concluding the first or opening the second. But in the Creek Nation, "allotment" meant much more. For this book, the moment of allocating deeds matters less than the quarter-century-long political struggle over whether the Creek Nation would accept allotment and how it would be enacted there. The pressure by the American colonial power on Creeks to accept allotment and the dissolution of their national government propelled a long debate over the fundamental issues of who belonged to the nation and what belonging meant. Indeed, a colonial policy that attempted to force Creeks to reduce their nationhood to a piece of land to be carved up favored the narrowest conceptions of what it meant to be Creek. Ultimately, the imposition of allotment, the political conflict it engendered, and the way it was executed encouraged a shift by many Creeks toward a racial conception of the Creek Nation.

"Intruders," Boomers, and Jeffersonian Agrarianism

After the Civil War, non-Indian "intruders" (as the unauthorized immigrants were known to Indian governments) began to trickle into the Creek Nation. At first they arrived in small numbers. But in the 1880s and 1890s, the number of intruders rose rapidly, until in 1890 the federal census found that 3,289 whites and 4,621 blacks inhabited the nation along with 9,999 Indians.[3] Most of the whites and some of the black people had entered the nation illegally. The promise of landownership was a powerful draw for both groups, and in the next chapter we will see the special meaning it held for African Americans. Yet it was the beliefs and actions of whites that would upend the Creek Nation, and so it makes sense to focus first on them.

In the three decades following the Civil War, white pressure on Creek lands intensified on several fronts. First, many whites called for the "opening" of Creek and other Indian Territory lands for white settlement. The 1862 Homestead Act and a series of similar acts transferred millions of acres of the public lands to private hands, but these only whetted the demand for still more lands.[4] Beginning in 1880, would-be homesteaders and land speculators, known as Boomers, massed on the Kansas–Indian Territory border and repeatedly ventured into Indian Territory to seize land, only to be ousted by federal troops after Creek authorities requested their removal.[5] Simultaneously, the Creek Nation was subject to another, quieter, and more successful incursion as white Americans settled there. A fraction of them had Creek Nation licenses or permits to work as traders or in the skilled trades. Most farmed either as squatters or as tenants who worked the lands of wealthy Creeks, only some of whom obtained a Creek

Nation permit to hire a noncitizen laborer, as the law required. William Luker recalled that when his family came from Tennessee they just "slipped into this country" rather than pay the permit fee.[6] The Creek authorities had no effective jurisdiction over whites, and federal authorities took only occasional and ineffectual action to remove intruders, and so they stayed. Over the years, more and more "slipped into" the nation. Perry and Tilda Brasfield came from Arkansas in 1890 and rented 160 acres a few miles southeast of Eufaula. The two-room log cabin, the homemade furniture and farm implements, and even the number of acres all recall familiar images of white homesteaders on the Great Plains.[7] But one important difference separated them from the idealized image of the homesteader: these whites were renting their 160 acres from an Indian, not homesteading it, and they could not legally own it.

To understand what the 160-acre stake meant for white settlers, it is worth looking more closely at the ideas of the Boomers. Unlike most white farmers of modest means, they made dramatic statements of their ideas and public demonstrations of their need for land.[8] The Boomers brought with them the racialized agrarianism that was their heritage. "Agrarianism," in this context, refers to the belief that farmers by rights are independent producers and that their independence derives in large part from owning their own land. Rooted in Jeffersonianism and republicanism and fed by the United States' expansion in the nineteenth century, this agrarianism was crucial to the creation of the state of Oklahoma and the development of insurgent farmer politics there.

The Boomers' demands for Indian lands expressed a hostility to (and an anxiety about) Indians' owning land that was imbued with American nationalism and beliefs about racial and gender hierarchy. To Boomers like W. T. Miller, it was axiomatic that Indian Territory land "does not belong to any Indian tribe or nation" but to "the people"—that is, white American people.[9] More than that, however, Indian land tenure threatened racial and gender degeneration. In an open letter to President Rutherford B. Hayes, another Boomer warned that white men in Indian Territory were reduced to marrying "squaws" in order to obtain land, thereby "filling the country with lawless half breeds."[10] In fact, a number of white American men, including prominent men in Creek affairs such as Louis Henderson Posey, were able to farm in the Creek Nation only because they had married Indian women. These men were commonly referred to in the white press as "squaw men," a derisive term that captures the ways that ideas of race and manhood came together in the agrarianism of the time. The ambiguity of the phrasing suggested that not only were these men married to "squaws" but they were themselves at least part "squaw." From the point of view of white American racial nationalists, the threat these men posed to the racial and gender order was therefore double. The perverse practice of Indian land tenure forced white men to lower themselves to marrying or becoming "squaws" in order to pursue their birthright as white American men: their own farmland.

The U.S. government did not permit the invasions as the Boomers wished, but federal policy turned decisively in favor of white settlers and against Indian land tenure at the end of the 1880s. In 1889, the federal government allowed would-be homesteaders to make a dash for a choice piece of the "Unassigned Lands," territory the Creeks had ceded to the United States in the treaty of 1866. In an iconic moment in the history of the American West, the hopeful settlers rushed on horseback, in wagons, and on foot to be the first to stake their claims on a desirable plot. As the 1890s wore on, still more Indian lands were distributed to settlers in a similar manner until the Creeks and other nations of the Five Tribes were surrounded by white farmers and governments hostile to their presence. In the eyes of many American observers and officials, Indian lands and governments became "anomalies."[11] Allotment would do away with these anomalies.

The story that white proponents of allotment told themselves was about creating idealized equality embedded in freedom and property. In reality, they used their colonial authority to enforce a rigid racial and gender inequality. Allotment sought to transform Indians into normative Americans as much as to impose a new landownership system on them. Specifically, reformers claimed that under land tenure in common, Native people were mere undifferentiated elements in a tribal mass.[12] With the private ownership of land, they would become the individuals of classical liberal theory—that is, rational economic actors and individual political citizens. Classical liberal theory, a foundation of American government, American capitalism, and American national self-conception, imagines individuals as abstractions. It is individuals' legal personhood—the right to make choices, the right to own things—that matters, not their particularities, and certainly not such supposedly physical attributes as their race or gender. The idea of the equality of persons is, moreover, inseparable from their abstract quality. By looking at how allotment actually worked in the Creek Nation, however, we can see that allotment did not create equals, and certainly not disembodied equals. It did create legal individuals, but at the very moment it did so, it legally and permanently marked those individuals with bodily differences of race and gender. Allotment enforced a hierarchy on the individuals it created, locking them in boxes called "Freedman," "full-blood," "mixed-blood," "male," or "female."

The Dawes Commission, "Full-Bloods,"
and Land Monopoly

In 1887, the reformers' zeal permitted them to get a mostly indifferent Congress to pass the General Allotment Act, usually known as the Dawes Act. The law provided for dividing up the tribal estate of American Indian peoples in preparation for extinguishing tribal government and extending American citizenship to Indian individuals. The vehement objections of the Cherokee, Chickasaw, Choctaw, Creek, and Seminole nations won Indian Territory an exemption from the act.[13] In the years after its passage, western legislators and businesses interested in land speculation militated for the allotment of lands in Indian Territory.[14] These demands for more allotment legislation came to fruition in 1893, when Congress empowered a commission to negotiate agreements with each of the tribes to provide for the allotment of Indian lands and the end of tribal government. Dawes, recently retired from the Senate, was appointed to head a three-member commission that became known as the Dawes Commission.[15] The commissioners traveled almost immediately to Indian Territory to begin negotiations, arriving there in early 1894.[16]

The Dawes commissioners and other reformers saw in Indian Territory a crisis of land monopoly, a terrible racial and class injustice that they aimed to resolve through allotment. Historian Alexandra Harmon demonstrates that many white Americans perceived a problem of land distribution in the states of the Union, and they accused the nations of Indian Territory of excessive land concentration, as well. In addition to serving to condemn wealthy Indians, these accusations underlay the moral self-justification of white Americans who called for allotment. Allotment, they claimed, would restore justice to land distribution and benefit especially "the masses," which the commissioners identified with "the full-bloods."[17] Indian commissioner Archibald McKennon argued that in the Creek Nation communal tenure was a sham. "A few men," he maintained, "hold many thousands of acres each; others only a few acres. Those who hold so many acres would not be benefited by a chan[g]e, but the masses would be."[18] Commission members repeatedly made it clear that they believed the impoverished objects of their protection to be "full-bloods" whose rights to land were being overwhelmed by wealthier "mixed-bloods."[19] Newspapers that backed the allotment cause were quick to take up the refrain, charging that elite politicians had intimidated "full-blood" Indians from voicing their true feelings of support for allotment.[20]

In the late nineteenth century, "the vanishing full-blood," the disappearing Indian of purely indigenous ancestry, occupied a large place in the Anglo-American imagination. These real Indians were doomed, so the story went, to die away as a new generation of "mixed-bloods," ignorant of the ancient ways, took their place. This tragic but inevitable demise made the figure of the "full-blood" all the more poignant.[21] When non-Indian reformers claimed that they were the true champions of the rights of "full-blood" Indians, they thus portrayed themselves as protecting real Indians from the voracious greed of racially mixed, inauthentic Indians. This eulogy before the fact deflected blame for land pressure from whites to Indians of mixed racial ancestry. It also declared that Indians were doomed by history, part of the past and not the future.

Because of his famous defense of land tenure in common, Isparhecher, a leading figure among Creek conservatives, frequently represented the "full-blood" in the imagination of white proponents of allotment. The editorialist of a pro-allotment newspaper, for example, invoked the trope of the tragic "full-blood" when he rhapsodized that Isparhecher was "a model of the type that we read of in Cooper's novels. Strongnatured [sic], honest, and thoroughly Indian." The writer's admiration for this idealized figure centered on Isparhecher's call for resistance to allotment, which the writer termed "a cry from a breaking heart." Yet the editorialist maintained that resistance was futile because "progress is inexorable. It moves steadily forward, crushing beneath its iron wheels all things that stand in its path."[22] The concern that white advocates of allotment elicited for the welfare of the "full-blood Indian" was inseparable from the belief that "the great expanding God of our Anglo-Saxon worship" doomed Isparhecher and the protest he represented to be "sacrificed to [the] triumphal progress" of Anglo-American settlement.[23] Never mind that Isparhecher was hardly content to be relegated to the past. In fact, this editorial was prompted by a pronouncement by Isparhecher that rejected allotment based on very contemporary legal arguments and analogies to the experiences of other tribal nations and the Hawaiian Islands. Still, in the minds of reformers, he and his nation were of the past. The idea that Indian authenticity was lodged in "the full-blood," and that it and he faced destruction by the forces of progress, informed the commissioners' insistence that Indians of mixed white ancestry were opposing allotment so that they could continue to benefit from a situation that robbed "full-bloods" of their rights.

Home Rule and White Prerogative

A sense of white American manhood and its prerogatives revealed the relation between demands for allotment and statehood. As the *Vinita Indian Chieftain* newspaper wryly noted, "The lustiest cries of 'home rule' come from the throats of men who never saw the country until a short time ago."[24] These people were white Americans who expected, along with the right to own land, the right to govern—"home rule." Standing before a white audience in the Choctaw Nation, Orville Platt, a Massachusetts senator and a member of the Dawes Commission, lamented that in Indian Territory "the white man" was reduced to the status of a "ward of the Indian, and a neglected ward at that." The racial inversion, and the implied infantilization and feminization of dependency, were outrageous. "Home rule" was their right as white American men, regardless of the fact that they were in another nation. "An Indian said to me to-day," Platt claimed, "that the white man had no right to complain" about being ruled by Indians. This same Indian had even told Platt "that if you did not like it you could go away." Platt scoffed that anyone who shared this opinion did not know the true nature of the white man. In colonial adventures and conquests from Puerto Rico to Hawai'i to the Philippines, Americans at the time were forging a sense of whiteness that spanned what they had earlier considered the different European races. Platt evoked this far-flung imperial whiteness and tied it to the colonial domination of continental sites like Indian Territory. He declared that it was "inborn in the Saxon, the Celt, and the Teutons, where he plants himself, he stays." White American men had the right to take lands, remain on them, and govern them as they saw fit. Indeed, according to Platt, doing so was part of their inborn nature.[25]

A wide social, educational, and economic gulf separated whites of modest means like Joe Grayson and the Boomers, on the one hand, from the ideologists of allotment and statehood, on the other. Nor were their agendas identical; one cannot confuse would-be settlers from self-defined reformers. Yet the two groups shared assumptions that linked race, American nationhood, and gender to private property in land. "Intruder" and Boomer men aimed to achieve their right, as white American men, to own lands and to govern them. For their part, the reformers wished to transform "the Indian" into a proper American and a proper man and to reduce his racial liability of difference, tasks that they believed entailed "giving" him private property in land while taking away his self-government. By the late 1880s, the settlers and reformers had not achieved the goals of "opening" the Creek Nation or imposing allotment on it, but they would succeed in making allotment the central—and divisive—issue in Creek politics.

Isparhecher: From Citizenship to Blood

The effects of that change can be seen in Isparhecher's changing ideas regarding citizenship, race, and land. In the summer of 1891, Isparhecher was happy to accept the nomination of the National Party for principal chief of the Creek Nation. Isparhecher was a farmer who had long been prominent among the faction of the nation who tilled their small farms, ran their herds on the commons, and resisted the land enclosures and political ambitions of wealthier, school-educated, English-speaking cattlemen, planters, and landlords. Though unable to read and write, Isparhecher was renowned for his eloquence and intelligence.[26] The National Party was the most recent iteration of the political organization of small-scale farmers, conservative towns, and their black town allies. Isparhecher noted with pride that the party had opposed measures permitting Creeks to enclose large tracts of the commons for private pastures and had been "outspoken in opposition to the sectionalization of our land"—in other words, allotment. In the tradition of the 1880s black-conservative alliance, Isparhecher linked the defense of land tenure in common to the respect of the equal rights of all Creek citizens.[27] "I will recognize," he assured the nation, "all people as equals whether *white, red* or *black*."[28]

But in the struggle in the 1890s to defend their political sovereignty and to halt allotment in the face of unrelenting pressures from the federal government, many Creeks adopted an increasingly rigid racial sense of Creek nationhood. This was the case for Isparhecher himself. By 1898, Isparhecher had abandoned his fight against allotment. He simultaneously abandoned his stand for racial equality in the nation. Indeed, he began to argue that Creeks of different races had different and unequal rights to land. Isparhecher now maintained that in the allotment of lands "Indians" should receive 160 acres of land but black "freedmen" should be entitled to only 40.[29] In 1891, Isparhecher had endorsed a racially neutral vocabulary of citizenship. Seven years later, he used a terminology of race: "Indians" and "freedmen." "Indians" might be "full-bloods" like himself or "mixed-bloods" with varying degrees of European ancestry. But "freedmen" were not "Indians," "Indians" were not black, and the two mutually exclusive groups had different rights to land.[30]

The meaning of Isparhecher's change of heart and of terminology becomes clearer in the light of an exchange he had with the chief justice of the Creek Supreme Court in 1896—which itself can be understood only in the light of U.S. pressure on Creeks to divide up the common lands. By that time, many conservatives had begun to distance themselves from their longtime black allies. Isparhecher had inquired whether the council had the authority to extend citizenship to "any colored persons" who were not included in the nation as part of the 1866 treaty. Chief Justice T. J. Adams replied that such people could not be "adopted" (granted citizenship) because it would take lands from Creek citizens in a zero-sum struggle for property in land: "The effect of adoption would be to take a portion of the property belonging to each citizen and bestowing it on the adoptee." Adams's statement is a remarkable one because it nearly reduced citizenship to a property right in "the common estate of the tribe."[31] In one sense, access to the national lands had always been central to Creek citizenship. Yet Adams's reply bore the clear marks of the allotment period. It depended on a new, but unstated, situation: the U.S. government would soon force that common estate to be divided into individual parcels. Adopting blacks therefore threatened to reduce the lands that other Creeks would receive as their own.

Isparhecher's changing rhetoric on race and citizenship, and the idea that citizenship was fundamentally about a personal ownership stake in the national lands, mark an important shift in thinking on race, on citizenship, and on Creek nationhood. Federal pressures to accept allotment catalyzed this shift, and the way federal authorities implemented the colonial policy of allotment reinforced the change. Washington made land a divisive force in the nation: not something Creeks had in common but something to be fought over. The rules of this zero-sum game were mostly set by Washington. In order to engage, or even oppose, the process of allotment, it became almost impossible not to resort to the American government's racial categories. The reformers who called for allotment hoped it would dissolve tribal identities. In fact, allotment did quite the opposite.[32]

Allotment was race law as much as it was property law, a colonial policy that codified tribal and racial categories.[33] It encouraged a racialized notion of politics and of nationhood. Resistance did endure: Creek citizens of different races cooperated in a militant effort to fight off allotment as late as 1902. Such cooperation was becoming increasingly difficult, however, as allotment progressed. By 1906, on the eve of Oklahoma statehood, the politics of allotment had refashioned the relationship between race and citizenship in Indian Territory.

Class, Blood, and the Opposition to Allotment

Even before Dawes and his associates reached Muskogee in January 1894, Creeks were denouncing allotment, and the arrival of the commissioners intensified this opposition. The opposition was already established, of course. Creeks had spoken directly to senators on the issue in 1878. None of the governments of the Five Tribes would negotiate an allotment agreement with the Dawes Commission.[34] In a response that merged a critique of Indian land tenure with Indian politicians—and by extension Indian sovereignty—the Dawes Commission members voiced the belief that allotment would protect "real Indians" from politically powerful "mixed-blood" land hogs. They faced, however, unified opposition that transcended the very real divisions of race and class in the Creek Nation. The debate between commissioners and Creeks reveals that different factions in the nation all believed that they had economic, political, and cultural interest in defending the commons and the nation. But the Creek Nation was, as always, a confederation, and Creeks had multiple affiliations and loyalties. Some black Creeks felt they were part of a black nation that spanned the political boundaries between Creeks and African Americans. These black Creeks came to endorse allotment because they felt it would serve that broader racial community.

Although the senators claimed wealthy "mixed-bloods" were using a fiction of common ownership to exploit poor "full-bloods," Creek opposition to allotment and statehood transcended lines of class and of ancestry. In March 1894, delegates of the Cherokee, Choctaw, Chickasaw, and Creek nations listened as the commissioners argued that only wealthy "mixed-blood" landholders would object to allotment. Yet every delegation of every tribe was unanimous in its opposition.[35] In the Creek delegation and the broader Creek leadership, there were some whom the Dawes Commission expected to oppose allotment, men like George Washington Grayson and Pleasant Porter. Grayson was the educated son of a prominent mixed-race family, a Confederate veteran, and a man involved in extensive cattle ranching.[36] His wealth was paltry, however, in comparison with that of Porter, son of a white planter and his Creek wife who had owned one of the most impressive plantations worked by enslaved people in the nation. He was educated in mission schools, fought for the Confederacy, and then built a ranching empire that came to encompass thousands of head of cattle and tens of thousands of acres. It was precisely this sort of wealthy Indian of mixed ancestry the Dawes Commission expected to oppose allotment.[37] But the Creek delegation that voiced its opposition to allotment in March 1894 also included Creeks such as Hotulke Emarthla and Isparhecher. These Creeks were the sort of individuals whom the Dawes Commissioners termed "full-bloods" and expected to benefit from allotment. Hotulke Emarthla was one of the most venerable figures in Creek politics. He had led his town, Okchiye, on the long trail from Alabama half a century before. A leader in Creek politics since the Civil War, Hotulke Emarthla was part of the "full-blood" faction that so often opposed the interests of cattlemen like Grayson and Porter. Isparhecher was a younger leader in this same faction and one well positioned to bridge the political and cultural divisions in the Creek Nation. In the Civil War, he had fought briefly for the Confederacy before allying himself with the Union. He was a committed Methodist but also "wise in medicine and tribal tradition."[38] The Dawes Commission's expectations of "full-bloods" missed the complexities of individuals like Isparhecher, and they missed the reasons that they opposed allotment as surely as Pleasant Porter did.

This is not to say that the different factions in the nation all resisted the Dawes commissioners for precisely the same reasons. In fact, the commissioners understood neither that the Creek land system gave economic incentives to people of all classes to oppose allotment nor that a dedication to Creek nationhood gave Creeks, whether rich or poor, reasons to oppose allotment that were not simply economic. Allotment threatened rich ranchers and planters because the equal division of lands meant they would lose the large estates that they had amassed. It threatened the poor because the common lands upon which they depended would disappear. It threatened all Creeks because it meant the dissolution of their government and the imposition of a new state. Principal Chief Legus C. Perryman offered Dawes Commission members Meredith Kidd and Archibald McKennon a vivid demonstration of this united opposition in March 1894 when he called on all Creek voters (men over twenty-one) to assemble near the national capitol in Okmulgee. Perryman told the crowd of two thousand (roughly a third of the Creek electorate)[39] that people in Washington had been claiming that "half breeds and educated full-bloods" dominated the wealth of the nation and were discouraging "full-bloods" from voicing their support for allotment. After the commissioners had made their case, the principal chief asked those who favored a new government and allotment to step to the left of the square and those who opposed to go to the right. Every single person present moved to the right, demonstrating his opposition. Perryman pointedly claimed that the majority of these two thousand were "full blood Creeks." Although the event bore the marks of political theater, it also bears witness to Creek opposition to allotment and Creek sensitivity to the charge that the issue divided the nation into factions of class and race.[40]

In defense of their great estates, some wealthy Creeks went so far as to echo the sentiments of white Gilded Age ideologues on the benefits of concentrated wealth in a society. They maintained that their holdings served as a salutary influence upon the less market-oriented "full-bloods." Principal Chief Perryman claimed that those who "own[ed] larger tracts" had earned them through "their own industry in fencing and pasturage"—conveniently erasing the labor of those who had actually cleared, fenced, and worked the land.[41] In 1894, prominent and wealthy members of several of the nations together wrote to the U.S. president and Congress contending that, in Indian Territory as in the United States, "the best friend the poor and uneducated man has is the man with means." The wealth of the rich, they argued, spurred the poor to emulate their industriousness. The council warned that allotment would "mean financial ruin, moral degradation and final annihilation to the full-blood and uneducated Indians."[42]

In contrast, statements that included small-scale Creek farmers sometimes indicted private property in land on the grounds that it inevitably led to inequity. In April 1894, the Creek National Council as a whole declared that the practice of private ownership of land impoverished not only Indians but Americans more generally. Allotment, then, would only replace the inequalities of land use in the Creek tenure system with the more entrenched inequalities of private land title. Like the other Indian Territory figures whom Alexandra Harmon has studied, Creeks asserted that their land system had a "moral distinctiveness" because it neither made land into a commodity nor reduced citizens to landlessness.[43] Without the national lands, small-scale farmers would no longer have a place to which they could always turn to make their farms. Even though conservatives had demonstrated that they agreed with the Dawes Commission that vast pasturelands were contrary to the spirit of tribal tenure, they did not agree that allotment was the answer. Thus both wealthy ranchers and small-scale farmers had an economic stake in opposing allotment.

But Creeks contended that allotment was a cultural threat as much as an economic one because common tenure was basic to the nature of their society. Because it struck at the foundations of the nation, it was more dangerous even than removal six decades earlier.[44] Chief Perryman elaborated the point, claiming that what was at stake was not any particular piece of land but the nation itself. "The holding of their lands in common," he declared, "is a custom of the Creeks as old as the history and traditions of the tribe." The two were coeval, and the nation and its land system survived removal together: "The custom has been carried with them in all their changes of habitation and practiced by them wherever they dwelt."[45] The continuation of the Creek land system therefore was part and parcel of the endurance of the nation. As Alexandra Harmon argues, because their land system "symbolized the opposition between their traditions and the American agenda," Indians came "to regard tribal land as a defining feature of a cherished Indian identity." They, and whites also, further understood that Indian land tenure created the space for the sovereignty of Indian tribal nations—what Harmon terms "discreet political, social, and geographical enclaves."[46] The bond between land and nationhood was far more than symbolic; the two were fused in Creek political thought and practice, as the conservative-black town alliance's defense of the common lands in the 1880s demonstrated. Furthermore, allotment was understood by all to be part of "territorialization" and doing away with Indian governments. Allotment, along with the replacement of tribal governance with a territorial or state government, would mean the end of the national lands, the way of life and the communities they sustained, and the nation itself.

The conservative faction fought allotment while keeping up its opposition to the enclosure of large pastures. This is the program that Isparhecher put forth in 1891 (cited earlier in this chapter) and again in 1895. In 1895 it won him the principal chieftaincy of the Creek Nation by a landslide in which he outpolled his nearest rival by nearly two to one. Isparhecher had vowed to resist allotment, work for the removal of all noncitizens, and prevent wealthy cattlemen from using too large a share of the nation's lands for their private pastures. The candidates of the five other parties had all also pledged to hold off the Dawes Commission, but Isparhecher's antiallotment stance was backed up by his broad and long-term dedication to the protection of the common lands and national sovereignty.[47]

The way that most black Creeks opposed allotment demonstrates their enduring commitment to these same principles and the way this commitment was rooted in Creek oral history. Canadian Colored Town lay between

Wetumka and Weleetka on the North Canadian River.[48] When federal officials attempted to convince residents of the town that they should embrace allotment, Jim Parkinson, a white merchant, held up a candy bucket filled with $10,000 to illustrate the wealth that allotment would bring. The town *micco*, Parah Bruner, ignored this condescending visual aid and stood to make it clear that he opposed the policy as a Creek and in the same terms as Creeks who were not black. Bruner told the townspeople that, like removal, allotment would lead to the dispossession of their land. Like removal, said Bruner, it would end in "people with packs and bundles on their backs having to leave their homes." Reminding his people that the 1832 treaty guaranteed that the lands would be the Creeks' "as long as the water ran and the grass grew," Bruner based his rejection of allotment on the fact that his townspeople were *Creeks*.[49] Political memory of land loss ran deep among black Creeks and offered cautionary notes to any politician who would favor signing away the nation's land. Jake Simmons, a black resident of the Choska Bottoms who was born in 1865, was told by his grandparents about "a fellow by the name of McIntosh, a half-breed," who had helped get "these treaties signed" without the authorization of the people. His grandparents told him the man was killed for the offense. Jake Simmons's grandparents had transferred to him correctly the gist of the Treaty of Indian Springs and the execution of William McIntosh in 1825.[50] Historical memory rooted Creeks, including black Creeks, in the nation and taught them that land loss threatened the nation. The power of that history can be sensed in the Creek council's rejection of allotment in 1894.[51]

The pressures to accept allotment were enormous, however, and by 1895 a minority of Indian citizens, often of mixed heritage, reluctantly endorsed allotment—while rejecting the notion that their thinking was driven by race or economic self-interest. These Indian officials, newspaper editors, and others argued that, because members of Congress and the Dawes Commission had explicitly stated that the lands of the Five Tribes would be allotted regardless of their wishes, the nations would do better to negotiate an advantageous agreement than be forced to accept a punitive one. The *Eufaula Indian Journal*, for example, intoned, "Do this now before congress does it for you."[52] In fact, the *Indian Journal* suggested that it was even time to accept statehood in order to protect allotment lands. The newspaper discounted worries that statehood would mean taxation of allotment lands, arguing that enfranchising Indians (at least Indian men) would permit them to better protect their interests. Furthermore, if Indian Territory and Oklahoma Territory were to join to make one state, the state could be funded by taxing lands in Oklahoma Territory, leaving allotment lands untaxed.[53] The pro-allotment minority emphasized the role of class and ideology, not race, in determining Indians' outlook on allotment. They rejected the Dawes Commission's charges that elites of mixed ancestry were opposing allotment. Grayson, for example, claimed that the western-educated, "progressive" Indians (who tended to be wealthier) favored allotment whereas the "masses" did not and never would.[54]

In the end, Washington assaulted the nation as land and the nation as polity by unilaterally imposing allotment and the end of effective national sovereignty on the unwilling Creek Nation and its neighbors. In June 1898, Congress passed the Curtis Act, decreeing that Washington would allot the lands and the tribal governments would be dissolved. The federal government would begin the enrollment process, determining who was entitled to a share of the national lands. The laws of the United States, particularly the laws of the neighboring state of Arkansas, would rule and would be administered by federal officers and federal courts, Creek officials and courts being forbidden to act. The Creeks could avoid this fate only by negotiating and approving another agreement acceptable to the federal government by October 1, 1898. Washington allowed Creeks only the sovereignty to negotiate the end of their effective sovereignty. The first attempt to ratify such an agreement failed when Creek voters narrowly rejected it by referendum. The Creek National Council finally secured ratification by referendum of an allotment agreement in February 1899, with a still narrow margin of 485 votes.[55] The agreement provided that each Creek citizen regardless of age or gender would choose (or, for minors, have chosen for them by their parents or guardians) an allotment of 160 acres. The citizens would designate 40 acres of the 160 as their "homestead," which would "be nontaxable and inalienable and free from any encumbrance whatever for twenty-one years." These limitations on taxation, sale, mortgaging, liens, and so on were known as "restrictions," and there were no restrictions placed on the remaining 120 acres of allotments, which were termed the "surplus" portion of their lands. The existing large estates, such as fenced pastures, would be broken up as an effect of the selection of allotments. The agreement dictated that the National Council could make no decision "in any manner affecting the lands of the tribe, or of individuals after allotment, or the moneys or other property of the tribe, or of the citizens thereof" without approval of the American president.[56]

The Process of Allotment:
Division of Lands and Divisions in the Nation

The Dawes Commission began the task of enrollment and allotment of the Creek Nation in April 1899.[57] It was a complex task. The Creeks numbered about eighteen thousand citizens belonging to a confederation of forty-seven widely scattered towns. Each town enjoyed a degree of autonomy within the confederation, and although the central Creek government officially held the power to decide matters of citizenship, in actuality officials in each town determined eligibility as late as 1890.[58] Furthermore, the Creek Nation had experienced significant immigration by African Americans and whites since the Civil War. Clustered around the Missouri, Kansas, and Texas railroad tracks, near the bustling trading town of Muskogee, and on farms and ranches in the agricultural districts were thousands of white and African American immigrants who had been arriving in rising numbers for decades. Many had married citizens of the Creek Nation. Others were accepted as town members by the black Creek towns. Some were legally entitled to Creek citizenship, but many who were not also wanted to secure a place on the rolls and thus an allotment.

Remarkably, for all the opposition they had voiced to allotment, many Creeks rushed to be enrolled and choose an allotment as soon as the Dawes Commission began making allotments in the Creek Nation on April 1, 1899.[59] One official reported to Dawes that when the doors of the office at Muskogee opened, there were "500 or 600 people waiting to get inside." By June 30, 1899, 3,800 citizens had selected their allotments. The number had topped 6,500 by December 5 and 10,000 by June 30, 1900. By September 1901, 13,600 citizens (5,000 of them black Creeks) had selected allotments, and 1,000 more were still expected to do so.[60] Still, deeds to the allotments had not been passed out, and in December 1901 both houses of the National Council passed a joint resolution asking that deeds be issued immediately.[61]

Why would Creeks eagerly enroll and select allotments while simultaneously electing officials who voiced opposition to allotment? One must bear in mind the strategic decisions individuals had to make. Creeks knew their opposition to the final division of lands might prove unsuccessful, and so there was considerable incentive to hedge one's bets and accept an allotment. There would be only one chance to get an allotment: once allotment was over, individuals would be permanently disqualified from getting a portion of their nation's land. Furthermore, not all land was equal in productivity or value. The nation encompassed everything from rich bottom-lands to barren hillsides, and the need to secure a usable plot added to the incentive to choose an allotment. Even though a cash payment after allotment was planned to compensate those who received less valuable land, the inequality of lands added to the already considerable pressure to choose an allotment despite opposition to the process.[62]

Historically rooted racial and class divisions in the nation would become more apparent as the U.S. government continued pressuring Creeks to accept allotment. The broad-based Creek resistance to allotment had demonstrated the way the Creek land and land tenure system created a bond that transcended divisions in the nation, but those divisions were still real. This was a composite nation born of a confederacy that only three decades earlier had practiced racial slavery. Creeks' complex and layered identities and loyalties are apparent in black Creek reactions to the push for allotment.

Although most Creeks initially followed the path of unified resistance endorsed by Parah Bruner and suggested by Jake Simmons's grandparents' stories, others favored the division of lands. To black Creeks who embraced economic individualism and capitalism, allotment represented an opportunity to be seized. Before emancipation, Morris Rentie of Canadian Colored Town had been a slave to John Yargee. By the time of allotment, he was not only a "farmer and stockman" but "a business man with an eye to the future." Given his market orientation, it is not surprising that his son recalled that his family favored allotment. Some other black Creeks followed suit.[63]

A distinct black identity and black political agenda that transcended Creek national boundaries also encouraged them to enroll and choose allotments. In the late 1890s, some black Creek men joined non-Creek black men in publicly espousing allotment because they believed that it would help them as a racial group and as citizens of the United States. These black leaders contended that all people of African descent in the Indian Territory, Creek or non-Creek, were one group with common interests. William H. Twine, a black lawyer, newspaper editor, and entrepreneur who had come to Indian Territory from Texas and who was not Creek, was a prime advocate of this cause. In 1898, Twine urged black citizens of Indian nations to hurry and enroll for allotment.[64] He argued that allotment had the potential to create a broad class of black landowners, a prospect that he relished. Twine looked forward to a day "not far distant" when allotment would ensure that "each citizen of the various Tribes will own his share of the soil in fee simple"—that is, with all the rights of private ownership common in the United States then and now. Allotment would also put land on the market, allowing the largely immigrant African American communities in towns and cities such as Muskogee to secure "title to their homes." This last point stands in sharp contrast to the alarm and dread that many Creeks expressed when considering the prospect that allotment lands would be sold and to the dominant way historians have portrayed allotment land sales—as the loss of a heritage and of a nation. Instead of fearing that individuals would be swindled or a nation dissolved, Twine hoped that the sale of blacks' allotments would foster the growth of an affluent and landed black community that included African Americans from the states. He and others like him thought of themselves as belonging to a racial community that spanned the boundaries of nation.

Indeed, in 1898 Twine used the pages of his newspaper, the *Muskogee Pioneer*, to boost the Inter-National Afro-American League, whose executive committee was headed by I. A. Rentie, a black Creek. The name of the organization crystallizes the complex loyalties of blacks in Indian Territory. It made clear that the tribal nations were indeed nations, and this at a time when their sovereignty was under attack. At the same time, it represented something "Inter-National," something that went beyond those nations.[65] While some black Creeks, like Parah Bruner, asserted the primacy of Creekness to their past, their identity, and their future, others were beginning to take I. A. Rentie's path, emphasizing the salience of blackness. One position did not necessarily exclude the other. Black and Creek identities and loyalties were simultaneous, and many black Creek people could and did embrace both Creek nationhood and the idea of a black identity that was "Inter-National."

Many nonblack Creeks also enacted an international consciousness that linked their identity and interests to other Native American people in the late nineteenth century. In the 1870s, that consciousness had been manifested at a series of councils held at Okmulgee at which representatives of the Five Tribes had met with representatives of Indian Territory's Plains nations in the unsuccessful effort to create "a federal union similar to that of the United States."[66] Cooperation of Indian nations continued in the late nineteenth century, as we have seen, in the opposition to allotment. In the light of the Inter-National Afro-American League, it is worth asking whether a sense of specifically racial solidarity played a role in furthering such efforts at intertribal cooperation.

A racialized sense of the nation is evident in the efforts by nonblack

Creeks to reduce the political power of black Creeks and their conservative allies in the 1890s. In 1892, a number of (evidently nonblack) members of the National Council met at Okmulgee to develop a strategy to "check . . . the ascendancy of the Negro race in the Nation." Alarmed that there were now seventeen members of the council and a number of national officers who were "of simon-pure African descent," the lawmakers blamed the growth of the black population and the black towns. Some called for "altering" the treaty of 1866 to disenfranchise blacks in the nation. The *Muskogee Phoenix* newspaper hinted that allotment might be "the only remedy for the state of affairs."[67] But treaties could not simply be altered (a message not clear to the American government), and few Creeks would have looked upon allotment as an acceptable cost for disenfranchising black Creeks. Another proposed solution came up for a referendum in 1894. The Creek electorate considered doing away with proportional representation in the council. Instead, each town would be represented by only one member in the House of Warriors. Given that the three black towns were the largest in the nation, making up nearly a third of the population, the proposed change would have sharply cut their representation in council. George Washington Grayson voiced the racial argument for the change, claiming that black council members had "no more ideas of government than the Bedouins of the plains of Arabia."[68] The popular referendum defeated the measure — which means that a substantial number of nonblack Creeks voted on the side of the black town voters, who opposed it with near unanimity. Black Creeks could not ignore the antagonism against them in the nation, but it is clear that many nonblack Creeks were willing to work with them to defend Creek land tenure and the Creek political order. In fact, the *Eufaula Indian Journal* lamented that, while black Creeks voted as a bloc, nonblack Creeks did not, and that fact was responsible for what it considered the sad state of Creek politics.[69]

Allotment in Practice: Race and Citizenship

U.S. policy was more consistent in insisting on a racial political order: it used allotment to impose its racial categorizations far more systematically and rigidly than Creeks had ever done. Allotment required enrollment — a listing of every citizen of each nation classified by race. Prior to 1896, the Creek Nation had never conducted a census that attempted to classify individuals according to the exact proportion of white and indigenous ancestry. A few censuses and rolls had registered individuals under the rubrics of "mixed-blood," "full-blood," and "negro" or "Freedman" (meaning former slave).[70] The Dawes Commission, however, sought mathematically precise racial categorizations. Each person seeking enrollment came before a Dawes Commission official either at the Dawes Commission's offices in Muskogee or at one of the field camps the commission established while traveling the countryside. Generally working with an interpreter, the official quickly interviewed each person about his or her ancestry, asking about the racial background of each person's ancestors. If the person did not claim to be a "full-blood," the official questioned the individual about her or his parents and grandparents. This interview established the individual's "blood quantum": three-quarters, one-half, three-eighths, and so on. This number was recorded on the individual's enrollment card.[71] Being enrolled meant being permanently and unchangeably classified into a racial group: "full-blood," "negro," or "mixed-blood."[72]

In practice, of course, such simple "blood quantum" figures could not capture the complexity of the population of the Creeks or of Indian Territory. A long history of intermarriage between tribes, especially between Creeks and Seminoles, meant that many people had parents and grandparents from two different tribal nations. In keeping with the law and practices in the Creek Nation, an applicant's tribal affiliation was decided by the mother. Superimposing ideas of "blood quantum" on this matrilineal system resulted, however, in absurdities. For example, when a woman was recorded as a "full-blood" Creek and her husband was enrolled as a "full-blood" Seminole, the commission would place their children on the Creek rolls as one-half Indian "by blood"—a matter that could have great importance in later years as laws on allotment lands evolved.[73]

Even more tellingly, the Dawes Commission considered that any individual with any African ancestry would be enrolled as a "Freedman," no matter what the other elements of his or her ancestry. Thus in cases in which the commission placed a woman on the "Creek by blood" rolls and her husband on the "Creek Freedman" rolls, the couple's children would be recorded as Creek Freedmen—racial status thereby overriding the generally matrilineal rule of Creek enrollment. Whether or not one had white or indigenous ancestry, the Dawes Commission made a policy of registering any person with known African ancestry as a Freedman.[74] In doing so, they were following the Anglo-American principle of racial hypodescent, which held that one "drop" of African "blood" established that a person was "Negro."[75] Though familiar in the United States in the late nineteenth century, this concept of race had never been dominant in the Indian Territory. Enrollment relegated some Creeks to the less prestigious status of Freedmen, even though other Creeks had considered them to be "mixed-bloods"—that is, "mixed" with white ancestry, not African. Some Creek citizens who were enrolled as Freedmen because of their African ancestry resisted the imposition of the "one-drop rule" when they sought to be reclassified as Creeks "by blood."[76] Exceptions did exist. Some alleged that Pleasant Porter's mother "had a decided strain" of black ancestry, yet he was enrolled as one-half Indian "by blood"—thus without African ancestry.[77] Political and social prestige, along with a lack of strongly African phenotypical features, probably allowed him to escape the liability of his reputed African ancestry. Similarly, the family of former principal chief Legus C. Perryman, whose African ancestry was reportedly visible in his features and dark skin, was enrolled as "full-bloods."[78] But as a general rule, enrollment established a more rigid racial order that differentiated people of African descent sharply from other Creek citizens on the basis of "blood" and differentiated among nonblack Creeks on the basis of "blood quantum."

The fact that Dawes Commission staff used race as the determinant of enrollment status gave vigor to the suspicions of some Creeks that many or even all black Creeks were not Creeks at all. In 1894, for example, one Creek warned that many black Creek citizens were nothing more than "intruders" who were "robbing our children of land and money." If allotment was inevitable, the writer hoped that Muscogee Indians would "stand shoulder to shoulder" to ensure that "each Indian" of Indian "blood" received a fair share and African American "intruders and robbers" would be expelled.[79] These ideas were not entirely new; in the 1880s, opponents of the conservative-black town alliance had also voiced concerns about black towns illegally extending citizenship to black immigrants and thus swelling black power. But the 1894 statement bore the distinctive mark of the racializing zero-sum game of allotment. The terminology of "blood," the particular concern about "land and money," and the sense that the inheritance of the Creeks' "children" was at stake bound race, citizenship, and property together in a way that was characteristic of the allotment period. This same array of ideas underlay the logic of the opinion, cited earlier in this chapter, that Creek chief justice T. J. Adams rendered to Isparhecher. Adams suggested that citizenship was fundamentally a property right when he asserted that the nation could not grant citizenship to outsiders—and specifically, in the context, black outsiders—because it would be tantamount to giving them part of the property of those who were already citizens. The colonial attempts to impose allotment, and the debates they unleashed in the Creek Nation, lent authority to these ideas and to racial conceptions of the Creek Nation. Since Washington insisted there would be no Creek Nation in a few years' time, and since Washington insisted that the Creek government's final act would be to dissolve its lands in a racially determined policy of allotment, it is hardly surprising that Chief Justice Adams suggested that Creek citizenship was primarily a right to property in land.

Noncompliance, Electoral Politics, and Militant Resistance

Some other Creeks rejected allotment, rejected Creek and American governmental authority, and asserted instead the kind of composite Creek nationhood, bound to common land, that conservatives and black towns had defended in the 1880s. The most common form of resistance was the refusal to be enrolled or to choose an allotment.[80] In November 1899, one Dawes Commission fieldworker estimated that three-quarters of those who had not enrolled (perhaps 6,750 of 9,000 who had not enrolled) were "absolutely opposed to enrollment and allotment" and the rest were "indifferent."[81] Opposition to enrollment ran particularly strong in the western sections of the nation, the center of conservative power. Thousands of Creeks resisted enrollment and allotment for years after the process began in 1898.[82] Disgruntlement over allotment was also registered, especially in elections, by Creeks who had acceded to pressures to enroll and choose plots despite their misgivings about dividing the lands and dissolving the government. A strongly antiallotment, antistatehood flavor characterized the politics of the Creek Nation from about 1898 to 1906, the final years before statehood. Allotment remained very much a live issue at the time of the 1899 election—a moment when the social disarray of allotment was compounded by a smallpox epidemic in the nation.[83] Isparhecher had been elected in 1895 to oppose enrollment and allotment, but he had come instead to participate in them. When he chose his allotment in May 1899, he lost all legitimacy in his former supporters' eyes. In the election that year, most of them chose not to participate rather than give their vote to Isparhecher. With their vote thus weakened, Pleasant Porter, the prominent rancher, businessman, and emerging land speculator, won the principal chieftaincy.[84]

The political opposition shifted to a new, more militant phase. Faced with this disappointing election result and the allotment agreement, a minority of Creeks initiated a militant and interracial resistance that claimed to be the true expression of Creek nationhood and drew on the political alliance of the 1880s. The new alliance of the turn of the twentieth century advocated open defiance of the authority of the Creek and U.S. governments. At its height, it claimed the loyalties of about five thousand Creeks, a third of the nation's population.[85]

The movement's leading orator and organizer, Chitto Harjo of Arbeka town, brandished a copy of the treaty of 1832, assuring his listeners that it remained in effect and that the lands of the Creek Nation were still the common property of all Creeks.[86] He stated that the allotment agreement held no legitimacy and that Creeks must refuse to participate in it. This was not a new message. Indeed, there was a line of continuity between Isparhecher and Chitto Harjo and between the dissidents in the 1880s and those at the turn of the century. Daniel Starr remembered accompanying Chitto Harjo to Isparhecher's house for frequent visits. The two men discussed politics at length, especially emphasizing the need to "stand for continued existence of the old Indian laws." At these visits, a tradition of Creek resistance was passed on.[87] It was a tradition that other Creeks sustained as well, and soon a large and interracial movement of opposition to allotment was coalescing. Lahtah Micco, the first leader of the movement, brought in Chitto Harjo as his *heneha*, or spokesman. The orator, whose name a nervous press translated as "Crazy Snake," emerged as a new leader so prominent that outsiders assumed that all those who resisted allotment were his followers, and they called them "Snakes" after him.[88] The movement seems to have been centered at Hickory Ground.

The movement's defense of the common lands and Creek national sovereignty attracted black Creeks. Indian, white, and black observers agreed that (in the words of Daniel Starr) "many negroes had been included or had joined in his band."[89] Indeed, Chitto Harjo and other speakers actively fostered black support for the movement. In the 1930s, Billie Brant described himself as a former "follower of Chitto Harjo." He recalled that Chitto Harjo and other speakers came into black communities warning that allotment and statehood meant "the Indians would be forced to abandon their freedom and be forced to live under rules that would be hard to understand and interpret." Chitto Harjo's message carried a utopian tone that linked ideas of property to freedom: "The idea was of a free country without restrictions," freedom to gather at a berry bush wherever it might be, freedom to follow game without concern for property lines.[90] In describing the movement, Brant continuously returned to the theme of freedom and autonomy. Chitto Harjo's "great idea," he said, "was to bring to his people the difference between the real freedom and being subject to others who would tell them what to do."[91] The appeal of this kind of freedom for black Creeks at the turn of the twentieth century—a time when Jim Crow and racial disenfranchisement and a bloody wave of lynchings were on the rise in the South—was enormous. The Creek Nation was still a place where black Creeks could govern their own towns and where black men had the same voting rights as other men and held positions of national political authority. Allotment and statehood threatened to bring an end to all of that.

In response to this danger, the dissidents affirmed Creek nationhood but rejected the Creek national government that was acceding to American wishes. Unsympathetic observers of the time tended to portray the Snakes as a rebel band or a town splintering from the nation. The terminology of *micco* and *heneha* and the centering around a stomp ground (Hickory Ground) do suggest that the movement partly followed the model of Creek town politics. Those close to the movement referred to it as a "band," which is a possible translation of *talwa* and the one usually used by Seminoles.[92]

However, Snakes' actions make it clear that by 1900 they were establishing a parallel national government to defend Creek nationhood and Creek land tenure. They were not splintering off from the nation but attempting to preserve it by redirecting it. In October 1900, the Snakes chose a legislature and national officers. Although Chitto Harjo was the most visible leader and is sometimes referred to as principal chief, it appears that Lahtah Micco continued in that role.[93] The Snakes set their "council grounds" at Hickory Town, where Chitto Harjo "camped for days at a time to attend to the business councils with his people."[94] The new government placed itself squarely in the tradition of the alliance of conservatives and black towns of the 1880s. Lahtah Micco proclaimed that Indians should farm only their home places, not spread out to use adjacent parcels—a jab at the wealthy and large planters and a defense of the broad use of the national lands. The Snakes linked this defense of lands to the defense of national sovereignty.

Refusing allotment and refusing American citizenship were part of this defense. Advocates of allotment and territorial government claimed that the Curtis Act ensured that an Indian would be treated like any other "American citizen."[95] This claim was mistaken: it was not the Curtis Act but rather the Dawes Act of 1887 that stated that Indians who accepted allotments automatically became U.S. citizens.[96] Still, it meant that the issue of U.S. citizenship was a powerful incentive to discourage Creeks from accepting allotments, as the Snakes did. By refusing to take allotments, Snakes refused to take the action that could be assumed to lead up to the imposition of U.S. citizenship and the dissolution of the Creek national state. They understood that allotment, the dissolution of Creek national government, and American citizenship were all of a piece. In 1901, Washington did with citizenship what it had done with allotment: it unilaterally imposed citizenship on all Indians in Indian Territory, including those who refused to take part in allotment.[97] Nonetheless, many Snakes continued to refuse allotments in the defense of the national lands and national sovereignty.

The parallel government set itself to passing and attempting to enforce a legal code that centered on the defense of land tenure in common. The faction posted and sometimes enforced its laws forbidding Creeks to file for allotments, rent land to non-Creeks, or hire white (and thus not Creek) labor. The dissidents repeatedly subjected Isparhecher to their discipline. On one occasion a mile of his barbed wire fence was cut down as punishment for renting out a parcel of his land to a non-Creek farmer from Tennessee.[98] On another, his home at Beggs was stormed, and he was threatened for flying the U.S. flag.[99] Such militancy and audacity inspired dissidents in the other Five Tribes. The press and federal officials circulated reports that Chitto Harjo's followers had sent emissaries to and recruited members from other nations.[100] Soon, the press was discussing antiallotment dissidence throughout Indian Territory as a unitary "Snake movement." Such terminology can lend a too centralized and formalized air to much resistance that was localized and spontaneous. Still, the Snakes were instrumental in building intertribal opposition to allotment and to the Indian governments and politicians who were making allotment agreements.

Contemporary characterizations of the Snakes as atavistic "full-bloods" desperately clinging to tradition were far too simplistic, ignoring Snakes' willingness to change in the defense of the common lands and the common nation. The *Indian Journal* claimed that the Snakes were fighting a losing battle against the laws of nature, especially that favorite law of Gilded Age ideologists, "the survival of the fittest." Given this immutable law, "Chitto Harjo (Crazy Snake) and his people are doomed. They cannot compete with this white civilization which is so mighty, so selfish and so natural."[101] The Snakes, however, were less convinced of their imminent demise and far more willing to adapt strategically to white pressures than the *Indian Journal* recognized. One Creek man, Joe Bruner, remembered that the Snakes were not opposed to leasing national lands to non-Creeks for mining or grazing but wanted a system by which all Creeks would receive an equal share of lease income.[102] In other words, what mattered was defending a shared national commons—even if it was a commons in a new form—not just following old ways. Chitto Harjo may also have considered the same strategy that Creeks had tried with the 1832 treaty in Alabama—to accept the form of allotments but attempt to continue the practice of common ownership and town governance. One Choctaw who was sympathetic to the Snakes and who said his family had left that nation rather than accept allotment recalled that Chitto Harjo was willing to accept allotment as long as deeds were never issued and common lands were set aside for towns. The reasoning was that as long as deeds were not issued, land "could not be taxed nor sold. In that way it would be of no use to anyone but the Indians." Snakes were neither blind traditionalists nor unaware of the realities of modern life but rather knew quite a bit about fee-simple property, deeds, taxes, and their dangers.[103]

The movement's phase as a government was spectacular but short lived. By January 1901, the Snakes claimed to have five thousand members (men, women, and children) and to exercise jurisdiction over a twenty-five-square-mile area along the Deep Fork River, a center of conservative Creek life. That jurisdiction ended January 25, however, when one U.S. marshal and a small posse succeeded in dispersing the rebels and arresting Chitto Harjo and 96 other men without shedding blood.[104] In March, the U.S. attorney "secured indictments for 253 named Creeks for 'conspiracy to deprive unknown persons of their personal liberty' and 'detaining them without lawful authority'"—in other words, enforcing the Snakes' laws. Legal historian Sidney L. Harring describes this as "the most massive indictment of American Indians in United States history," accounting for roughly 12 percent of the adult male population of what the United States termed "Creeks by blood." In a plea bargain, all 253 pleaded guilty, and all were pardoned.[105] The crackdown on the Snakes did not do away with them or the broader movement of opposition to allotment, but it did reduce their visibility.[106]

But even in its opposition to allotment, even in its continuation of an interracial nationhood of resistance, the Snake movement bore the marks of how allotment was eroding that kind of nationhood. This is apparent in one listing of 118 Creeks who were arraigned in 1901. On the one hand, the list suggests that the Snake movement transcended racial, town, and factional boundaries. Men from thirty-eight of the forty-four nonblack towns were arraigned. Some of the most heavily represented towns were conservative strongholds like Nuyaka and Pukon Tallahassee (eight arraignments each), but members from most of the other towns, including ones that whites considered more "progressive," were also arraigned. Still, in keeping with most descriptions of the Snake movement as predominantly "full-blood," men who bear that racial designation dominate the list. One hundred and eight were listed as "full-bloods," eight as "mixed-bloods," and only two as "freedmen"—Pompey Phillips, age fifty-five, of Canadian Colored Town, and Pompey Perryman, age forty-five, of Tuskegee Town.[107]

It is striking how few black Creeks were arrested in the crackdown. Two factors explain these small numbers of black Creek arrests. First, the profile of those arrested was probably not representative of the movement as a whole. Reports indicate that American authorities sought to arrest and prosecute the people they identified as movement leaders. The small number of arrests concurs with accounts in newspapers and oral histories that indicate that black Creeks took part in the movement but do not describe them as leaders in it. The two black Creek men who were arraigned may or may not have been leaders among blacks in the movement. Furthermore, authorities probably focused their energies on arresting those people who had been most vigorous in enforcing the Snakes' laws. It is possible that black Creeks were less likely to take part in these activities and that black Creeks took part in the Snake movement in greater numbers than the arrests suggest.

Nonetheless, the numbers point to the way the politics of allotment and impending statehood was undermining the basis of nonracial Creek national political life. As we have seen, some black Creeks joined with black Americans to argue that allotment was in the interests of all black people. Calls for black political organization in preparation for statehood suggest that the political ground had shifted under the strain of allotment politics. Some black Creeks were turning toward political action based on race rather than nation. Meanwhile, the kind of nonblack Creeks who had supported the interracial Creek alliance of the 1880s were starting to embrace a form of racial nationalism they had once resisted. This trend was illustrated by Isparhecher's change of heart on race, citizenship, and nationhood, noted earlier in this chapter. In 1891 he had declared that he and the National Party opposed "sectionalization" and favored equal rights for all Creek citizens regardless of race. By 1898, when he had accepted allotment, he called for racially discriminatory land distribution. The politics of allotment—spurred by the intervention of federal authorities, white reformers, and other non-Creeks—was literally taking away the ground upon which black Creeks and conservative Creeks had built a shared sense of nationhood.

Race, Resistance, and the Four Mothers Nation

The common ground for the alliance was eroding even among Creeks such as Chitto Harjo who continued to resist allotment into the twentieth century. Unlike Isparhecher, Chitto Harjo did not accede to the division of lands, but he and many like him similarly came to see black Creek citizens as a threat to the property of other Creeks. In 1906, before a senate select committee that had traveled to Indian Territory to investigate allotment, Chitto Harjo came forward to make his case against it.[108] Following the dictates of Creek oratory (and confusing and annoying the senators in the process), Chitto Harjo spoke in the person of the Creek Nation and built his position on a deep historical foundation. He began with 1492, when "Columbus first discovered me," establishing the prior right of Native Americans to the American continent.[109] Chitto Harjo recounted how he (the nation) had made a series of agreements with "the white man" but still retained the right to the Creek lands. He recalled that in 1832, at the time of removal, the United States had promised the Creeks a home in "the direction of the setting sun." Chitto Harjo reminded the senators, in an often quoted passage, that Washington had promised the Creeks these lands "as long as the sun shines, grass grows, and water runs." It followed, to Chitto Harjo, that the land still belonged to the Creeks.[110] Yet the orator did not end with this memorable passage. He lodged specific complaint that "the Government is cutting up my land and is giving it away to black people." He asked, "These black people, who are they?" Chitto Harjo answered his own question, and not by affirming, as Creek opponents of allotment had fifteen years before, that the "black people" were citizens entitled to equal rights to the common lands. Rather, Chitto Harjo stated, "They are negroes that came in here as slaves. They have no right to this land. It never was given to them. It was given to me and my people and we paid for it with our land back in Alabama."[111]

Also testifying before the senators in Tulsa, representatives of a movement that called itself the Four Mothers Nation seconded and extended Chitto Harjo's objections to allotment. The group portrayed itself as the champion of tradition but actually marked a new departure in Indian notions of race and citizenship by creating a new intertribal nation based on "full-blood" identity. Creek dissident Eufala Harjo described the group as "24,000 full-blood Indian people" in the Creek, Cherokee, Choctaw, and Chickasaw nations "that don't want to take their allotments of land." While the numbers of members that Harjo claimed were likely inflated, the opposition he described was real.[112]

The political battles over allotment had remade ideas of nation and citizenship among the dissidents. Race and nation merged in the minds of Eufala Harjo and other proponents of the Four Mothers Nation. In their mind, the nation transcended old borders to include Creeks, Cherokees, Chickasaws, and Choctaws. But these dissidents no longer envisaged the multiracial nation of the Creek past. Eufala Harjo insisted that the Four Mothers Nation was a nation of "full-blood Indians." There was no place in it for the "half breeds and negroes" who had "taken all the land" until "there is nothing left for the full-blood Indian at all." Allotment had so sharply exacerbated racial differences that, to dissident Creeks like Eufala Harjo, the recourse was to a nation of "full-bloods."[113] The term probably did not have the same narrow, mathematical meaning for Eufala Harjo as it did for Dawes Commission agents who calculated "blood quantum" into so many fractions. But in the context of the charges against "half-breeds" and "Negroes," "full-blood" took on a distinctly biological and racial tone that bears the imprint of allotment politics. In their battle against allotment, the dissidents had broadened the idea of nation to include Creeks, Cherokees, Chickasaws, and Choctaws. In the process, they had also narrowed the idea of nation to the single criterion of race. The dissidents—the same political group that had been so important to the black-conservative alliance two decades before—now deployed racial ideas of nationhood to exclude black people whom they had once treated as Creeks and allies. How could the alliance survive? The bases on which it was built—the lands and government of the Creek Nation—were being dissolved. A few areas of mutual concern existed for black Creeks and other Creeks, and for African Americans as well. Around 1906, blacks and Indians together interfered with the building of railroads through their communities in actions that railroad employees looked upon as "riots."[114] Interracial action was still possible, but these examples suggest that they occurred when both groups had something at stake—which was less commonly the case now that the national lands and government were being dissolved.

THE INDIAN TERRITORY had changed much in the fifteen years since Isparhecher had declared his opposition to allotment and his promise to treat "all people as equals whether *white, red* or *black*." In defense of communal-land ownership, men like Isparhecher rallied behind a definition of Creek citizenship that transcended race. In the years from 1891 to 1905, the politics of allotment gave new power to a racial definition of what it meant to be Creek. Allotment policies, and enrollment in racial categories, did not create racialized definitions of Creek citizenship, or racial tensions in Creek society, out of thin air. But the politics of allotment did undermine a notion of the Creek Nation in which people of all races could be equal citizens. Both allotment policies and the political debate over them tended to advance the notion that real Creek identity derived from indigenous ancestry, and the remainder of the nation could meaningfully be understood in terms of racial categories. Making property and codifying race were two inseparable parts of the American attempt at unmaking the Creek Nation and remaking its people.

The fate of the Creek Council House in Okmulgee similarly illustrates the decline of a sense of a Creek nation that encompassed a disparate population. That council house, a stout stone building built in 1878, still stands in what was the central square of the Creek Nation. It most visibly resembles the substantial county courthouses that Americans built throughout the Midwest. But when one looks past the neoclassical facade to consider what happened inside it, and when one places it in the landscape of Okmulgee and the Creek Nation, one can see a different political heritage at play. This was a place where representatives of all the towns of the composite Creek Nation assembled, a place where phenotypically white and black and indigenous Creeks debated one another as Creeks. It was a rectangular building placed in the center of a square in the center of a nation. Just like the council arbors of Creek towns, traditionally placed in the middle of a square ground in the middle of a town, it is oriented to the cardinal directions. It was not the same as a brush arbor where town officials and elders conferred, though it carried that heritage with it. Nor was it the county seat it resembled: it was the national capitol of an Indian nation. The Creek Council House captures the complexity of the political and historical situation of the Creeks in the late nineteenth century better than any words by Isparhecher or Checote or Pleasant Porter could, and it was the place where Creeks of different races had came together as a nation to debate.

In 1902, the United States placed the Creek Council House up for sale. While awaiting a buyer, the United States rented it for use as a courthouse.[115] There can be no better symbol of the blow that the U.S. government dealt to Creek sovereignty at the turn of the twentieth century. There can also be no better symbol of the decline, precipitated by this same attack by the U.S. government, of a Creek nationhood that could encompass people of different races and could in fact bring those people together in its defense. As always, it was not just an abstract nationhood that was at stake. It was one rooted in places: in the Creek Council House, in the square around it, in the town of Okmulgee, and especially in the land that stretched out for miles to the north, south, east, and west. Creek land, like the council house, had held a nation together. With the American imposition of a racialized foreign land law though allotment, Creek land could also drive its people apart and redraw the lines of nation and race.

Living under Allotment

RACE AND PROPERTY

In the early twentieth century, allotment, statehood, and a host of land-related policies made land ownable and made race a fixed and powerful legal category. Policy made a world where all land was owned, where some people were propertied and others were propertyless, where some could be landlords and others would be tenants. How would eastern Oklahoma's increasingly sharp class conflict shape relations among the state's Indian, black, and white residents? Part III is divided into three chapters, each of which emphasizes how one group—Creeks (Chapter 4), people of African descent (Chapter 5), and whites (Chapter 6)— attempted to navigate this context and shape it to their ends. For each of these three groups, the racial politics that emerged was as much about dynamics within the racial group as it was about relations with other racial groups.

4

Policy and the Making of Landlords and Tenants

ALLOTMENT, LANDLESSNESS, AND

CREEK POLITICS, 1906–1920S

In 1912, a frustrated farmer wrote a letter to a left-wing Oklahoma Cotton Belt publication that addressed his fellow farmers. "Ten years ago," he reminded the readers, "you were eager to unfold your plans of acquiring and fitting in a snug little farm house for the maintenance of yourself and your family." He went on to ask them, "How did your plans pan out?" He answered the question for them: "The fact that you are still renting is deemed sufficient answer."[1] Tens of thousands of white and black men like him had come to Oklahoma to become landowners and yet found themselves working the fields of a landlord, paying rent in shares or in cash. With 55 percent of Oklahoma farmers working as tenants in 1910, only five states, all in the Deep South, had a higher tenancy rate.[2] The contrast between expectation and reality was sharp and bitter. It was not only landless white and black men, however, who were dissatisfied with the realities of Oklahoma land tenure. In May 1915, Dallas Dunzy, a twenty-four-year-old Creek woman, wrote to the assistant commissioner of Indian Affairs in Washington, D.C., to protest his refusal of her petition for permission to sell a portion of her allotment land. She wrote the letter on the stationery of her family's store (The People's Grocery), which listed her as proprietor. The letterhead implicitly threw doubt on the commissioner's judgment that her lack of business experience made it unwise to permit her to sell her allotment land. To add insult to injury, she informed him, in his previous letter he had addressed her as "Mr." "I am affraid," she wrote, "you have misconstrued all around by not having knowledge of me." Not only was she a woman and properly addressed as "Miss," she wrote, "I will ashure you that if I own any thing I want [it] to be mine." By this she meant "I can do as I please just when I get ready to do so, as I am a free independent Born woman and do not need your assistance." This statement expressed a belief that making decisions regarding sale was her right as a property owner. It also called upon the feminism of the time to assert her abilities as a woman. By law, however, because the Dawes Commission had enrolled her as three-quarters Creek by blood, she did not have effective control of her land under the property regime of allotment.[3] Both the white farmer and the Creek allottee were dissatisfied, finding that allotment did not create the property system they had expected.

In the first decade of statehood, rural east-central Oklahoma became a society dominated by landlords and landless tenant farmers. This outcome resulted largely from the workings of American federal, state, and local government policy—the law, the way it was applied, and even the way it was broken in swindles that benefited from official complicity, corruption, and neglect. Policy shaped who would own land and who would be landless. The division of the Creek Nation's land was foundational in this process, but land policy entailed more than just allotment. Land policy encompassed allotment, taxation, credit, and even racial categorization.

Indeed, ensuring that a person's race was legally fixed and unchanging was crucial to the making of a capitalist order in eastern Oklahoma. Of course, policy had shaped Creek land tenure before statehood, as well. Land law and its enforcement had been a central political issue in Creek government. But Creek law was more visible and explicit than American law in the way it determined land tenure: Creek law stated who was Creek and who was not, and thus who could take up land and who could not. In contrast, after statehood, the effect of policy on landownership was less visible. That is because allotment began the process of creating a market in lands, and most Americans are used to thinking of markets as akin to natural forces. Similarly, laws regulating allotment lands were structured around race, and most Americans are used to thinking of racial categories as natural and unvarying. But in early twentieth-century Oklahoma, the fact that land was just entering a market and was being structured racially

House of a white tenant farmer near Warner, Oklahoma, 1939. (Photographer: Lee Russell; Library of Congress, Prints & Photographs Division, FSA/OWI Collection, LC-USF34-033526-D)

through allotment meant that it was a matter of considerable political debate how policy would determine who would own what and who would be called what race. Race and class were powerful forces in a wide array of land-related policies and their application, and they did much to determine the racial and class distribution of land. A look at these laws, the way they were enforced, and the way that they were debated suggests that policy, rather than markets, encouraged the emergence of a rural order characterized by landlords, tenants, and sharp inequalities of race.

For Creek people, the power of federal, state, and even county land policy and their lack of authority over it encapsulated the political challenges of the statehood era. Policy oversaw allottees more closely than any other group of landowners. Creeks, however, had very little purchase over law after statehood and the loss of effective, national, sovereign authority over the region. Nonetheless, Creek politics had not come to an end. A second Snake "rebellion," in 1909, was the most spectacular manifestation of statehood-era Creek resistance, but a more long-lasting avenue of Creek politics was the everyday action of Creek people. Creeks continued to use their land to work toward their own goals rather than succumb to being remade into yeomen or proletarians by reformers and officials. Creek autonomy in the new era was restricted, as Dallas Dunzy's fruitless letter to a far-off bureaucrat demonstrates. Still, Creek political life and Creek nationhood survived allotment and the imposition of state and local governments.

Debating the Place of Race in Land Law

While Washington was still busy carving the Creek Nation into separate parcels, debates over postallotment land law were well under way. In 1906, a Senate select committee traveled to Indian Territory to hold public hearings. The question at hand was how law should govern allotment lands after they were distributed. Although many people in Indian Territory still questioned the wisdom or validity of the allotment process, from the point of view of federal authorities, allotment was a foregone conclusion. The issue that remained was what would happen to Indians and their allotments in the market economy of the future state of Oklahoma. Even before federal authorities considered the conflicting ideas of Indian Territory residents, though, the answer was far from clear. The reformers who had initiated allotment were attached to two contradictory ideals: the profit-seeking liberal individual and the Jeffersonian yeoman farmer. The two ideals emerged from different economic ideologies and suggested opposing principles in land legislation. The liberal individual was the central figure in the mythology of Gilded Age capitalism, a free actor in the "free market." As such, he (the figure is gendered male in this image) had the right to sell his allotment and spend or reinvest the proceeds as he saw fit. Creating yeomen, however, required tying allottees to the land. After all, the yeoman emerged from a different, agrarian strand of American mythology and was defined by his relationship to the land he owned and worked. The reformers believed that tying allottees to the land would give landownership the time to work a slow alchemy of racial transformation. Indian people would gradually learn the whitening culture of capitalism. If allottees (as liberal individuals) merely sold or rented out their newly acquired lands, they would not learn these lessons. The problem was to empower allottees as individuals while restraining them from selling their land. In order to ensure that Indians would retain and work their land, these reformers and their supporters in government favored limiting the right of allottees to sell or lease their lands for a set period of time.[4] This compromise position, which the senators brought with them to the Indian Territory hearings, reflected the reformers' already conflicted ideas. At the hearings at Tulsa, the senators would encounter even more vigorous disagreements.

In their testimony at the hearings, some Creek citizens, including black Creeks, and their white allies proceeded from a racial logic to favor restricting Indian property rights with regard to allotments. They turned to notions of racial difference to argue that law had to temper the effects of the market to take into account the unequal needs of people of different races. Some contended that Indians, especially "full-bloods," were inherently childlike people who needed to be protected from whites, whom they associated with adult status and cupidity.[5] Creek House of Kings member Cornelius Perryman told the senators that whereas the "full-bloods" needed restrictions, the "half breeds" were as capable of managing their own affairs "as the average full blood white man."[6] Alice Robertson, a white woman who long taught in the Creek schools, deemed that while the abilities of "full bloods" and "half bloods" might be equal, "the mixed bloods on account of the strain of white in them are more assertive."[7] Perryman and Robertson attributed neither the presumed disability of "full-bloods" nor the more developed business capacities and assertiveness of the "mixed-bloods" to educational opportunities, experience, or cultural exposure but to race. It followed from this logic that the greater the degree of Indian "blood" allottees had, the greater need they had for protection from the market.

For their part, advocates of protective restrictions on the allotments of black Creeks differed as to whether their need was biological or cultural. M. L. Mott, a white attorney who represented the Creek Nation in its relations with the United States, followed the norms of racist theory when he argued that black Creeks were constitutionally incapable of understanding business: "Their heads are not built right." A Freedman knew "no more about the rules of business and trading and commerce than a child." In contrast, J. Coody Johnson, a black Creek attorney and member of the House of Warriors, argued that black Creeks needed protective restrictions, not because they were mentally deficient, but rather because they had little experience with the market. Being unused to economic planning and therefore thinking only of their immediate wants, he warned, black Creeks would quickly sell their allotments for insignificant sums and be reduced to landlessness. Johnson was not as optimistic about allotment as were Dawes and the white reformers. Nonetheless, he shared their belief that allottees could eventually learn the culture of capitalism but needed protective restrictions lest they lose their land before that apprenticeship was complete.[8] This solution suggested that the black Creeks were economic individuals in the making, much like children or students.

Creeks and their allies who emphasized the need for long-term protection of allottees did not do so with the same racist pessimism as did federal officials who assumed that Indians were inherently and irremediably incapable. That idea gained power in Washington, especially as allotment proceeded after 1905, and led some whites to conclude that it was best for whites to control allottees' lands, whether by buying them or leasing them.[9] This notion was not one embraced by Cornelius Perryman, Alice Robertson, M. L. Mott, or J. Coody Johnson. Neither Perryman's nor Robertson's words or actions suggest that they would welcome Creeks' losing control of their allotments. Mott may have served as the attorney for a national government whose leadership was at times hostile to black Creek allottees, he himself did not speak in that vein in his testimony before the senators. Johnson, himself a black Creek attorney and a vigorous defender of black Creek rights, reasoned that black Creeks were hampered by their experiences, not their race, but needed protective restrictions just the same. Far from following federal officials' line that allottees' would inevitably surrender control of their land, the local brand of biological determinism, rooted in the Creek Nation, suggested the need for long-term vigilance by the federal government in the interest of protecting Creeks' allotment lands. Simultaneously, for Perryman, the argument bolstered the idea that mixed-ancestry people like himself, who he believed were biologically equal to whites in their capacities, were entitled to full control of their allotment lands.

This final notion—that allottees deserved full control of their lands—was advocated for self-interested reasons by the white businessmen and land speculators who were thronging to the territory in search of opportunity. To the senators, they argued that the immediate creation of an unencumbered market in land would be a boon not only to the state but to Indian people as well. They complained that with so much of the land in Indian Territory nontransferable, it was impossible to sell lands to prospective farmers. Bankers warned that they could develop no profitable business if allottees could not mortgage their lands and if potential settlers could not buy them. Political hopefuls pointed out that with so much land nontaxable, the state and county governments of the future state would have to struggle for revenues. One newspaperman summed up the beliefs of those opposing allotment when he wrote, "Let the Indian sell his allotment (not his homestead) and the Indian himself will be benefited," the white buyer would be benefited, and, ultimately, "the country in general will be benefited" by a rise in the value of land.[10]

These champions of a free market in land emphasized to the senators the equality of all citizens as liberal individuals while ignoring or sweeping aside the specifics that others cited as reasons to limit allotment rental and sales. There is a striking similarity to a discursive move described by J. Kēhaulani Kauanui in her analysis of the debate over a Hawaiian homestead law in 1921. There, white colonial elites "evok[ed] an abstract logic of citizenship and equal rights" in their support for creating a racialized and racializing system of denying lands to indigenous people.[11] At the Tulsa hearing, those who advocated removing all restrictions on allotment lands argued that it was the right of Indians to do as they pleased with their own property. They further argued that, with few exceptions, Indians were capable of managing their own affairs and protecting themselves against any white man who sought to take advantage of them. In the words of C. M. Bradley, who dealt in Indian lands, it was "un-American" to keep this "noble race of people" from selling their land.[12] He sounded much the same note as Commissioner of Indian Affairs Francis Leupp, who deemed it "un-American" to restrict some allottees from selling their land because of their race.[13] Whereas Creek defenders of land tenure in common and Creek nationhood had once mobilized the discourse of equal rights of all citizens, it was now the rallying cry of those who wanted a free market in Indians' allotment lands—but for very different reasons. The champions of this position, mostly whites who had arrived relatively recently in the territory, told the senators that the economic development of the region depended on the lifting of restrictions. Obviously, they expected their own future prosperity to depend directly or indirectly on bringing more lands onto the market.

Instead of making such an obviously self-interested argument to the senators, these men couched it in terms of protecting Indians' interests. They contended that protective restrictions distorted the market to Indians' disadvantage. Even before deeds were issued to allottees, a market had emerged in which Indians sold to a speculator the right to purchase their land once the restrictions were removed, and at a prearranged price. Because of the speculative and probably illegal nature of the investment, allotments sold in this manner fetched prices far inferior to what they would be worth on an open market. In addressing the senators, bankers and land speculators used this kind of free-market argument, depicting their criticisms of restrictions as a defense of the rights of Indian people.[14]

As Laura Edwards argues, "Inequality is central to the conception of individual rights." The converse was also true in making allotment policy: asserting individual rights served to build racial and class inequality.[15] In fact, this equal rights argument was tied to a belief in racial inequality—that whites' racial characteristics suited them to lead the new state and that whites' interests must therefore be defended. Whites such as D. S. Sleeper, a Tulsa lawyer, complained to the senators that if restrictive legislation exempted homestead lands from taxation, whites would have to pay most of the taxes. They argued that protection of Indian interests therefore amounted to discrimination in favor of Indians over whites.[16] Whites, they claimed, had been the most valuable residents of the territory. W. J. Gregg, who said that he spoke as "a representative of the white man," pointed to "the fertile farms" and "splendid cities" of Indian Territory as the product of "the energy and activity of the white man," of "his energy, his capital, and his skill," and of his civilizing tendency.[17] A convention in Okmulgee told the senators that these same characteristics would make whites the most valuable citizens of the new state, as their "industry, intelligence, and high character must create, in large degree, the great values in Indian Territory."[18] To impede the flow of lands from the hands of Indians and blacks into the hands of whites would be to discriminate against those who were racially destined to lead the state to greatness. Opponents of restrictions argued that a free market was essential to transforming the territory into a Jeffersonian democracy of white landowning farmers. Alluding to the future state they expected would soon take the place of Indian Territory, prominent white men such as Robert Lee Williams argued that if Indian and black allottees could not sell or mortgage their land, it would be impossible to create a class of autonomous, landowning white yeomen. Williams, a lawyer in the Choctaw Nation who was making himself a prominent figure in the territory's Democratic Party, linked the future of the state to such a class of white, and presumably Democratic, farmers. If allottees could not alienate their lands, the dominance of such a class, and by implication the dominance of the white race, would be thrown into question in the new state.[19]

Designing Race into Law

In the end, Congress came up with a series of compromises. The Creek allotment agreement provided that each allottee would divide his or her allotment into a "homestead" portion and a "surplus" portion. Policy makers intended that the homestead remain in the allottees' hands for an extended period, whereas allottees would be permitted to sell or rent the surplus after a relatively short delay. The original Creek agreement, ratified in 1901, held that allottees would each declare 40 acres of their 160-acre allotment to be their "homestead." The remainder was termed their "surplus." The homestead would be inalienable and nontaxable for twenty-one years from the ratification of the allotment treaty. It could not be sold to, mortgaged to, or seized by any person or any government and was not subject to taxation. The surplus was covered by these "restrictions" (as they were known) for only five years. At that time, the surplus would be subject to all the normal laws governing real estate. Legislation further prescribed the duration of agricultural, grazing, and mineral leases that allottees could grant. The agreement provided that, upon approval of an appeal from the allottee, the secretary of the interior could approve the lifting of these restrictions to allow the sale, mortgage, or extended leasing of land.[20] In the agreement, these restrictions on property applied to all allottees, no matter the racial category to which the Dawes Commission had assigned them.

But race would be a pillar of land law and a means of alienating lands from allottees. In 1904, bowing to demands of bankers, speculators, and other would-be land buyers, Congress injected racial difference into the previously race-blind restriction laws. This made it possible for whites to acquire the lands of the least favored allottees in the Creek Nation. Allotment had left some of the richest lands in Oklahoma in the hands of black Creeks. Many of them had selected their allotments in the region they had inhabited and farmed since slavery: the fertile valley of the Arkansas River. Restrictions delayed the legal transfer of these lands to eager speculators and farmers. Congress voted in April 1904 to remove all restrictions on the 120-acre surplus lands of adult allottees who were "not of Indian blood."[21] In the Creek Nation, this meant black Creeks, and so the law made 549,480 acres belonging to them immediately purchasable.[22] The act allowed whites to purchase hundreds of thousands of acres from black Creeks. It also made it possible for white buyers to get legal title to land they had already purchased through illegal contracts. One black Creek reported that on the day the law went into effect, a number of white buyers had each bought the surplus lands of fifteen to twenty black Creeks.[23] The law also made black allottees liable for taxes on their surplus lands once the state of Oklahoma and its counties began taxing real property. The local press heralded this important decision, which was part of the Indian Appropriation Bill of 1904. That same act permitted Indians "by blood" to apply for the removal of restrictions on their land.[24]

Meanwhile, eastern advocates for reform of Indian policy continued to lobby for further restrictions on the sale of the allotments of Indians enrolled as "full-bloods." In April 1906, they won passage of the Five Tribes Act, which denied any "full-blood Indian" of the Five Tribes the "power to alienate, sell, dispose of, or encumber in any manner" any part of his or her allotment for twenty-five years (that is, until 1931). Thus for Indians registered as "full-bloods," restrictions would not only last longer than provided for in the original agreements but would also cover their entire allotment, homestead as well as surplus.[25] The act further stipulated that the tribal rolls drawn up by the Dawes Commission were to be considered conclusive as to "degree of Indian blood." People who were enrolled as Freedmen could not have their enrollment changed to "citizen by blood," even if they demonstrated Creek "blood" ancestry.[26] Combined with the 1904 act, the Five Tribes Act had the effect of creating three racially defined levels of restrictions on allottees, depending on whether they were labeled "full-blood," of partial Indian heritage, or not of "Indian blood." Allotment policy and politics had not conjured these categories out of the void, but it had given them legal salience that underscored their political salience.

The senatorial committee's 1906 visit to Indian Territory discussed above emboldened those who sought to remove most or all of the restrictions on the transfer and taxation of allotment lands. Oklahoma local officials and aspiring land speculators aimed an intensive lobbying effort at federal legislators in their efforts to bring allotment lands onto the market and the tax rolls. They succeeded in 1908. Federal legislation (summarized in table 1) removed all restrictions on the entire allotments (both "homestead" and "surplus" portions) of allottees whom the Dawes Commission had enrolled as "Negroes" or as less than one-half "Indian by blood." For allottees whom the commission had determined to have at least half but less than three-quarters Indian ancestry and no African ancestry, Congress lifted restrictions on the "surplus" portion of their allotment but left restrictions in place on the forty acres they had chosen as their homestead. Congress left all restrictions in place on the sale, rental, leasing, and taxation

TABLE 1 Race and Restrictions on Allotments in the Act of May 27, 1908

Dawes Commission Racial Categorization	Restrictions on 40-Acre Homestead Allotment	Restrictions on 120-Acre Surplus Allotment
Whites, "Negroes," and "Mixed-bloods" of less than one-half blood	No restrictions	No restrictions
"Mixed-bloods" of at least one-half blood but less than three-quarters blood	Restricted until May 31, 1931	No restrictions
"Mixed-bloods" of at least three-quarters blood, and all "full-bloods"	Restricted until May 31, 1931	Restricted until May 31, 1931

Source: Compiled from "An Act for the Protection of the People of the Indian Territory, and for Other Purposes" (30 Stat. 495: Act of June 28, 1898), in Lawrence Mills, *The Lands of the Five Civilized Tribes* (St. Louis: F. H. Thomas Law Book Co., 1919), 538–41.

of the entire allotment of Indians the Dawes Commission had classified as having at least three-quarters Indian "blood."[27]

Racial Fixity, Land Law, and the Sale of Lands

At the center of land regulation stood race, and racial fixity was therefore essential to capitalist growth. By legislating three racial categories and applying different real estate law to each, Congress enshrined in law a hierarchy of paternalist protection, suffused with white supremacy, based on the racial classifications in the Dawes Commission enrollment records. The legislation presumed that the higher the degree of one's indigenous heritage, the less capable one was of looking out for one's own interests in property, and the longer one needed to retain one's allotment to learn the life of the idealized white yeoman farmer. The legislation established a graduated level of protection for people of mixed white and indigenous parentage. Congress accorded none of this paternalist protection to those people whom the Dawes Commission had deemed to be "Negro," no matter how much indigenous or white heritage they might have. The "one-drop rule," the American precept that any African ancestry whatsoever made one black, took a prominent place in Oklahoma land law.

Placing race at the center of land policy meant that land markets—and thus the very functioning of capitalism in this agricultural society—depended on the ability to determine with certainty the legal racial categorization of an individual. Again, the ironies of the creation of a liberal economic order come into view because while that order was in theory based on the abstract equality of the individual, it depended in practice on the racial inequality of legal individuals. The land market was premised on the power of the state to decide what race a person was. One could be secure in the title to allotment land that one bought only if one could be sure that the seller had a right to sell it, which depended on the seller's degree of Indian "blood." This meant, for example, that no title was more secure than one that had been bought from a person enrolled as a Freedman. By definition, black Creeks' allotments were excluded from any of the restrictions on sale that applied to the allotments of persons enrolled as Indians by blood. If, as Cheryl Harris has put it, whiteness is property, blackness was the ability to sell property.[28] Thus when Joseph Tiger sold his entire 160-acre allotment in 1907, it was essential knowledge to the buyer that he was legally and indisputably a "Negro." Tiger later challenged the sale and argued before a federal court that he was, in fact, an "Indian by blood." Being categorized as an "Indian by blood" would mean that he was unable to sell the allotment land, and it would have nullified the transfer of deed. But the federal court decided that the Dawes roll was conclusive for the determination of race; Tiger was and would remain "Negro." The *Daily Oklahoman* newspaper celebrated the economic ramifications of this decision. "The decision is far reaching, affecting 5000 Creek freedmen and throwing the restrictions from the barter and sale of 800,000 acres in the Creek nation." The editors knew that racial fixity was the foundation for capitalist economic growth, and the significance of the decision making race inalterable was emphasized in their headline: "Releases Rich Lands for Sale."[29]

Land policy encouraged black landlessness by first ignoring illegal sales of black Creek lands and then legalizing such sales. Even before the federal court had ensured that racial fixity would secure whites' claim to land titles in Oklahoma, tens of thousands of acres of black Creek lands had already changed hands. Almost as soon as the process of choosing allotments was under way, land speculators swarmed the Indian Territory. Before they could purchase land, they used cheap leases (often as low as one dollar per year) to secure the advance right to buy land once it could be sold legally. Some lands were encumbered with mineral leases as soon as preliminary allotments were made on them. Though these leases violated federal restrictions, they were often effective and permitted land companies to sublease allotments to settlers at much higher prices. Prior to statehood, one company in the Creek Nation had 80,000 acres under such leases. Furthermore, black Creeks had gained the authority to sell their surplus allotment lands in 1904, and thousands had parted with their deeds almost immediately. Although firm figures on landownership by race are not available, contemporary reports contend that more than four out of five Freedmen had sold their surplus allotments before statehood. If correct, this would add up to roughly 653,664 acres of land in the Creek Nation, 60 percent of the approximately 1,089,440 acres black Creeks received in allotment.[30] The nonenforcement of restrictions prior to 1904, followed by the liberalizations of 1904 and 1908, added up to policy in favor of black landlessness.

For their part, nonblack Creeks seized upon the liberalization of restrictions to use their lands as a sellable or leasable resource instead of making them the path to yeoman farming. The removal of restrictions that began in 1904 and was extended in 1908 had the intended effect. It permitted the wholesale transfer of millions of acres of land from "by blood" allottees as well as black allottees to new buyers, mostly white but some of them African Americans. After passage of the 1904 act, more than fourteen hundred Creeks immediately applied to have the restrictions on their land lifted, but only fifteen received approval.[31] Other Creeks petitioned for removal of the restrictions on their surplus lands, and with the approval of the local Indian agent and the secretary of the interior, many "full-bloods" were renting out their homestead and surplus.[32] In 1908, land transfers accelerated. The end of all restrictions on the lands of black allottees and all Creeks whom the Dawes Commission had classified as less than one-half "Indian by blood" meant that hundreds of thousands more acres of Creek lands would be available for purchase. White citizens celebrated this as the emancipation of their state from the bondage of protective restrictions. In June 1908, the residents of Muskogee, the largest city in eastern Oklahoma and the center of the region's land trade, celebrated the impending removal of restrictions with a "jubilee."[33] In the days before July 27, 1908, when the lands became available for sale, thousands of allottees converged on county seats in eastern Oklahoma, as land sales had to be registered with county clerks. They were met by land speculators from Oklahoma, Texas, St. Louis, Kansas City, and Chicago. Newspapers and witnesses reported that, in their eagerness to

Indian tenant farm couple, McIntosh County, Oklahoma, 1939.
(Photographer: Lee Russell; Library of Congress, Prints &
Photographs Division, FSA/OWI Collection, LC-USF34-033559-D)

keep allottees away from other prospective purchasers, speculators in Muskogee and Wewoka (in the former Seminole Nation) put allottees in hotels, lodging rooms, business offices, camps in the woods, and whatever other space was available, furnished them with food and drink, and posted guards to keep away the competition. One speculator allegedly invited sellers to a dice game the day before the lifting of restrictions. He then notified the police of the game, ensuring that the allottees would be held in jail, safe from competitors until the next morning, when he arrived at the jail with the deeds ready for them to sign.[34] In Muskogee County alone, more than 25,000 acres of land, equivalent to 625 homestead allotments, changed hands in the two weeks following the 1908 lifting of restrictions.[35] The land sales continued, and roughly five years later, reports suggested that fewer than 10 percent of Freedmen and "mixed blood" Creeks still owned any of their allotment lands.[36] Removing all restrictions on the lands resulted in the massive transfer of lands out of allottees' hands, making many landless. The power of law to shape the distribution of property was tremendous.

Allotment as an Ongoing Process:
Protection, Restriction, and Conflict

Allotment was an ongoing and contested process, not just the selection of lands and the issuance of deeds. For allottees whose lands were still under allotment restrictions, Office of Indian Affairs agents had considerable leeway in deciding how it would be applied. For decades after the Dawes Commission completed its task, Indian Affairs agents continued the work of allotment in their management of Indians' allotment lands and income from lands. They used their trust authority over allottees' land and their income from land in their efforts to fulfill a number of agendas: to remake Indians, to prevent the sale of lands of those who deserved protection, to facilitate the sale of lands of those who did not, and to maximize lease income from allotment lands. The conflict over allotment continued as well, this time between agents and allottees. Creeks resisted the limits placed upon them and the goals that agents had for them, and they pursued their own agendas by using their land. The law limited allottees' control over their allotments and income, however, and gave Indian agents the crucial power to judge allottees' racial makeup and to adjust the application of the law accordingly.

In accordance with national policy, local Office of Indian Affairs agents attempted to use control over Indians' land and moneys to force them to engage the market economy as proletarians who conformed to American gender and kinship expectations. In 1904, Congress provided a means for Indians "by blood" to request that federal authorities lift the restrictions on their land, giving them authority to sell, rent, mortgage, or otherwise handle their lands as they wished.[37] In practice, this meant that allottees applied to the field agent of the Office of Indian Affairs for permission to do these things. The field agent, with the assistance of a field clerk, made a recommendation as to approval or denial to his superiors. Similarly, agents were charged with leasing out lands for allottees and holding their income in trust, distributing it as they deemed appropriate. Together, these measures gave agents control over land and income from it. In effect, agents used their power to control allottees' finances to control allottees themselves. In 1909, the Office of Indian Affairs in Washington decreed that no Indian would be "allowed to draw a monthly allowance or to expend any of his retained individual funds in the purchase of food or clothing." The stated goal was to conserve the funds of allottees who were "able-bodied and capable of supporting themselves and those properly dependent upon them." Yet the policies also aimed at changing Indian work habits and Indian kinship and community standards. The directive aimed to force "able-bodied" Indians to be workers who supported only the sort of immediate kin that white Americans thought of as "properly" dependent on them, not the network of kin and clan for which many Creeks felt responsible.[38]

The Indian Service of the Department of the Interior supervised restrictions on the Indian lands, and it was to their local agent that Creek allottees needed to apply if they wished to sell, rent out, or mortgage their land. In 1908, when Adolphus Tiger, age twenty-three, petitioned for permission to sell forty acres of his homestead allotment, the agent in Okmulgee declared that he was "an unsteady, erratic youth" who would just "dissipate" the money from a sale "as fast as he gets it." As Tiger was, in the agent's opinion, "strong and capable of doing a full day's manual labor," he should not be allowed to "simply idle away his time and squander his money." To force Tiger to become a manual laborer, the agent recommended denying him the opportunity to profit from his land.[39] Constraining Tiger's use of his allotment was a tool to force him to conform to the agents' expectations of his class and gender. The gendering of these expectations is more evident still in the case of Edward Webster. The agent refused to recommend approval of his request to sell eighty acres of land on the grounds that "he is an able-bodied man and well able to earn a good living for himself and wife."[40] Restrictions on allotments were used to try to force male allottees to labor and to conform to American norms of behavior for their class and gender. It is noteworthy that this represented a step back from the earlier stated goal of turning allottees into independent yeoman farmers and a step toward turning them into proletarians in the agricultural economy of rural Oklahoma. This shift corresponded to the transition from an optimistic policy that aimed to make Indians capable of overseeing their own allotments to a pessimistic one that assumed that Indian racial incapacity made it inevitable that whites would control their lands.[41]

Still, there remained the larger goal of discouraging or impeding Creeks from seeking to live off income derived from their land, whether by selling it or renting it out. Yet allottees frequently chose to rent out land, and field agents were charged with making advantageous lease agreements and preserving land as a source of lease income. Thus when Katie Tiner, a fifty-eight-year-old woman enrolled as one-half blood, made a petition to sell restricted land in 1908, the field agent recommended refusing it on the grounds that she depended on the lease income from it.[42] In effect, they were protecting her lease income. Different gender expectations made lease arrangements more palatable, from the point of view of field agents, in the case of female allottees like Tiner than men like Tiger. Tiner and other women were not expected to make their living from manual labor but rather to attach themselves to men who might make a living and provide for them. Nonetheless, field agents did also oversee the lease arrangements of men.

In considering petitions, field agents (like federal agents during the creation of the Dawes Rolls) imposed racial categories upon Creek individuals, shaping their economic future and the racial distribution of land tenure in the region. In fact, agents often disregarded racial status as indicated by enrollment records and adjusted their decisions in accordance with the way they perceived allotees' racial makeup. In doing so, they varied from the formal rules of allotment but remained true to its principle of imposing protection and restriction on people deemed "Indians by blood" and not on people deemed of African descent. At first, this appears to be a noteworthy exception to the way that legal racial fixity made a market in land possible. After all, the federal courts had ruled that Dawes Commission racial categorizations were authoritative as to race, making title secure. Yet when field agents made their own determinations as to race that were at variance with Dawes enrollment records, they did not undermine the security of land title in the land market. Rather, they were determining whether lands would be allowed onto the market at all. If they approved a sale of land, title could be bought and sold with confidence.

This practice hastened the transfer of lands out of the hands of people who appeared to the agents to be of African descent but were not enrolled as such. This was the case for Winey Bullwer, a twenty-six-year old woman who made a petition in 1913 to have the restrictions removed on eighty acres of her land so that she could sell it. Her husband, Henry Bullwer, a non-Creek, was facing a trial for murder. The Indian Office field clerk was convinced of his innocence. Winey Bullwer stated she would use part of the proceeds to hire an attorney and part to improve the lands that would remain after the sale. (This final statement was perhaps crafted to fulfill what she knew was a priority for the Indian Office, the improvement of Indian lands, and reflected the sophistication of the ways that allottees approached the federal bureaucracy.) The Dawes Commission had enrolled Winey Bullwer as a "full-blood" Creek. Because of the belief that "full-bloods" were the Indians least prepared to oversee their own economic affairs, Indian Office employees were particularly loath to remove restrictions on their lands. In this case, however, the district agent and the agent in Muskogee made an exception, and not only because Henry Bullwer faced a likely death sentence. The field clerk reported that Winey Bullwer was "enrolled as a full-blood Creek Indian but as a matter of fact, she is a mixed blood, the mixture being Indian and Negro. Her appearance indicates an equal mixture of Negro Blood." Her marriage to Henry Bullwer, "a mulatto" not enrolled as a Creek citizen, further disqualified her as an Indian deserving of protection. He was, wrote the field clerk, "a copper-colored negro who has the appearance of being part Indian, but as a matter of fact he has no Indian blood in his veins." He decided that his racial judgment overrode the fact that the Dawes Commission had enrolled Winey Bullwer as a "full-blood." His superior, the Indian agent, concurred: "In ordinary cases I would not approve this plan," he wrote, "but these people are very much Negroes."[43] In keeping with the spirit of the law, this meant they needed and deserved less protection.

In other cases, agents' determinations varied in relation to what they guessed the proportion of indigenous and white ancestry was. They believed that Indian "blood" made a person less economically capable. When deciding the petition of Butler Deer to sell some of his allotment land, the acting superintendent of the agency in Muskogee reasoned that "full-bloods" had an "inherited tendency of the mind to regard personal property" as like the common property of the pre-allotment period. This made it "difficult for the Indian, without previous training, to place a true value on property." The superintendent termed Deer "an ordinary full-blood Indian" and thus determined that the Indian Office should deny the petition. In contrast, when superintendents approved petitions to sell land of people they deemed to be largely white, they proceeded from the principle in allotment law that European ancestry made a person more economically capable. Thus the superintendent noted Louisa B. Smith, age sixty, had "the appearance of not more than one-sixteenth Indian blood"—even less than her enrollment of one-eighth Indian "blood" suggested. This made her "practically a white woman" in his eyes. Not surprisingly, then, she was "perfectly capable of looking after her own affairs."[44] In cases in which Office of Indian Affairs agents thought petitioners' proportion of Indian and European ancestry was roughly equivalent, other factors came into play. For example, the Dawes Commission had enrolled Thomas McIntosh as a "full-blood," but the agent judged he had "the appearance of a half-blood." Faced with this ambiguous proportion, the agent decided that the benefits of whiteness did not override the liabilities of Indianness because McIntosh derived a "comfortable living" from his land. The hundred acres of land that were cleared, fenced, and cultivated with a two-room house brought McIntosh $1,000 to $1,200 in lease income annually. The agent decided that allowing him to sell it would be unwise.[45]

The agents' paternalist interventions also reached inside Creek families, again demonstrating how the oversight of allottees' lands continued the work of allotment. In the eyes of agents, Creek men in general and Creek husbands in particular were suspicious. In accordance with long-held beliefs among whites, agents thought Indian husbands worked too little and drank too much. In a number of cases, the agents therefore refused to remove restrictions from the lands of female allottees on the grounds that their husbands would convince their wives to sell the land unwisely to get hold of the money.[46] The theorists of allotment had hoped to make Indians conform to Anglo-American gender norms, and the agents used their control of allotment lands to pursue this agenda. In cases such as these, in which they denied Creeks the permission to sell their land, the agents also undoubtedly kept allotment lands in Creek hands longer.

Yet many Creeks were eager to sell or mortgage their land. Histories of allotment rightly focus on the loss of lands and rightly term that dispossession a tragedy. But it is essential to note that from the point of view of the individual allottees, mortgaging or selling land could serve both the short-term goal of obtaining money or goods and the long-term goal of sustaining their communities and remaining part of them. Sometimes selling an allotment served these goals. This was particularly true in the many cases in which officials assigned allotments to individuals. Followers of the Snake movement, for example, refused to participate in the process of allotment as an act of protest and were marked down for plots that had nothing to do with their actual settlement patterns or communities. Looking at a similar situation at the White Earth Anishinaabe Reservation in Minnesota, Melissa Meyer concludes that in such circumstances mortgaging or selling "allotments that many had never even seen for cash to be used for horses, furniture, sewing machines, or groceries can be seen as an entirely rational decision."[47] The restrictions that aimed to protect allottees' landownership got in the way of their pursuit of their short- and long-term goals.

Not surprisingly, allottees resented these restrictions. Though sometimes effective, the restrictions were also meddlesome, intrusive, and patronizing. Creeks bristled at the implication that they were unable to manage their own property. Dallas Dunzy's letter at the opening of this chapter is a case in point. When Dallas Dunzy, age twenty-four, and her brother, Nathan Dunzy, age twenty-one, petitioned for the removal of restrictions on parts of their allotments, which would permit a sale, a field clerk informed his superiors that "the allottees are young and have had no experience in business matters." He noted, however, that the siblings (enrolled as three-quarters "blood") came from the influential family of J. R. Dunzy, the *micco* of Tuckabatchee town. The two had had "the advantages of their white neighbors." He thought it likely they would "cherish a sense of wrong" if the agent refused their application.[48] His expectation was correct. After the refusal, their father wrote to the commissioner of Indian Affairs in Washington in complaint. He warned the commissioner, "You are dealing with a civilized Indian & not any savage Race or Reservation Indians." The statement tried to alter the meaning that the commissioner assigned to their racial status, arguing that Indianness did not, as allotment policy would have it, mean incapacity.[49] His son Nathan similarly informed the commissioner: "[The fact] that you take us Indians to be all fools . . . shows you have no Experience in the Indian problem."[50] Both father and son also suggested that corrupt purposes might lie behind the decision. Dallas Dunzy, like her father and brother, spoke directly to the issue of dignity and autonomy and also asserted that her gender in no way disabled her from looking after her land and its disposition. As "a free independent Born woman," she was capable of managing her own affairs.[51] The Dunzys' letters spoke to central issues in the struggle over the ongoing practice of allotment as manifested in the ways that the Office of Indian Affairs controlled their lands and the income from it. The Dunzys declared that the practice of allotment was demeaning, premised on a notion of Indian incapacity, and failed to give allottees effective control over their own property. They did not succeed, however, in convincing officials in Muskogee or Washington to reverse their decision. The work of allotment continued, and the Dunzys and other Creeks had limited power over restrictions, the race that officials assigned to them, or the meaning officials assigned to that race.

Farm Tenancy and Landlessness

Boomers and other white agrarians had expected that property would create a landed white yeomanry, but instead property worked to create white propertylessness. It created a region of landlords and proletarians, not a republic of yeomen. As early as the first decade of Oklahoma statehood, a landlord elite came to dominate the rural economy and hold sway in the politics of eastern Oklahoma. They were enriched by land, much of which speculators had swindled from allottees in corruption so rampant and so tolerated that it must be understood as a pillar of Oklahoma's land policy. Politically connected whites got themselves named Indians' guardians in order to milk their lands for profit, buyers induced allottees to sign deceptive deeds of sale, and speculating "grafters" engaged in the many other schemes that historian and reformer Angie Debo amply documented in 1940 (so amply, in fact, that they are not discussed in depth here).[52] Men like Robert Lee Williams turned speculation in Indian lands into landed wealth and political dominance. A white attorney, Williams used his legal skills to transform limited capital into an empire of tenant farms in southeastern Oklahoma. His wealth fed a cycle of power: landownership won him influence; influence made it easier for him to accumulate more land; and his growing landholdings fed his growing power. Williams built a political career that won him the posts of state supreme court chief justice and then governor.[53] What a few men like Williams did at the state level was repeated a hundred times by locally prominent men like C. Guy Cutlip, whose family's speculation in Seminole allotment lands laid the basis for his career as a judge and Democratic Party leader in Seminole County.[54] Landlords like Williams and Cutlip and their allies in Oklahoma City and county seats throughout the old lands of the Indian Territory steered policy in their favor.[55]

As the wealth of landlords like Williams and Cutlip suggests, farm tenancy remained high in the new state, frustrating the would-be farm owners' agrarian vision of prosperous colonies of yeomen. Even before allotment, tenancy was widespread among the black and white immigrant farmers because the law forbade them to own land.[56] But allotment did not, contrary to expectations, open the door to farm ownership for many of these tenants. Indeed, the number of owner-operated farms in the area of the former Indian Territory barely changed between 1899 and 1908: it rose from 45,505 to 47,634, a change of only 4 percent.[57] Allotment only gave the opportunity to possess land to those who already had access to sufficient capital. The majority who lacked such funds, however, continued to rent. In Muskogee, Okfuskee, and Okmulgee counties, which included the most developed agricultural areas of the former Creek Nation, tenancy rates among whites ranged from 76 percent up to 84.5 percent, as table 2 shows. In all these counties, tenants worked smaller farms that were worth less money than farms that owners operated themselves. Three groups made up the category of "tenants." The best off paid their rent in cash, supplied all their own equipment and inputs (e.g., implements, draft animals, seed, fertilizer), and kept the entire harvest. These were few. More numerous were sharecroppers, who used their landlords' equipment and inputs and generally paid half the harvest as rent. The largest group was made up of share renters, who supplied their own equipment but used the landlords' inputs and generally paid the landlords one-third of the cotton and one-half of the corn as rent on the land.

Most striking is that in all these counties tenancy rates were *higher* for whites than they were for nonwhites—which made this region very distinctive in the history of American agriculture. A small but growing number of Indian farmers in Oklahoma were tenants. What made the low rate of Oklahoma nonwhite farm tenancy most remarkable, however, was black landownership. In 1910 and throughout American history, slavery, law, and practice have conspired to concentrate capital in the hands of whites, not African Americans. Nationwide, whites were more likely than African Americans to own land and African Americans more likely to rent. But in 1910 in eastern Oklahoma, allotment had placed land into the hands of many black Creeks. To a limited extent, restrictions on the sale of real estate had slowed the transfer of their lands to white people. Both allotment and restrictions, therefore, tended to lower the tenancy rate among nonwhites and increase it for whites. There are difficulties in using these census data: the Census Bureau racial categories do not correspond to the complexities

TABLE 2 Farm Tenancy in Counties Located within the Former Creek Nation Boundaries, 1910

| County | Tenancy Rate | | Average Acreage | | Average Value | |
	White (%)	Nonwhite (%)	Tenants	Owners	Tenant-Operated Farms	Owner-Operated Farms
Creek	81.5	72.2	245.1	134.8	$1,698.85	$3,263.28
Hughes	84.3	51.4	76.5	110.2	1,192.42	1,857.35
McIntosh	83.8	61.9	76.9	108.7	1,543.55	2,260.58
Muskogee	76.0	50.6	83.4	134.3	3,071.84	4,309.99
Okfuskee	84.5	82.3	85.0	138.6	1,235.94	2,374.06
Okmulgee	83.0	73.5	179.3	163.1	3,029.43	4,615.75
Tulsa	78.7	43.9	127.9	165.2	3,492.76	5,604.21
Wagoner	83.1	72.9	85.1	149.3	2,359.04	4,014.13

Source: Compiled from U.S. Bureau of the Census, *Statistics for Oklahoma, Thirteenth Census of the United States, 1910* (Washington: Government Printing Office, 1913), 634–49. Rogers County and Seminole County, which were located partly in the Creek Nation and partly in the Cherokee and Seminole nations, respectively, are not included here.

of race in eastern Oklahoma. The Census Bureau differentiated neither between Indian and African American farmers nor between Freedmen and newcomer African Americans. Furthermore, it is very likely that census enumerators counted as "whites" Creek allottees who had much white ancestry and resembled, to the enumerators, white people. The greatest weakness of the census data for the purposes of this study is that they report only the race of the people who operated farms, not the race of the farm owner. For that reason, one cannot determine the racial distribution of landownership for this period from the census data.[58] Nonetheless, the figures attest to the unusual situation that allotment and restriction had created in eastern Oklahoma.

In spite of the relatively high ownership rate among nonwhite farmers, most of the newcomer African Americans were working as tenant farmers, as both the census data and statements from 1910 to 1920 suggest.[59] This explains why rates of farm tenancy among nonwhites were significantly higher in Okmulgee and Okfuskee counties, areas where many African American newcomers settled. Many of them were unable to purchase land by 1910, despite the agrarian dreams that had drawn them to Oklahoma and even though so much Freedman land had come on the market in Okfuskee County. Even in the other counties, more than half of nonwhites, probably mostly African Americans, farmed as tenants.[60]

Indian Landowners, Tenancy, and Suspect Whiteness

To the extent that whites and African Americans commented on the place of Indians in farm tenancy, they blamed Indian landholding for causing the problem. In 1909, the state created a system of agricultural extension agents to bring the gospel of technically improved commercial agriculture to the state's farmers. The extension service, like the rest of Oklahoma government, was segregated, with only one black agent serving the state's entire black population and no agent dedicated to Indian farmers. White extension service agents were sympathetic to the racially specific Jeffersonian agrarian dream that so many white migrants had brought to Oklahoma, and they wished to see those dreams fulfilled. But the realities of a land tenure situation shaped by allotment frustrated this dream. White and African American agricultural extension agents reported that it was difficult to reduce the rate of tenancy because Indians owned too much land. The officials charged that allottees leased their lands out to speculators who subleased them to white farmers. Already in 1909, the head of the white extension service argued that landownership by Indians and African Americans and speculation in land by whites were twin evils that denied "poor, white tenant farmers" the "chance to get a home."[61] Extension officials continued to blame Indians for tenancy in Oklahoma into the 1920s.[62]

Affluent whites warned that the intolerable racial inversion of nonwhite people renting out land to poor whites was attracting a species of degraded tenants whose whiteness was suspect and whose agricultural practices were backward. The Eastern Oklahoma Agricultural Association, an organization founded at and centered on Muskogee and dominated by white bankers, businessmen, and large farmers and landholders, declared that eastern Oklahoma was not achieving its agricultural potential and was lagging behind its neighbors. The source of the problem was not in doubt: "The present retarded state existing here is due to the presence of the Indian."[63] Indian landownership meant that many whites were reduced to renting "poorly improved" lands from nonwhites. As a result, eastern Oklahoma had "bad tenants" rather than "good farmers."[64] Others characterized these tenants as "ignorant . . . of both the first principles of farming and of business methods" and fretted that there was "an absence of thrifty white farmers."[65] Better whites would, presumably, refuse to rent from Indians. It is worth noting that these tenants supposedly lacked precisely those traits that a number of whites businessmen had, at the 1906 senate select hearings in Tulsa, stated were characteristic of "the white man": his "energy and activity," his "industry [and] intelligence," and perhaps even his "high character."[66] Indian landowners were a threat to whiteness.

In the minds of some whites, they were also a threat to the fertility of the land itself. The logic was that Indian landownership meant a tenant form of agriculture, and tenants had little stake in maintaining the fertility of land they did not own. They therefore abused that soil. Thus Indian landownership led to soil depletion and erosion. Some who espoused this view placed it in a larger context of what they considered excessive concentration of landownership in eastern Oklahoma, but even then, they often placed particular blame on Indian landowners and particular hope on facilitating the sale of Indian lands to whites. C. R. Smith wrote to Governor R. L. Williams in 1914 to warn that the soil of eastern Oklahoma could be preserved only by "tenants becoming land owners," and the surest way to achieve that was to force any person owning more than 160 acres to sell off land. Smith favored an even more stringent limit for "Restricted Indians," who would be allowed only a 40-acre homestead. Barring that, he argued, forcing Indians to rent out their lands on leases of at least ten years would give renters a stake in preserving soil fertility. The evident racial intent of the proposal—to force Indians to transfer lands to whites—was reinforced by Smith's statement that his idea was in the interest of all those "who pay taxes." This was a racially loaded statement in Oklahoma, given that restricted allotment lands were nontaxable. The racial transfer of lands would effect a transformation of the wasted Oklahoma countryside into a veritable Jeffersonian Eden. "Make home owners of all tenant farmers," Smith predicted, "and the state will rapidly become the land of contentment, peace, righteousness and prosperity."

Oklahomans at the time were not unaware that one of the reasons so many Indians were renting out land rather than farming it or selling it was the restrictions constraining them. In order to keep allottees from parting with their lands, restrictions not only forbade selling land but also mortgaging it. Restricted allottees could therefore not secure the funds to purchase the animals, equipment, seed, fencing, and labor they needed to transform their allotments into profitable farms.[67] Added to the fact that these allottees—those termed "full-blood" or nearly so—were among the least likely to have experience in commercial agriculture, these restrictions constituted good reason for allottees to lease out their lands rather than farm them.[68] The restrictions that Indian policy reformers had intended to make Indians into yeoman farmers had the perverse effect of discouraging them from engaging in commercial farming. Thus high rates of tenancy did in part result, as extension agents claimed, from Indians leasing out their land to speculators, but that behavior needs to be understood in the context of the broader policies that constrained Indian allottees.

Aware of the impact of restrictions on the land market, though unsympathetic to the constraints they placed on Indian allottees, many whites called for legal change. J. F. Darby, the president of the Eastern Oklahoma Agricultural Association, urged "the removal of restrictions on alienation upon the greatest possible acreage."[69] Another affluent, educated, and urban white man who blamed Indian landowners—or, specifically, the legal restrictions on alienation that preserved Indian landownership—optimistically suggested that what policy had done it could undo. "Thrifty white farmers," he predicted, would "descnend [sic] upon the lands by thousands the moment the Creek is permitted to sell his realty."[70] This would effect a central goal of the Eastern Oklahoma Agricultural Association, "the immigration of a desirable class of farmers."[71]

Credit, Taxation, and Landownership

Far more than just restrictions on allotment land was creating this situation of tenancy. A whole array of laws, all enforced in ways that discriminated in favor of large landholders and against small landholders, was reinforcing the proletarianization of farm tenants. These same laws, moreover, affected allottees. The advent of state and county governments after 1907 meant that new authorities and new policies would do much to decide who owned land. Most politicians in the state espoused an agrarian rhetoric that championed the white yeomanry. In practice, however, state and county governments introduced credit and taxation policies that favored landownership for better-off whites, on the one hand, and facilitated landlessness for poorer African Americans, whites, and Indians, on the other.[72]

When state legislators created a subsidized mortgage program to assist those who wanted to own land, the stated goal was to address the problem that private banks provided few mortgages and interest rates were among the highest in the United States. In the second decade of the 1900s, both long-term and short-term interest rates in Oklahoma were frequently the highest in the nation, and when they were not, they came close to it.[73] In 1918, for example, the average farm mortgage rate charged by Oklahoma banks was nearly 9 percent, and 55 percent of mortgaged debtors paid more than 10 percent. These rates were frequently double those charged in the northeastern states because Oklahoma was distant from markets and sources of capital and Oklahoma farmers faced environmental risks from winds, erosion, and drought. Only 2 percent of bank loans in Oklahoma were mortgages, most farmers having to settle for much more costly short-term loans, often secured by their expected crop as collateral. All farmers faced these problems, but racial discrimination by banks made it particularly difficult for African American farmers to secure mortgages. Credit for them meant loans secured by crops and collateral other than land, at effective rates of interest that frequently exceeded 100 percent.[74]

These conditions made governmental credit programs a potentially powerful tool in helping farm tenants obtain land. Beginning in 1908, the state offered publicly subsidized mortgages at rates of 4 and 5 percent.[75] These loans did not, however, all reach farm buyers. Many (some claimed most) of the loans instead went to the friends and loyal supporters of state officials. In 1916, one reform-minded state commissioner described as common the practice of lending money to landlords at preferential rates so that they could relend it at higher interest to "some less fortunate neighbor"—very likely their own tenants. By using the loans to reward friends and to profit affluent landlords, the credit policy favored an accelerated concentration of wealth and landownership rather than farm ownership by the landless.[76]

Taxes on land hit small landholders disproportionately hard, adding cost to landownership and sometimes resulting in forced sales for back taxes. When the federal government removed restrictions on the sale of land, it simultaneously permitted states and counties to impose taxes on the unrestricted allotment lands of Freedmen and Indians. The imposition of these taxes created a cost for retaining allotment lands, and those interested in buying land welcomed additional incentives for owners to sell it. In 1905, when federal officials were considering imposing taxes on all allotment lands except homesteads, one newspaper in Oklahoma commented that "any white man in the territory today" would welcome the change because "when land is made taxable, it is made alienable."[77] Federal officials and Congress eventually removed restrictions and imposed taxation on a racially graduated basis. This meant that among allottees, black Creeks and "Indians by blood" of more than half white ancestry were the first to have to bear the burden of taxation. Studies of farm taxation in the early and mid-twentieth century have found that officials assessed smaller properties at levels that were higher in proportion to their market value than those of larger properties. This meant that owners of little property faced a higher effective tax rate than owners of much property.[78] Furthermore, larger and more affluent landowners could borrow money in order to pay taxes on time, but small landholders could not, and many thus ended up paying late-payment penalties of 18 percent.[79] If they failed to pay their taxes, farmers risked having their land seized by the county and auctioned off. When problems with taxation arose, poor farmers generally lacked the resources to hire an attorney and were thus at the mercy of county authorities.[80] Because African American landowners were almost exclusively small landholders, this disadvantage affected them especially severely. Agrarian legislators at the state constitutional convention and in the earliest years of statehood did secure passage of legislation that favored small landowners, such as a graduated tax on land and a law that required the bank that held a mortgage, rather than the debtor that took out a mortgage, to pay the taxes on mortgaged land. Complaints surfaced, however, that landlords and banks frequently evaded these taxes.[81]

While landlords and creditors evaded their taxes, counties were wrongly taxing restricted allotment lands, resulting in still more sales of allotment lands. When negotiating allotment treaties, Indian nation representatives had taken pains to ensure that allotments that were restricted in terms of sale would be free from taxation. These provisions covered taxation by any governmental body. Counties, however, depended on land taxation for the majority of their income. Many non-Indian Oklahomans argued that the law unjustly discriminated in favor of allottees and placed an unfair tax burden on other landowners—a racially loaded argument that suggested that Indians were shifting their tax burdens onto the backs of whites.[82] Despite the clear legal language on the matter, Bureau of Indian Affairs officials regularly received complaints that counties were assessing taxes on restricted lands. To make matters worse, when allottees did not pay these improper tax bills, they risked losing their land. In 1909, 1910, and 1911, federal authorities found that counties were posting for sale restricted, nontaxable lands for nonpayment of taxes, a process to which the Creek National Council (now very much less powerful than before allotment and statehood) vehemently objected. Despite warnings from the Office of Indian Affairs that both the taxation and sale of restricted allotment lands were illegal, the counties continued the practice.[83] When allottees like Bessie Brown English, a Creek woman, did not pay these taxes, counties threatened to seize their lands. English (with the help of the Creek Nation's lawyer) appealed the case to the U.S. Supreme Court, which decided in English's favor in 1913. Still, counties continued to levy and collect taxes on restricted allotment lands and, in an unknown number of cases, seized and sold them when taxes were not paid.[84]

Credit and taxation policies and their discriminatory enforcement underscore the close relationship between class, race, political power, and landownership in early twentieth-century Oklahoma. Officials were likely to enforce laws in ways favorable to individuals with wealth and whiteness and power and in ways unfavorable to those who were poor, nonwhite, and less powerful. For landlords, owning extensive land carried with it informal political power that helped them benefit from credit policies and avoid taxation laws that aimed to mitigate the concentration of landownership in the state. The fact that counties imposed taxes on tax-exempt allotment lands serves as a reminder that what ultimately mattered was the way that laws were enforced, rather than the laws themselves.

A New Phase in Creek History

By the second decade of the twentieth century, Creeks were less prominent than ever before in the land that many whites considered a "white man's country." The federal government barely recognized the existence of a Creek national government, mostly calling on it to complete the work of allotment. Still, though it no longer exercised jurisdiction over the region, this was the Creek Nation. Allotment, and even the dramatic land losses of the first years of statehood, must be seen as the beginning of a new phase in Creek history, not its end. After statehood was established, most of these actions took place beyond the bounds of the Creek national government. To the white press and white officials, Creek politics looked all but exhausted with only occasional outbursts of backward-looking resistance. But a more attentive look at the ways the Creeks engaged in tribal town life, lived on their allotments, and used them reveals that in this period Creek people embraced a politics that insisted that they were still present and still directed their own lives. They would not be denied their voice, their presence, or their identity. Dallas Dunzy insisted in the letter at the opening of this chapter that she be known as a woman, not a man, and as a landowner in charge of her own affairs, not a hapless ward. This was an insistence that Creeks would remain an active presence in Oklahoma on their own terms—a kind of politics that the Anishinaabe literary scholar and cultural critic Gerald Vizenor calls "survivance." It is by moving beyond narrow, state-oriented definitions of politics that we can discern Creek politics at a time when Americans denied that the Creek Nation existed. It is, furthermore, by remaining attentive to the words, actions, and choices of individual Creeks like Dallas Dunzy that we can see how Creeks made themselves an active presence at the center of the new Oklahoma.[85]

For decades after allotment began, Creeks attempted to act through their national government, but the scope of Creek formal political action at the national level was severely limited.[86] Until the mid-1930s, the federal government generally recognized the Creek government only insofar as it was useful in finalizing the distribution of allotments and dissolution of national lands. Moreover, Washington chose the chief executive of this much diminished government. Pleasant Porter, elected in 1899, was the last principal chief elected for decades. When he died in 1907, the U.S. secretary of the interior appointed his replacement, Moty Tiger. Tiger's replacements (George Washington Grayson in 1917 and his son, Washington Grayson, after him in 1921) were also appointees of the U.S. government.[87] Representatives of towns continued to meet to confer as a national council. They attempted to shape the ways that other governmental entities, especially the federal Office of Indian Affairs and its field representatives in Creek country, applied policy to Creek people. Their ability to act was limited, however, because they were subject to the actions of a chief who was appointed by Washington. For example, in 1909 the Creek National Council sent a resolution to Principal Chief Moty Tiger making note of a number of pressing issues: the Dawes Commission was enrolling people as Creeks that the council believed were not eligible for citizenship; Creek national funds were being disbursed without the council's approval; and the state of Oklahoma was imposing taxes on citizens whom, because of their "blood quantum," the allotment agreement had exempted from taxation. The council members called on Tiger to allow them to convene officially (and thus legislate), reminding him that to deny them this opportunity would "deprive a large class of citizens of their means of proper representation." The letter calls attention to Creek attempts at maintaining a scope of formal political action but also to the restraints upon those actions. The council was clearly convening without the chief empowering them to do so, and the council pushed him to allow them to act. It also is noteworthy that one of the leading lights of black Creek political life, the attorney J. Coody Johnson, still served as clerk of the council at the time it wrote the letter. But just as important as these facts are the limits the council faced: when the chief would not convene it, he denied it the power to act in the interest of the nation it represented.[88]

Governance and political action continued at the town and international (i.e., intertribal) level in these years and, indeed, through the twentieth century. New conditions meant, however, that more and more of Creek life was outside the purview of these entities. Creek town government had always functioned at the intimate face-to-face and oral level, and so few documents attest to towns' actions, especially in the twentieth century, when records of their dealings with the Creek national government dwindle. Yet occasional references in written records to town *miccos* and other town officers concur with the contention of Creeks that the *talwa* (tribal town) continued to function as a fundamental unit of social and political life. Towns sent representatives to the National Council and convened for the Green Corn festival and other events in the Creek ritual calendar.[89] It is in these cyclical ritual gatherings, moreover, that we can most clearly perceive how the political, social, and spiritual dimensions of town life intertwined. At such gatherings, town officers and elders discussed current matters, town members reaffirmed social bonds, and town members safeguarded the life of the community through their ritual action.[90] Indeed, these same three components merged in the Creek church. These mostly Baptist and Methodist congregations often took on the same political, social, and spiritual roles as the towns, sometimes operating in parallel with them and in some communities mostly supplanting towns. Town and clan membership continued to pass to children matrilineally, despite many Creeks' adoption of patrilineal family names and inheritance practices.[91]

For some Creeks, the town and the clan did not retain the prominence they had before allotment and the near dissolution of Creek government. Some Creeks, for example, no longer participated in the town-centered ritual cycle. Evidence of black Creek town political (or social) life after allotment is particularly scant, suggesting that these towns lost their political power quickly. Perhaps these recent, postemancipation creations were not deeply embedded in black Creek life. As for clans, by the 1920s, some Creeks went so far as to ignore the fundamental requirement that they marry outside their clan. The predominance of non-Creek people in the population and the rise of county and state governments also meant that many Creek people's dealings were with non-Creeks and thus to a large degree outside of the purview of towns and clans. Yet, despite these changes, for many Creeks towns continued to function as fundamental polities of Creek life, and clan affiliation determined kinship loyalties and shaped marriage patterns along the lines of clan exogamy.[92]

Creek political life continued also at the international level, in ways that lead us to consider the place of spiritual activity in political action. For years after statehood, Creeks, along with Cherokees, Chickasaws, and Choctaws, continued their international political and spiritual organization through the organization known as Ecke Ostat (Four Mothers) in Creek. Community members donated funds to send delegations and petitions to Washington, including a trip to that city by Earnest and Jack Gouge of Hillabee Canadian town (nephews of Opothleyahola) and representatives from other tribes. The struggle against allotment, to defend political sovereignty, and to halt land losses remained important to the Four Mothers Nation (or Four Mothers Society, as it was increasingly being known, using the terminology of intertribal and secret societies). It would be a mistake, however, to understand it, or other traditionalist movements, as purely political in the conventional sense. The members of the Four Mothers were ceremonialists.[93] A comparison with tribal towns is instructive. Towns' ritual activities were just as important to the preservation of the community as their participation in national governance. Cherokee historian Tom Holm treats the Four Mothers Nation (or Society, as he calls it), the Snakes, and the Cherokee Keetoowah Society as parts of a broader resistance to American efforts to annihilate tribal nations and Indian people, which he calls "the vanishing policy." He writes, "At the heart of the resistance were the beliefs that religion was organically connected with the land and that societies were living entities that could not be changed without creating a degree of chaos. . . . The resistance to the vanishing policy was a spiritual as well as political movement."[94] One could say that in these movements the spiritual was political and the political was spiritual, and both centered at a time of uncertainty on the preservation of, to use Holm's words, "societies as living entities." The defense of Creek nationhood and Creek people therefore required, in addition to state-oriented action that is easily recognized as political (sending delegates and petitions to Washington), action the political valences of which a historian might more easily miss. Maintaining spiritual activity and building ritual bonds between tribal nations were political acts, and Creeks played a prominent role in these intertribal efforts with such neighbors as the Cherokees—activities that have received far less scholarly attention than they deserve.[95]

The Second Snake Rebellion

The same cannot be said of the second Snake "rebellion," which took place in 1909. The spectacular nature of armed conflict and the romance of a disappeared Indian leader have drawn writers' attention. Unfortunately, the drama of the story has perhaps contributed to an overly simplistic analysis of the events. Changes in the Snake movement in the years after statehood shed light on the way that allotment and statehood were redrawing lines of race and nation in the Creek Nation and the difficult politics that emerged from this context for Creeks (black and nonblack) and African Americans. In March 1909, whites accused black people encamped at Hickory Ground, the center of Snake activity, of stealing some smoked meat. A white posse confronted the Hickory Ground settlement, and in the shootout that followed a number of people—between ten and twenty, accounts varied—were injured, some on each side. The residents scattered, some hiding in ditches and covering themselves with brush, but the posse arrested forty-two people. Deputy U.S. marshals with the assistance of local officials were dispatched to Chitto Harjo's home twenty miles away. They were greeted with gunfire. Chitto Harjo was wounded in the gunfight and disappeared—perhaps to die soon thereafter at the home of a Choctaw friend as his family claimed. Other, evocative stories circulated, though: perhaps he lived secretively among the Creeks for years, the spirit of resistance incarnate; perhaps he fled to Mexico, a warrior who lived to his old age in exile; perhaps he was burned in his cabin by a posse, to some a martyr, to others a troublesome Indian who got what he deserved.[96]

The Snake movement in 1909 captures a moment of transition in the politics of race and nation, reflecting both the alliance between blacks and Indians and the social distance between them. Most or all of the people at Hickory Ground at the time of the battle were black. After the arrests of 1901, the Snake movement was considerably less visible than in its days of publicly proclaiming itself the legitimate Creek government with jurisdiction over Creek lands. These events, combined with the progress of allotment and the establishment of state and local governments, forced the Snakes to take another tack.[97] Black Creeks were already part of the movement prior to 1901, but black people became even more prominent at Hickory Ground in the years that followed. According to the oral histories (collected in the 1930s) of two black men who said they took part in the Snake movement, Snakes actively sought to recruit people of African descent into the movement, including non-Creeks. "After statehood Crazy Snake's followers diminished," reported Harry Jacobs, who as a young man had taken part in the movement at Hickory Ground. "He allowed all negroes that had Creek blood in them and state negroes to join him." According to M. C. Hickman, a white man who lived near the Hickory Ground, Chitto Harjo promised blacks "that when they got the country back, they would be considered citizens of the Creek Nation, regardless of color and have the rights of an Indian."[98] The recruitment of non-Creek blacks suggests not only a late manifestation of the black Creek–conservative Creek alliance of the 1880s and 1890s but an extension of it to include African Americans from the states.[99] If this is the case, it is tremendously significant. It would suggest that Creek people who were racialized as black, Creeks who were figured as "full-bloods," and black newcomers to the region used a Creek national resistance movement as the foundation of an effort to counter the racial and economic order of the statehood period. Nonetheless, "full-bloods" still maintained a social distance from black Creeks and black Americans. Snakes began to build shelters at Hickory Ground, but the "full-bloods" soon left. Once "the negroes and half-breeds outnumbered the fullbloods," recalled Jacobs, "the fullbloods left for their homes."[100] Thus in 1909, the encampment at Hickory Ground was composed of about fifty people who were mostly or entirely seen as black by groups who lived as Indians, as whites, and perhaps by themselves as well. On the one hand, the Hickory Ground marked one of the later moments of an interracial political coalition of black Creeks and other Creeks. On the other, the departure of "the fullbloods" from it represents the deepening racial divisions among Creeks and the emerging racial solidarity between black Creeks and African Americans from elsewhere.

But in the years that followed, individuals and groups continued to give voice to their opposition to allotment and to statehood, sometimes evoking bonds between Creeks and black people.[101] Just as allotment continued on into the century in the supervision of allottees and their property, and just as the Creek Nation and its National Council continued to exist as a government despite the lack of federal recognition, Creek resistance to allotment, the state it helped create, and the racial order it sought to seal went on. The Four Mothers Nation remained active for decades. Other, smaller groups appear in the record from time to time, often because they elicited the concern of state and federal officials. In 1919, eight to ten Creek families had gathered in a settlement and gave their support to Ellen Perryman, a Creek woman collecting money to travel to Washington to "get their lands back for them."[102] In other cases, individuals voiced their opposition to allotment. In May 1912, Carrie Peck wrote to the governor of what she called (disputing the legitimacy of statehood five years after it had been imposed) "this territory, a so call state." Peck identified herself as a descendant of slaves to Creeks and warned him that the injustices the United States had done "the Redman" would not go unpunished by God. While she wrote on behalf of Native Americans, she spoke as a member of the "Black Race." In proclaiming this racial identity, she demonstrated how some former Creek slaves remained loyal to the Creek Nation but also to a racial identity that bound them to other, non-Creek black people.[103] The story of allotment, of statehood, and of a new racial order might have been settled for some officials in 1906, but not for all Creek people.

Land and Everyday Resistance to Allotment's Goals

The most important form of resistance to allotment, however, was the least dramatic: simply pursuing one's own goals rather than those of the reformers and officials who sought to use allotment to remake Indians in the image of white yeoman farmers. It is essential to note that the Snake insurrection and the Four Mothers Nation continued a tradition of resistance, but it is equally essential to remember that most Creeks, probably the majority, did not participate in these sorts of resistance. However, that does not mean that most Creeks accepted the goals of allotment and the statehood apparatus that sustained the new order, and it does not mean that Creeks had become marginal figures flitting on the edges of Oklahoma society. Here it is important to remember what the goals of allotment were. Reformers sought the dissolution of tribes, the replacement of tribal bonds with individualism, the replacement of communal economic life with individual economic life, the creation of yeoman farmers, and the creation of male-headed households. White state builders and white would-be farmers sought the transfer of Indian lands into white hands in order to create a society of prosperous, white yeoman. Although many allotments were sold, to a significant degree Creeks and other Indians frustrated the goals of white reformers, state builders, and farmers. Creek people resisted allotment and its goals in the ways they lived their lives, used their land, and engaged their communities after allotment. Their acts of resistance are easy to miss because they were in no way spectacular; in fact, they often consisted in what Creeks did not do as much as in what they did do. None of this means that Creeks flourished economically or politically in the early twentieth century; indeed, some of the ways in which they pursued their goals and frustrated those of allotment deepened their impoverishment and extended the sale of lands. But allotment achieved the transformation, individualization, and detribalization of Creek people far less than it achieved the loss of Creek lands. What is more, Creeks retained enough land well into the twentieth century that the ways they used it mattered to the state of Oklahoma.

The way they chose allotments and the ways they used them demonstrate that Creeks were determined to try to use the new land system to sustain kinship and community ties rather than to embrace the economic individualism that allotment was meant to accomplish. On maps of allotments, surnames appear in clumps on the landscape. Most Creeks tried to select parcels that related to existing settlement patterns, where members of kinship groups lived in rural neighborhoods. Furthermore, children and infants were entitled to allotments just as adults were, and parents typically selected plots for their children that adjoined their own. These selection patterns are visible in the grouping of people with the surname Long on the allotment map of the area around the tiny town of Yeager, in the western portion of the nation near the conservative Creek town of Wetumka. Longs had lived in the Wetumka area for some time. George Long, for example, had been the head of the Creek Lighthorse (police) for the district.[104] Under allotment, more than twenty people with the surname Long chose allotments in close proximity to one another there. It is quite possible that some of the other families clustered in the area—Harjos, Yargees, and others— were kin as well.[105] Longs remained clustered in the area for decades; they persist in the 1910, 1920, and 1930s censuses.[106] Soon after allotment, of course, many allottees sold their land. Even then, however, Creeks often went to live on the allotments of friends and kin who still owned their land. So too did Creeks whose allotments were located far from their kinship and community networks. This situation—having an allotment far from family and friends—occurred when Creeks did not select their own allotment, often because they opposed allotment. In such cases, Dawes Commission employees assigned them a plot. Thus when Jackson Barnett received an allotment in a place that meant little to him, he was sheltered in the homes of friends and kin.[107] Allotment disrupted and altered but did not succeed in fully replacing the way Creeks used land and settlement to sustain community and kinship.

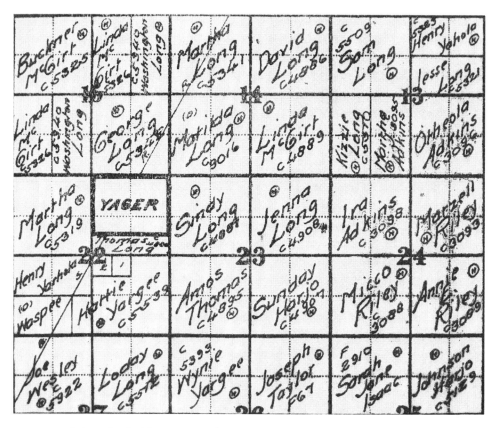

MAP 6. Long Family Allotments, Hughes County. (From E. Hastain, *Hastain's Township Plats of the Creek Nation* [Muskogee: Model Printing Co., 1910].)

Creeks similarly countered allotment's goals when they chose to be landlords rather than yeomen. Judged on its own terms, one of allotment's most spectacular failures was in its effort to transform Creeks into yeoman farmers. In fact, allotment hastened the decline of a Creek agricultural tradition. A society that had been firmly rooted in small-scale agricultural production with a subsistence basis and limited market engagement in the 1880s was, within years of allotment, no longer a predominantly farming population. Some still farmed, of course. Many produced gardens and crops of corn for consumption and cotton for marketing. But no longer did most Creeks pursue the strategy of small-scale production and limited market engagement they had used to maximize their autonomy and minimize their dependency in the decades after the Civil War. They retained these goals, but many turned to another strategy to pursue them: renting or leasing their land to farmers or oil companies. To become farmers or laborers would have dramatically reduced their economic autonomy. Renting out land or leasing mineral rights for oil extraction created a compromise: clearly they became fully part of the cash economy, but their land itself continued to offer them sustenance. Rules against mortgaging allotment lands made it difficult to borrow the capital to farm them commercially, which further encouraged this strategy. The process of agricultural renting and mineral leasing emerged before allotment was complete and was fully institution- alized in the second decade of the twentieth century. The Office of Indian Affairs managed the renting of restricted allotment lands for Creeks with the stated goal of maximizing their return. Some other Creeks preferred to bypass the Indian agents and rent or lease their allotment lands directly. In either case, the practice became a central fact of Creek economic life for allottees. In 1938, the Bureau of Indian Affairs office responsible for most of the area of the Creek Nation reported that, by its count, only one in seven Indians there were "entirely self-supporting from their own industry and thrift."[108] Four years before, the bureau had abandoned the allotment policy and the effort to transform Indians into yeomen. Still, the old ideas imposed some blinders on agents as they looked at Indian land use. Federal officials lamented that "the Indian" played "the role of a petty capitalist, idly sitting by while someone else works his assets." They recognized that "certain forces over which he has little control"—presumably including re- strictions on mortgaging allotments—made renting land out rather than farming it an attractive option.[109] They did not, apparently, perceive that rent seeking was also a strategy to maintain some level of autonomy in Oklahoma's rural economy.

Creeks used payments for oil under their lands in similar ways. Public officials and the press dedicated significant attention to the fortunes a few Creeks were making by leasing out oil-rich allotments. The vast Midconti- nent oil pool lay beneath much of the area of the Creek Nation, and the rich strikes that prospectors made there brought enormous profits in the form of lease royalties to a few allottees. Newspapers and magazines nationwide reported on what they considered an absurdity: uneducated Indians, men like Jackson Burnett, "the world's richest Indian," who did not speak stan- dard English and had always lived a simple rural life, found themselves to be the recipients of great wealth, able to live lavishly, and the targets of non- Indians eager to get a hold of their oil revenues. These reports were full of a derisive disbelief that so much money could come to such undeserving individuals.[110] Only a few made such fortunes, of course. Most allottees did not have oil under their lands, and most of those who did benefited from oil royalties without becoming wealthy. Those royalties served the same purpose that rentals from agricultural leases did: they allowed Creeks to use their lands to engage the market economy without entering it as a laborer or a farmer and thus to maintain a greater level of autonomy.

Land Law and the Limits of Autonomy

It would be wrong, however, to exaggerate the level of autonomy Creeks could maintain by renting their land or leasing its mineral rights. Allotment had commodified land and made a market for it. The economic well-being of those who rented their land or mineral rights was, therefore, subject to the whims of that market, the farming practices of tenants, and how long the oil lasted. If one's land was rich and fertile or adjacent to a growing town or lay above a deep pool of oil, the rental market could bring significant income. But allottees whose land was thin and rocky, far from the nearest town, and unlikely to yield oil found there was much less to be earned on the rental market. Furthermore, rental and mineral lease incomes were unstable. Because of share rental agreements, landlord income was just as subject to volatile agricultural prices as tenant income. The collapse in cotton prices in 1920 and the persistent low prices of the 1930s, for example, translated into hard times for sharecrop landlords, including Creek landlords. Oil income was particularly rich but also particularly unstable: when wells ran dry, the lessor's income evaporated. Finally, Oklahoma's farmers were mining the soil as quickly as oil companies were mining the oil. By 1919, agricultural extension agents were warning that farm tenancy gave tenants no stake in farming the land in a sustainable manner. From a regional point of view, the erosion and soil depletion that inappropriate farming techniques inflicted on the land were a long-term economic threat. From the point of view of the individual landowner, erosion and soil depletion meant that the principal source of income was being made worthless.[111]

The sale of allotment lands captures the paradoxical nature of forms of resistance to allotment: land sales frustrated some of the goals of reformist allotment advocates, furthered other of their goals, and allowed Creek people to pursue their own agendas even at the risk of deepening their long-term poverty. Creeks sold the great majority of their lands soon after those lands could legally be sold and sometimes before—unrestricted lands were sold on the open market, and restricted lands were sold after securing permission from the Office of Indian Affairs to do so. Securing cash meant that Creek people could use the money for goals as varied as buying cars, buying houses, hiring lawyers to defend relatives, investing in the inputs they needed to farm their remaining land, or simply to pay for living expenses. It meant that they could pursue their own personal and familial agendas, which only occasionally coincided with the goals of the reformers who had advocated allotment or of the Indian agents who oversaw allottees' economic affairs. It also meant, however, that their land was gone for good. It could never again be turned to as a means of support or a place to live.

Allotment and the imposition of state government over the area of the Creek Nation marked a decisive turn in Creek politics, but it did not bring an end to Creek political life. Creek national government continued and Creek towns and clans still functioned, though in ways that had been altered and restricted by changed circumstances. International politics and spiritual action became, if anything, more urgent in a time when Creek national life and Creek communities faced overwhelming numbers of settlers in their midst and the imposition of an economic order that threatened to marginalize Creek people. They resisted marginalization, however, in the very ways in which they sought to survive and to preserve their autonomy. When they resisted becoming either yeoman farmers or proletarianized workers by renting land to farmers and leasing mineral rights to oil companies, Creek people placed themselves at the center of the new commercial economy that was imposed on their nation. This had not necessarily been their goal. Rather, they had aimed to survive and maintain a measure of autonomy. Still, when Creeks rented or leased out their land, they put themselves in a crucial (though insecure) position in the new Oklahoma.

■ ■

We Were Negroes Then

POLITICAL PROGRAMS, LANDOWNERSHIP, AND

BLACK RACIAL COALESCENCE, 1904–1916

On November 16, 1907, Indian Territory and Oklahoma Territory were bound together to make a new state. From the point of view of many of Oklahoma's black residents, statehood also bound together the fates of two black populations: black Indian citizens and recently arrived African Americans. To J. E. Toombs, editor of the *Muskogee Comet*, this coming together created both opportunities and perils for black people. In June 1904, he advised the readers of that African American newspaper that once Indian Territory became part of the new state of Oklahoma, they could turn landownership into political power. "There are many townships and some counties," he claimed, "that can be controlled and officered by colored men, for they own the land and have the votes which if properly handled will land in office whosoever they will." Toombs warned that the greatest threat to this future of wealth and power was divisiveness among "colored men"— whether they were black Creeks or newcomer African Americans. "There is no time for denominational contentions among us," he wrote, "for while we contend for the rights of this denomination or that denomination, the white man is busy buying land." Toombs gave voice to hopes and fears shared by thousands of African Americans who migrated to Indian Territory and by Creeks of African descent who lived there. Like Toombs, they believed that land would be a foundation of their political power and that political unity was necessary to obtain and keep land. They feared that divisions among them would frustrate these hopes. "Let us throw down our contention and meet on common ground," Toombs urged his readers, "that we may be able to buy land (not sell), get homes, save money, and thus prepare for the political battles which are not far in the distant future."[1] Ethnic conflicts between blacks from the South and from the Creek Nation, and class differences among black people, opened fissures that made it hard for black people to create "common ground." Toombs was preparing his readers for the politics of landownership once allotment was complete and statehood was achieved. He suggested that this politics required suppressing ethnic and class conflicts in favor of racial unity.

Like whites in early twentieth-century Oklahoma, people of African descent believed that landownership was inseparable from political aspirations, and they understood these goals within the rubrics of race and nation. Although Toombs directed his words at black people, the many whites who came to the region to farm also looked at struggles for land and political authority as mutually reinforcing and embedded in class conflict. Whites of modest means came to Oklahoma to claim what they believed was their birthright as white Americans: the chance to own land, to farm it as independent yeomen, and to vote into office politicians who would serve their interests. For African Americans from the southern states, the defeat of Reconstruction, the imposition of Jim Crow, and the denial of voting rights across the South gave particular urgency to the quest for landownership and political self-determination.[2] They had come to Oklahoma in large part because the South that they left denied most African Americans both economic self-sufficiency and political rights.

Looking at the ways that people of African descent engaged the problem of land, political authority, and nationhood in this period shines a light on two important themes in early twentieth-century African American history. First, the struggle for black advancement was a holistic one. Historians often have turned to Booker T. Washington, W. E. B. Du Bois, and Marcus Garvey to personify three streams of African American response to the era of Jim Crow: the goal of racial uplift through economic "self-help," the call to political action, and emigrationist nationalism, respectively. Yet historians also have noted that this shorthand represents an abstraction that not even Washington, Du Bois, and Garvey, let alone less famous black men and women, always respected in action.[3] Indeed, examining the ways that African Americans in Oklahoma tried to fashion their future makes clear that they saw all three strategies as parts of one effort to make a prosperous and secure place for themselves. For rural black Oklahomans, economic uplift, political agitation, and mass migration represented three components of a unified political program in which landownership loomed large. Second, this story also serves to shift our gaze from "race relations" and toward the complex issues of ethnic diversity, class conflict, and racial unity *among* people of African descent. The study of black peoples' encounter with white people and white supremacy must frame this story. It should not, however, obscure the interior dynamics of what appears, in a "race relations" model, to be a monolithic black community. Toombs's words at the start of this chapter suggest that the meaning and political uses of community were very much in play in Indian Territory in this period.[4] Sometimes black Indian citizens and newcomer African Americans came together in the ways that Toombs hoped they would, but often they formed distinct and sometimes antagonistic groups.

In the decades after the Civil War, small numbers of African Americans from the South had filtered into Indian Territory. Towns, families, and settlements of Creeks of African descent incorporated these few newcomers without much difficulty. Beginning in the late 1880s, however, tens of thousands of African Americans poured into Oklahoma. The mass migration created strains between black Creek citizens and newcomers. They expressed these tensions as ethnic differences. Even though economic uplift, political agitation, and mass migration came together in a unified political program, it was not always a unified people who put that program forward.

Allotment and the advent of statehood in 1907, however, placed black Creeks and newcomers on similar, and similarly precarious, economic and political footing. This gave them the incentives to create a more unified community as "Negroes." The elimination of citizenship distinctions between black Creeks and black newcomers, the creation of a market in allotment lands, the widespread landlessness of black Creeks and black newcomers—all of these spurred African Americans from the South and black Creeks to cooperate to fight Jim Crow and to regain the vote in order to defend their political and economic interests, which they understood as conjoined. All these developments must be understood in the context of the imposition of white supremacy, a political, economic, and ideological structure that made white men dominant in the state of Oklahoma. In the eyes of Toombs and many other blacks in Oklahoma, white supremacy made African American racial unity necessary. It could not, however, make black racial unity a reality. To the extent that such a thing came to exist, black racial coalescence in eastern Oklahoma was a political project that drew on the inheritances of black Indian citizens and African Americans from the South and emerged out of the particular political and economic context of the early twentieth century.

Black Immigration to Indian Territory:
Black Yeoman Independence

For two decades before statehood in 1907, the African American and white populations of Indian Territory had been growing at a tremendous rate. By the 1880s, Indian governments were already concerned about the influx of African Americans and whites into their territory. Between 1890 and 1907, the African American population of Indian Territory increased more than fourfold, surging from less than 19,000 to more than 80,000. In the same seventeen-year period, the white population jumped from 109,400 to 538,500, while the Indian population remained stable at roughly 61,000.[5]

These figures, which are for Indian Territory as a whole, underestimate the numerical prominence of the black population in the Creek Nation because African Americans tended to settle there and in the neighboring Seminole Nation. Given the tensions that erupted between the groups, this requires some explanation. It is certain that the rich lands of the Canadian and Arkansas river valleys drew black farm families, as did the fact that a large number of blacks from the South had already settled in the region. The black population grew as African American settlers were joined by family members and others from their social networks. The city of Muskogee, with its large black population and a number of black business owners, probably also served as a magnet to blacks going west. The black settlers made their homes especially in areas that became part of Okfuskee and Okmulgee counties, but also in Muskogee, Wagoner, Seminole, and other counties that would make up Oklahoma's "Black Belt." These counties were between 20 and 41 percent African American (see map 7), but even these statistics understate the concentration of the black population. Some townships within the counties were well over 80 percent African American. These figures are hardly comparable to the those in the Black Belt that ran from Georgia through Alabama and into Mississippi, but they were quite distinctive in Oklahoma.

The growth of the black population of Indian Territory was one of a number of black westward migration movements of its time but is unique

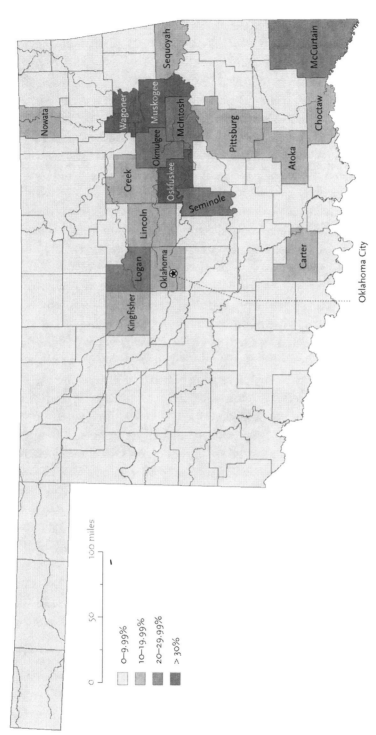

MAP 7. African American Population by County, 1910. (Population data from U.S. Bureau of the Census, *Thirteenth Census of the United States Taken in the Year 1910*, vol. 3, *Population 1910* [Washington: Government Printing Office, 1913], 466–78.)

Oklahoma City

0–9.99%
10–19.99%
20–29.99%
> 30%

0   50   100 miles

among them because it brought blacks from the South to a place where there was *already* a large and ethnically distinct black population. The black "Exodusters" who moved to Kansas settled in an almost exclusively white area. Similarly, whites surrounded the areas of African American settlement in Oklahoma Territory (a jurisdiction Washington had carved out of the western half of Indian Territory after the 1889 Land Run).[6] Indian Territory, in contrast, was already home to significant populations of African descent—black Creeks but also black Cherokees, Choctaws, Chickasaws, and Seminoles. That fact made the story of Indian Territory the site of complex negotiations of race between black Indian citizens and black newcomers from the South. This began a complex relation that reveals much about the complexities of black identities and communities in American history.

To understand this relation, we must understand the ideas that brought African Americans to leave the South and move to the region. Emigrationism—the belief that mass migration was a viable strategy for African Americans to achieve prosperity and self-determination—was a founding principle of African American migration to Indian Territory just as surely as it fueled later calls for an exodus to Africa.[7] The majority of the African American immigrants, like the majority of white newcomers, were farmers in search of their own land.[8] A large proportion of them came from the southern states, especially Tennessee, Texas, Mississippi, Alabama, and Arkansas, where many African Americans' hopes of landownership were foundering on the rocks of debt peonage and tenant farming.[9] Oftentimes, Indian Territory was the second or third stop on a westward march in search of land, prosperity, and autonomy. Many migrants had moved to Texas from the states to the east before heading north into what would become Oklahoma. Tennessee had been the home of the African Americans who headed west to Kansas in the "Exoduster" migration of the late 1870s. Joanna Draper and her husband followed the path to Kansas when they left Mississippi because they had heard whites were "better to the Negroes up in the North." In fact, they found "they ain't no better there." They moved on to the Creek Nation.[10] Like the Drapers, many blacks looked to Oklahoma Territory and Indian Territory as the places to achieve their dreams of yeoman independence.

Newcomer African Americans in eastern Oklahoma espoused and practiced a program of Washingtonian racial uplift rooted in landownership.[11] In an appeal for migrants to come to the town and region, the *Boley Progress* sadly noted, "[Many of] our people . . . are on the farms and plantations of white men, just as they were twenty or thirty years ago, with every-

"Pomp Hall, Negro tenant farmer, reading newspaper to which he subscribes, Creek County, Oklahoma," 1940. Publishing and reading newspapers—from the *Boley Progress* to the white-owned *Tulsa Daily World*—were important to the region's politically active and informed African American and black Creek population from at least the 1890s forward. (Photographer: Lee Russell; Library of Congress, Prints & Photographs Division, FSA/OWI Collection, LC-USF34-035235-D)

thing mortgaged so they cannot get away." The problem would endure, the booster editorial argued, until African Americans were economically sovereign, no longer "working upon [white people's] farms and trading in their stores."[12] This call for black landownership rather than black tenancy was echoed many times by African American leaders in eastern Oklahoma. In it, one can sense the appeal of the ideology of economic uplift most often associated with Booker T. Washington. Washington made a career and won the support of prominent whites by preaching to African Americans the gospel of racial uplift, that African Americans should develop their skills in agriculture, trades, and service and use those to gain advancement economically. This, he claimed in his public pronouncements, was the path to progress and harmony with the white race, not the reckless pursuit of political equality, desegregation, or other citizenship rights. In essence, Washington championed a nationalist form of accommodation. The builder of a black college in Alabama's Black Belt, he held that African Americans had the duty to "lift up the race" by developing their own economic and educational institutions at the same time that they maintained good relations with whites by accepting disenfranchisement and segregation.[13] Washington won the admiration of the boosters of Oklahoma's African American towns, who reported on his words and deeds in their newspapers. The founders of Bookertee even named their town in Washington's honor. All the town promoters were dedicated to the notion of African American economic advancement through agriculture and trade.

Freedmen and African American settlers in Oklahoma, however, almost never embraced the political quiescence that Washington counseled, preferring instead the political agitation for which his rival, Du Bois, was growing famous. The *Progress* encouraged African Americans to leave the South and move to the Boley area, "where you can buy a cheap farm" and "where you can make your own laws to govern your own affairs in a town and community populated by colored people."[14] African American political self-determination, in this vision, was intimately tied to African American economic self-determination based on landownership. When Washington reported on a tour he made through Oklahoma in 1905, he noted that he "was pleased to learn that an unusually large number of these black immigrants had become owners of land in the city and in the country" and that African Americans had prospered especially in the Creek Nation. Nonetheless, he noted that in general, blacks had not achieved the economic success of whites. Washington attributed this to the wrongheaded political aspirations of the African American settler who was attracted by "the notion that he could vote or would in some way have more freedom or respect here than he had at home." Washington perceived the political ambitions that African American settlers embraced, but he refused to recognize that the settlers believed political self-determination and economic sovereignty to be mutually dependent.[15]

J. E. Toombs, whose words open this chapter, also believed that specifically *male* landownership would foster proper order in African American society in the region. When Toombs spoke of the imperative for Freedmen to sell their land to "colored brothers" and his hopes for government by "colored men" who owned land, he was alluding to what he believed was the foundation of a stable African American community: male landownership. Toombs exhorted "young men" to "buy a home" instead of "throwing away your means in riotous living."[16] A community of households headed by landowning men lived in "peace, quietness and prosperity." In contrast, Toombs warned, a community where men rented land was an "unchained hell" where men loafed while women made "the living honorably if they can, dishonorably if they must."[17] Toombs warned that dishonor to African American women, and therefore to the racial community, loomed on the horizon if African American men did not possess land.

Toombs's ominous words reflect a patriarchal merging of domestic and Jeffersonian agrarian ideologies and evoke a history of African American men and women's struggles over women's work outside the home and in the fields. Some African American men saw in emancipation the opportunity to prove their proper manhood in part by restricting black women to their homes rather than permitting them to work outside, especially in the fields—an idea that was not entirely unwelcome to black women.[18] The sentiment that Toombs expressed demonstrates a further development of this domestic ideology. In Toombs's version, the honor of black people was lodged in the sexual virtue of black women, virtue that was threatened when black women engaged in wage labor, perhaps even paid sexual labor. Black honor thus required keeping black women out of wage labor, which in turn depended on the financial independence of the family. To Toombs and men like him, that independence was founded upon male landownership. In defense of African American honor, then, this patriarchal ideal wed domestic ideology with the Jeffersonian vision of the autonomous yeoman farmer. Thus for African American men, settling in Indian Territory and owning land there could mean economic opportunity, political opportunity, and even the setting aright of family relationships and gender hierarchies. This land of opportunity constituted unity and strength and honor for the race.

Some whites looked on the pairing of black landownership and the assertion of black manhood with an amusement that scarcely concealed their own economic, racial, and gender anxieties. The white-run *Vinita Indian Chieftain* newspaper printed a letter, written in a pejorative pseudo–African American dialect, that purported to be an inquiry from an African American in Illinois. The letter asked about the possibilities that Indian Territory offered for settlement. The supposed author had heard from a friend that "Mr. Jackdaws" (Senator Charles Dawes) had gotten through Congress an act to drive out all whites and let blacks take their farms. But it was not only land the "author" sought; it was also women—perhaps Indian, perhaps white. He reports having heard that "dar am lots purty gals in de Injin nation." Given such economic and sexual opportunities to displace white men, the "writer" announced the intention to move to Indian Territory and "cibilize dat kentry." The satirical letter deployed two familiar tropes in the white racial imaginary of the United States at the turn of the twentieth century—the pompous black buffoon and the sexually ravenous black beast. It also voiced the fears to which black settlement gave rise among whites in Indian Territory.[19]

Divisions between African American Newcomers and Freedmen

African American immigration into Indian Territory opened a rift between black settlers and Indian Territory Freedmen, a division based in large part on access to land. Prior to statehood, newcomers lacked citizenship rights in the Indian nations, and therefore they could not make the land their own by clearing and tilling it. African American settlers who wished to farm could either squat on the lands of the Indian nations or work as tenants for an Indian landlord. Both of these choices placed them in conflict with black Creeks, who had worked with their conservative allies in the 1880s and 1890s to put a halt to squatting and the taking up of the commons by tenants who worked for large landholders. Thus before allotment and statehood, the politics of landownership separated black Creeks from African American newcomers.

Faced with these impediments to farming and attracted by the commercial opportunities in the towns and cities of the rapidly growing region, many African Americans settled in some twenty smaller communities that had been founded as "all-black towns." The development of the towns (and of the mostly African American countryside surrounding them) speaks to the newcomers' and black Creeks' nationalist beliefs, their intertwined motives of race uplift and personal profit, and the complex ways that they accommodated their nationalism to the constraints of African American life. The largest and most prominent of these communities were Langston, founded in 1890 in Oklahoma Territory, and Boley, promoted beginning in 1903 in Indian Territory. These two towns both grew out of explicitly nationalist commitments to creating places of African American self-governance and self-reliance in the American West, but they were also business ventures. They, like the other African American towns, were part of the same entrepreneurial town-site speculation that fed the development of predominantly white towns throughout Oklahoma. Freedmen and newcomers sought to grow wealthy by developing black towns.[20]

The development of these African American towns highlights the social distance that separated the African American immigrants from black Creeks. Most towns, such as Langston in Oklahoma Territory, were far from the historical centers of the black Indian populations. Even those that were physically close to or even on black Creek allotment lands, however, were socially distant from the black Creek communities. This was certainly true of Boley, which was located close to black Creek population but where the conflict between black Creeks and black newcomers sometimes spilled into violence. Boley residents complained that Freedmen not only disrupted their church services but also even periodically rode through town at night, terrorizing the population by shooting out windows. One report maintains that the attacks ceased only when Boley's security officer killed several of the Freedmen in an altercation, but the animosities remained.[21]

The division between black Creeks and immigrant African Americans stands as a reminder of the plasticity of race and the importance of land in marking race differences in the Creek Nation at this time. In the late nineteenth century and the first years of the twentieth, the two groups expressed disapproval of marriages between Freedmen and newcomers. They avoided socializing with each other, as well. One black Creek who attended school in Clearview later recalled that newcomer children outnumbered black Creek children, prompting the latter to remain warily apart from outsiders—or as he put it, "I buddied with my own." The division between the groups is nowhere more apparent than in the terms they used to refer to each other. The newcomers in Boley and other towns called the black Creeks "natives." Black Creeks similarly set themselves apart from the immigrants by referring to them in English as "States Negroes," "States people," or more pejoratively by calling them by the Muskogee word "*wvcenv*" when speaking English. The epithet suggests a sense of racial difference between the groups, as the term generally means "white person." More important, however, the word suggests that race and identity were not purely a matter of biology in the minds of black Creeks. Here they operated in a long Creek tradition. In the eighteenth century, Creeks had called any intruder upon their lands a *wvcenv*, not only white people. The marker of difference that the term represented, then, was lodged more in relationships of citizenship and land than of supposedly biological race.[22]

The coming of Oklahoma statehood in 1907 qualified white and African American immigrants for citizenship and erased all U.S. citizenship distinctions between Freedmen and newcomer African Americans. All citizens of the Creeks (as well as the Cherokees, Chickasaws, Choctaws, and Seminoles) were made citizens of the United States in March 1901.[23] They retained their Indian citizenship, but statehood meant that the federal government abandoned all pretense of recognizing the sovereignty of the Creek, Cherokee, Chickasaw, Choctaw, and Seminole governments, and Indian citizenship was not at the center of early statehood politics.[24]

The citizenship rights of people of African descent in Oklahoma were distinctly second class. In the elections for representatives to the state constitutional convention, white Democrats pledged that they would enshrine Jim Crow into the state's organic law and reserve the franchise for white men, promises that helped the party win a commanding majority in the convention. African Americans responded by forming such organizations as the Anti–Jim Crow League and the Afro-American Independent Suffragist League, calling mass meetings, distributing petitions, and pressuring Republican candidates to protect the voting rights of African American men. Newcomers took an active role in these efforts, but so did black Creeks such as J. Coody Johnson and A. G. W. Sango.[25] Black Creeks and black newcomers cooperated in the various efforts. In the end, the constitutional convention voted to require Jim Crow rail coaches, waiting rooms, and schools but rejected limiting the franchise to white men. Such a provision, delegates argued, ran the risk of convincing Republican president Theodore Roosevelt to block Oklahoma's constitution. Roosevelt met personally with a delegation of African Americans from Oklahoma and heard their objections to the Jim Crow clause, but he accepted the constitution nonetheless.[26]

In addition to mandating segregation, the state constitution made a step toward defining the legal meaning of race in Oklahoma. Native American representatives to the constitutional convention expressed concerns that the segregation provisions of the constitution, worded as they were to separate "whites" from "the colored race," would result in Indians (as nonwhites) having to share facilities and schools with African Americans. Eager to assuage their worries and to win Indian votes for the ratification of the constitution, Democratic delegate Robert Lee Williams, a white resident of the Choctaw Nation, proposed an amendment. It stated that for the purposes of the constitution, "the word or words, 'colored' or 'colored race,' 'negro' or 'negro race,' . . . shall be construed to apply to all persons of African descent. The term 'white race' shall include all other persons."[27] In effect, the provision defined Indians as legally white. This definition became part of the 1907 constitution.

Of course, Indians did not by fiat of law become socially or culturally homogeneous with white Oklahomans. Creeks continued to settle close to members of their families and nations. Religious practices, whether fasts for the Green Corn festival or services at Creek churches, continued to bind Indians together and set them apart from other Oklahomans. Rates of intermarriage between Native Americans and whites were high, but intermarriage was no novelty to Creek life. Finally, federal restrictions on the sale, rental, or mortgage of allotment lands of some Native Americans remained as a legal distinction separating them from the remainder of the population. The distinction between Indian and white remained powerful despite the constitution's provisions.[28]

The constitutional definition of race proceeded from the notion that all people of African descent belonged to one group, but black people in Oklahoma did not all agree. Though they attended segregated schools together, sat in segregated waiting rooms together, and rode on segregated trains together, for many black Creeks and newcomer African Americans "the Negro"—a unitary race—was not a reality. Some black Creeks continued to remain aloof from "States Negroes," while some immigrants still looked with disdain on "the natives." Nonetheless, by eliminating citizenship differences among people of African descent, the legal creation of whiteness and blackness provided one of the conditions that encouraged black coalescence. When black Indian citizens and black newcomers sought to defeat Jim Crow and defend their voting rights, they were emphasizing the U.S. citizenship that linked them rather than the different citizenships that divided them. Shared political and economic difficulties would similarly encourage Freedmen and newcomers to come together.

Removal of Restrictions, Land Transfers, and
Black Creek–Newcomer Relations

Land was a cause of both contention and coalition between Freedmen and immigrant African Americans. The 1904 and 1908 changes in the law made it possible for African Americans to purchase land in the region for the first time, exacerbating tensions between Freedmen and African

American newcomers. African American immigrants were buying Freedmen's allotment lands just as surely as white people were. It was, in fact, the sale of Freedmen land that made it possible for many of the newcomers to purchase the farmland surrounding Boley.[29] Land buyers preferred land that had been the allotments of Freedmen to lands that had been the allotments of "Indians by blood." Some restrictions remained on the lands of the latter group, and so sales of their lands were liable to be challenged. In contrast, all lands of black Creeks had been cleared of restrictions, and titles to it were therefore more secure.[30]

African American newcomers charged Freedmen with disloyalty to the race if they sold their lands to whites. They turned the Freedmen's charge that the newcomers were "white man's Negroes" against them. The *Muskogee Comet*, an African American newspaper that dedicated much of its editorial energies to the need to build a prosperous community among African American immigrants, accused Freedmen of refusing to sell to willing African Americans and selling instead to white "sharks" (unethical land speculators.) The newspaper laid much of the blame for "the lack of confidence" between Freedmen "natives" and newcomers on the claim that "when a colored man approaches his native brother and proposes to buy land of him he is turned away as if nothing had been said." To make matters worse, "the native brother goes on to the office of the shark and there barters away his fortune for a mere song, and THAT song is set to a very poor TUNE."[31]

The market in allotment lands gave rise to class divisions that ran across the boundaries of ethnicity dividing Freedmen from newcomers. Not only did the sale and lease of allotments bring African American newcomers into the black Creeks' districts, but the black allottees who sold or leased out their lands to African American newcomers realized at least some return on the transaction. This return was paltry, however, compared with what land speculators could achieve. In search of those profits, black allottees as well as whites and newcomer town-site developers engaged in the land business. In 1904, a group of black Creeks along with one African American newcomer established the Creek Citizens' Realty Bank and Trust Company in Muskogee. Like white land speculators, the company advertised its eagerness to buy, sell, lease, and mortgage Freedmen's allotment lands and encouraged newcomer African Americans to buy them "before the prices go skyward." The development of Boley and other towns similarly depended on black allottees and African American newcomers working together in land speculation. The trade in land was a bond between black Indian citizens and African American newcomers of this class. The deeds, mortgages, and leases that were the land dealer's stock in trade also represented, however, the tools that were used to separate black Creeks from their land, land that represented the only remainder of the Creek national lands. The trade that enriched some rendered others landless. In the development of business bonds between black Indian citizens and newcomer African American entrepreneurs lay the potential for rifts along class lines.[32]

Some black Creeks, however, used their homes and their land to help African American newcomers. The evidence is scant (not surprising given the ways that black Creeks were caught up in a whirlwind of change), but it is suggestive of how land could be used to bridge the divisions among black people. This reminds us that the bonds that linked the groups were not wholly the creation of the statehood period and that land could serve as a place where black people came together. One account maintains that "the freedmen did a great deal to help the immigrants get a start, frequently taking them in and housing and feeding them for long periods of time."[33] Such acts of generosity would have been a tremendous assistance to migrants from far away, many of whom had to live in tents until they built themselves a shelter. Tom Grayson, a black Creek, ensured that newcomers would have even more permanent shelter. In 1904, he gave up a piece of his allotment so that "states folks and their family" would have a place to be buried.[34]

The Vote and Landownership

Given the impact of public policy on landownership, landownership depended in part on electoral power. For African Americans in Oklahoma, it was impractical to follow a Washingtonian strategy of economic uplift without also pursuing political rights in the way that Du Bois advocated. The vote meant a chance to fight for better schools, fairer trials, police protection rather than harassment and brutality, and many other things, one of the most important of which was the chance to have a voice in the policies that would affect African Americans' ability to obtain and keep land.[35]

After statehood, however, African Americans in eastern Oklahoma soon faced a threat to their ability to have such a voice. Between 1907 and 1910, African American men used their votes to elect members of their own race to local offices in areas of dense African American settlement. African American voters in Logan County even succeeded in sending A. C. Hamlin, a Republican and African American farmer, to the state legislature, much to the chagrin of many of their white neighbors.[36] Hamlin would serve only one term, however, because in 1910 the state's voters approved a ballot initiative to disenfranchise African Americans. Modeled on other states' laws, the Oklahoma Grandfather Clause tried to circumvent the Fifteenth Amendment by imposing strict literacy requirements on African American voters but not on whites or Indians. The Democratic Party was particularly eager to eliminate a group that was largely loyal to the Republican Party. African Americans mobilized two organizations—the Negro Protective Association and the Negro Suffrage League—to protest the change, gathering more than eight hundred people at one meeting in Boley. They also sought relief from Republican lawmakers, but Grand Old Party leaders, unwilling to risk their prospects for white votes, were timid at best in the defense of the voting rights of African American men. With the assistance of sympathetic white Republican lawyers and the young National Association for the Advancement of Colored People, a group of African American Oklahomans brought the issue through the courts to the attention of the U.S. Supreme Court, which struck down the clause in 1915. The Oklahoma Grandfather Clause had been the last such law to be written into a southern state constitution, and it became the first to be ruled unconstitutional.[37]

In eastern Oklahoma counties with large African American populations, white political activists looked on the 1915 Supreme Court decision with horror. One warned that "the negro . . . will swarm at the polls after he as been advised of this decision like flies before a meat shop."[38] The Young Men's Democratic Club of Wagoner County reminded Democratic governor Robert Lee Williams that its members still felt "the bitter experience suffered immediately after statehood of negroes dominating our elections and negro office holders participating in the administration of our county."[39] J. E. Harston of the Oklahoma State Board of Agriculture voiced the concerns of white editorialists and politicians when he urged Williams to "provide some means of keeping Oklahoma a white mans [sic] country," as whites in eastern Oklahoma faced the imminent threat of "Negro supremacy."[40]

Ever vigilant in the defense of white supremacy, Williams called a special session of the state legislature to craft another, constitutionally sounder Grandfather Clause act. Like the earlier law, it would have instituted a literacy requirement for voting. Registrars could require prospective voters to write out and explain parts of Oklahoma's constitution, an invitation to selective disenfranchisement. In an effort to pass constitutional muster, however, it eliminated the explicit devices that the former

Grandfather Clause used to protect whites from disenfranchisement. The dropping of these devices aroused widespread fears that poor white men, especially tenant farmers, would be denied the vote. Agrarian Democrats and the state's growing Socialist Party (discussed in the next chapter) objected vehemently. Oklahoma voters defeated the measure in 1916.[41] The Democratic-controlled legislature was not content to let the issue go at that, and it passed a restrictive voter registration law in 1916 that made it easy for registrars to avoid placing African Americans on the polls. By creating a brief window of time in which to register and penalizing people who moved frequently, the law made it easy for registrars to selectively disenfranchise black tenant farmers because many of them moved from farm to farm frequently. Supporters of the measure argued that it worked in the interest of "the yeomanry of the country." In doing so, they revealed the racial connotation that "yeoman" held for them and for other conservative agrarians because the measure successfully disenfranchised most (but not all) African Americans until the 1930s.[42] In 1918 in Okfuskee County, of 1,700 African Americans who were by state law eligible for the vote, only 90 succeeded in registering.[43] A resident of Vian complained that the registrar, "a man with his heart as black as mid night," had refused to register even a single African American voter "on account of our skin being dark."[44]

Racial Uplift, Land, and Political Action

In the aftermath of the 1910 Grandfather Clause and in the context of widespread farm tenancy, two important trends emerged in African Americans' efforts to expand landownership in their communities. Both had their roots in the founding ideas of eastern Oklahoma's African American communities, but they emphasized two different aspects of those ideas: racial uplift and emigrationism. Invoking the Washingtonian rhetoric of racial uplift, town-dwelling African American professionals and businessmen increased their efforts to convince farmers that with hard work and self-help they could improve their situation and buy land. Proponents of emigration, for their part, found their supporters among landowning farmers of more modest means. They saw in a return to the ancestral home of Africa the promise of prosperity and political autonomy, a strategy that would be associated in coming years with Marcus Garvey. For all their differences, however, neither group abandoned the effort to link political self-determination to landownership.

The model of agricultural education of practicing farmers, or "cooperative extension," constituted a lasting influence of Booker T. Washington's Tuskegee Institute on African American agriculture in eastern Oklahoma. In Alabama, Tuskegee sent African American agronomists out to the surrounding farms to instruct farmers on improved techniques in crop and animal production.[45] In 1908, J. R. Council, a Tuskegee Institute graduate, brought this model to the farms around Boley. He began, apparently without any government support, practicing extension work with African American farmers in Okfuskee County. The next year, the state placed him on its payroll as the first and only African American extension agent in Oklahoma, at two-thirds the pay of a white agent.[46]

Council and later African American extension agents mixed a strong dose of self-help into the technical advice they dispensed to the African American farmers, mostly tenants, in the region. African American farmers should aspire to own land, they maintained, and this goal was achievable though individual effort. Unfortunately, when it came to landownership, black extension agents could generally offer tenants little more than exhortations to stay on the farm, produce efficiently, and save their money.[47] The agents made clear how much they valued landownership when they reported in glowing terms the success of farmers who had achieved landowning prosperity through self-help. In 1917, extension agent B. F. Brown reported that the farmers around Boley had much to learn from Sam Callahan, who had used diversified farming and careful savings to build up holdings of four hundred acres, mostly bought with cash.[48] Extension agent Levi Nelson informed his superiors, "At all of my meetings, among the farmers, club meetings etc I laid special emphasis on this one thing": the need to buy land. He found the results in 1919 "very pleasing": nine tenants had bought farms.[49] Although 1919 was a year of exceptionally good conditions, the fact remains that a minority of African American farm tenants did succeed in buying land despite the problems they faced.

The African American businessmen and professionals who celebrated and advanced the strategy of racial uplift through individual economic advancement did not, however, necessarily abandon politics or accept disenfranchisement, as would have been consistent with Booker T. Washington's philosophy. Although dedicated to self-help, they were fully engaged in the effort to protect or win back African American voting rights. J. Coody Johnson, the former member of the Creek House of Warriors who was at the time a lawyer in Wewoka and reportedly owned a number of farms, lent his support to such uplift projects as the Okfuskee Negro County Fair and then organized the Co-operative Negro Farmers Industrial State Fair. At the fairs, farmers could examine one another's produce and improve their skills to improve their standard of living, in full accordance with the Tuskegee ideal of self-help. Johnson also headed, however, the Negro Protective League and later the Suffrage League, through which he militated for suffrage rights from the time of the state constitutional convention through the fight over the second Grandfather Clause.[50] E. O. Tyler of Boley publicized the work of county demonstration agents in familiarizing farmers with hybrid cottonseed perfected at Tuskegee and promoted Washington's Negro Business League. Meanwhile, he denounced the Grandfather Clause as an illegal act and joined with other prominent African Americans to protest it to Oklahoma's governor.[51] Self-help and the defense of political rights constituted two parts of the same program for such men.

Furthermore, for all their emphasis on self-help, the African American extension agents recognized that individual initiative needed to be supplemented by cooperation among farmers. To that end, they encouraged farmers to join together in improved stock clubs, improved cotton clubs, soil amelioration clubs, and general "community associations" in which to share ideas and experiences. The agents often met with frustration in this area, however. In 1919, Seminole County African American extension agent E. R. Moore was disappointed that his best efforts had convinced only a handful of African American farmers to join "community farmers clubs." In fact, there was only one such club for African Americans in the county, and Moore was happy to report that he had helped to organize it.[52]

Emigration, Once Again: Chief Alfred Sam's Back-to-Africa Movement

Moore admitted that the task had been made easier by the fact that the area had "been organized two times [by] 'Back too Africa' Organizers" including a Chief Alfred Sam.[53] The emigrationism that had brought African Americans to leave the South and head west to Kansas and Oklahoma remained alive. It was turned, however, to another, even more symbolically potent destination that also resonated for black Creeks: Africa. There, many black farmers hoped to redeem the promise that Oklahoma had once held out: landownership supporting political rights and political action sustaining landownership.

To appreciate what "Back-to-Africa" movements of the time reveal about the making of a unified "Negro" identity in Oklahoma, we must turn for a moment back to the 1880s and 1890s. As the debate raged over the fate of Creek national sovereignty and Creek lands, some black Creeks looked for their future abroad. In 1887, several groups of black Creeks left the area of Muskogee for Liberia. Just how many emigrated is unclear, but the migration would go on for several years. More black Creeks left for Liberia in 1889 and 1890. Those who contemplated the voyage were encouraged by the reports of such emigrants as Moses Cade. Cade had settled with his wife, Clarissa, in the region of the St. John River in Liberia and reported that the happiness he had found had well warranted the forty days of travel from Muskogee. The Cades' labor had led to material comfort. Cade boasted, "My land is drawn, my house is built," and not only were the crops in the ground, but "breadstuffs are coming up plentifully." Cade assured his friends that what he had found, so too could they, for "there is plenty of land here, and good land it is." He intimated that prosperity awaited the emigrant.[54] But ultimately, what Cade advocated was not emigration to Liberia but *return* to Africa. Cade did not call his friends out of Indian Territory and to Liberia for the simple sake of material success but rather as part of an explicitly nationalist project. He enjoined them to "come home to Liberia," for it was "our home where we can truly praise God who made us under the flag of liberty." Cade made clear that this banner was not the Stars and Stripes but rather the "lone star of Liberis." Cade's was a specifically racial form of nationalism; he proclaimed that he had arrived in "the land of the Negro Race." For Cade, this was what gave meaning to the material gains he had made in Liberia. After returning to his African home, he could declare, "I am happy under my own vine and fig tree."[55] Not all the emigrants sent back reports of such glowing success, and yet for some, the movement retained its appeal.[56] The emigration movement continued to gather adherents, with the Creeks' neighbors also participating. In 1892, a group of twenty-five families struck off for Liberia from the Sequoyah District of the Cherokee Nation but were unable to secure the transportation they needed from New York.[57] In 1899, newspapers reported that two rail cars full of African Americans from Oklahoma Territory set off for Liberia.[58]

Judging from news reports, African emigration movements quieted at the turn of the century. Although it is risky to venture a guess why, this period coincided with massive transformations in the region. When they moved to Indian Territory, newly arrived African Americans from the southeastern states had just completed a major act of emigration in the hope of bettering their lives. Perhaps this made them less likely to pick up and move again, this time across the Atlantic Ocean. Meanwhile, the changes that the area was undergoing—allotment was all but completed by 1907, when the new state government of Oklahoma replaced the governments of the Indian nations—may have occupied the attentions of the Freedmen who would otherwise have looked for their future in Africa. Finally, the influx of African Americans from the southern states, and the resulting tensions between black Creeks and black newcomers, may have placed strain on the racial pan-Africanism that underlay appeals for a return to Africa. Whatever the reason, African American emigrationist movements in the area seem to have quieted during the first decade of the twentieth century.

They gained new intensity after 1909. That year, Dr. P. J. Dorman, an African American teacher in Mantee, Oklahoma, founded a society to favor the emigration of African Americans to Africa. That society apparently included only a few members. Those members, however, followed the news of African emigration movements elsewhere in the country. In 1913, Dorman learned about a Chief Alfred Sam, an African who was organizing a trading company and intended to lead African Americans to settle in Africa. Dorman and his fellows put themselves in correspondence with Chief Sam and arranged for him to come to Oklahoma. By May 1913, Chief Sam was in Oklahoma, speaking in small towns, making quite a stir in the area of dense African American settlement that stretched through the lands of the old Creek and Seminole nations.

In late October 1913, Chief Alfred Charles Sam addressed more than one thousand African Americans at the First Baptist Church in the town of Weleetka. Sam informed the crowd that he came from Apaso in the western Akyem district of the British colony of Gold Coast (present-day Ghana). He announced that there was "more than ample room in Africa for the American Negro to settle." African Americans who moved there, he told the audience, would find unequaled opportunity and would build the race. Sam offered his listeners the chance to be part of this enterprise. Sam said he had purchased forty-five square miles of fertile land in the region and had founded the Akim Trading Company. Anyone who bought a share of this company would receive passage to the Gold Coast and the chance to start over on that land. Many who were present already knew about this opportunity to emigrate to Africa and had already decided to follow Sam there. When Sam finished speaking, they took the pulpit and testified that Sam's word was good and his plan not only was solid but offered the chance for individual prosperity and the redemption of the race. The testimonials continued the next day, when the manager of the Akim Trading Company announced that shares in the company would be sold in front of the church for $25 apiece. In a matter of hours, the company sold more than $6,000 in stock, more than 240 shares. By the end of the emigration effort, the company would sell $72,000 in shares.[59]

Sam had been in eastern Oklahoma since May, drawing the interest of farmers and the ire of town developers. He had chosen a time and a place that made his plan very appealing to farmers interested in buying land and gaining greater sovereignty. The boll weevil had reached southeast Oklahoma four years earlier and had been spreading northward ever since.[60] Cotton prices in 1913 were stagnant. Farm owners often found it hard to earn what it cost them to operate their farms. Meanwhile, the opportunity to own land that had drawn so many African Americans to Oklahoma had turned for many into a life of labor on tenant farms, an existence little better than what African Americans had known in the South that they had risked so much to leave. Disenfranchisement and lynching had followed them all the way to Oklahoma.[61] As C. G. Samuels of Boley put it, "The ballot box has been taken from us and we can not act as a man and [our] peoples are treated so crual . . . , lynched for most any little frivulus crime with the cord of law and . . . jim Croed in the courthouse and in all publick places." Given such a disappointment, Samuels decided it would be better to "make it to our native land."[62] Statements such as Samuels's explain why historians have classed Chief Sam's movement with "escapist responses to segregation" that sprang from "the despair and seeming hopelessness of black Oklahomans in the years following the establishment of Jim Crow."[63]

Such interpretations, however, mischaracterize the people who favored emigration to Africa and misunderstand their motivations. Certainly this was a response to Jim Crow, but it was not an escapist movement of the desperate so much as a calculated, though romantic, move by men and women of some modest means. Accounts from the time suggest that the emigrants were drawn not from the poorest elements of Oklahoma's black population but rather from landowning and home-owning farmers. Many of those who were planning to leave sold their farms in preparation for the move, a decision that struck their critics as the height of recklessness.[64] Joe Murff, an affluent landowner, planned to set off with Sam but was taking a more cautious path. He would accompany Sam to the Gold Coast to verify that the plan would work and report back to a group of other Oklahomans interested in emigrating.[65] The letters and editorials of concern that the movement generated never refer to tenant farmers or laborers leaving. It may be that the businessmen and professionals who opposed the emigration plan were less concerned about tenants and laborers departing from the area than landowners, but the reports may well be correct. It is worth noting that, although the figure was not out of their reach, the twenty-five dollars required to buy into the Akim Trading Company and secure passage to the Gold Coast would have constituted a large investment for the poorest residents of the Black Belt.[66]

In contrast to the enthusiasm of farmers for emigration, town-based African American professionals and businessmen expressed their alarm and hostility at the project.[67] In letters to white officials, they warned that Sam was "inducing hundreds of negroes to give up their home."[68] A Boley attorney, W. S. Peters, reported with disapproval that "the country Negroes" were "wildly excited" by the emigration movement, which town dwellers of Peters's class feared would destroy their communities.[69] No less an authority than Booker T. Washington warned a crowd of hundreds in Boley "not to follow 'Chief Sam or Chief anybody else.'"[70] Sam himself recognized that the opposition to his plan came from town-dwelling professionals when he told audiences "to pay no attention to the sceptic lawyers, doctors and school teachers" who wanted farmers to stay in Oklahoma and give them business rather than seek a better life in Africa.[71]

A few important exceptions to the pattern of town-dwelling professionals voicing hostility to the plan shed light on the power of emigrationist black nationalism to bring together not only farmers and businessmen but also newcomers and Freedmen. Two newcomer African Americans, one a teacher and the other a doctor, headed Chief Sam's organization. The legitimacy of the emigration effort gained a boost, however, when it won the endorsement of J. Coody Johnson, the same black Creek attorney who promoted respectable uplift and political action efforts. One newspaper reported that Johnson "made the speech of his life" in favor of emigration, a discourse so moving that it "brought tears and groans from the audience." Such a stamp of approval led even the skeptical editor, a newcomer to Oklahoma, to believe that exodus to Africa was inevitable.[72] Just as the defense of American citizenship rights could bring Freedmen and newcomers together, so too could the hope to build a nation far from American shores.

Emigration was a means to achieve landownership as Booker T. Washington urged *and* to get a secure hold on the political rights that Du Bois emphasized, and for Sam's advocates, emigration, uplift, and political rights were bound into a unitary strategy of liberation. R. C. Lee, a minister in Nuyaka who was the secretary of a local club of Sam supporters, summed up the appeal of emigration to the Gold Coast: Sam told African American Oklahomans "that they will have a home there always without price and without taxation and that the Government is run absolutely by negroes."[73] In short, the emigrants saw in the Gold Coast the same promise of land and political self-determination that had drawn migrants to Oklahoma's black towns and their hinterland. The emphasis on freedom from taxation was a new addition to this hope-inspiring formula, but then again, black Creeks' and African Americans' experiences of landownership in Oklahoma had done much to demonstrate the power of taxes to threaten the security of land titles. The would-be emigrants' hopes for Africa were rooted in their own experiences of government and race. What struck town-dwelling professionals as a risky scheme or clever confidence game appealed to the ideological background and experiences of small landowning black Creek and African American farmers in eastern Oklahoma.

Chief Sam was not operating a confidence game, but the emigration effort ended in failure for most. By February 1914, hundreds of would-be emigrants gathered to make camp at Weleetka and then at Galveston, Texas, the port of departure. Difficulties with hostile port authorities and the antiquated steamer Sam had bought meant months of waiting, during which time many would-be emigrants exhausted their supplies and funds. The ship was far too small to carry all who held stock in the company, and only sixty passengers were aboard the *Liberia* when it left port on August 20, 1914. After a difficult voyage and a delay of several months in Sierra Leone, imposed by the British authorities, the ship finally arrived in Gold Coast on January 13, 1915. Contrary to the skeptics' predictions, Sam did in fact have lands ready for the immigrants to settle, and they were well received by Sam's people. The crops, tools, and methods of agriculture were unfamiliar, however, and illness may have weakened many of the settlers. Sam disappeared, according to reports, into "self-exile" in Liberia. Although a few settlers stayed in Africa and thrived as planters and business operators along the coast, the bulk of the settlers returned to the United States. Reports of the emigrants' failure reached Oklahoma even before the impoverished emigrants, featured prominently in the newspapers that had opposed the plan.[74]

Despite this disaster, which had cost families their farms and shareholders more than $72,000, pan-Africanism and emigrationism would retain their force in Oklahoma for years. Oklahoma was a western stronghold of Marcus Garvey's Universal Negro Improvement Association, a reminder that the organization's appeal extended well beyond Harlem. Between 1921 and 1933, thirty-one chapters of the association were active in the state, far more than Texas's ten, and even more than southern states like South Carolina and Alabama, which had substantially larger African American populations. Small all-black towns such as Lincoln City, Red Bird, and Tullahassee sustained chapters. Even Bookertee, named for Booker T. Washington, boasted a chapter of the organization that repudiated more forcefully than any other the ideas of Booker T. Washington, who had told African Americans, "Cast down your buckets where you are"—to seek their fortunes in the South.[75] Emigration, along with uplift and political agitation, was a founding principle of the black communities of rural eastern Oklahoma, and it retained its power for many well into the twentieth century.

AS THE DISTINCTIONS of class and ideology that separated the advocates of self-help and emigration came into focus in the second decade of the twentieth century, references to divisions between black Creeks and immigrant African Americans grew rare. The story of the transformations of the first fifteen years of statehood reveals that their economic and political struggles in that period provided the means and the incentive to come together as a race. Constitutional definitions of race, the end of Indian citizenship, the removal of restrictions, disenfranchisement, and discrimination had created shared conditions for black Creeks and newcomers. A few Freedmen and newcomers had together achieved prosperity through the building of African American towns and land speculation. Many more black Creeks and newcomers were joined in landless poverty and tenant farming. In addition to these shared conditions, African Americans from both groups had joined together in political action in defense of their rights as citizens of the American nation. Nationalism of a different stripe also brought together those who favored emigrating to Africa to build a nation there. Finally, even before these changes, the two groups had been aware of a shared heritage. All these conditions created common ground on which black Creeks and black newcomers could make their common identity as "Negroes" a politically potent force.

The lives of Lucy Grayson, Napoleon Davis, and the improbably named Jefferson Davis suggest how individuals negotiated the fluid ground of racial identity. Born around 1890, Lucy Grayson was a Creek Freedman. (As a term describing African American members of the Creek Nation, the same term was used for men and women.) Like other Freedmen, she received 160 acres in the allotment of the Creek Nation. She did not own the land for long, however. Like many allottees, she sold it. When I was so fortunate as to meet her son, Napoleon Davis, he recalled, "She said she 'lost' the land. But she didn't lose it; she sold it, two or three times. She didn't know what she was doing." Lucy Grayson remained an enrolled Freedman, but she no longer had the property that made that a distinctive status, and the law no longer set her apart from other African American women in any way. When she married in 1913, Lucy Grayson became Lucy Davis, the wife of Jefferson Davis. Jefferson Davis was from Louisiana, a "State Negro." Lucy Davis gave birth to their first child in June 1914 and named him Napoleon.[76]

Napoleon Davis, asked decades later whether it was surprising that his mother would marry a newcomer African American, denied any differences. "We were Negroes then," he said of his childhood. Nonetheless, as a child, Davis was aware that his mother was a Freedman, and he had some sense of what that meant. Neither Davis nor his mother spoke Muskogee, but he sometimes heard black people who were speaking English use the word "*wvcenv*" in referring to African Americans whose families had come from the states to the east. Black Creeks retold stories of and retained pride in their distinctive history through the early twentieth century, and Napoleon Davis manifested his pride in his mother's heritage by dedicating the years of his retirement from bricklaying to building an Oklahoma Creek Freedman Memorial and Shrine. Still, when speaking of his childhood, he says, "We were Negroes then."[77]

For African Americans in early twentieth-century eastern Oklahoma, racial identity had emerged out of the particular political context and the particular system of law, land, and labor in which Lucy Davis and her family lived. Napoleon Davis's father (a newcomer) faced discrimination when he tried to register to vote because he was African American. Although they were Creek Freedmen, his mother's brothers faced the same racial discrimination, as did his mother after the passage of the Woman Suffrage Amendment in 1920. After Davis's father died, a victim of the influenza epidemic of 1918–19, his mother moved the children from the white man's land they had been farming on shares to another white man's land where they again farmed on shares. In this simple move of an impoverished family across the land, one can see the working of two decades of politics and law that had built racialized markets in land and labor. Indeed, it is possible that neither the two white landlords nor the farmers of African descent in the area saw a Creek Freedman family move from farm to farm but rather a "Negro" family move from farm to farm. After all, that was what most "Negroes" did.[78]

■ ■

The Battle for Whiteness

MAKING WHITES IN A WHITE MAN'S COUNTRY, 1916–1924

What did it mean to be a Klansman? N. Clay Jewett, the Grand Dragon of the Oklahoma Ku Klux Klan, spread the word about what he considered the highest of callings. "Klankraft," as he put it, meant "the exemplification of the noble ideals of chivalry." It required the defense of "the chastity of our women" and "the protection of our homes." It proceeded from a "spirit of pure patriotism" and a "sublime reverence for our Lord and Savior, Jesus Christ." To Jewett, the Klan represented "honor and justice in all things." Almost needless to say, it called white men to do battle for the "maintenance of white supremacy."[1] The Klan's mission was capacious, bringing together matters political and spiritual, affairs public and intimate. But in this long litany of Klan virtues, a listener hears no reference to an issue that so dominated the political life of the state that it had helped motivate its creation: landownership. Closer examination reveals that this silence was part of a larger absence: there is no reference to class in Jewett's listing of the nature and purpose of Klankraft. In a state riven by violent class conflict and insurgent agrarianism, this silence on land and class constituted an act of suppression. Jewett, the Klan, and others on the right in Oklahoma in the 1920s aimed to redirect whiteness away from the issue of land—a potent part of class conflict in the region—in their effort to harness whiteness for their own political purposes.

They had reason to do so. The years that stretched from 1916 to 1924 witnessed fierce class conflict during a period of economic transformation in the region. In this period, oil extraction increasingly overshadowed agriculture in east-central Oklahoma's economy. This transformation intensified battles between tenant farmers and landlords and between wage laborers and employers. Furthermore, tenants and oil workers largely lived in rural areas and the boomtowns that sprang up among the farms, whereas landlords and employers inhabited what passed for more settled towns and cities in the young state. This pattern encouraged Oklahomans to experience and express class conflicts as struggles pitting the rural poor against the town-dwelling rich.

Both racism and class consciousness were part of white agrarianism. For white Oklahoman agrarians, whiteness was no "false consciousness" distracting them from the reality of race. Rather, whiteness and class were equally real parts of one whole: the way they understood themselves. Since statehood, white working-class farmers and mine workers had given the power of their racialized class consciousness to a variety of causes that posited that the central issue in Oklahoma politics was the exploitation of white men at the hands of profiteering capitalists. This racially infused class politics threatened the political and economic security of Oklahoma's landlords, land speculators, and mine owners and operators. More threatening still, from the point of view of Oklahoma's business classes, was the growth of interracial working-class action in the years immediately preceding World War I. In response to what looked like an emerging alliance among white, black, and Indian working-class people, Oklahoma's small-town and urban business classes promoted a politics of unity that fused race and nation: a unity of white Americans. The Klan provided the most infamous support for this politics of white American unity, but it came in many other guises—especially campaigns for wartime loyalty, 100 percent Americanism, and moral uprightness. Each of them asserted that white American people needed to draw together to defend and purify American whiteness. For these white middle-class and affluent Oklahomans, drawing together as white people and as Americans meant that white tenant farmers and oil workers had to reject class politics. It meant that the poor had to live as decent white people according to racialized, middle-class standards of propriety. Fundamentally, it meant that poor whites needed to conceive of themselves in terms of race first, not class. This notion, promulgated by the white business classes, resonated with the racism that was part of white agrarianism. It was strikingly different from white agrarianism, however, in that it removed land and class from the meaning of whiteness, thus discouraging class conflict.

This story helps us understand the political, social, and economic stakes in what it meant to be white—that is, what "whiteness" meant. In early twentieth-century rural Oklahoma, to be a white American man meant to deserve the economic sovereignty of owning land. In other words, agrarianism provided the linkage (some would say the articulation) between race and class—both of which were suffused with ideas of gender and nation.[2] This insight helps us to extend our understanding of the relationship of whiteness to the history of capitalism, especially in rural areas. W. E. B. Du Bois wrote that whites received a "public and psychological wage" from their race.[3] Yet in rural Oklahoma poor whites received something they held more dear than wages: they received the promise that they would one day own land. After all, the hope was that landownership would mean not needing wages, a crucial achievement of yeoman independence. Landownership is what separated a landed farmer from a landless tenant, sharecropper, or laborer.

When both the landed and the landless were white, the unfulfilled promise of white landownership became a political problem. "Free land" for whites had served as a powerful unifying narrative for whites in Oklahoma until the second decade of the twentieth century, but the consolidation of a white rural proletariat after statehood had given the lie to that hope. Prior to allotment, whites like the Boomers, other squatters, and would-be settlers thought of themselves as a frustrated yeomanry, denied their right as whites to own land by tribal and federal governments and a wrong-headed recognition of Indian treaty rights. But by around 1914, many white Oklahomans had concluded that they lived in a class society of landowning and landless classes, of employers and wage earners. Now there was such a thing as a white proletariat that recognized itself as such, rather than angry whites who thought their entry into the yeomanry was delayed. The intensification of class politics in that decade had everything to do with this realization. This is not to say, as Frederick Jackson Turner would have it, that "free land" had provided a safety valve from radicalism nationwide, but in Oklahoma, whites had believed they were on the cusp of coming into their own as landowners with allotment. But instead of creating a vast class of white yeomen, the creation of fee-simple property in land created landlessness for most whites and landed wealth for a few.

Frustrated Expectations: Farm Tenancy
and White Agrarian Politics

In the second decade of the twentieth century, many white farmers' agrarian hopes to achieve yeoman independence were frustrated by a high level of white tenancy. In 1910, more than seven out of ten white farmers rented their land in most of Oklahoma's cotton-growing counties.[4] White farmers' frustrations sprang from the ideological power that landowner-ship held for white settlers. As was true for black settlers, the white men who came to farm in Oklahoma linked race, landownership, political em-powerment, and gender. These ideas, however, bore the marks of different experiences and different expectations than those of the African Ameri-can settlers. In their lived experience, the poor southern and midwestern whites who settled in eastern Oklahoma hardly constituted the most privi-leged members of their communities. They played, however, a privileged role in the agrarian ideology of white American yeoman democracy that powerful southern white politicians had long celebrated. That contrast be-tween experience and expectation would be at the heart of white rural poli-tics for decades to come.[5]

White agrarianism was already a potent force in Indian Territory prior to statehood. It gave power to the call for allotment. Interestingly, although the People's ("Populist") Party was the torchbearer for agrarianism in the South and the American West in the 1880s and 1890s, it was never in much evidence in the Creek Nation. Among Creeks, politics in those decades was consumed with the question of allotment, not the American political parties. Among Indian Territory whites, the Farmers Union rather than the Populists bore the torch of agrarianism.[6] The territorial branch of this moderate agricultural organization voiced the hostility of small farmers to land speculators and large landowners, arguing, "Because some old fogy managed to rake together a big lot of land and managed to hold it 'till it became valuable is no sign that he did anything toward gettingrich [*sic*]." The Farmers Union was a fairly conservative organization—its program centered on education for farmers' children and the creation of marketing cooperatives. Still, it had a broad appeal that extended beyond its white farmer base. Among the publications that sympathetically followed its ac-tivities in the state was an African American Republican newspaper—and this at a time when neither African Americans nor the Republican Party was notably warm to white agrarian politics.[7]

Blacks remained cool to this politics because whiteness and white

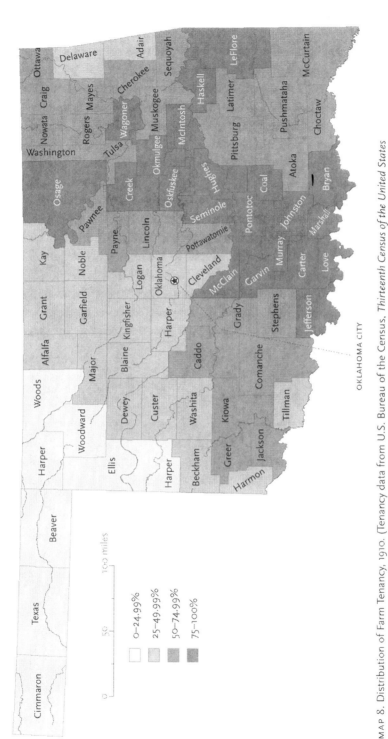

OKLAHOMA CITY

MAP 8. Distribution of Farm Tenancy, 1910. (Tenancy data from U.S. Bureau of the Census, *Thirteenth Census of the United States Taken in the Year 1910, vol. 7, Agriculture 1909 and 1910* [Washington: Government Printing Office, 1913], 374–79.)

0–24.99%

25–49.99%

50–74.99%

75–100%

0   50   100 miles

supremacy were tightly bound up with agrarianism in the South and in Oklahoma. Southern white leaders had effectively wed white supremacy to agrarianism and given it a decidedly southern accent. In the aftermath of Reconstruction, southern politicians such as "Pitchfork" Ben Tillman crafted a political and social order that left many poor whites landless and with little political authority, all the while claiming to defend "the yeoman" and "the farmers."[8] According to Tillman and other agrarians, these noble figures were menaced by class antagonists: powerful white landlords and creditors. They also faced the threat of racial antagonists, however: African Americans whose inherent savagery made their disenfranchisement imperative. This was a point Tillman no doubt drove home in the fall of 1906 when he lectured at Muskogee on the topic of "the Negro and the South."[9] The settlers' loyalty to agrarianism, and to national political figures who had so ably tied it to ideologies of race and nationalism, left its mark on the very map of the state. A traveler on the Red River passes alongside Oklahoma counties named for Ben Tillman and other giants of the American agrarian tradition: Thomas Jefferson, Andrew Jackson, and William Jennings Bryan.[10]

Agrarianism and Socialism in Oklahoma

By making itself the primary vehicle for this kind of white agrarian politics in the state, the Socialist Party made exceptional electoral gains in the decade from 1910 to 1920.[11] Democrats had initially won the loyalty of many small-scale white farmers in the new state, but soon a landlord elite came to dominate Democratic politics. Landlords and their allies in Oklahoma City and county seats around the state steered the Democratic Party away from policies favored by its "dirt farmer faction."[12] As the Democratic Party moved to the right, more white farmers migrated into the Socialist Party. The Socialist Party was growing nationally, but the party's growth in Oklahoma was unparalleled. Whereas the party had won fewer than 10,000 votes statewide in 1907, it claimed almost 25,000 in 1910 and more than 41,000 in 1912. In five years' time, then, the party more than quadrupled its votes, winning seats for a number of local and state officials and legislators.[13] By 1914, Oklahoma Socialists had a larger membership than any other state branch of the party, measured both in absolute numbers and as a percentage of the electorate. That year, Oklahomans voted five Socialists into the state house of representatives, one into the state senate, and more than 20 percent of voters cast their ballots for the Socialist gubernatorial candidate. More than one hundred Socialists won local and county offices.[14]

The politics of white landownership was central to Socialist success. Socialist calls for broadening landownership became a centerpiece of the party's appeal to poor white tenants and small landowning farmers who constituted the bulk of the party. State party leaders in Oklahoma City had initially hewed to Marxist orthodoxy. The 1910 Socialist state platform, for example, declared the party's intention to "bring into collective property the land," consistent with the idea that the means of production must be in the hands of the state.[15] At times, the party suggested awkward ways of bringing agrarianism and Marxism together. One idea (bearing a similarity to land tenure practices in a number of Native American nations) held that the commonwealth would hold title to the land but farmers would own use and occupancy rights. But those positions ran counter to the agrarian dream of many small farm owners and tenants. Because their political heritage emphasized individual landownership, calls for state or communal land tenure acted as a brake on the growth of the party. Historian Jim Bissett persuasively argues that the turning point for the party came when the rural rank and file forced it in 1912 to endorse the notion that all farmers should have title to their own land. Still, the party grew because white farmers believed the Socialist Party was as dedicated as they themselves to farmers owning their own land. In Oklahoma, Socialists won electoral success by accommodating white agrarians.[16]

Embracing white agrarians entailed ignoring or even expressing hostility to American Indians and African Americans. The state's Socialist Party initially sought and received African American support, but from the start it mostly ignored American Indians. Given the fact that many agrarians in Oklahoma placed some of the blame for the extent of white farm tenancy on Indian allotment owners, it is not surprising that the Socialist Party had little say about or to Indians. As for African Americans, the early leadership of the party had included a significant portion of educated, immigrant, northern-born, and labor-union-oriented white Marxists. These leaders had emphasized that African Americans were part of the proletariat and their concerns were the concerns of the Socialist Party. As the issue of landownership came to dominate the party, however, so did white farmers, many of whom expressed the same dedication to white supremacy as their Democratic adversaries. At its height, the Socialist Party in Oklahoma had only a small African American membership, much of it in Oklahoma City.[17] The few indications of Socialist sympathies for black rights after the party had dedicated itself to agrarianism are far from conclusive. For example, after the U.S. Supreme Court struck down the state's first Grandfather Clause law, Socialist voters were an important part of the successful effort to defeat a 1916 ballot measure to impose a literacy test on voters. White Socialist voters, and other whites who voted against the law, may have been seeking to protect their own suffrage rights, though, not blacks'. Much of the white working class had very limited literacy skills, and agrarians, including Socialists, feared the law would be used to disenfranchise white men. D. Bryan, for example, appealed to Governor Robert Lee Williams "on behalf of the farm renters of Oklahoma who constitutes A large part of the states population" not to use a literacy test to disenfranchise them. Such a law "would take from them the last vestige of liberty which they now posess."[18] The governor, like other advocates for the measure, assured concerned whites that he did not want to disenfranchise any white man but rather wanted "to see the white people have supremacy in this state."[19] The Socialist Party, though wary of opposing the measure for fear of alienating white voters, denounced the clause, which voters defeated. The state legislature then passed a registration law designed to discriminate against very mobile populations—including black farm tenants, but white farm tenants, also.

This new registration law contributed to a decline in the party's fortunes after 1914. Historians have speculated that favorable economic conditions for farmers lessened the Socialist appeal at a time when party activists were already exhausted from their efforts in 1914. With prices up for commodities, especially cotton, the kinds of farmers who had supported the Socialist Party may have felt less urgently the need to effect radical social change.[20] In 1916, Socialist fortunes began to sour in the state. In that year's elections, the Democrats routed the Socialists, who lost all their seats in the state house.[21]

The Working Class Union

In this context of Socialist decline, some landless Oklahoma farmers made a shift away from land-based politics and toward a class-based organization that opened up new avenues of interracial action: the Working Class Union (WCU). One of its most important characteristics was what it was not. It was not centrally concerned with expanding landownership. This was a turning point in the history of race, class, and landownership in Oklahoma. Unlike parties and organizations from the Farmers Union

to the "dirt farmer" Democrats to the Socialists, the WCU did not emphasize broadening landownership. Instead, it asserted that tenant farmers and
wage laborers had the same interests. By joining the WCU, tenant farmers
called themselves "working class," not would-be yeomen. This meant that
the farmers who took part in it were expressing the idea that (unlike the
white Boomers, squatters, and land-seeking settlers of a decade earlier)
they did not expect to own land. They sought to improve their lot through
identifying as people without capital ("workers") rather than as people who
aspired to capital. This important shift in the agrarian tradition facilitated
the making of an interracial alliance among whites, blacks, and Indian
people. Indeed, the WCU became for a time the principal vehicle of insurgent agrarian politics in Oklahoma, and its activists would set off a remarkable but disastrous rebellion in 1917. When rural working-class politics
broke out of racial boundaries, the repression would be swift and brutal.

The WCU's activities demonstrated its members' dedication to militant
action as rural proletarians. The group had its origins in Louisiana, where
it had been founded by members and former members of the Industrial
Workers of the World (IWW) and the Brotherhood of Timber Workers, two
of the most successful radical unions in American history. By 1914, the
WCU was active in Sequoyah County, Oklahoma (in the former lands of
the Cherokee Nation), where farmers had organized to seek prosecutions
of landlords and bankers who charged rates of interest above that allowed
by state antiusury laws.[22] At first WCU activists sought legal and electoral
remedies. Soon members of the group began taking more direct means:
threats, arson, and beatings targeting exploitative landlords and the tenants
who agreed to work their lands.[23] These acts of guerrilla class warfare were
few, but aided by rumors that the WCU was an affiliate of the Industrial
Workers of the World, they terrified Oklahoma's newspaper editors and
politicians.[24]

This militant, rural working-class politics was shaped by the rise of wage
labor and mining in this mostly agricultural region and farmers' contact
with militant unionism. Transformations in Oklahoma's economy were
bringing farmers, especially white men, into closer contact with wage labor,
industrial workers, and new ideas about class politics. In the second decade
of the twentieth century, some men from rural Oklahoma, especially young
white men, found seasonal work in the wheat harvest in Kansas and western
Oklahoma, where they encountered the organizing efforts of the Agricultural Workers Organization, a union affiliated with the Industrial Workers
of the World.[25] Mineral exploitation, especially oil fields discovered under

the old Creek Nation, provided longer-term and closer contact with radical labor ideology. Since statehood in 1907, Oklahoma had witnessed tremendous booms in coal and especially oil, booms that required the settlement of large numbers of workers in the areas of mineral development.[26] Most of the full-time miners and oil workers came to the state from elsewhere, but farmers did have many points of contact with them. Some men in the farm population found part-time or full-time employment in the mines and oil fields, which paid better than farming. Charlie Storms was only fourteen years old when he got a job in the oil fields near Dropright in 1915 during the summer vacation from school, but he was able to earn five dollars a day. This was ten times the fifty cents per day he could earn chopping cotton.[27] Miners came into contact with a variety of American Federation of Labor–affiliated craft unions as well as the iww-affiliated Oil Workers Industrial Union, which enjoyed some organizing success in Oklahoma. One former miner, H. H. "Rube" Munson, became the state organizer for the wcu, bringing the ideas and methods of the miners' unions with him. These contacts and experiences, historian Nigel Anthony Sellars argues, added a syndicalist radicalism and expansive working-class consciousness to the already potent agrarian and Socialist political background of eastern Oklahoma's tenant farmers.[28]

iww-affiliated unions also introduced ideas of class-based mobilization that crossed racial boundaries. In both the oil fields and the wheat harvests, employers reserved jobs almost exclusively for white men. In keeping with the practices of employers nationwide, they tried to subvert labor organization by threatening to replace whites with African American or Mexican workers.[29] They were not always successful: the Agricultural Workers Organization met the strategy of racial division head-on by planning to hire African American organizers to bring the blacks into the union.[30] Ultimately, the employers never brought in the black workers. In harvest and mining work, Oklahomans encountered and helped to build class organizations that crossed racial lines.

This fact is important because the wcu grew in racially mixed farming areas and an unknown number of rural blacks and perhaps Indians took part in its meetings. It is difficult to know just who formally joined the union. Not surprisingly, the wcu did not publicize membership lists, as it was engaged in illegal activities and its members faced prosecution and retaliation by officials, landlords, and employers. Nonetheless, testimony in the trials of members indicates that the organization admitted men and women "irrespective of color." Blacks clearly participated, and it seems likely that Indians did, as well.[31] Farmers joined chapters of the secret organization in Sallisaw, Muskogee, Hughes, Seminole, and Pontotoc counties and other localities in the eastern section of the state, all areas with racially mixed rural populations. The WCU enjoyed particular success among the impoverished tenant farmers in the hills surrounding Sasakwa and in the valley of the Canadian River in the southern portions of the old Seminole and Creek nations. These areas had large African American, Creek, Seminole, and black Creek and Seminole populations.[32] In April 1916, a WCU activist boasted that the new Muskogee County chapter had already attracted 1,800 members.[33] Contemporary newspapers' estimates of the WCU's membership ranged from 18,000 to 35,000. Whatever the figure, the appeal of the WCU to working-class solidarity clearly won it the support of many Oklahomans.[34]

The shift among Oklahoma's landless farmers toward a broader proletarian politics and away from a central focus on land was evident as the WCU more directly addressed the concerns of wage laborers. At a 1916 convention in Sallisaw, the organization adopted a platform that was familiar to Oklahoma Socialists: "the abolition of rent and the wage system; the eight-hour day, workers' compensation and old age pensions; child labor laws; free school textbooks, and the initiative, referendum, and recall in the state government."[35] The WCU's agenda thereby joined landless farmers' dissatisfaction with their exploitation as tenants and wage laborers' concerns with the wage labor system and tied both to issues that were of concern to both farmers and wage earners, such as pensions, schooling, and the powers of the citizenry in the electoral process.

In 1917, this class politics came to focus on the war in Europe and the draft. Broadsides warned that the sons of the poor would be sacrificed on the battlefield for a war that profited wealthy speculators. Taking up a formulation familiar in America since the time of the Civil War, they decried the conflict as a "rich man's war" but a "poor man's fight."[36] The conflict in Oklahoma escalated as federal agents arrested WCU members and other radicals on charges of conspiring to obstruct the draft. Explosions attributed to the WCU (sometimes mistakenly referred to as the IWW) rocked one town's water tower and tore open the sewer mains in another.[37]

The outcome of all of this agitation was a brief and disastrous event termed the Green Corn Rebellion or the Roasting Ear Rebellion. On July 27, 1917, men began to gather at the farm of John Spears after he raised two flags—one the Stars and Stripes, the other the red banner of socialism. The farmers intended to march to Washington to bring their case against the war to President Woodrow Wilson. They carried small-bore hunting rifles to protect themselves along the way.[38] The grand revolt ended almost before it started. On August 2, members of the group ambushed a sheriff and his deputy near Sasakwa. Posses immediately converged on the group. Gunfire killed three men. For days, posses and state authorities scoured the surrounding countryside, taking 450 men prisoner, 184 of whom faced charges and about 150 of whom were convicted and sentenced to prison terms ranging from sixty days to ten years.[39]

Class War and Interracial Action

What made the resistance to the draft and the war in east-central Oklahoma so exceptional was the way that class politics underpinned interracial action. In most of the South, race simultaneously motivated and divided the resistance to the draft. Rural white working-class men resisted conscription on class grounds but were infuriated that segregation in the military had the effect of keeping blacks in support roles and therefore out of the line of fire.[40] Meanwhile, most African American resistance to the draft was far less overt. Historian Jeannette Keith argues that "southern black men's primary strategy of resistance" to the draft was to take up "the classic weapons of the weak: evasion, prevarication, and foot dragging."[41] There is little evidence of coordinated draft resistance linking Native Americans and either whites or African Americans.[42]

Events looked quite different in east-central Oklahoma in 1917, where militant interracial action opposed the draft. Those arrested in the Green Corn Rebellion included a small but noteworthy number of African Americans and Native Americans. The five men who ambushed the sheriff and his deputy near Sasakwa in the first clash of the rebellion were all reportedly African American members of the wcu.[43] One of the three men killed in the conflict was an African American tenant farmer named Clifford Clark.[44] At least ten men with distinctly Seminole or Creek names were arrested, and more were likely involved, as many Native people in the area had Anglo-American names. Reports also repeatedly mention the participation of "Snake" Indians in the rebellion—that is, Native Americans who had opposed allotment and the advent of U.S. government in the area.[45]

What is perhaps most striking is that this interracial cooperation took place even though the wcu was nearly silent on issues of race. Similarly, one finds scarcely a word on racial cooperation in the transcript of a trial of

Green Corn participants—a document consisting of more than a thousand pages.[46] The willingness of Oklahomans of different races to collaborate in this way is noteworthy, of course, and constituted a significant political statement in and of itself. Still, given that most Americans who opposed the draft did so in racially bounded ways, how were these poor farmers able to build an interracial movement?

Whites, African Americans, and American Indians joined together in the WCU and the Green Corn Rebellion because they insisted on class unity in pursuit of class warfare, not because they sought a liberal antiracist agenda. The WCU's single-minded attention to class and the Green Corn rebels' focus on resisting the draft were thus interracial (but not antiracist) because of a class consciousness born of specific circumstances. Both movements emerged at a moment when an entrenched tenant farming system, a growing wage labor sector, and contact with leftist labor unions had led a number of poor white Oklahomans to stop considering themselves as white landowners-in-waiting and start seeing themselves as workers. Many African American and Indian tenant farmers found themselves in similar straits. In these particular historical conditions, the class consciousness of this self-proclaimed union of working-class people overrode the strong racial divisions in rural Oklahoma. Furthermore, this class consciousness emerged out of a specific geography of race. The Canadian River valley—an area of strong WCU activism and the center of the rebellion—was farmed not only by poor whites but also by large numbers of Seminoles, Creeks, Freedmen, and African Americans whose families had migrated to Oklahoma. These black and Indian farmers were part of the same rural economy as white tenant farmers and shared many of the same economic problems—landlessness, indebtedness, economic insecurity. Although the lines dividing blacks and whites and Indians were no mere illusions—indeed, Jim Crow law and restrictions on allotted lands made them a matter of public policy—the lines of class that bound tenant farmers and workers together were not illusions either. Once the United States entered the war in Europe, poor whites, African Americans, and Native Americans had yet another thing in common: all faced conscription into what radical Americans termed a "rich man's war."

Furthermore, Native Americans and African Americans could draw on a heritage of resistance when they took part in the WCU and the rebellion. The Little River area near Sasakwa, near the center of the rebellion, was a place that one white policeman described as a settlement of black people, mostly "native," who were bold in their disregard of the law and willing to defend their own when the law came after them.[47] That boldness had antecedents that government reports and the press alluded to when they called the Creeks and Seminoles who took part in the disturbances "Snakes." In resisting conscription into the U.S. Army, Creeks and Seminoles (including black Creeks and Seminoles) could draw on the recent heritage of the Snake defiance to the imposition of allotment and state government only a decade before.[48]

This was a draft resistance movement that owed little to pacifism but much to class warfare, a fact that is apparent in the way the rebels conscripted farmers into their efforts. Like Doc White, an African American farmer who was charged in the Green Corn Rebellion, some blacks testified in their defense that neighbors (white and black) had coerced them into taking part. It was certainly in the interests of defendants to claim they did not participate of their own free will, but there is every reason to believe that Green Corn rebels, white, black, or Indian, would have intimidated African Americans into participating. After all, the wcu had warned farm tenants, "We have ways of making you join."[49] When class solidarity was lacking in the eyes of wcu activists, they were willing to enforce it through intimidation. They were ready to turn the tool of violence against people they considered class traitors—tenants who worked the lands of boycotted landlords or patronized boycotted gins, for example. Division would have weakened their efforts and strengthened the hand of landlords and the business class.

Indeed, racial divisions had weakened every major class-based movement in Oklahoma. White agrarian racism meant that the dirt-farmer faction of the Democratic Party pursued the disenfranchisement of black men, not the votes of blacks or Indians who might have helped them to tip laws in the favor of landless farmers. The racism of white Socialists had kept that party from pursuing the rural and small-town African American and American Indian support that might have permitted Socialists to advance an agenda that would favor tenants and renters. The racism of white miners had permitted employers to rein in the miners' demands by threatening to hire black or Mexican workers. Now, the wcu and the Green Corn rebels had assembled a movement that included white, African American, and American Indian support in the pursuit of class war. The interracial nature of the wcu and the Green Corn Rebellion signaled a danger to the power of Oklahoma landlords and businessmen.

World War I created an opportunity to answer this challenge. Oklahoma businessmen and politicians fought interracialism by reasserting whiteness but in a modified form. During World War I, officials and businessmen promulgated an intensely nationalistic form of whiteness that muted class conflict among whites. This had the effect of making the kind of class-based interracial action of the wcu or the Green Corn Rebellion more difficult to effect. Landlessness had facilitated white rural radicalism because it made it clear to white tenants and laborers that they would not achieve the status of yeomen. Recasting whiteness, emphasizing nationalism over agrarianism, worked to restrain radicalism by making land and class peripheral to whiteness.

The massive and ongoing repression of working-class politics, black and Indian assertion, and white working-class people during and after World War I was pivotal to retraining radicalism. The crushing of the Green Corn Rebellion was just a first glimpse of the repression of interracial or class-based movements that World War I would legitimate in Oklahoma. The following years would bring the full weight of right-wing mobilization. During World War I, the use of deputized posses like the one the state had used to stop the Green Corn Rebellion would expand. Militarized organizations that had the power of the state but were not answerable to the citizenry played a crucial role in enforcing the will of Oklahoma's government.

The role that posses would play is apparent in events in Tulsa in November 1917. The city was the capital of Oklahoma's oil boom, the headquarters of Phillips Petroleum, and the home to thousands of oil workers, many of them former farmers from Oklahoma and farther afield. iww organizers enjoyed success in their recruitment efforts among workers there, despite official repression and harassment. After a bomb exploded on October 29 at the home of an oilman, police raided iww offices, eventually taking twelve men into custody. Although the men (and their five defense witnesses) were quickly convicted, courtroom justice was not enough to satisfy some Tulsans. On November 9, the last day of the trial, the *Tulsa Daily World* urged its readers to "get out the hemp." "Kill 'em just as you would kill any other kind of a snake. Don't scotch 'em; kill 'em. And kill 'em dead." That night a group of about fifty, calling itself the Knights of Liberty, seized the seventeen men, whipped, tarred, and feathered them, then ran them out of town.[50] The members of the posse were no working-class ruffians. They carried weapons obtained from a local militia and included a former assistant police chief and other policemen.[51] Civilians of the business class—what the *Daily World* called a "sterling element of citizenship"—made up the bulk of the posse.[52]

These same sorts of town-dwelling, better-off white men would also dominate the militias that rallied support for the war and enforced loyalty through the war years. The Councils of Defense were para-state organizations, mandated nationwide by Congress in 1916, that oversaw the actions of county Home Guard militias. Though the governor named the businessmen, bankers, editors, lawyers, and landlords who led the county councils, they remained largely independent of governmental oversight.[53] Via their militias, the Councils of Defense rallied support for the war, enforced loyalty, sold war bonds, and punished Oklahomans whom they deemed traitors or "slackers." Their methods ranged from splashing yellow paint on "slackers'" barns, to harassing individuals who had not properly demonstrated their patriotism, to publishing their names, to refusing to sell them goods or extend credit to them, to abducting, beating, tarring, and feathering people the councils suspected of disloyalty.[54] The crusade was national in scope but was particularly active and violent in Oklahoma, if only because it had so much resistance to suppress.[55] The relative success of radical tenant and working-class politics in Oklahoma (the WCU, the Green Corn Rebellion, the Socialist and Wobbly movements) explains the particular virulence of reactionary repression in the state during World War I.

In another way, however, the reaction in Oklahoma was typical of repression nationwide: it emphasized a patriotism that was strongly racialized. In Oklahoma and elsewhere, many of the kind of people who called themselves "old-stock Americans" associated dissidence and working-class insurgency with foreign ideas and foreign people. There was a certain irony to this in Oklahoma, a place that attracted few immigrants and where the Socialist Party, the WCU, and labor organizations were all largely made up of native-born white farmers and workers with deep roots in the American soil. Conservatives could seize on the fact that a German-born Socialist, Oscar Ameringer, spearheaded the growth of the Socialist Party in Oklahoma.[56] But even that was hardly the point because, for the opponents of radicalism, left-wing ideas were by definition foreign. Wartime reaction and government-sponsored propaganda campaigns in Oklahoma and elsewhere in the United States emphasized that citizens must embrace a totalizing patriotism called "100 percent Americanism." This meant an unquestioning endorsement of American nationalism, American goals in the war, and "American ideals."[57] What is essential to note here is that all these concepts were imbued with racial meaning. To those who championed it, men from Theodore Roosevelt down to heads of county Councils of Defense, "100 percent Americanism" required whiteness. Of course, as many historians have noted, the definition of white was in flux at this time. It was not yet true (as it is today) that just because all of one's ancestors came from Europe one would be called white. To many Anglo-Americans, the whiteness of Jews, Italians, Slavs, Greeks, and others from southern and eastern Europe was highly questionable. Not coincidentally, so was their loyalty to "American ideals." In Oklahoma, whites were less concerned with the state's small European immigrant population than with its much more visible Native American and African American populations.

Patriotism and racial fears merged in the minds of some white Oklahomans, as can be seen in words of the leader of one small organization, the True American Order of the White Brotherhood of the World. J. R. Lamb, a white resident of the old Creek town of Eufaula, was the chairman of the organization, which was also known as the White Order of True Americans. During World War I, Lamb warned that the service of African American men in the war threatened "White Supremacy in these United States." African American men were no longer "satisfied with subordinate relations with white people." Indeed, unless drastic measures were taken, Lamb foresaw that the war would result in "equalization of the black and white races of America at the ballot box and the marriage altar." The resulting miscegenation would prove the downfall of the United States.[58] The True American Order was an obscure organization, but the rantings of its chairman expressed beliefs that would enjoy great currency after the war. Indeed, the fears that African American men would return from war with new determination to resist white supremacy not only were well founded but also underlay a postwar backlash that resulted in lynchings of black veterans throughout the South.[59] In that way, then, Lamb and his True American Order anticipated the future of white supremacism in the period between the world wars.

It is essential to note, however, that Lamb's white supremacist thought was rooted in a form of land-oriented white politics that would soon be superseded in Oklahoma white supremacism. Lamb took pains to term himself a "country farmer." Part of his program of global racial segregation was a call for the U.S. government to purchase "surplus" land from landlords and sell it in 160-acre plots to landless white people. This appeal, echoing as it did calls for the allotment of Indian lands and the redistribution of the lands of corporations and monopolists, found its roots in the agrarianism that had fed the Oklahoma Boomers and even rural socialism in the state. Twenty years earlier, agrarians had called for wresting lands from American Indian control. During World War I, Lamb took this further, demanding global segregation and white supremacy.[60] But the True American Order, with its call for redistributing landlords' holdings so that landless whites might achieve their birthright as yeomen, represented a form of white land-oriented supremacism that would face a formidable challenge from the Ku Klux Klan in the postwar period.

Agricultural Crisis

Meanwhile, the land tenure situation for white farmers worsened in the postwar years as wartime hopes pushed overexpansion that ended in disaster for many of them. Even before the United States entered the conflict, the need to clothe and equip American forces had increased demand and boosted cotton prices. In 1916, cotton prices rose from eleven cents per pound to sixteen cents per pound. The next year, prices doubled and then remained stable through 1918. Even though production was uneven (there was a falloff in 1918), these tremendous gains in price did much to fatten the purses of Oklahoma's small farmers. These farmers, like those throughout the Cotton Belt, responded by putting more and more acreage into cotton. This trend, which the federal government encouraged as part of the war effort, increased farmers' expenditures—growing less of their own food and feed meant farmers had to purchase these. Hoping to profit from higher cotton prices, landlords pressured sharecroppers and share tenants to dedicate their energies to planting cotton. With prices, Washington, and landlords all encouraging cotton production, farmers in eastern Oklahoma responded by planting the crop (to use the clichés of the time) "from hedgerow to hedgerow" and "to the very doors of their cabins."[61] Some white farmers increased their risk when they took out loans in order to buy land, assuming that high cotton prices would allow them to pay off their debts. The discovery of oil in east-central Oklahoma furthered this tendency, as farmers hoped that the next big oil strike would occur on their land.

Joined to this increase in demand for land was an increase in "supply." Even after the successive removal of restrictions on the allotment lands of many Creeks in 1904 and 1908, the lands of most "full-bloods" had remained restricted, keeping some land off the market. In the course of the next decade, many of these lands came on the market. Some of these land sales were voluntary. As children who had received allotments reached the age of eighteen, they gained the ability to sell their land, and many promptly did. Some restricted allottees successfully petitioned to be able to sell their land. In other cases, Native American landowners were forced to sell their land. Among the least abusive of such sales were those in which an allottee died leaving several heirs, one of whom wished to sell his or her inheritance. In what one historian terms "a suspicious number of cases," the state courts deemed that the land could not be properly divided among the heirs to facilitate a partial sale, and the courts therefore ordered the entire allotment sold and the proceeds divided. These court orders, of course, brought more acres on the market. More coercive still were sales and leases of allotment lands by allottees' court-appointed guardians. Around 1913, the county courts began to declare in thousands of cases that not only Indian children but adults, too, were legally incompetent. To protect their interests, the courts appointed guardians, many of whom had never met their wards and some of whom were "professional guardians" with dozens of wards. Investigations by reformers in the state revealed that thousands of acres of Indian land were sold when corrupt guardians sold their wards' lands to colleagues or family members instead of conserving the property as the law required.[62]

The oil boom and high cotton prices spurred a steep rise in land prices. By 1923, demand for land in areas of oil production such as Okmulgee County had priced much land out of the agricultural market.[63] Agricultural extension agents had always encouraged tenants to buy land, but now they fretted that new farm buyers were engaging in "wild adventures or speculative dealings." When white tenants took out loans to buy their first land and when white small landholders mortgaged their plots to buy more land, they paid a premium, and the value of their new land depended on the vagaries of war and subterranean geography.[64]

The outcome was a land tenure crisis for whites. Cotton and other agricultural prices slumped after the war, and only a minority of landowners grew rich from oil production. Many white Oklahomans had to sell their land. By 1921, county extension agents were reporting that "there probably never was a time when there was a greater feeling of insecurity or a more general despondency among the farmers." Cotton prices were so low that farmers were forced to sell it at a loss, and "many farmers were unable to meet their obligations with bankers and business men."[65] The result in many cases was foreclosure.[66] Between 1920 and 1925, there was a sharp drop in the number of white farmers who owned their land in most eastern Oklahoma counties. In Creek County, the numbers of such farmers fell 12 percent, from 507 to 444. In Muskogee County, the drop was less severe—only 6 percent—but still, 53 fewer farmers there owned the land they tilled in 1925 than was the case in 1920. In Seminole County, the drop was precipitous. The decline from 790 to 603 meant that only three white owner-operators were farming in 1924 for every four who had been doing so five years earlier.[67]

Meanwhile, many nonwhite farmers were making visible gains in land-ownership. (Census reports did not differentiate between African Americans and Native Americans in land tenure figures.) In Creek County the numbers of nonwhite owner-operators swelled from 145 to 206 between 1920 and 1925. In Okmulgee County they rose from 228 to 274. In Okfuskee County, the increase was remarkable, from 490 to 728. These gains for nonwhite farmers were not evident everywhere; in Seminole County the 21 percent drop in the number of nonwhite owner-operators between 1920 and 1925 nearly matched the drop for whites.[68] Nonwhite farmers did not escape unscathed from the agricultural troubles of the early 1920s, but their still vulnerable position was in some ways improved in relation to that of white farmers. Discrimination in lending may have insulated some nonwhites from foreclosure. In the years 1910–19, whites had access to credit to purchase land, but when the wartime boom turned into an agricultural crisis, debt wiped many out. Nonwhite farmers, poorer but often less encumbered by debt, stood ready to buy land as whites were selling.

*The Ku Klux Klan, the Tulsa Riot,
and the Future of Whiteness*

In this racially explosive context, the Ku Klux Klan changed the subject away from land. As poor whites saw their progress outstripped by blacks and Indians, the Ku Klux Klan promulgated a form of whiteness that might contain potentially insurgent agrarianism. This was a postallotment, postagrarian whiteness that was far from calling for land reform—indeed, far from asserting any kind of working-class claims through race. Its largely middle-class and affluent advocates sought to replace rural whites' class-conscious whiteness with one that would tie them to the new landlord and business elite of the state. They needed to learn to see wealthy whites as their racial brothers and social superiors rather than their class enemies.

It would be foolish to pretend that the Klan aimed simply at suppressing class conflict among whites. This was, after all, an organization that was obsessed with what it saw as threats of racial mongrelization, white women's sexual impurity, Catholic cultishness, moral decay, primitive jazz music, and obscene jazz dance—a panoply of changes that white Americans faced in the 1920s. But as Nancy MacLean has argued, these concerns were enmeshed in the fears of small-town businessmen that class conflict between the poor beneath them and the rich above would crush them. Thus in the mind of Klansmen the struggle to preserve and defend what they called decency and racial purity was inseparable from preserving their own economic position. In Oklahoma, the primary focus of these concerns was the working class. The racial, gender, and cultural elements of 1920s white supremacy cannot be reduced to economic conflict, but they cannot be understood apart from it, either.[69]

THE LARGEST EPISODE of white supremacist violence in Oklahoma in this period, one of the largest in the nation's history, was a massive attack by whites on Tulsa's black neighborhood in 1921. It was not organized or instigated by the Klan, but it demonstrates the power of white supremacy in the state, the dangers it held for African Americans, and the vigor with which African Americans sought to defend their communities. On May 30, 1921, Dick Rowland, a nineteen-year-old African American man, was accused of grabbing a seventeen-year-old white woman who was operating the elevator in which he was riding. Tulsa had a particularly large, affluent, and empowered African American community. To prevent a lynching, three carloads of African American men converged on Tulsa's courthouse, guns in tow. White Tulsans took the assembly as a provocation. Soon mobs of whites were tearing through Greenwood, Tulsa's African American neighborhood. The mob burned homes, smashed businesses, and beat African American passersby. City police cooperated with the rampage, issuing guns to civilians and deputizing members of the mob. The National Guard was called out, and instead of protecting Greenwood residents, it sought to quell the supposed "negro uprising" by disarming black Tulsans and forcing them into camps. The degree of official complicity in the riot was so high that African American Tulsans gave wide credence to rumors that airplanes were mobilized to bomb Greenwood or coordinate the attack from above. Black Tulsa fought back, led by World War I veterans: the commander of the National Guard recalled he was "surprised by the number of negroes in army attire" who wore their army-issue helmets and were "well supplied with long range Winchesters, often provided with 20 or 30 rounds of ammunition." They were vastly outnumbered and outgunned, however. The white attacks burned thirty square blocks to the ground, destroyed two square miles of property, and left more than 1,250 African American families homeless. How many black Tulsans the rioters and authorities killed is unknown. A 2001 report commissioned by the state of Oklahoma found that the number of dead was likely between 100 and 300. In the first years of the twenty-first century, Tulsans were still searching for mass graves.[70]

The destruction of Greenwood was the harbinger of racial violence in the 1920s that is most vividly associated with the rise of the second Ku Klux Klan. The 1920s Klan was a powerful force nationwide, but Oklahoma's Klan was unusually large and successful, particularly in the eastern part of the state. The Ku Klux Klan probably came to Oklahoma in 1920, when "kleagles" (organizers) from Texas arrived in Tulsa.[71] From 1921 to 1924, the Oklahoma Klan grew quickly. At its height in 1922 and 1923, the group claimed about a hundred thousand members in the state.[72] This would represent more than one in five native-born white men of native white parentage.[73] There is no way of knowing whether this was an exaggeration, but there can be no doubt that the Oklahoma Klan grew rapidly in size and power in the early 1920s. Local Klan chapters, called klaverns, developed throughout the state, especially in the towns that dotted the farms and oil districts of eastern Oklahoma.[74] The "Invisible Empire" carefully made itself into a visible political force in the state. Reports circulated that by 1923 a majority of the state legislators were Klansmen and more had been elected with Klan support.[75] Although there were Klansmen and Klan-endorsed politicians in both of the major parties, it was in the Democratic Party that the Klan achieved more prominence and power.[76]

The Oklahoma Klan was a town-based, middle-class organization that enforced its racialized, nationalistic, middle-class morality on poorer, especially rural, whites in an effort to remake their whiteness and their politics. Although Oklahoma Klansmen denounced immigrants, Catholics, Jews, and radicals, most of all they railed against what they called immorality. As is clear in the quotations from the Grand Dragon of the Oklahoma Klan that open this chapter, issues of morality, gender, and family—notably the defense of "the chastity of our women" and "the protection of our homes"—stood front and center in Klan rhetoric.[77] The enforcement of moral, gender, and family norms also dominated Klan action. One tally of Klan attacks in Oklahoma found that purported offenses against Klan morality—the possession or sale of alcohol, sexual improprieties, the nonsupport or abuse of family, or couples' living together out of wedlock—together accounted for more than 60 percent of attacks in cases in which motivation could be determined.[78]

Ku Klux Klan rally in Oklahoma, 1923. (Western History Collections, University of Oklahoma Libraries)

For all the talk of morality and patriotism, white supremacy stood quietly at the center of Klan ideology. Klansmen understood this patriotic honor and this justice as white ideals, or more properly, ideal American whiteness. As a Klansman proclaimed to a crowd of twenty-five hundred in Muskogee in May 1923, "The salvation of the country today relies on the native born, white protestant Americans."[79] The Klan's broad social crusade thus depended on what Jewett called "the maintenance of the supremacy of that race of men whose blood is not tainted by the more colorful pigments."[80] The point is essential because in Oklahoma most Klan rhetoric did not explicitly concern race and much Klan violence was directed at white Protestants.[81] These facts do not undercut the tremendous violence that the 1920s Klan wrought on African American people or religious minorities. But even when it targeted only white Protestants, Klan rhetoric and violence remained racial to the core.[82]

The Beggs Klan and the Virtue of Whiteness

The class orientation of the Klan and its pedagogy of whiteness become clearer through an examination of one local Klan: the Beggs Klan, in Okmulgee County in the heart of the old Creek Nation. Beggs was situated in the center of the oil boom area, and its recent history epitomized the changes that were wrenching east-central Oklahoma.[83] In early 1918,

Beggs had been a quiet town of about eight hundred. A series of major oil strikes in 1918 and 1919 transformed the town and the surrounding country. The town population exploded to more than two thousand as wildcatters, speculators, oil workers, and others poured into Beggs. Land that adjoined major strikes sometimes leased for more than a thousand dollars an acre, although they had recently sold for just fifteen to twenty-five dollars per acre. Forests of oil derricks sprang up in the cotton fields.[84]

The rapid rate of change created profound social tensions that town residents expressed in the language of virtue, vice, and class. The presence of prostitutes and bootleggers, the occurrence of robbery and fatal fights between oil workers, and the hijacking of automobiles alarmed many residents of towns near the oil fields. The local newspaper reported that farmers sent their daughters to live elsewhere to protect them from the perceived sexual threat these men represented. Vice seemed to other Beggs residents to characterize this new working class of "roughnecks" and "roustabouts."[85]

Divisions of class, and of town and country, separated Beggs Klansmen from their victims. Beginning in late 1921, some middle-class and wealthy residents donned the robes of the Ku Klux Klan to enforce their moral vision through attacks on oil workers and farmers.[86] Witnesses and victims of Klan attacks and other local people consistently identified middle-class and professional urban white men as the attackers. The manager of a garage, a grocer, the principal of the school, a schoolteacher, a doctor, a druggist, a hotel manager, ministers, the chief of police, policemen—with very few exceptions, these were the sorts of "exemplary members of the community" whom witnesses consistently identified as Klansmen in Beggs.[87] Its membership made the Beggs Klan representative of the Oklahoma Klan as a whole.[88] Conspicuously absent from the Klan in Beggs and elsewhere in the state were farmers. In the words of historian Carter Blue Clark, "The urban Klansman left his city to strike at the rural farmer-Socialist."[89] In Beggs, oil workers, who were the region's other large group of proletarianized workers besides tenant farmers, made up a large proportion of the victims of Klan attacks.

Klansmen paired the support of the virtuous with the discipline of those they called immoral. By parading in their robes and masks into Sunday services at area churches and leaving behind cash donations, they demonstrated their embrace of order and virtue.[90] To the immoral, they made their message just as clear. After one ritual procession and donation at the Baptist church in the nearby town of Mounds, twenty to thirty Klansmen seized and blindfolded a white oil field worker named Norman Chesser.

They took him in a car a half mile from town and told the terrified man, "We are going to teach you how to live a better life." The Klansmen informed their unwilling pupil in morality that by neglecting his widowed mother, carrying a gun, and selling whiskey he had shown his need for such a lesson. They proceeded to whip Chesser.[91]

The Klansmen's charges against this worker expressed concisely the moral vision of the Klan, a vision the group expanded on in a notice in the local newspaper. It ordered sons to stop sponging off fathers, bootleggers and "dope peddlers" to leave the area, men living with women out of wedlock to marry the women, pool halls to put a stop to gambling, "pool room loafers" to get a job, hotels housing prostitutes to clean up or close, and pimps to leave town.[92] The Beggs Klansmen put this program into action when they thrashed white men on charges of abusing their mothers, buying homemade beer, selling whiskey, or indulging in general immorality.[93] Notably, few of the Klan's moralistic decrees specified precisely for whom they were intended. They were directed, however, at the unmarked category that the Klan took as the norm: whites, particularly white men.

The Klan in Beggs and in Oklahoma targeted Native American people less frequently than African Americans.[94] "The Indian" played a lesser role in the ideology of whiteness of the 1920s than in that of earlier decades. In the minds of many white Oklahomans, Native Americans had become picturesque reminders of a frontier past, not a real threat to white power. Some Native Americans did fall victim to the Klan's ire.[95] Yet Klansmen and other white supremacists in Oklahoma no longer defined whiteness in opposition to Native Americans. Whites in Oklahoma shifted the unenviable role as foil to whiteness from Native people to African Americans. African Americans were particular targets of Klan violence, and that violence was directed squarely at maintaining racial order. The beating of African American prisoner Charles Smith in 1922 for insubordination to his jailers, for example, demonstrated publicly that flouting white supremacy would bring dire results.[96]

Still, attacks on whites constituted the majority of documented Klan attacks in Beggs and elsewhere in Oklahoma.[97] Klansmen attacked working-class whites to teach and enforce whiteness. On the one hand, white supremacists in Oklahoma associated whiteness with virtue. By attacking working-class whites who fell short of their standard of virtue, Klansmen were defending what they understood to be true whiteness. On the other hand, white supremacists in Oklahoma associated vice with African Americans and punished whites who tainted their racial purity in their contacts with African Americans. In their newspaper manifesto, the Beggs Klan warned "that white men who associate with niggers will receive the same consideration as the niggers."[98] For example, masked men seized O. E. Arnold from his home in Beggs, hauled him to a pasture, and beat him with a piece of steel. The mob accused him of buying illegal whiskey and beer from African Americans before they let him go.[99] Another white Beggs resident, Leonard Matthews, was similarly kidnapped and thrashed, this time on charges of associating with African Americans and perhaps consorting with an African American woman.[100] The point is that, to the Klan, working-class whites were not acting white enough. To the Klan, being white was not just an issue of who your parents were. It was also a matter of how you acted. Put another way, race was a matter not merely of biology but of performance. Klansmen were attempting to enforce middle-class whiteness on the white working class.

This effort to narrow the bounds of the white race was a local manifestation of a regional and national phenomenon. The whiteness of southern, rural, poor whites was coming very much into doubt in the second and third decades of the century, under the influence of the "racial science" of eugenics. In the cotton country of central Texas, so much like the cotton country of eastern Oklahoma, white academics and politicians and planters cast a doubtful eye on poor white farmers and farm laborers, whom they considered nearly as lazy, stupid, physically repugnant, and immoral as African Americans and Mexicans. Historian Neil Foley has traced how more-affluent Texans came, in fact, to wonder just how white poor whites truly were. The situation was not unique to the South, the Southwest, or cotton-producing areas, however. Indeed, doubts about the racial capacities of poor whites drew inspiration from a host of eugenicist studies. Among the most famous was Henry Goddard's writings on a poor white clan in New Jersey, which concluded that half of the family was inherently "feeble-minded" and easily led into a life that is "vicious, immoral, and criminal."[101]

In Oklahoma, the political stakes in the battle over whiteness are particularly clear. The violent enforcement of this standard of middle-class whiteness was an attempt to contain the intense class-based opposition that had arisen in Oklahoma in the decade after statehood. White agrarians and labor activists in Oklahoma had demonstrated a dangerous tendency to think of class in terms of economic interest, a tendency that had led poor whites to cooperate with African Americans and Native Americans to confront the power of wealthier whites. The Klan's moralistic campaign sought to undercut such radical potential by convincing poor whites that to maintain their racial status they had to act like proper whites. To act like proper whites, they had to comport themselves like middle-class whites. And to do that, class could no longer play the role in their whiteness that it had for white agrarians. At the most basic level, the Klan said that poor whites should act respectably in order to preserve their race, not act radically in order to defend their class.

The White Class Politics of the Klan War

White farmers and workers, however, resisted the Klan's effort to suppress the class consciousness embedded in agrarian and working-class whiteness. White agrarianism's continued vigor and its deep dedication to white supremacy came to the fore in a political battle over the role of the Klan in Democratic politics in the state. In 1923, Democratic Oklahoma City mayor Jack Walton was elected governor with the support of a group of former Socialist leaders, labor activists, and agrarians working within the Democratic Party. Walton's victory was a challenge to the rising, conservative, business-oriented faction of the Democratic Party, a faction that Walton and others identified with the Klan. He attempted to crush the Klan (and thereby boost his political fortunes) in 1923. To eradicate it, he declared martial law, first in Okmulgee County, then in Tulsa County, and finally in the state as a whole.[102]

White farmers and workers manifested the class-based, agrarian antagonism they felt for the Invisible Empire and its brand of whiteness in their support for Walton's war on the Klan. G. R. Cundiff of Choctaw County swore to Walton that "the farmer of the grass root" was on his side in the Klan fight, urging the governor, "Give the KKK's H——!"[103] S. M. Abbott, Wallace Brown, and W. H. Deshazer pledged their support of his anti-Klan crusade "as farmers, and as Citizens of the State of Oklahoma."[104] These men evidently voiced the feelings of many of their neighbors, since rural districts gave their votes to Walton and the Reconstruction League while voting against Klan-affiliated or Klan-endorsed candidates.[105] Opposition to the Klan and support for Walton was broad among farmers: members of the moderate Farmers Union offered Walton their support in the battle, but so did farmers in the radical Farm-Labor Union, which suggested that laborers (including "dirt farmers") and wage workers mount a boycott to fight the Klan.[106]

This opposition to the Klan aimed to defend the white working class and its whiteness. Gardner Knupp, a farmer from Wagoner County, believed that farmers were "slaves to the capi[ta]list," and their hope lay in men such as Walton who were willing to challenge the Klan. Knupp's evocation of slavery reveals the race politics enmeshed in white agrarians' opposition to the Klan. It echoes the language of white workingmen in the antebellum era. Historian David R. Roediger has argued that when such men voiced fears of enslavement by employers they were expressing their concern that their disadvantage as a class threatened their status as white men. Similarly, many whites in Oklahoma perceived the Klan in the 1920s as an attack by white men—small-town landlords, merchants, and professionals as well as urban businessmen—on white farmers and workers and opposed it as such. To enforce class unity, farmers opposed to the Klan adopted one of the same tactics as the Working Class Union when they threatened to burn the homes of tenants who rented from Klansmen.[107]

Defending their class interests meant defending their whiteness as well. Despite the efforts of the Klan, race and class fused to form one identity for these white agrarians. This fusion is obscured by the fact that such men took their whiteness as so fundamental and so much the norm that they did not name it. Leaving the racial category "white" unmarked expresses how powerful a thing whiteness was. When R. C. Tyre championed the rights of "the good laber clase," or when Knupp, Abbott, Brown and Deshazer expressed their fears for the future of "the farmers," they did not need to identify the race of the people about whom they were speaking. Their whiteness constituted part of their class identity.[108] Fighting the Klan on the grounds of class meant also opposing it on the grounds of their own white race.

White agrarian enemies of the Klan were by and large champions of white supremacy, and none was more eloquent in this belief than Walton himself. Walton mocked the Klan's claim to advocate for white supremacy. "The supremacy of the white race needs no advocacy," he declared. Walton argued that it would be as reasonable for the Klan "to say that it advocates or intends the sun to shine as to say that its purposes are to maintain the supremacy of the white race." The sun did shine; whites were supreme. He took pains, though, to honor the memory of the Reconstruction-era Klan. This "little band of heroes" had saved the South from "the horror of the domination of an ignorant, misguided and superstitious race"—that is, African Americans. Walton opposed the Klan of the 1920s on the grounds of defending religious freedom and even the rights of ethnic minorities like German Americans, but not on the basis of protecting the rights of African Americans.[109] Furthermore, like the many Oklahoma farmers who endorsed his battle against the Klan, Walton generally did not make pronouncements about white supremacy because he and they took it for granted.

The Titan of the Oklahoma Klan did not take white supremacy for granted because he believed it was threatened by class conflict. He proclaimed that his organization aimed at nothing less than "to unify all antagonistic forces," to forge a union of "labor and capital, Democrats and Republicans."[110] The aim was the safe unity of whiteness, which required suppressing conflicts among whites. The promise of white landownership had not been kept. Allotment did not create a broad class of property owners but a limited class of landlords and a large class of tenants, and a smaller group of landowning farmers. Oklahoma now had a white proletariat that knew that it was not just a delayed or frustrated yeomanry. Whiteness represented for some whites the hope to contain the conflict between affluent town-based whites and the restive white agrarians and white workers of Oklahoma in the 1920s. Whiteness contained the possibility of holding off the danger of poorer whites joining with blacks and Indians in a class alliance. The nationalist whiteness of the Klan offered white unity within safe middle-class whiteness. It offered its champions in the Klan a way past the cultural, social, and class conflict of the period: the tumult of the oil boomtowns, the revindication of African American rights, urbanization, labor conflict, and especially the kind of interracial, class-based, insurgencies like the Working Class Union and the Green Corn Rebellion. Whiteness offered them the hope of a safely conservative peace.

The mid- and late 1920s brought that peace after the violent years that stretched from the Green Corn Rebellion, through wartime repression, the Tulsa riot, and the attacks of the Klan. Both the Invisible Empire and its white agrarian opponents faded in power in Oklahoma.[111] White small-town merchants and professionals and their white big-city businessmen allies successfully won the battle to secure their power in a new economy where oil and industry had begun to overshadow agriculture. By recasting whiteness to survive the end of the dream of a white landowning yeomanry, middle-class and affluent white Oklahomans had secured the new order of postallotment Oklahoma. Though the Klan dwindled, the battle for whiteness that it represented had been won for the time being. Not that the Klan had brought an end to moral disorder, eliminated African American resistance, or succeeded in making all whites accept its understanding of patriotic whiteness. Nor was farm tenant politics definitively defeated, as the

Southern Tenant Farmers Union and agrarian Oklahoma politicians would demonstrate a decade later. But the postallotment economic and political order had been secured.

Radical politics did not fall into disarray only in Oklahoma but nationwide in the 1920s. And while repression is undoubtedly part of the story, it is not all of it. The kind of unifying, nationalist whiteness that the Klan had advocated gained power in Oklahoma and the United States in the 1920s. When white farmers or workers accepted this racial ideology, it made it difficult for them to make or to heed explicit appeals to class politics. Class politics lay outside the proper performance of whiteness, and to engage in a class-based insurgency would be a threat to the racial standing of white working-class people, whether rural or urban. The Klan and its allies won a significant victory in the 1920s. Its campaign for a unifying, nationalist whiteness could not eliminate white working-class challenges to the political and economic order of the day. It did, however, succeed in discouraging white working-class politics in years to come in a place the Klan called "WHITE mans Country."[112]

Newtown

UNSETTLING OKLAHOMA, UNSETTLING AMERICA

By the late 1930s and early 1940s, a visitor to Oklahoma could be forgiven for thinking that the paradoxes and conundrums of the past were as dead and buried as the Indian leaders of the previous century. Wasn't it obvious what it meant to own land? Wasn't it clear who was Creek, who was white, and who was black? Didn't everyone know that there was only one nation here and that was America? All these questions might seem part of the remote past, like the larger-than-life characters who animate the conflicts of late nineteenth-century Creek history. Those figures had been replaced by Indians who might seem disappointingly familiar by the 1930s—poor and middle-class Indian people like Sallie Johnson, who lived at Hanna, or the Gouge brothers, who lived nearby, or Agnes Kelley living in Okmulgee. These Creek people simply lived in Oklahoma, reminders of what was, in the romantic imagining, a much more interesting but distant frontier past.

But if we go beyond the most casual glance, individuals like these indicate the surprising proximity of the past and its pertinence to the present—whether that present was the 1930s or our day. Sallie Johnson was the granddaughter of Hotulke Emarthla (also known as Edward Bullett), the *micco* of Okchiye who rekindled his town's fire on the ashes he had carried from Alabama to Indian Territory, reestablishing a new ceremonial ground so that the town might live on in the new land.[1] The Gouge brothers were the nephews of Opothleyahola, the Loyal Creek leader during the Civil War.[2] Agnes Kelley was the daughter of Samuel Checote, leader of the Confederate-allied Creeks.[3] The nineteenth-century Creek past was not terribly distant after all. It was as close and as easily recounted as memories of parents, aunts, uncles, and grandparents.

And just as the leaders of the past still were present in the stories told about them, so were the issues of property, race, and nationhood that had run through their political battles. A closer look at one family can open a window onto the history of race, nation, and land in the Creek Nation and eastern Oklahoma. By taking the time to examine the history of one family and the place they lived, we can perceive the intimate relationship between race, nation, and landownership in this region. And when we consider how the encounter with that history and that place can unsettle our established notions, we can see that the study of race, nation, and landownership in Oklahoma can disrupt our understandings of the American past and compel us to think again about America and its nations.

RUFUS COX WAS BORN in June 1949 and lived with his parents on the grounds of the Newtown Creek Methodist Church outside Okmulgee. When I was fortunate enough to interview him for this book, he explained that about a dozen Creek families called the church grounds home during his boyhood. They lived in a variety of rough camp houses. Some, like the Coxes, dwelled in log structures. Others' homes were built from milled lumber. But all the homes were old and in various states of disrepair. None had electricity or running water. The people who lived in them were poor, so poor that they had come to live on the grounds of the Creek church. The Newtown church grounds were, without a doubt, a rural settlement of impoverished Indians. But the residents were also individuals with a very particular lineage and relationship to the church grounds on which they had come to live.[4]

To tell the story of Rufus Cox's ancestors and how he came to spend his boyhood living on a church ground is to summarize much of the history of the wrenching changes that eastern Oklahoma witnessed from the late nineteenth century to the 1940s. Rufus (everyone called him "Buddy") was born into a family with an illustrious past. His paternal great-grandparents personified the landed wealth and political power of the post–Civil War Creek elite. Great-grandfather Samuel Haynes hailed from a Creek family that had prospered in commerce and controlled large amounts of land. Haynes, an educated man who practiced law, was a member of the Creek council and served as the last chief justice of the Creek high court.[5] As was befitting a man of his stature in the nation, he married Sarah Lerblance,

In June 1939, Lee Russell took this photograph of a Native American boy standing between portraits of his ancestors near Sallisaw, in the Cherokee Nation. While the boy is probably Cherokee, the photo suggests the same kind of proximity to the past that Buddy Cox grew up with about seventy miles to the west, on the grounds of the Newtown Creek Methodist Church. (Library of Congress, Prints & Photographs Division, FSA/OWI Collection, LC-USF34-033721-D)

daughter of Elijah Hermigine Lerblance, a wealthy Creek from Checotah.[6] In addition to other assets, by the end of the nineteenth century Lerblance owned a half interest (with his relation, W. E. Gentry) in a firm having 2,500 head of cattle, a general store in Checotah with merchandise valued at $12,000, and a cotton gin.[7] During his tenure as a judge in the 1890s, Lerblance had demonstrated his sympathies for pasture owners who rented out land for the use of non-Indians' cattle.[8] For all their class similarities, however, cultural differences did exist between the bride's and groom's families. The Lerblances had been one of the first Creek families to embrace Christianity, but the Hayneses were (according to Buddy Cox) one of the last among the elite to make that change. Still, in accordance with Sarah's wishes, Samuel Haynes built a one-room cabin at his wife's church where she could stay during revivals.

When allotment came, the Hayneses' fortunes rapidly began to turn, exemplifying the decline of Creek wealth and power in the new state of Oklahoma. Each member of the family took an allotment. Samuel and Sarah's daughter Stella chose hers near the town of Beggs, close to the allotments of several family members. But allotment brought an end to the kind of ranching and extensive farming that had profited wealthy Creeks in the nineteenth century. According to Buddy, the elite Creek families had been accustomed to living well prior to allotment, and they tried to continue to do so after allotment, supplementing their diminished incomes by spending their savings and selling their assets as time went on. A substantial section of the growing town of Okmulgee was built on twenty acres of land that Sam Haynes sold to a white man.[9] Soon, the people who had occupied the pinnacle of the social hierarchy in the Creek Nation became, from the point of view of white outsiders, relatively unexceptional Indians of modest means in the new state of Oklahoma. Within the Creek world, their position was still important. Samuel Haynes chaired the Creek House of Kings from 1901 into the 1930s, and in 1933 he visited Washington to meet with John Collier, chief of the Bureau of Indian Affairs.[10] Economically, however, the position of Creeks like Haynes had declined, and they felt this decline acutely. Buddy remembers that his grandparents' generation, such as his Grandma Stella, used to comment that it was better never to have had money than to have had it and lost it.

An indication of the family's changed position can be found in the marriage that Stella Haynes made. Whereas her mother had married a wealthy Creek legislator and jurist, Stella wed a white telegraph lineman named Porter Cox, who, like so many other settlers, arrived in the Creek Nation in the 1890s. Similarly, the fate of Stella's allotment land serves as a reminder of how the allotment process made land loss possible. Stella sold her allotment to bankroll a dairy farm for herself and her husband to work. They did fairly well in dairying (with Porter allegedly supplementing their earnings by selling bootleg liquor in the dry state) until Porter died of pneumonia in 1927. At that point, times turned harder for Stella. The dairy farm failed, and her children grew up in dire poverty. They were assisted through the hardest times by the kindness of Creeks who not only still retained their allotments but also were so fortunate as to have profitable oil reserves beneath them. The generosity of these allottees sustained many in the Creek community through the depression of the 1930s.

Stella's son Rufus (Buddy's father) worked his way up from construction work to electrical work and then fought in the Pacific in World War II. Upon his return, he married a local woman, Dorothy Kailey. Dorothy, who also grew up in the Okmulgee area, appeared white to most people but had some Cherokee and Choctaw ancestry. This helped her to be accepted among Creeks, but more important was the fact that she learned quite a bit of the Creek language. She had plenty of opportunity to practice it because the couple found it necessary to move to the Newtown Creek Methodist Church grounds, where Creek was frequently spoken. Rufus's wages in construction and Dorothy's earnings from taking in laundry and waitressing were insufficient to afford much of a home, a problem likely worsened by the housing crunch that hit much of the nation after the war. As a result, Rufus and Dorothy moved into the log camp house that Rufus's grandmother had used during revivals at the church. It was there that Buddy Cox lived the first years of his life.

THE MEANING OF that cabin for the family had changed in the roughly fifty years between the turn of the century, when Samuel Haynes had built it for his Christian bride, and the post–World War II years, when Rufus and Dorothy Cox made it their home. When the family had enjoyed landed affluence, the house had been a convenient little cabin where Sarah and others could stay to be near the church and socialize with other Creek people. Allotment, however, had shrunk the wealth of the family. It provided each person with one piece of property, one chip of capital. Stella had played and lost that chip when she tried to turn it into a dairy farm that would sustain her family into the future. As the wealth of the family diminished, the importance of the camp house at the Newtown church grew. Rufus and Dorothy did not, like Samuel and Sarah Haynes, have land on which they could live. They did not have capital to liquidate and reinvest in starting a farm, as had Stella Cox. They were landless people who lived by their labor. When they could not find jobs or did not make enough at that labor, they had to move into a cabin that had once been just a convenient place for Rufus's grandmother to spend a few nights.

It is strange but nonetheless true that one of the reasons that Rufus and Dorothy Cox could still live in the camp house was that the family had never owned the land on which it stood. The grounds belonged to the New-town Creek Methodist Church, not to any individual in particular. Thus the land was relatively protected from alienation. No individual could sell it for money to invest or cash on which to live. No individual could be tricked out of the land by marking an "X" or signing a paper that was purportedly a lease but really a deed. And as church property, the grounds could not be taxed and could therefore not be lost in a tax forfeiture proceeding. The church grounds, in a greatly diminished way, came as close as was possible in the 1940s to playing the role that the Creek commons had prior to allot-ment. This was land on which members of the community—in this case, the members of the church—could make a secure home for themselves. But just as the meaning of the Cox camp house had changed in fifty years, so too had the meaning of the church grounds. Once they had been just a small patch of a Creek Nation that spread for thousands of square miles all around. Now they were an island of Creek land in the middle of the state of Oklahoma.

When we turn from the churchyard to the church congregation, we are also reminded of some of the racial complexities of the history of the re-gion. Buddy remembers that the church played a part in his learning about the history of the interaction of people of indigenous and African descent in the Creek Nation. Two of the members of the church were a very old black Creek couple. The church services were conducted in the Creek language, and over time it dawned on the little boy that this couple spoke, prayed, and sang in Creek as well as the other old people around, and the old man could not even speak English. This surprised him because all the other black people he had seen spoke in English. He asked why these people spoke Creek, and he was told, "Because they are some of the original Freed-mans." He recalled, "That was when I learned what a Freedman was." This was a lesson that involved learning about slavery in the Creek Nation and that hinted at the ambiguities of racial identity that the Jim Crow signs on display around Okmulgee's business district sought to deny.

Those ambiguities existed within Buddy Cox's own family as well, as he would find out over time. In his adulthood, an interest in the history of his family led Cox to make a curious discovery. Looking at microfilm of the manuscript census from 1910, he found the entries for his grandparents: there was his grandfather, Porter Cox, listed as a white man, and there was his wife, Stella, listed as an Indian woman. All was as he expected. Going to the next decennial census, however, Buddy was taken aback: every member of the family—father, mother, and children—was listed as a "mulatto."[11] What had happened between 1910 and 1920? The family's ancestry obviously had not changed in those ten years, and yet the words projected on the microfilm reader's screen clearly indicated that something had happened.

The census enumerator's markings brought back memories. Buddy had heard whispers that the Coxes were part black. He had never really thought much of it because the whispers, coming from Creeks, were not particularly unusual. All Creeks knew that many people who lived their lives as Creek Indians, not as "Negroes," had some fraction of black ancestry. Among Creeks it was a matter worthy of comment and perhaps derision that a person was part black, but it was so common that there was nothing particularly shameful about this information. Nonetheless, it seemed surprising to Buddy and his family that, whereas Stella was listed as "mulatto," only a few lines away on the census other members of her birth family appeared as "Indian."

This difference in racial status, coupled with other mysteries about his grandfather's background, led Buddy Cox to a rather startling inference: perhaps the alleged black ancestry in his family came not from the Creek Haynes side, as he had assumed, but from the supposedly white Cox side. After all, when Porter Cox had come from Tennessee and began living as a white man, no one knew anything about his faraway kin. Was he, perhaps, a black person who was passing himself off as white? Was that the reason that someone had drawn a hat on his portrait photograph—to hide suspiciously kinky hair? The genealogist reasoned that people in Okmulgee may have found out his grandfather's secret sometime between 1910 and 1920, perhaps from another migrant from Porter Cox's Tennessee hometown. The census enumerator might then have assigned this newly discovered racial status to Cox's children and wife, as well. The explanation, while plausible, is probably unprovable, and the reason for the temporary change in his family's racial categorization in the census remains unknown.

It is nonetheless a reminder that the racial complexity of the region and the ambiguities that shot through its racial order between the 1830s and the 1930s are less exceptional than they might at first appear. After all, the presumed source of Porter Cox's racial ambiguity was Tennessee, not Oklahoma. Although the history of the Creek Nation and the history of eastern Oklahoma have certain particularities, they do not differ fundamentally from developments in other areas of the United States. Among the Creeks, the presence of African American citizens made enrollment a process that was particularly fraught, but for all Indian peoples enrollment and allotment gave power to the politics of blood and the language of race. Lines of ethnicity that divided people of African descent from one another were particularly sharp in this region in the first two decades of the twentieth century, and white racism elicited an especially strong nationalist response from black people in eastern Oklahoma, but the division of ethnicity and the unity of nation characterized African American communities elsewhere, as well. In no other state did the Ku Klux Klan enjoy such success on the heels of the suppression of so vigorous a Socialist Party, but patriotic and white supremacist racism obscured divisions of class among whites throughout the nation after 1919. The Creek Nation, and later east-central Oklahoma, was a place unlike any other in the United States, but the politics of race, nation, and landownership that unfolded there shed light on the historical transformation of the United States in the nineteenth and twentieth centuries.

Still, while the history of eastern Oklahoma may not be unique, it is unsettling. Buddy Cox thought he knew who was who and what was what in the history of his family, but the historical record surprised him. Indeed, the historical record of the region disrupts many common narratives of American history. It documents that race was fluid, that the boundaries of the nation were long contested, and that the relationship between race and nation shifted and evolved in the contest over the land that Cox's ancestors called their own. Buddy Cox encountered the unexpected racial complexity of the Creek Nation as a child in his experiences with black members of his Creek community and as an adult in his discovery of the inconsistencies of census racial classifications. He has reacted by digging deeply into Creek history in Oklahoma in his effort to understand his family's past. By disrupting the expected narratives of the American past, the history of the Creek Nation and eastern Oklahoma can spur us to try to understand how Americans of all races have lived the abstractions we call race, nation, and class.

Notes

ABBREVIATIONS

Cruce Papers	Lee Cruce Papers, General Correspondence (1913),
	Record Group 8-B-1, Oklahoma State Archives, Oklahoma City
IPH	Works Progress Administration, *Indian Pioneer History*
	Collection, edited by Grant Foreman (1937; Oklahoma City:
	Oklahoma Historical Society Microfilm Publications, 1978);
	notes reference volume numbers, not microfilm reel numbers
NA	National Archives, Washington, D.C., and College Park, Maryland
NA-FW	National Archives and Records Administration Center,
	Fort Worth, Texas
OHS	Oklahoma Historical Society, Manuscripts Division,
	Oklahoma City
OSA	Oklahoma State Archives, Oklahoma City
RG 33	Record Group 33: Records of the Extension Service
RG 75	Record Group 75: Records of the Bureau of Indian Affairs
RG 83	Record Group 83: Records of the Bureau of
	Agricultural Economics
T-881	*Extension Service Annual Reports: Oklahoma, 1909–1944*,
	RG 33: Records of the Extension Service, National Archives
	Microcopy T-881
USDA	United States Department of Agriculture
WHC	Western History Collections, University of Oklahoma, Norman

ACKNOWLEDGMENTS

1 Mary Kawena Pukui, *'Ōlelo No'eau: Hawaiian Proverbs and Poetical Sayings* (Honolulu: Bishop Museum Press, 1983), 67.

INTRODUCTION

1 Black belt: "In the Black Belt of Okfuskee County, Oklahoma," *Boley Progress*, January 13, 1910. White man's country: Sarah Deutsch, "Being American in Boley, Oklahoma," in *Beyond Black and White: Race, Ethnicity, and Gender in the U.S. South and Southwest*, ed. Stephanie Cole and Alison M. Parker (College Station: Texas A&M University Press, 2004) 121 n. 44. Indian homeland: Ronald N. Satz, *American Indian Policy in the Jacksonian Era* (Lincoln: University of Nebraska Press, 1974), 130. Black promised land: Jimmie L. Franklin, "Black Oklahomans: An Essay on the Quest for Freedom," in *Alternative Oklahoma: Contrarian Views of the Sooner State*, ed. Davis D. Joyce (Norman: University of Oklahoma Press, 2007), 38. White heartland: Lynn M. Itagaki, "Transgressing Race and Community in Chester Himes's 'If He Hollers Let Him Go,'" *African American Review* 37 (Spring 2003): 74.

2 John Steinbeck, *The Grapes of Wrath* (1939; New York: Viking, 1986), 42–43.

3 In Creek County, for example, the 1930 population of 64,115 fell to 55,503 by 1940 and to 43,143 by 1950. University of Virginia, Geospatial and Statistical Data Center, "Historical Census Browser," <http://fisher.lib.virginia.edu/collections/stats/histcensus/index.html> (July 20, 2008).

4 Michael Omi and Howard Winant, *Racial Formation in the United States: From the 1960s to the 1990s* (New York: Routledge, 1994); Theodore Allen, *The Invention of the White Race* (London: Verso, 1994); Karen Brodkin, *How Jews Became White Folks and What That Says about Race in America* (New Brunswick, N.J.: Rutgers University Press, 1998); Matthew Frye Jacobson, *Whiteness of a Different Color: European Immigrants and the Alchemy of Race* (Cambridge, Mass.: Harvard University Press, 1999).

5 The major exception is Neil Foley, *The White Scourge: Mexicans, Blacks, and Poor Whites in Texas Cotton Culture* (Berkeley: University of California Press, 1997), which considers the way whites imagined their racial difference from Mexicans and African Americans though landownership and landlessness. My work benefits from Foley's insights to place white racial and national self-constructions in historical dialogue with those of Creeks and African Americans. See also María E. Montoya, *Translating Property: The Maxwell Land Grant and the Conflict over Land in the American West, 1840–1900* (Lawrence: University Press of Kansas, 2005), 13.

6 See, for example, Edward J. Blum, *Reforging the White Republic: Race, Religion, and American Nationalism, 1865–1898* (Baton Rouge: Louisiana State University Press, 2005); Gary Gerstle, *American Crucible: Race and Nation in the Twentieth Century* (Princeton, N.J.: Princeton University Press, 2001); Rogan Kersh, *Dreams of a More Perfect Union* (Ithaca, N.Y.: Cornell University Press, 2001); Cecilia Elizabeth O'Leary, *To Die For: The Paradox of American Patriotism* (Princeton, N.J.: Princeton University Press, 1999); Noah Pickus, *True Faith and Allegiance: Immigration and American Civic Nationalism* (Princeton, N.J.: Princeton University Press. 2005); Lyn Spillman, *Nation and Commemoration: Creating National Identities in the United*

States and Australia (Cambridge: Cambridge University Press, 1997); and David Waldstreicher, *In the Midst of Perpetual Fetes: The Making of American Nationalism, 1776–1820* (Chapel Hill: Omohundro Institute of Early American History and Culture/University of North Carolina Press, 1997). Francesca Morgan makes a significant contribution by demonstrating the place of African American clubwomen in the broader history of American nationalism. Francesca Morgan, *Women and Patriotism in Jim Crow America* (Chapel Hill: University of North Carolina Press, 2005).

7 Edmund Sears Morgan, *American Slavery, American Freedom: The Ordeal of Colonial Virginia* (New York: Norton, 1975). Other landmark works in the study of how American nationalism was elaborated in opposition to racial "others" include John Higham, *Strangers in the Land: Patterns of American Nativism, 1860–1925* (New Brunswick, N.J.: Rutgers University Press, 1955); Reginald Horsman, *Race and Manifest Destiny: The Origins of American Racial Anglo-Saxonism* (Cambridge, Mass.: Harvard University Press, 1981); and Gail Bederman, *Manliness and Civilization: A Cultural History of Gender and Race in the United States, 1880–1917* (Chicago: University of Chicago Press, 1995).

8 Foley, *White Scourge*; Brodkin, *How Jews Became White Folks*; Noel Ignatiev, *How the Irish Became White* (New York: Routledge, 1995); David R. Roediger, *The Wages of Whiteness: Race and the Making of the American Working Class* (London: Verso, 1991); Omi and Winant, *Racial Formation in the United States*; Barbara J. Fields, "Ideology and Race in America," in *Region, Race, and Reconstruction: Essays in Honor of C. Vann Woodward*, ed. J. Morgan Kousser and James M. McPherson (New York: Oxford University Press, 1982); Matthew Frye Jacobson, *Barbarian Virtues: The United States Encounters Foreign Peoples at Home and Abroad, 1876–1917* (New York: Hill and Wang, 2001); Jacobson, *Whiteness of a Different Color*.

9 George M. Fredrickson, *The Black Image in the White Mind: The Debate on Afro-American Character and Destiny, 1817–1914* (New York: Harper and Row, 1971); Winthrop D. Jordan, *White over Black: American Attitudes toward the Negro, 1550–1812* (Chapel Hill: University of North Carolina Press, 1968); Gary B. Nash and Richard Weiss, eds., *The Great Fear: Race in the Mind of America* (New York: Holt, Rinehart and Winston, 1970); Ronald T. Takaki, *Iron Cages: Race and Culture in Nineteenth-Century America* (New York: Knopf, 1979); Richard Drinnon, *Facing West: The Metaphysics of Indian-Hating and Empire-Building* (Norman: University of Oklahoma Press, 1997); Alden T. Vaughn, "From White Man to Redskin: Changing Anglo-American Perceptions of the American Indian," *American Historical Review* 87 (October 1992).

10 Mia Bay, *The White Image in the Black Mind: African-American Ideas about White People, 1830–1925* (New York: Oxford University Press, 2000); Nancy Shoemaker, "How Indians Got to Be Red," *American Historical Review* 102 (June 1997). On the creation of identities in opposition to "the Other," see Tzvetan Todorov, *The Conquest of America: The Question of the Other* (New York: Harper and Row, 1984).

11 David E. Wilkins, *American Indian Politics and the American Political System* (Lanham, Md.: Rowman and Littlefield, 2002), 45–66.

12 A foundational work on "tribalism" is D'Arcy McNickle, *Native American Tribalism:*

Indian Survivals and Renewals (New York: Oxford University Press, 1973). James Clifford has influenced efforts to bring historical and political context to the traditional ethnographic interest in identity. James Clifford, *The Predicament of Culture: Twentieth Century Ethnography, Literature, and Art* (Cambridge, Mass.: Harvard University Press, 1988), 277–346.

13 Graham D. Taylor, *The New Deal and American Indian Tribalism: The Administration of the Indian Reorganization Act, 1935–45* (Lincoln: University of Nebraska Press, 1980); William T. Hagan, "Tribalism Rejuvenated: The Native American since the Era of Termination," *Western Historical Quarterly* 12 (January 1981); William T. Hagan, "Full Blood, Mixed Blood, Generic, and Ersatz: The Problem of Indian Identity," *Arizona and the West* 27 (Winter 1985); Loretta Fowler, *Shared Symbols, Contested Meanings: Gros Ventre Culture and History, 1778–1984* (Ithaca, N.Y.: Cornell University Press, 1987); Melissa L. Meyer, *The White Earth Tragedy: Ethnicity and Dispossession at a Minnesota Anishinaabe Reservation, 1889–1920* (Lincoln: University of Nebraska Press, 1994); Alexandra Harmon, "Tribal Enrollment Councils: Lessons on Law and Indian Identity," *Western Historical Quarterly* 32 (Summer 2001); Alexandra Harmon, *Indians in the Making: Ethnic Relations and Indian Identities around Puget Sound* (Berkeley: University of California Press, 1998).

14 On pan-Indian movements, see Hazel W. Hertzberg, *The Search for an American Indian Identity: Modern Pan-Indian Movements* (Syracuse, N.Y.: Syracuse University Press, 1971); Gregory Evans Dowd, *A Spirited Resistance: The North American Indian Struggle for Unity, 1745–1815* (Baltimore: Johns Hopkins University Press, 1992); R. David Edmunds, *Tecumseh and the Quest for Indian Leadership* (Boston: Little, Brown, 1984); R. David Edmunds, *The Shawnee Prophet* (Lincoln: University of Nebraska Press, 1983).

15 Craig S. Womack, *Red on Red: Native American Literary Separatism* (Minneapolis: University of Minnesota Press, 1999), 14. See also Craig S. Womack, "The Integrity of American Indian Claims (or, How I Learned to Stop Worrying and Love My Hybridity)," in *American Indian Literary Nationalism*, ed. Jace Weaver, Craig S. Womack, and Robert Allen Warrior (Albuquerque: University of New Mexico Press, 2006).

16 Michael A. Gomez, *Exchanging Our Country Marks: The Transformation of African Identities in the Colonial and Antebellum South* (Chapel Hill: University of North Carolina Press, 1998); Sterling Stuckey, *Slave Culture: Nationalist Theory and the Foundations of Black America* (New York: Oxford University Press, 1987); Sidney J. Lemelle and Robin D. G. Kelley, eds., *Imagining Home: Class, Culture, and Nationalism in the African Diaspora* (London: Verso, 1994).

17 Winston James, *Holding Aloft the Banner of Ethiopia: Caribbean Radicalism in Early Twentieth-Century America* (London: Verso, 1998); Irma Watkins-Owens, *Blood Relations: Caribbean Immigrants and the Harlem Community, 1900–1930* (Bloomington: Indiana University Press, 1996); Philip Kasinitz, *Caribbean New York: Black Immigrants and the Politics of Race* (Ithaca, N.Y.: Cornell University Press, 1992).

18 A number of books and anthologies have appeared, including Kenneth Wiggins Porter, *The Black Seminoles: History of a Freedom-Seeking People* (Gainesville: University Press of Florida, 1996); Claudio Saunt, *A New Order of Things: Property, Power,*

and the Transformation of the Creek Indians, 1733–1816 (Cambridge: Cambridge University Press, 1999); James Brooks, ed., *Confounding the Color Line: The Indian-Black Experience in North America* (Lincoln: University of Nebraska Press, 2002); Claudio Saunt, *Black, White, and Indian: Race and the Unmaking of an American Family* (New York: Oxford University Press, 2005); Tiya Miles, *Ties That Bind: The Story of an Afro-Cherokee Family in Slavery and Freedom* (Berkeley: University of California Press, 2005); Tiya Miles and Sharon Patricia Holland, *Crossing Waters, Crossing Worlds: The African Diaspora in Indian Country* (Durham, N.C.: Duke University Press, 2006); Gary Zellar, *African Creeks: Estelvste and the Creek Nation* (Norman: University of Oklahoma Press, 2007); and Celia Naylor, *African Cherokees in Indian Country* (Chapel Hill: University of North Carolina Press, 2008). Unfortunately, Zellar's and Naylor's important contributions appeared too late for their insights to be incorporated into the present volume.

19 Muscogee (Creek) Nation, *Constitution of the Muscogee (Creek) Nation* ([Okmulgee, Okla.]: Muskogee (Creek) Nation, 1979), art. II, sec. 1.

CHAPTER 1

1 Benjamin Hawkins, *Letters, Journals, and Writings of Benjamin Hawkins*, ed. C. L. Grant (Savannah, Ga.: Beehive Press, 1980), 80j–81j.

2 This paragraph depends on a number of depictions of Creek village fields in the eighteenth and early nineteenth centuries. William Bartram, *Travels through North & South Carolina, Georgia, East & West Florida, the Cherokee Country, the Extensive Territories of the Muscogulges, or Creek Confederacy, and the Country of the Chactaws; Containing an Account of the Soil and Natural Productions of Those Regions, Together with Observations on the Manners of the Indians* (Philadelphia: James and Johnston, 1791), 193–94, 510; William Bartram, "Observations on the Creek and Cherokee Indians" (1789), in *William Bartram on the Southeastern Indians*, ed. Gregory A. Waselkov and Kathryn E. Holland Braund (Lincoln: University of Nebraska Press, 1995), 158–59; Robbie Ethridge, *Creek Country: The Creek Indians and Their World* (Chapel Hill: University of North Carolina Press, 2003), 140–47; Claudio Saunt, *A New Order of Things: Property, Power, and the Transformation of the Creek Indians, 1733–1816* (Cambridge: Cambridge University Press, 1999), 40–41. William Bartram's notes on the Creek Indians in the 1770s differ from most accounts by suggesting that men directed and executed labor in the fields. Bartram, "Observations on the Creek and Cherokee Indians," 152, 159.

3 "Phoebe Banks," in *The WPA Oklahoma Slave Narratives*, ed. T. Lindsay Baker and Julie P. Baker (Norman: University of Oklahoma Press, 1996), 30–33.

4 Steven C. Hahn's work presents a breathtakingly detailed narrative of what he terms the "invention of the Creek nation." His work, however, examines the origins of what is, in my terminology, the Creek national state rather than the nation itself. Steven C. Hahn, *The Invention of the Creek Nation, 1670–1763* (Lincoln: University of Nebraska Press, 2004). My argument here follows Claudio Saunt's in tracing the creation of the National Council to the Creek elite who espoused it. See Saunt, *New Order of Things*, 80, 190.

5   Ethridge, *Creek Country*, 143; Saunt, *New Order of Things*, 38–42; Angie Debo, *The Road to Disappearance: A History of the Creek Indians* (Norman: University of Oklahoma Press, 1941), 19. This description also draws on Norman Graebner's depiction of Creek agriculture in the years immediately following removal. Graebner argues that these practices continued those that had been followed in the Southeast. Norman Arthur Graebner, "Pioneer Indian Agriculture in Oklahoma," *Chronicles of Oklahoma* 23 (Autumn 1945): 233.

6   Linda S. Parker, *Native American Estate: The Struggle over Indian and Hawaiian Lands* (Honolulu: University of Hawaii Press, 1996), 20–23.

7   Ethridge, *Creek Country*, 23, 31, 58; Kathryn E. Holland Braund, *Deerskins and Duffels: The Creek Indian Trade with Anglo-America, 1685–1815* (Lincoln: University of Nebraska Press, 1993), 5–6.

8   John Lawson and Frances Latham Harriss, *Lawson's History of North Carolina, Containing the Exact Description and Natural History of That Country, Together with the Present State Thereof and a Journal of a Thousand Miles Traveled through Several Nations of Indians, Giving a Particular Account of Their Customs, Manners, Etc., Etc.* (1714; Richmond, Va.: Garrett and Massie, 1951), 213; Saunt, *New Order of Things*, 50–51; Bartram, *Travels*, 186.

9   Bartram, "Observations on the Creek and Cherokee Indians," 156; Saunt, *New Order of Things*, 51–52, 111; John Reed Swanton, *Social Organization and Social Usages of the Indians of the Creek Confederacy*, Bureau of American Ethnography Annual Report, vol. 42 (Washington: Government Printing Office, 1928), 48. Like Creeks, many West African societies were matrilineal, practiced nonchattel captive slavery, and allowed captives to become kin and thereby to enter society. These resemblances may have helped enslaved people navigate their way to freedom in Creek society. Barbara Krauthamer, "A Particular Kind of Freedom: Black Women, Slavery, Kinship, and Freedom in the American Southeast," in *Women and Slavery*, ed. Gwyn Campbell, Suzanne Miers, and Joseph C. Milled (Athens: Ohio University Press, 2008), 2:101. For an influential examination of the complexity of slavery and kinship, see James Brooks, *Captives and Cousins: Slavery, Kinship, and Community in the Southwest Borderlands* (Chapel Hill: University of North Carolina Press, 2002).

10 Edward J. Cashin, *Lachlan McGillivray, Indian Trader: The Shaping of the Southern Colonial Frontier* (Athens: University of Georgia Press, 1992), 74; Michael P. Morris, *The Bringing of Wonder: Trade and the Indians of the Southeast, 1700–1783* (Westport, Conn.: Greenwood, 1999), 66; Braund, *Deerskins and Duffels*, 78.

11 Saunt, *New Order of Things*, 111–16.

12 Cashin, *Lachlan McGillivray, Indian Trader*, 74; Morris, *Bringing of Wonder*, 66.

13 Daniel F. Littlefield, *Africans and Seminoles: From Removal to Emancipation* (Westport, Conn.: Greenwood, 1977), 40–43.

14 Ethridge, *Creek Country*, 79; Saunt, *New Order of Things*, 70. McGillivray's sister, Sophia Durant, owned eighty slaves. Ethridge, *Creek Country*, 84.

15 Saunt, *New Order of Things*, 117–20.

16 Edmund Sears Morgan, *American Slavery, American Freedom: The Ordeal of Colonial Virginia* (New York: Norton, 1975), 315, 328.

17 Saunt, *New Order of Things*, 131–33.

18 Andrew Frank, *Creeks and Southerners: Biculturalism on the Early American Frontier* (Lincoln: University of Nebraska Press, 2005), 84–86; Ethridge, *Creek Country*, 28–29, 64; Braund, *Deerskins and Duffels*, 6–7.

19 Benjamin Hawkins, *The Collected Works of Benjamin Hawkins, 1796–1810*, ed. H. Thomas Foster (Tuscaloosa: University of Alabama Press, 2003), 67s; Saunt, *New Order of Things*, 179; Duane Champagne, *Social Order and Political Change: Constitutional Governments among the Cherokee, the Choctaw, the Chickasaw, and the Creek* (Stanford, Calif.: Stanford University Press, 1992), 113.

20 Michael D. Green, *The Politics of Indian Removal: Creek Government and Society in Crisis* (Lincoln: University of Nebraska Press, 1982), 37; Saunt, *New Order of Things*, 180.

21 Champagne, *Social Order and Political Change*, 111–17.

22 Saunt, *New Order of Things*, 171–77.

23 Ethridge, *Creek Country*, 168.

24 Thomas Simpson Woodward, *Woodward's Reminiscences of the Creek, or Muscogee Indians: Contained in Letters to Friends in Georgia and Alabama* (Mobile, Ala.: Southern University Press, 1965), 17, 43, 68, 116; Champagne, *Social Order and Political Change*; Joel W. Martin, *Sacred Revolt: The Muskogees' Struggle for a New World* (Boston: Beacon Press, 1991), 156–57, 160–61, 163; John Grenier, *The First Way of War: American War Making on the Frontier, 1607–1814* (Cambridge: Cambridge University Press, 2005), 204; Ethridge, *Creek Country*, 240–41. For discussions of the spiritual dimensions of the Redstick movement, see Laura E. Donaldson, "The Breasts of Columbus: A Political Anatomy of Postcolonialism and Feminist Religious Discourse," in *Postcolonialism, Feminism, and Religious Discourse*, ed. Laura E. Donaldson and Kwok Pui-lan (New York: Routledge, 2002); Gregory Evans Dowd, *A Spirited Resistance: The North American Indian Struggle for Unity, 1745–1815* (Baltimore: Johns Hopkins University Press, 1992); and Martin, *Sacred Revolt*.

25 "Treaty with the Creeks, 1790," in *Indian Treaties, 1778–1883*, vol. 2 of *Indian Affairs, Laws and Treaties*, ed. Charles J. Kappler (New York: Interland, 1972), 25. It is noteworthy that what is generally termed the first Anglo-Creek treaty, signed in 1705, was in fact a treaty with the "Ochese Nation" (part of what came to be called the Creeks), demonstrating the difficulty in identifying a unitary Creek nation at early points in its development. On the treaty, see Hahn, *Invention of the Creek Nation*, 65.

26 Champagne, *Social Order and Political Change*, 123.

27 Francis Paul Prucha, *The Great Father: The United States and the American Indians* (Lincoln: University of Nebraska Press, 1984), 2:609–15, 621; Francis Paul Prucha, ed., *Atlas of American Indian Affairs* (Lincoln: University of Nebraska Press, 1990), map 24.

28 "Treaty with the Creeks, 1832," arts. 1, 2, and 12, in Kappler, *Indian Treaties*, 341–43; Green, *Politics of Indian Removal*, 146–48, 167–70, 181. For the initial Creek proposal, see Opothle Yaholo and others to Cass, March 19, 1832, in RG 75, microfilm publication M234B, *Letters Received by the Office of Indian Affairs, 1824–1881* (Washington: National Archives and Record Service, 1956–58), reel 222, frames 88–92.

29 Green, *Politics of Indian Removal*, 183–84.

30 Ibid., 185; Debo, *Road to Disappearance*, 103.

31 Debo, *Road to Disappearance*, 101.

32 Billy Byrd, "Ochai Tribe, an Interview with Hully Proctor . . . ," *IPH*, 40:481–82; Debo, *Road to Disappearance*, 106–1; Champagne, *Social Order and Political Change*, 200.

33 Mary Jane Warde, *George Washington Grayson and the Creek Nation, 1843–1920* (Norman: University of Oklahoma Press, 1999), 26, 35; Champagne, *Social Order and Political Change*, 164, 200–201.

34 Alexander Spoehr, *Changing Kinship Systems: A Study in the Acculturation of the Creeks, Cherokee, and Choctaw*. Field Museum of Natural History Publication 583. Anthropological series, vol. 33, no. 4 (Chicago: Field Museum, 1947) 221–22; U.S. Commissioner of Indian Affairs, *Annual Report of the Commissioner of Indian Affairs for the Year 1842* (Washington: Government Printing Office, [1843]), 442.

35 Warde, *George Washington Grayson*, 26.

36 Graebner, "Pioneer Indian Agriculture," 233.

37 Ethan Allen Hitchcock, *A Traveler in Indian Territory: The Journal of Ethan Allen Hitchcock, Late Major-General in the United States Army*, ed. Grant Foreman (Cedar Rapids, Iowa: Torch Press, 1930), 128.

38 J. Leitch Wright, *Creeks and Seminoles: The Destruction and Regeneration of the Muscogulge People* (Lincoln: University of Nebraska Press, 1986), 12–14; Graebner, "Pioneer Indian Agriculture," 233.

39 Graebner, "Pioneer Indian Agriculture," 233.

40 Debo, *Road to Disappearance*, 19.

41 Debo, *Road to Disappearance*, 99.

42 Slave population: Claudio Saunt, *Black, White, and Indian: Race and the Unmaking of an American Family* (New York: Oxford University Press, 2005), 66. Nonslave Creek population: Grant Foreman as cited in Craig S. Womack, *Red on Red: Native American Literary Separatism* (Minneapolis: University of Minnesota Press, 1999), 34. Saunt's number for 1860 is higher than that given by Daniel F. Littlefield, who reports 1,532 slaves (see Daniel F. Littlefield, *Africans and Creeks: From the Colonial Period to the Civil War* [Westport, Conn.: Greenwood, 1979], 154). This is because Saunt quite reasonably includes slaves of masters who were absent from the nation at the time of the census.

43 Warde, *George Washington Grayson*, 26; Jas. S. Buchanan, "Lewis, Phillip A. Interview," *IPH*, 6:213–20.

44 See, for example, "Mollie Barber," in Baker and Baker, *WPA Oklahoma Slave Narratives*, 42–43.

45 "Phoebe Banks," in Baker and Baker, *WPA Oklahoma Slave Narratives*, 30.

46 Billy Byrd, "An Interview with Alex Haynes: Slave Days," *IPH*, 62:3.

47 Tiya Miles offers an excellent summary of the literature on this topic. Tiya Miles, *Ties That Bind: The Story of an Afro-Cherokee Family in Slavery and Freedom* (Berkeley: University of California Press, 2005), 40.

48 On the transition in Creek slavery, see Graebner, "Pioneer Indian Agriculture," 242. On terminology, see Jack B. Martin and Margaret McKane Mauldin, *A Dictionary of Creek/Muskogee: With Notes on the Florida and Oklahoma Seminole Dialects*

of Creek (Lincoln: University of Nebraska Press, 2000), s.v. "slave," 313, and s.v. "*vpuekv*," 141.

49 Grace Kelley, "An Interview with Mr. Ned Thompson," *IPH*, 112:181.

50 Dawes Fife, "Interview with Richard Adkins," *IPH*, 12:128; Nettie Cain, "Interview with Ben F. Bruner," *IPH*, 89:258–60.

51 L. W. Wilson, "Interview with John Harrison (Colored)," 4:403.

52 Baker and Baker, *WPA Oklahoma Slave Narratives*, 30–31, 109, 112, 173, 175, 225; Orlando Patterson, *Slavery and Social Death: A Comparative Study* (Cambridge, Mass.: Harvard University Press, 1982), 181. On Creek slavery of this type, see also Kelley, "Interview with Mr. Ned Thompson," 180.

53 Littlefield, *Africans and Creeks*, 46.

54 "Treaty with the Creeks, 1796," in Kappler, *Indian Treaties*, 46–50; U.S. Commissioner of Indian Affairs, *Annual Report of the Commissioner of Indian Affairs for the Year 1842*, 442.

55 Littlefield, *Africans and Creeks*, 145.

56 The liberal theory of citizenship and rights was most influentially developed in T. H. Marshall, *Citizenship and Social Class and Other Essays* (Cambridge: Cambridge University Press, 1950).

57 Debo, *Road to Disappearance*, 127.

58 Grace Kelley, "Interview with Siegel McIntosh," *IPH*, 35:230–39.

59 Debo, *Road to Disappearance*, 127; Littlefield, *Africans and Creeks*, 144–45. Quotation is from Saunt, *Black, White, and Indian*, 74.

60 Littlefield, *Africans and Creeks*, 145.

61 L. W. Wilson, "Interview with Mrs. Sarah Odom," 81:236–37.

62 Annie Heloise Abel, *The American Indian as Slaveholder and Secessionist*, vol. 2 of *The Slaveholding Indians* (Cleveland: Arthur A. Clark Co., 1919), 86 n. 122.

63 John B. Meserve, "Chief Samuel Checote, with Sketches of Chiefs Locher Harjo and Ward Coachman," *Chronicles of Oklahoma* 16 (December 1938).

64 Debo, *Road to Disappearance*, 32, 34, 38, 110, 125, 140; Prucha, *The Great Father*, 2:137–38.

65 Abel, *American Indian as Slaveholder and Secessionist*, 58 and 58 n. 91.

66 "Phoebe Banks," in Baker and Baker, *WPA Oklahoma Slave Narratives*, 31–32; Littlefield, *Africans and Seminoles*, 182–83; Prucha, *Great Father*, 2:137–38, 140; John W. Morris, Charles R. Goins, and Edwin C. McReynolds, eds., *Historical Atlas of Oklahoma*, 3rd ed. (Norman: University of Oklahoma, 1986), map 28.

67 Fife, "Interview with Richard Adkins," 129.

68 Charles R. Freeman, "The Battle of Honey Springs," *Chronicles of Oklahoma* 13 (June 1935).

CHAPTER 2

1 "Nellie Johnson," in *The WPA Oklahoma Slave Narratives*, ed. T. Lindsay Baker and Julie P. Baker (Norman: University of Oklahoma Press, 1996), 224, 227.

2 "Treaty with the Creeks, 1866" in *Indian Treaties, 1778–1883*, vol. 2 of *Indian Affairs. Laws and Treaties*, ed. Charles J. Kappler (New York: Interland, 1972), 932.

3 Total Creek Nation population: U.S. Commissioner of Indian Affairs, *Report of the*

Commissioner of Indian Affairs for the Year 1866 (Washington: Government Printing Office, 1866), 21–22; former slave population: Claudio Saunt, *Black, White, and Indian: Race and the Unmaking of an American Family* (New York: Oxford University Press, 2005), 120. In 1870, in preparation for a payment for wartime losses to "Loyal Creeks," the American government counted fifty-eight "free colored" people. This number must be considered an undercount of the total free black population, as the roll was prepared specifically to reimburse soldiers and refugees. It therefore presumably leaves out those who claimed no wartime indemnities and those who were neither soldiers nor refugees during the war. The "free colored" and "freedman" people on the list include, for example, only one person who was under twenty-five at the end of the war. "1870 Loyal Creek Abstract," <http://freepages .genealogy.rootsweb.com/texlance/loyalcreek/index.htm#index> (July 20, 2008).

4 In this chapter, I have chosen my terms carefully from among a number of possibilities. Many at the time and since have referred to the people I term "black Creeks" as "Freedmen" or "Creek freedmen." Although the term was in use in the late nineteenth century, it not only has the liability of its gender marking but also defines these people in relation to what they had been, slaves. "Black Creeks" (even better, black Creek citizens) has the advantage of emphasizing what they had become: full members of the Creek Nation, though marked by race in ways important to their political and social lives. It correlates closely to the late nineteenth-century usage "colored Creek." Similarly, the individuals and towns that I refer to as "conservative" have appeared in the literature variously as "conservative," "full-blood" (a famously imprecise term that explains difference through race rather than political position), or "traditionalist" (which explains difference through cultural orientation rather than a political program). I prefer "conservative" because it emphasizes the political nature of the distinction and embeds it in the effort to "conserve" something—in this case, the land, land system, and sovereignty of the Creek Nation. "Conservative" should not be taken here to mean atavistic or reactionary; in the pursuit of their goals, Creek conservatives made novel use of old political ideas and structures, such as the nation as confederacy and town governance.

5 Grace Kelley, "Smith, Cora. Interview," *IPH*, 59:251–60. Cora Summers (later Cora Smith) is enrolled as Cordia Summers on the "Creeks by Blood" rolls opposite number 2,844. U.S. Commission to the Five Civilized Tribes, *The Final Rolls of Citizens and Freedmen of the Five Civilized Tribes in Indian Territory* (Washington: Government Printing Office, 1907), 519.

6 Daniel F. Littlefield, *Africans and Creeks: From the Colonial Period to the Civil War* (Westport, Conn.: Greenwood, 1979), 241.

7 Ketch Barnett, John McIntosh, Scipio Barnett, Jack Brown, and Cow Tom are identified as "delegates for the black population living among the Creeks and Euchees," and Harry Island is identified as "interpreter for the Creeks" in "Agreement with the Cherokee and Other Tribes in the Indian Territory, 1865," in Kappler, *Indian Treaties*, 1051.

8 Quoted in Saunt, *Black, White, and Indian*, 116.

9 U.S. Commissioner of Indian Affairs, *Report of the Commissioner of Indian Affairs for the Year 1866* (Washington: Government Printing Office, 1866), 10. Note that,

contrary to accounts such as Angie Debo's, Creeks were not merely "induced" to accept black citizenship. Some Creeks favored this as a just outcome. See Angie Debo, *And Still the Waters Run: The Betrayal of the Five Civilized Tribes* (Princeton, N.J.: Princeton University Press, 1940), 10.

10 The 1866 treaty is signed by Harry Island with his mark. He is identified as "United States Interpreter" on the treaty. "Treaty with the Creeks, 1866," in Kappler, *Indian Treaties*, 937. On interpretation, see Grace Kelley, "An Interview with Mr. Ned Thompson," *IPH*, 112:179.

11 L. C. Perryman, ed., *Constitution and Laws of the Muskogee Nation* (1890; Wilmington. Del.: Scholarly Resources, 1975), 32.

12 Michael Vorenberg, "Reconstruction as a Constitutional Crisis," in *Reconstructions: New Perspectives on the Postbellum United States*, ed. Thomas J. Brown (Oxford: Oxford University Press, 2006).

13 Saunt, *Black, White, and Indian*, 117, 120.

14 The effort was only beaten back thanks to united effort by black Creeks and leaders of the Sands faction. Already, just after the war, that alliance was being built. Ibid., 119.

15 Mary Jane Warde, *George Washington Grayson and the Creek Nation, 1843–1920* (Norman: University of Oklahoma Press, 1999), xvi, 87.

16 Saunt, *Black, White, and Indian*, 135.

17 Two works that have published selections from the Indian Pioneer History narrative are Baker and Baker, *WPA Oklahoma Slave Narratives*, and Terri M. Baker and Connie Oliver Henshaw, *Women Who Pioneered Oklahoma: Stories from the WPA Narratives* (Norman: University of Oklahoma Press, 2007). For a useful discussion of the difficulties and possibilities in using WPA narratives for historical research, see Mia Bay, *The White Image in the Black Mind: African-American Ideas about White People, 1830–1925* (New York: Oxford University Press, 2000), 114–16.

18 Grace Kelley, "Interview with Siegel McIntosh," *IPH*, 35:236.

19 Celia Naylor-Ojurongbe, "'Born and Raised among These People, I Don't Want to Know Any Other': Slaves' Acculturation in Nineteenth-Century Indian Territory," in *Confounding the Color Line: The Indian-Black Experience in North America*, ed. James Brooks (Lincoln: University of Nebraska Press, 2002).

20 Jerome M. Emmons, "Interview with Island Smith," *IPH*, 20:334; Jack B. Martin and Margaret McKane Mauldin, *A Dictionary of Creek/Muskogee: With Notes on the Florida and Oklahoma Seminole Dialects of Creek* (Lincoln: University of Nebraska Press, 2000), s.v. mekko-hoyvnēcv, 75; John Reed Swanton, *Creek Religion and Medicine* (Lincoln: University of Nebraska Press, 2000), 655; Clara Sue Kidwell, "Native American Systems of Knowledge," in *A Companion to American Indian History*, ed. Philip J. Deloria and Neal Salisbury (Malden, Mass.: Blackwell, 2002), 97; John K. Crellin, *Reference Guide to Medicinal Plants* (Durham, N.C.: Duke University Press, 1989), 102–4.

21 Kelley, "Interview with Siegel McIntosh," 236; C. Lee Phelps, "A True Story of Indian Missions," *IPH*, 8:216; Patrick N. Minges, *Slavery in the Cherokee Nation: The Keetoowah Society and the Defining of a People, 1855–1867* (London: Routledge, 2003), 85–86.

22 Amelia Rector Bell, "Creek Ritual: The Path to Peace" (Ph.D. diss., University of Chicago, 1984), 10–11.

23 Emmons, "Interview with Island Smith," 339.

24 Duane Champagne, *Social Order and Political Change: Constitutional Governments among the Cherokee, the Choctaw, the Chickasaw, and the Creek* (Stanford, Calif.: Stanford University Press, 1992), 230.

25 Grace Kelley, "Interview with Mrs. Willie Blair," *IPH*, 104:85, 89–93. The *IPH* narrative identifies Caledonia Perryman Morey as the sister of Chief Legus C. Perryman (p. 81), but she is not listed as one of the siblings or half siblings in a history of the family by John Meserve. See John B. Meserve, "The Perrymans," *Chronicles of Oklahoma* 15 (June 1937): 172. Caledonia Perryman Morey may be the person identified as Calley Morey on the "Creeks by Blood" rolls opposite number 2,237. U.S. Commission to the Five Civilized Tribes, *Final Rolls of Citizens and Freedmen*, 516.

26 L. W. Wilson, "Interview with Mrs. Sarah Odom," *IPH*, 81:235–40, 244–45. On the elaboration of corn foods, see Jerome M. Emmons, "Interview with Robert M. Hamilton," *IPH*, 27:249. On Creek women and their primary role in agriculture, see Kathryn E. Holland Braund, "Guardians of Tradition and Handmaidens to Change: Women's Roles in Creek Economic and Social Life during the Eighteenth Century," *American Indian Quarterly* 14 (Summer 1990): 242–43.

27 Billy Byrd, "Interview with Sunday Taylor, Okemah, Oklahoma," *IPH*, 10:333–37.

28 Grace Kelley, "Grayson, Joe. Interview," *IPH*, 26:359–64. On the affluence of Grayson's father, Simpson Grayson, see Saunt, *Black, White, and Indian*, 80.

29 Emmons, "Interview with Island Smith," 331–35.

30 Braund, "Guardians of Tradition," 243.

31 Byrd, "Interview with Sunday Taylor" 333–36.

32 Wilson, "Interview with Mrs. Sarah Odom," 237–39, 244–45, 247–48; Warde, *George Washington Grayson*, 90, 93–95.

33 Philip Deloria, *Indians in Unexpected Places* (Lawrence: University Press of Kansas, 2004), 6. See also Tanis C. Thorne, *The World's Richest Indian: The Scandal over Jackson Barnett's Oil Fortune* (Oxford: Oxford University Press, 2003), 18.

34 Wilson, "Interview with Mrs. Sarah Odom," 242.

35 Byrd, "Interview with Sunday Taylor," 336.

36 U.S. Commissioner of Indian Affairs, *Annual Report of the Commissioner of Indian Affairs to the Secretary of the Interior for the Year 1881* (Washington: Government Printing Office, 1981), lvii–liix; Swanton, *Creek Religion and Medicine*, 630.

37 Alan Gallay, *The Indian Slave Trade: The Rise of the English Empire in the American South, 1670–1717* (New Haven, Conn.: Yale University Press, 2002), 134; Kathryn E. Holland Braund, *Deerskins and Duffels: The Creek Indian Trade with Anglo-America, 1685–1815* (Lincoln: University of Nebraska Press, 1993).

38 Kelley, "Grayson, Joe. Interview," 362. Emmons, "Interview with Island Smith," 331–35.

39 Grace Kelley, "One of the Oldest Indians," *IPH*, 8:197; Grace Kelley, "Hitchita Town," *IPH*, 31:222.

40 Perryman, *Constitution and Laws*, 3–4; Craig S. Womack, *Red on Red: Native American Literary Separatism* (Minneapolis: University of Minnesota Press, 1999), 35.

41 Angie Debo, *The Road to Disappearance: A History of the Creek Indians* (Norman: University of Oklahoma Press, 1941), 192.

42 Grace Kelley, "Interview with W. B. Tiger," *IPH*, 10:514.

43 Perryman, *Constitution and Laws*, 3–4.

44 U.S. Congress, Senate, Committee on Territories, *Report*, 45th Cong., 3rd sess., 1879 (Washington: Government Printing Office, 1879), 684, 688; Saunt, *Black, White, and Indian*, 119.

45 The 1867 constitution that reconstructed the nation transferred authority over citizenship from the town *miccos* to the Creek federal government, but in practice the central government continued to depend on the towns to draw up lists of their members. See Kent Carter, *The Dawes Commission and the Allotment of the Five Civilized Tribes, 1893–1914* (Orem, Utah: Ancestry.com, 1999), 42; Debo, *Road to Disappearance*, 220, 369.

46 Quoted in Katja May, *African Americans and Native Americans in the Creek and Cherokee Nations, 1830s to 1920s: Collision and Collusion* (New York: Garland, 1996), 104. Stidham's comments are in U.S. Congress, Senate, Committee on Indian Affairs, *Report of the Committee on Indian Affairs, United States Senate, on the Condition of the Indians in the Indian Territory, and Other Reservations, etc.*, 49th Cong., 1st sess., 1885–86 (Washington: Government Printing Office, 1886), pt. 2:152.

47 U.S. Congress, Committee on Territories, *Report*, 710.

48 Arrell M. Gibson, *Oklahoma: A History of Five Centuries* (Norman, Okla.: Harlow, 1965), 281.

49 C. W. Turner, "Events among the Muskogees during Sixty Years," *Chronicles of Oklahoma* 10 (March 1932).

50 E. M. Morton, "Railroad Life in Indian Territory, Being the Personal Experiences of Mr. E. M. Morton," *IPH*, 7:322.

51 Rebecca Belle Bateman, "'We're Still Here': History, Kinship, and Group Identity among the Seminole Freedmen of Oklahoma" (Ph.D, diss., Johns Hopkins University, 1991), 102.

52 Debo, *Road to Disappearance*, 260.

53 Jas. S. Buchanan, "Annie V. Noble," *IPH*, 38:110; H. F. O'Beirne and E. S. O'Beirne, *The Indian Territory: Its Chiefs, Legislators and Leading Men* (St. Louis: C. B. Woodward Co., 1892), s.v. "Fisher, William," 214.

54 Billy Byrd, "Simmer. Interview," *IPH*, 9:379.

55 Effie S. Jackson, "Early Day Ranches (in the Tulsa Area)," *IPH*, 30:500; Donald A. Wise, *Broken Arrow: City of Roses and Pure Water* (Chicago: Arcadia, 2002), 8; Lon R. Stansbury, "George B. Perryman, Land Owner and Rancher," *IPH*, 10:96; Effie S. Jackson, "Mrs. Ella Perryman Kneedler," *IPH*, 32:360. Wise describes the Perrymans' claim as only about four miles north to south, whereas Jackson suggests it was twelve miles north to south. Given the descriptions of the land that they leased out, Jackson's larger description is more convincing.

56 Ella M. Robinson, "The Daugherty Ranch, Creek Nation," *Chronicles of Oklahoma*

38 (Spring 1960); Walter Prescott Webb, ed., *The Handbook of Texas* (Austin: Texas State Historical Association, 1952), s.v. "Daugherty, James M.," 466; Amelia F. Harris, "Interview with E. T. Pendley," *IPH*, 93:214; Effie S. Jackson, "An Interview with W. M. McCollough," *IPH*, 35:20.

57 Ella Robinson, "Reminiscences of D. H. Middleton," *IPH*, 7:197–98.

58 John A. Gardner, chattel mortgage deed copy, 1904, folder 2677–82, Frederick Severs Papers, OHS; John A. Gardner, chattel mortgage deed copy, 1900, folder 2677–82, Severs Papers, OHS.

59 Saunt, *Black, White, and Indian*, 143.

60 U.S. Commissioner of Indian Affairs, *Report of the Commissioner of Indian Affairs for the Year 1887* (Washington: Government Printing Office, 1887), 111; Danney Goble, *Progressive Oklahoma: The Making of a New Kind of State* (Norman: University of Oklahoma Press, 1980), 55.

61 Alexandra Harmon, "American Indians and Land Monopolies in the Gilded Age," *Journal of American History* 90 (June 2003): 107–8.

62 Saunt, *Black, White, and Indian*, 142.

63 *Turner v. United States*, 248 U.S. 354 (1919); Goble, *Progressive Oklahoma*, 54–55; Sidney L. Harring, *Crow Dog's Case: American Indian Sovereignty, Tribal Law, and the United States* (Cambridge: Cambridge University Press, 1994), 91–92.

64 Byrd, "Interview with Sunday Taylor," 334–35.

65 Saunt, *Black, White, and Indian*, 142.

66 Harring, *Crow Dog's Case*, 92.

67 Champagne, *Social Order and Political Change*, 120.

68 Harring, *Crow Dog's Case*, 92.

69 Thorne, *The World's Richest Indian*, 18.

70 For ways in which Creek nationalists from different factions mobilized narratives of the past in the defense of sovereignty, see Claudio Saunt, "Telling Stories: The Political Uses of Myth and History in the Cherokee and Creek Nations," *Journal of American History* 93 (December 2006).

71 Womack, *Red on Red*, 26.

72 Ibid., 17.

73 John Reed Swanton, *Social Organization and Social Usages of the Indians of the Creek Confederacy*, Bureau of American Ethnography Annual Report, vol. 42 (Washington: Government Printing Office, 1928), 54.

74 Swanton, *Social Organization*, 65, 67. For other tellings of this story that contain some variations but also emphasize the deliberate creation of an alliance, see "Muskogee: Coweta-Tuckabatchee Alliance (M7)" and "Muskogee: Tuckabatchee-Coweta Alliance (MT2)," in Bill Grantham, *Creation Myths and Legends of the Creek Indians* (Gainesville: University Press of Florida, 2002), 162 and 163–64, respectively.

75 Swanton, *Social Organization*, 69.

76 Ibid., 54, 59, 266; Grantham, *Creation Myths*, chap. 14, 159–66.

77 "Hitchiti: Hitchiti Origin (H1)," in Grantham, *Creation Myths*, 135.

78 Womack, *Red on Red*, 35–36.

79 John B. Meserve, "Chief Isparhecher," *Chronicles of Oklahoma* 10 (March 1932): 54–55.

80 Saunt, *Black, White, and Indian*, 125.

81 *Vinita Indian Chieftain*, November 7, 1889, 2; *Muskogee Indian Journal*, November 21, 1889, 4. The newspaper article situates the events in the "Bruner settlement." See also Donald A. Grinde Jr. and Quintard Taylor, "Red vs Black: Conflict and Accommodation in the Post Civil War Indian Territory, 1865–1907," *American Indian Quarterly* 8 (Summer 1984).

82 On conflicts in the Chickasaw, Choctaw, and Cherokee nations, see Barbara Krauthamer, "In Their 'Native Country': Freedpeople's Understandings of Culture and Citizenship in the Choctaw and Chickasaw Nations," in *Crossing Waters, Crossing Worlds: The African Diaspora in Indian Country*, ed. Tiya Miles and Sharon Patricia Holland (Durham, N.C.: Duke University Press, 2006), and Tiya Miles, *Ties That Bind: The Story of an Afro-Cherokee Family in Slavery and Freedom* (Berkeley: University of California Press, 2005).

83 Champagne, *Social Order and Political Change*, 231; Debo, *Road to Disappearance*, 193, 195, 214, 220, 222, 247–48.

84 Jerome M. Emmons, "Interview with Simon McIntosh," *IPH*, 35:244; L. W. Wilson, "Interview with Scott Waldo McIntosh," *IPH*, 35:244.

85 Debo, *Road to Disappearance*, 272.

86 Ibid., 268–69; Daniel F. Littlefield, *Alex Posey: Creek Poet, Journalist, and Humorist* (Lincoln: University of Nebraska Press, 1992), 30–31; Saunt, *Black, White, and Indian*, 134.

87 J. Leitch Wright, *Creeks and Seminoles: The Destruction and Regeneration of the Muscogulge People* (Lincoln: University of Nebraska Press, 1986), 17, 308. Littlefield favors Wright's interpretation here. See Littlefield, *Alex Posey*, 30.

88 *Vinita Indian Chieftain*, August 24, 1883, 2.

89 Saunt, *Black, White, and Indian*, 135.

90 "Message of Spiechee," *Muskogee Indian Journal*, January 3, 1884; Saunt, *Black, White, and Indian*, 135.

91 Debo, *Road to Disappearance*, 247, 242–43, 263, 268–69, 272, 281.

92 *Eufaula Indian Journal*, September 22, 1895; Debo, *Road to Disappearance*, 261.

93 Perryman, *Constitution and Laws*, 67–68.

94 Ibid., 95.

95 Ibid., 135, 138.

96 Ibid., 172–73.

CHAPTER 3

1 Grace Kelley, "Interview with Joe M. Grayson," *IPH* 26:367–84. This man is identified in the interview cover sheet as "Joe Grayson (White)" to differentiate him from the Creek men, both black and nonblack, who had the same name. Laura Ingalls Wilder, *Little House on the Prairie* (1935; New York: Harper and Row, 1971), 136–41, 233–34. On the history of the white incursions onto Osage lands in 1869, and the politics of Laura Ingall Wilder's narrative, see Dennis McAuliffe Jr., "Little House on the Diminished Osage Prairie," in *A Broken Flute: The Native Experience in Books for Children*, ed. Doris Seale and Beverly Slapin (Berkeley, Calif.: Oyate, 2006), 49–52.

2 U.S. Board of Indian Commissioners, *Annual Report of the Board of Indian Commissioners for the Year 1885* (Washington: Government Printing Office, 1886), 90.

3 Angie Debo, *And Still the Waters Run: The Betrayal of the Five Civilized Tribes* (Princeton, N.J.: Princeton University Press, 1940), 13.

4 Paul Wallace Gates, *History of Public Land Law Development* (New York: Arno Press, 1979).

5 Danney Goble, *Progressive Oklahoma: The Making of a New Kind of State* (Norman: University of Oklahoma Press, 1980), 7; U.S. Commissioner of Indian Affairs, *Annual Report of the Commissioner of Indian Affairs to the Secretary of the Interior for the Year 1881* (Washington: Government Printing Office, 1881), lxvii; U.S. Commissioner of Indian Affairs, *Annual Report of the Commissioner of Indian Affairs to the Secretary of the Interior for the Year 1883* (Washington: Government Printing Office, 1883), xxiv.

6 Henry Day, "An Interview with Mr. William J. Luker," *IPH*, 60:265–67.

7 Melvin Stites, "Interview with Mr. Bill Brasfield," *IPH*, 72:357–66.

8 On the social background of the Boomers, see John Thompson, *Closing the Frontier: Radical Response in Oklahoma, 1889–1923* (Norman: University of Oklahoma Press, 1986), 48.

9 W. H. Miller to Hon. G. H. Orth, January 22, 1882, letter M178, box 64, Special Case #78: Settlement of Indian Territory, entry 102: Special Cases, RG 75, NA.

10 Clipping "Biased Braves," attached to W. E. Savage to the Secretary of the Interior, envelope S412, box 64, Special Case #78: Settlement of Indian Territory, entry 102: Special Cases, RG 75, NA.

11 Jeffrey Burton, *Indian Territory and the United States, 1866–1906: Courts, Government, and the Movement for Oklahoma Statehood* (Norman: University of Oklahoma Press, 1995), 26.

12 The other major tool in this process was the Indian boarding school, which Joel Pfister has termed an "individualizing factory." Joel Pfister, *Individuality Incorporated: Indians and the Multicultural Modern* (Durham, N.C.: Duke University Press, 2004), 31, 35.

13 Francis Paul Prucha, *The Great Father: The United States and the American Indians* (Lincoln: University of Nebraska Press, 1984), 2:669, 737, 746.

14 Debo, *And Still the Waters Run*, 52–53.

15 Ibid., 26; Kent Carter, *The Dawes Commission and the Allotment of the Five Civilized Tribes, 1893–1914* (Orem, Utah: Ancestry.com, 1999), 4.

16 Goble, *Progressive Oklahoma*, 72; Debo, *And Still the Waters Run*, 22.

17 Alexandra Harmon, "American Indians and Land Monopolies in the Gilded Age," *Journal of American History* 90 (June 2003). As early as 1886, the commissioner of Indian Affairs had made this argument about land tenure among the Five Civilized Tribes. D. S. Otis, *The Dawes Act and the Allotment of Indian Lands* (Norman: University of Oklahoma Press, 1973), 43–44.

18 "Commissioner McKennon," *Eufaula Indian Journal*, March 22, 1894, 1.

19 "An Address from the Commissioners to the Citizens of the Five Civilized Tribes—They Say That a Change Must Be Made," *Eufaula Indian Journal*, February 15, 1894,

END

1; Carter, *Dawes Commission*, 8; "International Council," *Eufaula Indian Journal*, February 22, 1894, 1.

20 "The People and Politicians," *Eufaula Indian Journal*, May 11, 1894, 4.

21 On the discourse of "the vanishing Indian," see Brian W. Dippie, *The Vanishing American: White Attitudes and U.S. Indian Policy* (Middletown, Conn.: Wesleyan University Press, 1982), chap. 8.

22 "Editorial on Message by Isparhecher," *Purcell Register*, October 13, 1898, typescript copy in folder 24, box 1, Isparhecher Collection, WHC. The editorialist was referring, of course, to James Fenimore Cooper, author of *The Last of the Mohicans* and the Leatherstocking tales, romantic works that did much to popularize the discourse of the vanishing Indian. See Dippie, *Vanishing American*, 21–25.

23 "Isparhecher," *Claremore Progress*, September 28, 1895, typescript copy in folder 5, box 1, Isparhecher Collection, WHC; "New Item of Isparhecher," *Fort Gibson Post*, October 27, 1898, typescript copy in folder 33, box 1, Isparhecher Collection, WHC.

24 Reprinted in *Tahlequah Cherokee Advocate*, June 16, 1900, 2.

25 "Senator Platt Speaks," *Eufaula Indian Journal*, April 19, 1894, 1, 4.

26 Jerome M. Emmons, "Interview with Robert M. Hamilton," *IPH*, 52:248.

27 As early as 1878, the platforms of all three Creek political parties contained a provision assuring that all Muscogee citizens, no matter their color, were equal before the law. As is explained below, however, Isparhecher's pronouncements of racial equality carried particular weight because of his political background. See also Chapter 2 on this issue. Debo, *And Still the Waters Run*, 247. Isparhecher was reiterating a pledge he had made in 1884, when he proclaimed that "every Muskogee citizen, whether his skin be red, white, or black, has equal rights in this nation." "Message of Spiechee," *Muskogee Indian Journal*, January 3, 1884, typescript copy in folder 2, box 1, Isparhecher Collection, WHC.

28 "Letter of Isparhecher," *Muskogee Our Brother in Red*, August 8, 1891, typescript copy in folder 1, box 1, Isparhecher Collection, WHC (emphasis in the original).

29 *Fort Gibson Post*, December 1, 1898, typescript copy in folder 33, box 1, Isparhecher Collection, WHC.

30 Katja May argues that Isparhecher was "genuinely in favor of the rights of the black Indian citizens in the Muskogee Nation" and speculates that white newspapermen made up the 1898 quotation because they ("self-serving whites") did not want to share Indian Territory lands with black people. I argue instead that these words in 1898 mark a significant shift in Isparhecher's thinking on race and Creek citizenship because they are consistent with the changing political context and the opinions voiced by other Creek conservatives at the time. See Katja May, *African Americans and Native Americans in the Creek and Cherokee Nations, 1830s to 1920s: Collision and Collusion* (New York: Garland, 1996), 112–13.

31 "Decision of Supreme Court as to Creek Freedmen," *Muskogee Phoenix*, August 20, 1896, 1.

32 Alexandra Harmon, "Wanted: More Histories of Indian Identity," in *A Companion to American Indian History*, ed. Philip J. Deloria and Neal Salisbury (Malden, Mass.:

Blackwell, 2002), 248–65; Alexandra Harmon, *Indians in the Making: Ethnic Relations and Indian Identities around Puget Sound* (Berkeley: University of California Press, 1998), chap. 6.

33 On the broader history and politics of racial classification of Indian people according to schemes of "blood," see William T. Hagan, "Full Blood, Mixed Blood, Generic, and Ersatz: The Problem of Indian Identity," *Arizona and the West* 27 (Winter 1985); C. Matthew Snipp, "Who Are American Indians? Some Observations about the Perils and Pitfalls of Data for Race and Ethnicity," *Population and Policy Review* 5 (January 1986); Melissa L. Meyer, *The White Earth Tragedy: Ethnicity and Dispossession at a Minnesota Anishinaabe Reservation, 1889–1920* (Lincoln: University of Nebraska Press, 1994), 39–40, 163–71.

34 U.S. Congress, Senate, *In the Senate of the United States. March 24, 1896*, 54th Cong., 1st sess., 1896 (Washington: Government Printing Office, 1896), 3–5, 40, 247; Carter, *Dawes Commission*, 3–6; Angie Debo, *The Road to Disappearance: A History of the Creek Indians* (Norman: University of Oklahoma Press, 1941), 345.

35 "International Council," 1; "Local Notes," *Eufaula Indian Journal*, March 29, 1894, 4.

36 George Washington Grayson, *A Creek Warrior for the Confederacy: The Autobiography of Chief G. W. Grayson*, ed. W. David Baird (Norman: University of Oklahoma Press, 1988), 6–7; "Local Notes" *Eufaula Indian Journal*, February 22, 1894, 4; Debo, *Road to Disappearance*, 290.

37 Porter remained personally opposed to allotment until 1891, when he came to think it would be better to accept the plan. Nonetheless, he continued to work against allotment politically, Ralph William Goodwin argues, in order to represent the wishes of the Creek people. Ralph William Goodwin, "Pleasant Porter, Tribal Statesman" (M.A. thesis, University of Oklahoma, 1953), 12–16, 19, 55, 98, 104, 110. Porter's life and economic pursuits are detailed by his son in Effie S. Jackson, "Interview with Willie Porter," *IPH*, 40:233–45.

38 Debo, *Road to Disappearance*, 106, 246–47, 323, 346, 356.

39 I estimate the Creek electorate in the following manner: the 1907 final rolls of the Dawes Commission show 18,761. Allowing that 1,000 Creeks may have been left off the rolls, the total could be estimated at 19,761 Creeks. Assuming that half the Creeks were female and only two-thirds of the males were of voting age, the Creek electorate could be estimated at 6,587, and 2,000 voters would represent 30.3 percent of that electorate.

40 "Creek Council," *Eufaula Indian Journal*, April 12, 1894, 1.

41 L. C. Perryman, "Chief Perryman Speaks," *Eufaula Indian Journal*, May 11, 1894, 4.

42 "Protest against It," *Eufaula Indian Journal*, March 1, 1894, 1.

43 "Creek Council," 1; Harmon, "American Indians and Land Monopolies," 124.

44 "Protest against It," 1.

45 "Creek Council."

46 Harmon, "American Indians and Land Monopolies," 125.

47 It is possible that there is a hint of a coming political shift in the fact that, in the

three predominantly African American towns in the nation, Isparhecher lost out to Ellis B. Childers, also a conservative and foe of allotment. Note that in the 1906 senatorial hearings, discussed later in this chapter, Childers was the only witness that still called for racially neutral land legislation. Debo, *Road to Disappearance*, 361. On general resistance to allotment, see Carter, *Dawes Commission*, 9–10.

48 Grace Kelley, "Interview with George Looney, Weleetka, Oklahoma," *IPH*, 33:381–82.

49 May, *African Americans and Native Americans*, 108.

50 L. W. Wilson, "Interview with Mr. Jake Simmons," *IPH*, 9:346. For another black Creek who had a remarkably detailed knowledge of the history of treaty making, removal, and Creek politics, see L. W. Wilson, "Interview with Scott Waldo McIntosh," *IPH*, 35:208–28.

51 Carter, *Dawes Commission*, 5.

52 "Time to Act," *Eufaula Indian Journal*, February 15, 1894, 1. See also "Statehood," *Eufaula Indian Journal*, April 5, 1894, 1.

53 "The Facts," *Eufaula Indian Journal*, November 30, 1900, 3. For worries about taxation, see "Taxable Lands," *Cherokee Advocate*, April 22, 1905, 1.

54 "Statehood," *Eufaula Indian Journal*, March 8, 1894, 1; "Statehood," *Eufaula Indian Journal*, March 29, 1894, 1.

55 "Act of June 28, 1898 (Curtis Bill) 30 Stat. 495," in W. F. Semple, *Oklahoma Indian Land Titles, Annotated* (St. Louis: Thomas Law Book Co., 1952), 585–605; Prucha, *Great Father*, 2:748; Debo, *And Still the Waters Run*, 33–35; Carter, *Dawes Commission*, 43.

56 "An Act to Ratify and Confirm an Agreement with the Muscogee or Creek Tribe of Indians, and for Other Purposes," in *Indian Treaties, 1778–1883*, vol. 2 of *Indian Affairs, Laws and Treaties*, ed. Charles J. Kappler (New York: Interland, 1972), 729–39.

57 "Notice to Creek Citizens," *Vinita Indian Chieftain*, March 16, 1899, 1.

58 Carter, *Dawes Commission*, 41–42, 64.

59 Ibid., 45, citing Dawes Commission Report of April 15, 1899, to the Secretary of the Interior, OHS Microfilm, Dawes Commission roll 4.

60 "Creek Allotment," *Cherokee Advocate*, September 28, 1901, 2. By March 1902, almost all 10,000 enrolled Creeks and 5,000 enrolled Creek Freedmen had selected allotments.

61 "Crazy Snake Repudiated," *Cherokee Advocate*, December 7, 1901, 1.

62 "An Act to Ratify and Confirm an Agreement with the Muscogee or Creek Tribe of Indians, and for Other Purposes," 31 Stat. 861, sections 3 and 9, as reprinted in Lawrence Mills, *Lands of the Five Civilized Tribes: A Treatise upon the Law Applicable to the Lands of the Five Civilized Tribes in Oklahoma* (St. Louis: F. H. Thomas Law Book Co., 1919), 593, 598; Debo, *And Still the Waters Run*, 49.

63 Grace Kelley, "An Interview with Louis Rentie, Henryetta," *IPH*, 70:473–80. Both Morris Rentie and his wife, Katie McGilbray, were members of Canadian Colored Town. "1869 Dunn Roll, Creek Freedmen, Index Re-Se," <http://freepages .genealogy.rootsweb.com/texlance/dunnroll/dunnname17.htm> (May 25, 2008).

64 "The Inter-National Afro-American League," *Muskogee Pioneer*, June 24, 1898, 2. On W. H. Twine, who went on to edit the *Cimeter* newspaper, see Booker T. Washington, *The Negro in Business* (Coshocton, Ohio: Hertel, Jenkins and Co., 1907), 212; Frank Lincoln Mather, ed., *Who's Who of the Colored Race* (1915; Detroit: Gale Research Co., 1976), s.v. "Twine, William Henry," 1:269–70.

65 "Inter-National Afro-American League," 2.

66 Curtis L. Nolen, "The Okmulgee Constitution: A Step towards Indian Self-Determination," *Chronicles of Oklahoma* 58 (Fall 1980); Debo, *Road to Disappearance*, 195–210.

67 *Muskogee Phoenix*, October 13, 1892, 4.

68 Debo, *Road to Disappearance*, 244–45, 333.

69 Ibid., 353; *Eufaula Indian Journal*, June 15, 1894, 1; "A Quiet Election," *Eufaula Indian Journal*, June 15, 1894, 4.

70 Carter, *Dawes Commission*, 49.

71 Ibid., 46, 49.

72 Debo, *And Still the Waters Run*, 40.

73 Carter, *Dawes Commission*, 49.

74 Ibid. I accept Carter's statement to this effect, as he has closely researched enrollment and allotment and is the director of the Southwest Regional Records Center of the National Archives, where the records of the Dawes Commission are maintained. Note, however, that representatives of the Dawes Commission vigorously denied that they followed the practice of assigning all people with any African heritage to the category of Freedmen. On this issue in the Choctaw Nation, see U.S. Congress, Senate, Select Committee, *Report of the Select Committee to Investigate Matters Connected with Affairs in the Indian Territory with Hearings, November 11, 1906–January 9, 1907*, 59th Cong., 2nd sess., 1906–7 (Washington: Government Printing Office, 1907), 1:471–545.

75 Melvin Harris, *Patterns of Race in the Americas* (New York: Walker, 1964), 37; Christine B. Hickman, "The Devil and the One Drop Rule: Racial Categories, African Americans, and the U.S. Census," *Michigan Law Review* 95 (March 1997): 1171–87.

76 Carter, *Dawes Commission*, 49.

77 For Porter's reported black ancestry, see "Pleasant Porter," in Grant Foreman Collection (Accession 83–224), folder 1, box 12, OHS. For his Dawes enrollment, see roll number 6,220, census card number 1,991, U.S. Commission to the Five Civilized Tribes, *The Final Rolls of Citizens and Freedmen of the Five Civilized Tribes in Indian Territory* (Washington: Government Printing Office, 1907), 539.

78 For the reputed African ancestry and appearance of Perryman family members, see Claudio Saunt, *Black, White, and Indian: Race and the Unmaking of an American Family* (New York: Oxford University Press, 2005), 35, 117, 171, 189. For the enrollment of Legus C. Perryman, Arparye Perryman, Henry W. Perryman, and Homer Perryman, see enrollment card 910 of the Creek "by blood" rolls, U.S. Commission to the Five Civilized Tribes, *Final Rolls*, 520.

79 "Allotment," *Eufaula Indian Journal*, 22 February 1894, 1.

80 Goble, *Progressive Oklahoma*, 75

81 Carter, *Dawes Commission*, 52. This very rough approximation is based on reports that about 6,500 of the roughly 15,000 eligible Creeks had enrolled by early December 1899.

82 Many were still resisting in 1904. Editorial on Pleasant Porter, *Wagoner Weekly Sayings*, December 8, 1904.

83 Jesse Lee Blakemore, "Experiences of a Pioneer Doctor," *IPH*, 15:298–302.

84 "Editorial on Isparhecher," *South McAlester Capital*, June 1, 1899, typescript copy in folder 38, box 1, Isparhecher Collection, WHC.

85 Mace Davis, "Chitto Harjo," *Chronicles of Oklahoma* 13 (June 1935); Grace Kelley, "Ward, Leroy. Interview," *IPH*, 48:453.

86 For Arbeka as Chitto Harjo's town, see Charles Gibson, "Creek War Whoop," *Eufaula Indian Journal*, January 31, 1902, in *Selected Works of Charles Gibson*, ed. Thomas Murray, Digital Library, American Native Press Archives, University of Arkansas at Little Rock, <www.anpa.ualr.edu> (July 20, 2008). Chitto Harjo is listed under Arbeka in the Creek census of 1882.

87 Billie Byrd, "Wah-Sah-Shee Wa-Ke, An Interview of Daniel Starr, Age 85, Arbeka Town (Tulwa), Henryetta, Okla.," *IPH*, 57:353–54.

88 Kenneth Waldo McIntosh, "Chitto Harjo, The Crazy Snakes and the Birth of Indian Political Activism in the Twentieth Century" (Ph.D. diss., Texas Christian University, 1993), 46.

89 Byrd, "Wah-Sah-Shee Wa-Ke," 353.

90 Billie Byrd, "Interview with Billie Brant," *IPH*, 89:140–45.

91 No person by the name of Billie Brant appears on the Dawes rolls, although Brant suggested that he was descended from "slaves who had been owned by Indians." In an ambiguous reference, he suggested that the Coker family had owned his family. A number of Cokers appear on the Dawes rolls as Seminoles by blood. Ibid., 140.

92 Byrd, "Wah-Sah-Shee Wa-Ke," 353.

93 "Vain Threats Made," *Tahlequah Cherokee Advocate*, February 2, 1901, 1.

94 Byrd, "Wah-Sah-Shee Wa-Ke," 353.

95 "Vain Threats Made."

96 Section 6 of 24 Stat. 388, in Semple, *Oklahoma Indian Land Titles*, 920.

97 "Act of March 3, 1901, According Citizenship to Indians in Indian Territory" (31 Stat. 1447), Semple, *Oklahoma Indian Land Titles*, 925.

98 McIntosh, "Chitto Harjo," 48–49.

99 *Kingfisher Free Press*, February 27, 1902, 2; "Editorial on Isparhecher and Pleasant Porter," *Tulsa Democrat*, February 21, 1902, typescript copy in folder 40, box 1, Isparhecher Collection, WHC; McIntosh, "Chitto Harjo," 88.

100 McIntosh, "Chitto Harjo," 51–52.

101 "Reflections upon Crazy Snake," *Eufaula Indian Journal*, February 1, 1901, 4.

102 Dawes Fife, "An Interview with Joseph Bruner," *IPH*, 51:173.

103 Grace Kelley, "Ward, Leroy. Interview," *IPH*, 48:453.

104 Ibid.; McIntosh, "Chitto Harjo," 53–54, 56; *Vinita Indian Chieftain*, February 7, 1902, 2.

105 Sidney L. Harring, "Crazy Snake and the Creek Struggle for Sovereignty: The Native American Legal Culture and American Law," *American Journal of Legal History* 34 (October 1990): 374, 376.

106 "'Crazy Snake' Still Hostile," *Tahlequah Cherokee Advocate* (1904): 2.

107 McIntosh, "Chitto Harjo," 191–93.

108 Ibid., 101.

109 U.S. Congress, Senate, Select Committee, *Report*, 2:1246, 1248; McIntosh, "Chitto Harjo," 102, 194.

110 U.S. Congress, Senate, Select Committee, *Report*, 2:1249–51.

111 Ibid.

112 Ibid., 1:89–91.

113 Ibid., 92.

114 Elizabeth Ross, "Interview with Jesse Doyle," *IPH*, 65:487.

115 *Tahlequah Cherokee Advocate*, December 13, 1902, 2.

CHAPTER 4

1 Quoted in John Thompson, *Closing the Frontier: Radical Response in Oklahoma, 1889–1923* (Norman: University of Oklahoma Press, 1986), 145.

2 U.S. Bureau of the Census, *Agriculture 1909 and 1910*, vol. 5 of *Thirteenth Census of the United States* (Washington: Government Printing Office, 1913), 122–27.

3 Dallas Dunzy to Hon. Acting Commissioner Merritt, May 7, 1915, in file: Creek 306, folder 129013–14, box 4429, entry 121: Central Classified File, RG 75, NA. The 1910 census, which spelled her first name "Dallace," listed her as age twenty. See U.S. Bureau of the Census, Thirteenth Census of the United States, 1910, NA, microfilm T624, Oklahoma, Hughes County, Barnard Township, Enumeration District 98, sheet 1A, line 16. Dallas Dunzy is enrolled on the "Creeks by Blood" rolls opposite number 3,204. U.S. Commission to the Five Civilized Tribes, *The Final Rolls of Citizens and Freedmen of the Five Civilized Tribes in Indian Territory* (Washington: Government Printing Office, 1907), 521.

4 On the theory of allotment, see D. S. Otis, *The Dawes Act and the Allotment of Indian Lands* (Norman: University of Oklahoma Press, 1973), chap. 2. On restrictions on alienation, see ibid., 13, 50–51; Francis Paul Prucha, ed., *Americanizing the American Indians: Writings by the "Friends of the Indian," 1880–1900* (Cambridge, Mass.: Harvard University Press, 1973), 6; Alexandra Harmon, "When Is an Indian Not an Indian? The 'Friends of the Indian' and the Problems of Indian Identity," *Journal of Ethnic Studies* 18 (Summer 1990): 104; Frederick E. Hoxie, *A Final Promise: The Campaign to Assimilate the Indians, 1880–1920* (Lincoln: University of Nebraska Press, 1984), xii, 85.

5 U.S. Congress, Senate, Select Committee, *Report of the Select Committee to Investigate Matters Connected with the Affairs in the Indian Territory with Hearings, November 11, 1906–January 9, 1907*, 59th Cong., 2nd sess., 1906–7 (Washington, Government Printing Office: 1907), 1:425–26, 442, 592, 687–88, 864–65.

6 Ibid., 2:1255–56.

7 Ibid., 1:692.

8 Ibid., 441–433.

9 Hoxie, *Final Promise*, 164, 183.

10 Editorial on Pleasant Porter, *Okemah Independent*, October 14, 1904, typescript copy in folder 1, Alice Brown Davis Collection, WHC.

11 J. Kēhaulani Kauanui, *Hawaiian Blood: Colonialism and the Politics of Sovereignty and Indigeneity* (Durham, N.C.: Duke University Press, 2008), 125.

12 U.S. Congress, Senate, Select Committee, *Report*, 1:662.

13 Melissa L. Meyer, *The White Earth Tragedy: Ethnicity and Dispossession at a Minnesota Anishinaabe Reservation, 1889–1920* (Lincoln: University of Nebraska Press, 1994), 2.

14 U.S. Congress, Senate, Select Committee, *Report*, 1:415.

15 Laura F. Edwards, *The People and Their Place: Legal Culture and the Transformation of Inequality in the Post-Revolutionary South* (Chapel Hill: University of North Carolina Press, 2009), 25.

16 U.S. Congress, Senate, Select Committee, *Report*, 2:1334–35, 1339–40. For a similar mobilization of the notion of antiwhite discrimination, see Kauanui, *Hawaiian Blood*, 125.

17 U.S. Congress, Senate, Select Committee, *Report*, 2:1880–81.

18 Ibid., 1896.

19 David A. Y. O. Chang, "'The Land Owners Are Ruining the Land': Race, Class, and the Politics of Soil Depletion in Oklahoma, 1907–1940," paper presented at Social Science History Association Annual Meeting, Fort Worth, Texas, November 14, 1999, 3–4.

20 Lawrence Mills, *The Lands of the Five Civilized Tribes: A Treatise upon the Law Applicable to the Lands of the Five Civilized Tribes in Oklahoma* (St. Louis: F. H. Thomas Law Book Co., 1919), 445.

21 Ibid., 132.

22 The law applied only to adults, not minors, and provision was made permitting the Indian Department agent in Muskogee to remove restrictions. The law provided for some exceptions, and courts later decided that it permitted only voluntary transfers of land, not involuntary transfers such as seizures for unpaid taxes. Ibid., 129.

23 Angie Debo, *And Still the Waters Run: The Betrayal of the Five Civilized Tribes* (Princeton, N.J.: Princeton University Press, 1940), 114.

24 "Many Called, Few Chosen," *Vinita Weekly Chieftain*, November 3, 1904, 2.

25 W. F. Semple, *Oklahoma Indian Land Titles, Annotated* (St. Louis: Thomas Law Book Co., 1952), 719.

26 Debo, *And Still the Waters Run*, 90; Semple, *Oklahoma Indian Land Titles*, 709.

27 "An Act for the Protection of the People of the Indian Territory, and for Other Purposes" (30 Stat. 495: Act of June 28, 1898) in Mills, *Lands of the Five Civilized Tribes*, 538–41.

28 Cheryl I. Harris, "Whiteness as Property," *Harvard Law Review* 106 (June 1993).

29 "Releases Rich Lands for Sale," *Oklahoma City Daily Oklahoman*, May 29, 1907, 1.

30 This conservative estimate is based on the assumption that 80 percent of the 6,809 enrolled Creek Freedmen had received 160-acre allotments and sold their 120 acres of surplus lands. It does not take into account that some had already effectively sold their homestead lands through illegal contracts despite restrictions on it. Debo,

And Still the Waters Run, 47, 51; Danney Goble, *Progressive Oklahoma: The Making of a New Kind of State* (Norman: University of Oklahoma Press, 1980), 78. Mineral leases: Moses Starr and Hepsie Starr, "Indenture," 1900, folder 3, flap folder 8, box 3, Grayson Family Papers, WHC.

31 "Many Called, Few Chosen."

32 "To Remove Restrictions," *Vinita Weekly Chieftain*, April 14, 1904, 1.

33 *Muskogee Times Democrat*, June 12, 1908, 1.

34 *Oklahoma City Oklahoma News*, August 20, 1908; Debo, *And Still the Waters Run*, 181–82.

35 *Muskogee Times Democrat*, August 8, 1908, 8. A newspaper in Muskogee, the center of the trade in allotted lands, reported that the removal of restrictions could make available for sale 71,000 farms. *Muskogee Times Democrat*, July 30, 1908, 1.

36 Debo, *And Still the Waters Run*, 182.

37 "Many Called, Few Chosen."

38 Office of Indian Affairs, "Circular No. 279 (2nd Supplement)," in Departmental Circulars, vol. 1, no folder, box 1, entry 304: Records of the Five Civilized Tribes Agency: Circulars, 1907–50, RG 75, NA-FW.

39 Thomas J. Farrar to Dana H. Kelsey, August 27, 1908, in file: Creek 306, box 4409, entry 121: Central Classified File, RG 75, NA.

40 Dana H. Kelsey to Commissioner of Indian Affairs, January 8, 1909, in file: Creek 306, box 4409, entry 121: Central Classified File, RG 75, NA.

41 Hoxie, *Final Promise*, xii.

42 Katie Tiner, "Application for Removal of Restrictions," August 22, 1908, in file: Creek 306, box 4431, entry 121: Central Classified File, RG 75, NA; Thomas J. Farrar to Hon. Dana H. Kelsey, November 18, 1908, in file: Creek 306, box 4431, entry 121: Central Classified File, RG 75, NA.

43 Thomas J. Farrar, "Field Report upon Application for Removal of Restrictions," 1914, in file: Creek 306, box 4428, entry 121: Central Classified File, RG 75, NA; D.H.K. [Dana H. Kelsey], "Winey Bullwer, Restrictions No. 10793," 1914, in file: Creek 306, box 4428, entry 121: Central Classified File, RG 75, NA.

44 Dana H. Kelsey to the Commissioner of Indian Affairs, April 2, 1914, in file: Creek 306, box 4426, entry 121: Central Classified File, RG 75, NA.

45 Dana H. Kelsey to the Commissioner of Indian Affairs, January 14, 1909, in file: Creek 306, box 4409, entry 121: Central Classified File, RG 75, NA.

46 Case of Jennie Hickory, Dana H. Kelsey to Commissioner of Indian Affairs, January 8, 1909, in file: Creek 306, box 4409, entry 121: Central Classified File, RG 75, NA; Case of Stella Shawnego, Dana H. Kelsey to Commissioner of Indian Affairs, January 5, 1909, file: Creek 306, box 4409, entry 121: Central Classified File, RG 75, NA (1909).

47 Meyer, *White Earth Tragedy*, 156.

48 Gabe E. Parker to the Commissioner of Indian Affairs, February 15, 1915, in file: Creek 306, box 4429, entry 121: Central Classified File, RG 75, NA.

49 J. R. Dunzy to the Commissioner of Indian Affairs, April 14, 1915, in file: Creek 306, folder 129013–14, box 4429, entry 121: Central Classified File, RG 75, NA.

50 N. Dunzy to the Commissioner of Indian Affairs, May 6, 1915, in file: Creek 306, folder 129013–14, box 4429, entry 121: Central Classified File, RG 75, NA.

51 Dallas Dunzy to Hon. Acting Commissioner Merritt.

52 Debo, *And Still the Waters Run*, 92–126.

53 R. L. Williams, "Graduated Land License Tax Report," ca. 1914, folder 1, box 14, Robert Lee Williams Collection, OHS; "Name of Chief Justice Williams Is Brought into Land Graft," *Oklahoma City Times*, August 15, 1908, 1.

54 Sammah and Halia Harjo to Amo B. Cutlip, Warranty Deed with Relinquishment of Dower, February 2, 1907; Mary Fixico to Amo B. Cutlip, Warranty Deed with Relinquishment of Dower, February 9, 1907; Robert Johnson to Amo B. Cutlip, Warranty Deed with Relinquishment of Dower, February 12, 1907; Jacksey Watko to Amo B. Cutlip, Warranty Deed with Relinquishment of Dower, February 12, 1907; Sally and John Hulwa to Amo B. Cutlip, Warranty Deed with Relinquishment of Dower, February 16, 1907; A. W. and Mollie Butts to Amo B. Cutlip, Quit Claim Deed, March 11, 1907; George Hulbutta to Amo B. Cutlip, Warranty Deed with Relinquishment of Dower, March 22, 1907; Wesley Chupco to Amo B. Cutlip, Warranty Deed, April 7, 1909; J. Wesley to Amo B. Cutlip, Warranty Deed with Relinquishment of Dower, April 20, 1907; Thomas F. and Lillian Robertson to Amo B. Cutlip, Quit Claim Deed with Relinquishment of Dower, March 25, 1909. All these deeds are located in folder 17, box 9, C. Guy Cutlip Collection, WHC. Thompson, *Closing the Frontier*, 36–38.

55 James Green, *Grass-Roots Socialism: Radical Movements in the Southwest. 1895–1943* (Baton Rouge: Louisiana State University Press, 1978), 66–72; Garin Burbank, *When Farmers Voted Red: The Gospel of Socialism in the Oklahoma Countryside* (Westport, Conn.: Greenwood, 1976), 44–48; James R. Scales and Danney Goble, *Oklahoma Politics: A History* (Norman: University of Oklahoma Press, 1982), 20–43.

56 Immigration just prior to statehood exacerbated the problem of farm tenancy, which was widespread even before allotment. Between 1890 and 1907, the population of Indian Territory increased from 178,097 to 538,512. Most of the increase was made up of would-be farmers without citizenship rights and without the hope of getting an allotment. Debo, *And Still the Waters Run*, 182.

57 "Oklahoma Farms Average 149 Acres," *Vinita Weekly Chieftain*, December 24, 1909, 5.

58 For this reason, for information on the racial distribution of landownership and the persistence of ownership by Creek allottees, this chapter depends on reports from contemporary sources, which are themselves estimates.

59 Katherine Smith, Home Demonstration Report, Muskogee County, 1916, T-881, reel 1, [1]; E. R. Moore, "Report of the Work of the County Agent, Calendar Year 1919. Negro," T-881, reel 5; Dover P. Trent, "Report of Work of the County Agent, Calendar Year 1921," T-881, reel 10, all in RG 33, NA.

60 "In the Black Belt of Okfuskee County, Oklahoma," *Boley Progress*, January 13, 1910; W. D. Bentley, "Annual Report, Oklahoma State Department of Cooperative Demonstration Work, 1911," November 1, 1911, T-881, reel 1, RG 33, NA; Thompson, *Closing the Frontier*, 24.

61 Annual Report, Oklahoma State Director of Cooperative Demonstration Work, 1909, September 27, 1909, T-881, reel 1, 37, RG 33, NA. See also E. R. Moore, "Report of the Work of the County Agent, Calendar Year 1919. Negro," Seminole County, T-881, reel 5, page no. illegible, page heading is "Manure" and "Annual Report: Extension Division, Oklahoma A. & M. College, 1922–23," 1924, Extension Circular no. 195, General Series no. 32, T-881, reel 13, 2, both in RG 33, NA.

62 G. C. Gibbons, "Annual Report of Agronomy Work in Oklahoma," 1923, T-881, reel 10, RG 33, NA.

63 "Eastern Oklahoma Agricultural Association," in folder 6, box 1, Fred Barde Collection, OHS.

64 J. F. Darby, "Report of J. F. Darby to the Permanent American Commission on Agricultural Conditions and Needs of Oklahoma," folder 4, box 4, Cruce Papers.

65 Marion S. Lahman, "Report of Marion S. Lahman to the Permanent American Commission on Agricultural Conditions and Needs of Oklahoma," folder 4, box 4, Cruce Papers; "Arbeka Crossing, Ok, April 24," in folder 18, box 14, Barde Collection, OHS.

66 U.S. Congress, Senate, Select Committee, *Report*, 2:1880–81, 1896.

67 Allottees whom the Dawes Commission had enrolled as having more than three-quarters Indian "blood" were also forbidden to sell part of their lands to fund improving or farming the remainder. "An Act for the Protection of the People of the Indian Territory," in Mills, *Lands of the Five Civilized Tribes*, 538–41.

68 Debo, *And Still the Waters Run*, 127

69 Lahman, "Report."

70 "Arbeka Crossing, Ok, April 24."

71 "Eastern Oklahoma Agricultural Association."

72 On differential impacts of public policy on land tenure by race and class, see Thomas W. Mitchell, "From Reconstruction to Deconstruction," Research Paper no. 132 (Land Tenure Center, Madison, Wisconsin, 1999), 19–26; Donald A. Krueckeberg, "Who Rents America? Owners, Tenants, and Taxes," Working Paper no. 32 (Land Tenure Center, Madison, Wisconsin, 1999), 2–3; Manning Marable, "The Politics of Black Land Tenure, 1877–1915" *Agricultural History* 53 (January 1979).

73 "Long Term Interest Rates," unnumbered folder, box 15 (1915), entry 114: Records Relating to Rural Credit in the United States, 1913–19, RG 83, NA.

74 "Average Usual Rate Charged by Banks on Farm Mortgages, July 1, 1918," folder "Manuscripts," box 12; Office of Markets and Rural Organization, USDA, "Factors Affecting Interest Rates on Farm Mortgage Loans," ca. 1915, folder "Reports and Mms. [sic] on Rural Credit Conditions," box 23; USDA, "Short Time (Personal) Interest Rates—Comparative Statement," ca. 1913, folder 16b, box 12; USDA, "Distribution of Bank Loans, July 1, 1918," folder "Manuscripts," box 12; USDA, "Distribution of Farm Mortgage Loans Held by Banks on July 1, 1918, According to Interest Rates," folder "Manuscripts," box 12, all in entry 114: Records Relating to Rural Credit in the United States, 1913–19, RG 83, NA.

75 "Terms of State Loans to Farmers," ca. 1921, folder "Credit Union Laws in Different

States 1920–1921," box 7, entry 114: Records Relating to Rural Credit in the United States, 1913–19, RG 83, NA.

76 [Robert L. Williams] to E. W. Moore, June 14, 1915, folder 5, box 3, RG 8-C-3-1: Administrative File, Robert L. Williams Papers, OSA; E. B. Baum to G. A. Smith, January 12, 1916, folder 8, box 3, RG 8-C-3-1: Administrative File, Robert L. Williams Papers, OSA; "Credit Structure for Delta Area, Federal Reserve Data," ca. 1921, folder "Cotton Literature," box 5, entry 114: Records Relating to Rural Credit in the United States, 1913–19, RG 83, NA; Thompson, *Closing the Frontier*, 102–5; G. A. Smith to Members of the Oklahoma Legislature, ca. 1916, folder 6, box 3, RG 8-C-3-1: Administrative File, Robert L. Williams Papers, OSA.

77 "Will End Land Controversy," *Muskogee Pioneer*, November 4, 1905, 2.

78 Eric Englund, "Assessment and Equalization of Farm and City Real Estate in Kansas," June 1924, envelope: "Englund MS and memos," box 3, entry 119: Records Relating to Taxation Studies, RG 83, NA; E. C. Pasour Jr., "The Capitalization of Real Property Taxes Levied on Farm Real Estate," *American Journal of Agricultural Economics*, 57 (November 1975): 539.

79 Lee Cruce to W. P. Poland, July 25, 1912, folder 5, box 31, Cruce Papers.

80 Mrs. R. Robinson to Lee Cruce, February 16, 1914, folder 12, box 1, Cruce Papers.

81 Governor's Secretary to Arthur Capper, March 1915, folder 1, box 2, RG 8-C-1-1: General Correspondence, Robert L. Williams Papers, OSA.

82 "Does Indian Homestead Taxation Mean Practical Confiscation?—Opposing Views," folder 1, box 28, Barde Collection, OHS.

83 U.S. Department of the Interior, *Indian Affairs, Territories*, vol. 2 of *Reports of the Department of the Interior for the Fiscal Year Ending June 30 1910: Administrative Reports* (Washington: Government Printing Office, 1911), 182–183.

84 Central Classified File Creek no. 121, box 4400, entry 121: Central Classified File, 1907–36, RG 75, NA; I. J. Simpson to Hon. R. L. Williams, folder 4, box 4, Robert Lee Williams Collection, OHS; Bessie Brown English vs. H. T. Richardson, Brief of Plaintiff in Error, folder 14, box 12, Grant Foreman Collection, OHS; *English v. Richardson*, 224 U.S. 680 (1912); W. M. Baker to Mr. C. H. Drew, August 1, 1916, folder "Taxes," box 2, entry 648: Office Files of the Field Clerk at Wewoka, 1916–37, RG 75, NA-FW.

85 Gerald Vizenor, *Fugitive Poses: Native American Indian Scenes of Absence and Presence* (Lincoln: University of Nebraska Press, 1998), 15.

86 A similar point is made in Sidney L. Harring, "Crazy Snake and the Creek Struggle for Sovereignty," *American Journal of Legal History* 34 (October 1990): 378.

87 Ohland Morton, "Reconstruction in the Creek Nation," *Chronicles of Oklahoma* 9 (June 1931).

88 Sam'l J. Haynes, D. M. Hodge, Billy G. Barnett, et al. to Hon. Moty Tiger, October 26, 1909, flap folder 4, folder 6, box 2, Grayson Family Papers, WHC.

89 The functioning of the National Council in this period is little documented, given the fact that the Curtis Act had all but ended any federal recognition of the Creek government. The best collection on the Creek government in the first few decades of statehood is in the Rufus Cox Collection, OHS.

90 Lester Robbins argues that the fact that Creek ritual, including the Green Corn *poskita*, was embedded in town life contributed to its persistence through removal, allotment, and the twentieth century. Lester Eugene Robbins, "The Persistence of Traditional Religious Practices among Creek Indians" (Ph.D. diss., Southern Methodist University, 1976), iv.

91 Amelia Rector Bell, "Creek Ritual: The Path to Peace" (Ph.D. diss., University of Chicago, 1984), 9–11; Alexander Spoehr, *Changing Kinship Systems: A Study in the Acculturation of the Creeks, Cherokee, and Choctaw*, Publication 583, Anthropological series, vol. 33, no. 4 (Chicago: Field Museum, 1947), 203–4, 211, 213, 222, 225.

92 Spoehr, *Changing Kinship Systems*, 200, 208, 209–10, 220.

93 Earnest Gouge, *Totkv Mocvse/New Fire: Creek Folktales by Earnest Gouge*, ed. and trans. Jack Martin, Margaret McKane Mauldin, and Juanita McGirt (Norman: University of Oklahoma Press, 2004), xi, xix.

94 Tom Holm, *The Great Confusion in Indian Affairs: Native Americans and Whites in the Progressive Era* (Austin: University of Texas Press, 2005), 30. Lee Irwin describes the Four Mothers Society as a "renewal movement" within the general rubric of "religious resistance." Lee Irwin, "Freedom, Law, and Prophecy: A Brief History of Native American Religious Resistance," *American Indian Quarterly* 21 (Winter 1997). John A. Wickham emphasizes rather its state-based political action when he notes that "the first intertribal collective political action before Congress was initiated and called the Four Mothers Society" and describes it as the forerunner of such Progressive Era pan-Indian organizations as the Society of American Indians. John A. Wickham, "September 11 and America's War on Terrorism: A New Manifest Destiny?" *American Indian Quarterly* 26 (Winter 2002). On the Keetoowahs and the Four Mothers, see Janey B. Hendrix, *Redbird Smith and the Nighthawk Keetoowahs* (Park Hill, Okla.: Cross-Cultural Education Center, 1983), 62.

95 Cherokee Nation Cultural Resources Center, "Redbird Smith Story," <http://www.thepeoplespaths.net/Cherokee/RedbirdSmithStory.htm> (June 30, 2008).

96 The sensational news coverage of the events, and the politically and emotionally charged nature of the events, have made it difficult for historians to reconstruct these events with clarity. This summary is based on Kenneth Waldo McIntosh, "Chitto Harjo, the Crazy Snakes and the Birth of Indian Political Activism in the Twentieth Century" (Ph.D. diss., Texas Christian University, 1993), 118–26; Daniel F. Littlefield and Lonnie E. Underhill, "The Crazy Snake Uprising of 1909: A Red, Black or White Affair?" *Arizona and the West* 20 (Winter 1978); and Mel H. Bolster, "The Smoked Meat Rebellion: Early Oklahoma and Creek Unrest," *Chronicles of Oklahoma* 31 (Spring 1953): 41–44. See also Grace Kelley, "Interview with Mrs. Willie Blair," *IPH*, 104:95–97; Otis Hume, "An Interview with Henry Jacobs," *IPH*, 31:100–103. In the 1930s, some raised the possibility that Chitto Harjo was still alive: Jerome M. Emmons, "Interview with Mrs. Ada M. Roach," *IPH*, 52:347.

97 Alexander Lawrence Posey, *The Fus Fixico Letters: A Creek Humorist in Early Oklahoma*, ed. Daniel F. Littlefield and Carol A. Petty Hunter (Norman, Okla.: Red River Books, 2002), 14.

98 M. C. Hickman, "Moving to Our Claims, 1891," *IPH*, 29:43–49.

99 A skeptical white man offered another explanation for the new inclusiveness of the movement, claiming that Chitto Harjo charged each member ten dollars to join and thus "made plenty of money out of his scheme." Ibid., 48.

100 Hume, "Interview with Henry Jacobs," 102. Billy Brant also reported that he was a black Creek who took part in the Snake movement, but a number of incongruous details render his account problematic. Billy Byrd, "Interview with Billie Brant," *IPH*, 30:140–145.

101 Debo, *And Still the Waters Run*, 296–98.

102 E. J. Kersting to Adjutant General, February 6, 1919, folder 4, box 29, RG 8-D-1-1: General Correspondence, J. B. A. Robertson Papers, OSA.

103 Carrie Peck to Govenor Crues, May 14, 1912, and Mrs. Peck to Govenor Cruce, May 26, 1912, folder 5, box 31, Cruce Papers.

104 Nettie Cain, "An Interview with Lucendy Long Dunzy," *IPH*, 23:128.

105 E. Hastain, *Hastain's Township Plats of the Creek Nation* (Muskogee: Model Printing Co., 1910), 57.

106 See the manuscript censuses as follows: Yeager Township, Hughes County, Oklahoma, Thirteenth Census of the United States, 1910, NA, microfilm T624; Yeager Township, Hughes County, Oklahoma, Fourteenth Census of the United States, 1920, NA, microfilm T625; Yeager Township, Hughes County, Oklahoma, Fifteenth Census of the United States, 1930, NA, microfilm T626.

107 Tanis C. Thorne, *The World's Richest Indian: The Scandal over Jackson Barnett's Oil Fortune* (Oxford: Oxford University Press, 2003), 33–34.

108 "Annual Report of Extension Workers, Form B, Okmulgee District, Five Civilized Tribes," in folder "Annual Report," box "Okmulgee Farm Agent Reports, Correspondence," entry 637: Office Files of the Farm Extension Agent, Okmulgee District, 1935–38, RG 75, NA-FW.

109 Vance Rogers, "The C.W.A. Social and Economic Survey of Selected Indian Reservations," in folder "N.R.B. Compilation of Survey 1934," box 1, entry 292: Records of the Division of Extension and Survey, Records Relating to Social and Economic Survey, 1933–34, RG 75, NA.

110 That scorn was exemplified by the early press coverage surrounding Creek allottee Jackson Barnett. Thorne, *World's Richest Indian*, 61, 68.

111 T. A. Vincent, "Southeast District," in "Report of the Extension Division. A & M. College, Year of 1919–1920," reel 6, T-881, RG 33, NA; C. W. Callarman, "South Central District," in "Report of the Extension Division. A & M. College, Year of 1919–1920," reel 6, T-881, RG 33, NA; John A. Simpson, address to the Oklahoma Farmers Union, 1919, folder 23, box 6, John A. Simpson Collection, WHC; E. R. Moore, "Report of the Work of the County Agent, Calendar Year 1919. Negro," Seminole County, reel 5, T-881, RG 33, NA; Statistics Division of Research and Federal Emergency Relief Administration Finance, "The Western Cotton Growing Area, Choctaw County, Oklahoma," 1934, box 1, entry 156: Division of Farm Population and Rural Life and Its Predecessors: County Reports on Rural Problem Areas, 1934–35, RG 83, NA.

CHAPTER 5

1 "State-Hood," *Muskogee Comet*, September 29, 1904, 1.

2 On African American efforts to obtain and keep land during and after Reconstruction, see Edward Royce, *The Origins of Southern Sharecropping* (Philadelphia: Temple University Press, 1993); Eric Foner, *Reconstruction: America's Unfinished Revolution, 1863–1877* (New York: Harper and Row, 1988), 104–6, 374–77; Barbara Jeanne Fields, *Slavery and Freedom on the Middle Ground: Maryland during the Nineteenth Century* (New Haven, Conn.: Yale University Press, 1985), 175–81; Claude F. Oubre, *Forty Acres and a Mule: The Freedmen's Bureau and Black Landownership* (Baton Rouge: Louisiana State University Press, 1978).

3 See, for example, Robin D. G. Kelley and Earl Lewis, eds., *To Make Our World Anew: A History of African Americans* (New York: Oxford University Press, 2000), 378–79; Nell Irvin Painter, *Standing at Armageddon: The United States, 1877–1919* (New York: Norton, 1987), 222–23; Cary D. Wintz, ed., *African American Political Thought, 1890–1930: Washington, Du Bois, Garvey, and Randolph* (Armonk, N.Y.: Sharpe, 1996), 1–2, 6, 10; David Levering Lewis, *W. E. B. Du Bois: Biography of a Race, 1868–1919* (New York: Henry Holt, 1993), 175, 177; John M. Wortham, "The Economic Ideologies of Booker T. Washington and W. E. B. Du Bois: 1895–1915" (Ph.D. diss., Boston University, 1997); and Howard Bleeth, "A Black Elite Agenda in the Urban South: The Call for Political Change and Racial Economic Solidarity in Houston during the 1920s," *Essays in Economic and Business History* 10 (1992).

4 On the political uses of "community," see Miranda Joseph, *Against the Romance of Community* (Minneapolis: University of Minnesota Press, 2002).

5 Angie Debo, *And Still the Waters Run: The Betrayal of the Five Civilized Tribes* (Princeton, N.J.: Princeton University Press, 1940), 133; U.S. Bureau of the Census, *Extra Census Bulletin: The Five Civilized Tribes of the Indian Territory* (Washington: Government Printing Office, 1894), 7–8; U.S. Bureau of the Census, *Statistics for Oklahoma, Thirteenth Census of the United States, 1910* (Washington: Government Printing Office, 1913), 695.

6 Nell Irvin Painter, *Exodusters: Black Migration to Kansas after Reconstruction* (New York: Knopf, 1977); Jimmie Lewis Franklin, *Journey toward Hope: A History of Blacks in Oklahoma* (Norman: University of Oklahoma Press, 1982), 11–13.

7 On the long history of eighteenth- and nineteenth-century African American emigrationist and Back-to-Africa movements, see Edwin S. Redkey, *Black Exodus: Black Nationalist and Back-to-Africa Movements, 1890–1910* (New Haven, Conn.: Yale University Press, 1969), and Floyd J. Miller, *The Search for a Black Nationality: Black Emigration and Colonization, 1787–1863* (Urbana: University of Illinois Press, 1975).

8 Franklin, *Journey Toward Hope*, 21.

9 On land tenure in southern states in this period, see Neil R. McMillan, *Dark Journey: Black Mississippians in the Age of Jim Crow* (Urbana: University of Illinois Press, 1990), and Manning Marable, "The Politics of Black Land Tenure, 1877–1915," *Agricultural History* 53 (January 1979).

10 Painter, *Exodusters*, 256–61; Robert G. Athearn, *In Search of Canaan: Black Migration to Kansas, 1879–80* (Lawrence: Regents Press of Kansas, 1978), 277–79;

"Joanna Draper," *The WPA Oklahoma Slave Narratives*, ed. T. Lindsay Baker and Julie P. Baker (Norman: University of Oklahoma Press, 1996), 136. For an overview of post-Reconstruction-era migration from the South to the American West, including the migration to Oklahoma, see Quintard Taylor, *In Search of the Racial Frontier: African Americans in the American West, 1528–1990* (New York: Norton, 1998), 134–63.

11 Joel Williamson, "Black Self-Assertion before and after Emancipation," in *Key Issues in the Afro-American Experience*, ed. Nathan I. Huggins, Martin Kilson, and Daniel M. Fox (New York: Harcourt Brace Jovanovich, 1971), 230–31.

12 *Boley Progress*, March 16, 1905, 1.

13 Wintz, *African American Political Thought*, 1–6.

14 The editorial did allow that some settlers might "lease a good farm at from 15 to 25 cents per acre" instead of buying but swept aside the cautious statement with a more characteristically optimistic one: "You can own a home in the Creek Nation easier than rent." Untitled editorial, *Boley Progress*, March 16, 1905, 1. See also untitled editorial, March 23, 1905, 1.

15 Booker T. Washington, "The Negro in the New Southwest," December 30, 1905, reprinted in Louis R. Harlan and Raymond W. Smock, eds., *The Booker T. Washington Papers* (Urbana: University of Illinois Press, 1979), 8:472–73.

16 *Muskogee Cimeter*, July 21, 1904, 4.

17 *Muskogee Cimeter*, July 14, 1904, 4.

18 Paula Giddings, *When and Where I Enter: The Impact of Black Women on Race and Sex in America* (New York: Morrow, 1984), 62; Jacqueline Jones, *Labor of Love, Labor of Sorrow: Black Women, Work, and the Family from Slavery to the Present* (New York: Basic Books, 1985), 58; Gerald Jaynes, *Branches without Roots: Genesis of the Black Working Class in the American South, 1862–1882* (New York: Oxford University Press, 1986), 228–31.

19 "The Jubilee in Sight," *Vinita Indian Chieftain*, January 26, 1888, 2.

20 Kenneth Marvin Hamilton, *Black Towns and Profit: Promotion and Development in the Trans-Appalachian West, 1877–1915* (Urbana: University of Illinois Press, 1991), chaps. 3–4.

21 Ibid., 126; Norman L. Crockett, *The Black Towns* (Lawrence: Regents Press of Kansas, 1979), 28; Sigmund Sameth, "Creek Negroes: A Study in Race Relations" (M.A. thesis, University of Oklahoma, 1940), 56; Kaye M. Teall, ed., *Black History in Oklahoma: A Resource Book* (Oklahoma City: Oklahoma City Public Schools, 1971), 167.

22 William E. Bittle and Gilbert Geis, *The Longest Way Home: Chief Alfred C. Sam's Back-to-Africa Movement* (Detroit: Wayne State University Press, 1964), 22–23; Teall, *Black History in Oklahoma*, 167; Crockett, *Black Towns*, 28–29; Sameth, "Creek Negroes," 54, 56; Jack B. Martin and Margaret McKane Mauldin, *A Dictionary of Creek/Muskogee: With Notes on the Florida and Oklahoma Seminole Dialects of Creek* (Lincoln: University of Nebraska Press, 2000), s.v. "wvcenv," 150; Claudio Saunt, *A New Order of Things: Property, Power, and the Transformation of the Creek Indians, 1733–1816* (Cambridge: Cambridge University Press, 1999), 115–16.

23 "Act of March 3, 1901, According Citizenship to Indians in Indian Territory" (31 Stat.

1447), W. F. Semple, *Oklahoma Indian Land Titles, Annotated* (St. Louis: Thomas Law Book Co., 1952), 925.

24 Lawrence Mills, ed., *The Lands of the Five Civilized Tribes: A Treatise upon the Law Applicable to the Lands of the Five Civilized Tribes in Oklahoma* (St. Louis: F. H. Thomas Law Book Co., 1919), 16; "An Act to Amend Section Six, Chapter One Hundred and Nineteen, United States Statutes at Large Numbered Twenty-Four (31 Stat. L. 1447)," in Mills, *Lands of the Five Civilized Tribes*, 716.

25 "Suffrage League Convention," *Muskogee Cimeter*, October 4, 1907. Alex Sango appears on the Creek Freedman rolls opposite enrollment number 421. U.S. Commission to the Five Civilized Tribes, *The Final Rolls of Citizens and Freedmen of the Five Civilized Tribes in Indian Territory* (Washington: Government Printing Office, 1907), 577. This is likely the same man who appears on the 1910 U.S. census as Alax G. W. Sango. See U.S. Bureau of the Census, Thirteenth Census of the United States, 1910, NA, microfilm T624, Oklahoma, Muskogee City, Muskogee County, Muskogee City, Enumeration District 119, sheet 3B, line 75.

26 "That Washington Trip," *Muskogee Cimeter*, November 1, 1907.

27 Constitution of the State of Oklahoma, 1907, sec. 2, art. 23, and sec. 35, art. 6; [Robert Lee Williams], untitled manuscript, n.d., folder 4, box 1, Robert Lee Williams Collection, OHS.

28 Debo, *And Still the Waters Run*, 292–94; Alexander Spoehr, "Oklahoma Seminole Towns," *Chronicles of Oklahoma* 14 (December 1941); Jack M. Schultz, *The Seminole Baptist Churches of Oklahoma: Maintaining a Traditional Community* (Norman: University of Oklahoma Press, 1999), 40–45.

29 The purchase of town lots in Boley itself was complicated by the fact that the town was situated on a minor Freedman's land and restrictions remained on the land of minors after having been lifted on adults' allotments. The owner's father had arranged a lease with the intent to sell the land to the developers, but the buyers encountered years of legal difficulties before securing the right to do so. Hamilton, *Black Towns and Profit*, 121, 128–30.

30 "Land for Sale," *Boley Progress*, November 10, 1910, 4; Debo, *And Still the Waters Run*, 89–90.

31 "Some Things to Be Regretted," *Muskogee Comet*, August 25, 1904, 2.

32 "Land! Land! Land!" *Muskogee Cimeter*, June 2, 1904, 8; untitled, *Muskogee Cimeter*, June 23, 1904, 4; "Still Another Enterprise," *Muskogee Comet*, June 16, 1904, 1; "Freedmen's Land and Trust Co," *Muskogee Pioneer*, October 28 1905, 1; "Farm Loans," *Muskogee Pioneer*, October 28, 1905, 3.

33 Teall, *Black History in Oklahoma*, 167.

34 *Muskogee Comet*, August 11, 1904, 1.

35 "Negroes Were Disappointed," *Muskogee Pioneer*, December 2, 1905, 2; "Haskell News," *Muskogee Pioneer*, December 16, 1905, 8; *Muskogee Comet*, July 14, 1904, 2; "Great Territorial Mass Convention," *Muskogee Comet*, August 18, 1904, 1.

36 Teall, *Black History in Oklahoma*, 225.

37 Franklin, *Journey toward Hope*, 108–12; "Grandfather Clause—Believed by Prominent Men," *Vinita Indian Chieftain*, July 22, 1910, 3; [Robert L. Williams], to G. T. Searcy, May 11, 1910, folder 4, box 14, Robert Lee Williams Collection, OHS; W. H.

Carter to Hon. R. L. Williams, June 7, [1914?], folder 4, box 4, Robert Lee Williams Collection, OHS; Joel Williamson, *The Crucible of Race: Black-White Relations in the American South Since Emancipation* (New York: Oxford University Press, 1984), 244.

38 Charles R. Freeman to R. L. Williams, August 3, 1915, folder 4, box 11, RG 8-C-1-1: General Correspondence, Robert L. Williams Papers, OSA.

39 E. J. Broaddus and F. Sullivan to Hon. R. L. Williams, November 29, 1915, folder 2, box 1, RG 8-C-1-2: General Correspondence, 1916, Robert L. Williams Papers, OSA. The Democratic member of the state senate recalled that prior to disenfranchisement in 1910 African Americans had held local office and the end of the Grandfather Clause threatened to revive this state of affairs. J. H. Sutherlin to R. L. Williams, November 9, 1915, folder 2, box 4, RG 8-C-3-1: Administrative File, Robert L. Williams Papers, OSA.

40 J. E. Harston to Gov. Rob't. Williams, December 11, 1915, folder 10, box 3, RG 8-C-3-1: Administrative File, Robert L. Williams Papers, OSA; Garin Burbank, *When Farmers Voted Red: The Gospel of Socialism in the Oklahoma Countryside, 1910–1924* (Westport, Conn.: Greenwood, 1976), 84–85; Franklin, *Journey toward Hope*, 114.

41 Burbank, *When Farmers Voted Red*, 85–86.

42 Joel Williamson, *Crucible of Race*, 245. On the term "farmer," see Stephen Kantrowitz, *Ben Tillman and the Reconstruction of White Supremacy* (Chapel Hill: University of North Carolina Press, 2000), 110–12, 130–31.

43 Franklin, *Journey toward Hope*, 116; John Thompson, *Closing the Frontier: Radical Response in Oklahoma, 1889–1923* (Norman: University of Oklahoma Press, 1986), 134.

44 E. D. Mitchell to Gov. Williams, February 18, 1918, folder 7, box 4, Robert Lee Williams Collection, OHS.

45 Virginia Lantz Denton, *Booker T. Washington and the Adult Education Movement* (Gainesville: University Press of Florida, 1993), 106–19.

46 W. D. Bentley, Annual Report, Oklahoma State Director of Cooperative Demonstration Work, 1910, July 1, 1910, reel 1, T-881, NA, 11; W. D. Bentley, Annual Report, Oklahoma State Department of Cooperative Demonstration Work, 1911, November 1, 1911, reel 1, T-881, NA, 3, 27–28.

47 B. F. Brown, "Report of Work of the County Agent," 1917, filmed under "Payne, Okmulgee, Creek, Muskogee," reel 1, T-881, NA, n.p.; Bentley, Annual Report 1910, 2; "Narrative Report of County Agent Work," in James Edward Taylor, "Report of Work of the County Agent, Calendar Year 1921," reel 10, T-881, NA, n.p.

48 B. F. Brown, "Report of Work of the County Agent," 1917, filmed under "Payne, Okmulgee, Creek, Muskogee," reel 1, T-881, NA, n.p.

49 J. M. Daily, "Report of the Work of the County Agent, Calendar Year 1919. Negro," reel 5, T-881, NA, p. OEWS 920-cc.

50 Teall, *Black History in Oklahoma*, 179–80; Arthur L. Tolson, *The Black Oklahomans: A History, 1541–1972* (New Orleans: Edwards Printing Co., 1972), 131; C. Guy Cutlip, untitled manuscript on Seminole County history, 1930, folder 18, box 2, C. Guy Cutlip Collection, WHC.

51 "Demonstration Work," *Boley Progress*, December 3, 1910, 1; "Negro Business

League Notes," *Boley Progress*, August 6, 1915, 2; "The Grand Father Clause Is Not a Law," *Boley Progress*, December 3, 1910, 1; "The Grandfather Clause," *Boley Progress*, October 22, 1915, 1.

52 E. R. Moore, "Report of the Work of the County Agent, Calendar Year 1919. Negro," reel 5, T-881, NA, n.p., follows verso of pp. OEWS 920-cc, OEWS 920-A, OEWS 920-A2.

53 Ibid., n.p., follows verso of p. OEWS920-cc.

54 "Letter from Liberia, West Africa," in *Indians and Intruders*, ed. Sharron Standifer Ashton (Norman, Okla.: Sharon Standifer Ashton, 1998), 3:45.

55 Ibid.

56 "Liberia," *Muskogee Phoenix*, November 8, 1888, 1.

57 "Territory News," *Muskogee Phoenix*, February 25, 1892, 1; untitled, *Muskogee Phoenix*, February 25, 1892, 4.

58 *Twin Territories*, March 1899, 79, cited under "Negroes, Emigration to Africa" in Muskogee Newspaper Index cardfile, Newspaper Division, OHS.

59 Bittle and Geis, *Longest Way Home*, 79–81.

60 "Annual Report, Oklahoma State Director of Cooperative Demonstration Work," 1909, September 27, 1909, reel 1, T-881, NA, 4, 6–7.

61 Folder "SUG File—Lynching—Oklahoma," box C-364, NAACP Papers, Library of Congress Manuscript Reading Room, Washington, D.C.; Franklin, *Journey toward Hope*, 131–35.

62 Bittle and Geis, *Longest Way Home*, 76.

63 Franklin, *Journey toward Hope*, 57.

64 S. A. Clark to Lee Cruce, folder 11, box 2; B. W. Warren to Lee Cruce, folder 11, box 2; "Governor" [Lee Cruce] to C. M. Pearson, folder 11, box 2, all in Cruce Papers.

65 Bittle and Geis, *Longest Way Home*, 74, 85; "Chief Sam Has Many, Many Places to Visit," *Clearview Patriarch*, September 27, 1913; "Africa," *Clearview Patriarch*, November 25, 1913.

66 Bittle and Geis, *Longest Way Home*, 91–92.

67 One town developer favored, however, another sort of emigration plan. J. E. Thompson called for a movement to push the U.S. government to set aside an area for exclusive African American settlement to be governed exclusively by African American people. Like Chief Alfred Sam, Thompson represented African American farmland tenure as one of the principal attractions of his scheme. Thompson was also the founder of an African American fraternal organization named the Patriarchs of America, and his emigration plan may have reflected the same concern for the establishment of patriarchal domestic order as J. E. Toombs evinced. J. E. Thompson, Address to the Farmers' Conference at Clearview, *Clearview Patriarch*, May 25, 1911.

68 Warren to Cruce.

69 Bittle and Geis, *Longest Way Home*, 74. For letters of concern about Sam's activities and their effects on African American communities, see also S. A. Clark to Lee Cruce, December 19, 1913, folder 11, box 2; B. W. Warren to Lee Cruce, October 6, 1913, folder 11, box 2; Rev. James E. Fair to Lee Cruce, October 6, 1913, folder 11, box 2, all in Cruce Papers.

70 *Annual Report of the Fifteenth Annual National Business League*, Muskogee, Oklahoma, August 19–21, 1914, cited in Crockett, *Black Towns*, 136.

71 *Wewoka and Lima Courier*, November 11, 1913, quoted in Bittle and Geis, *Longest Way Home*, 82.

72 "African Delegation Meets," *Wewoka and Lima Courier*, November 21, 1913, 1.

73 R. C. Lee to Secretary of the Interior, October 17, 1913, Cruce Papers, quoted in Bittle and Geis, *Longest Way Home*, 77–78.

74 "Chief Alfred Sam," in *The Marcus Garvey and Universal Negro Improvement Association Papers*, ed. Robert A. Hill (Berkeley: University of California Press, 1983–2006), 1:542–46; Bittle and Geis, *Longest Way Home*, 173–212; Teall, *Black History in Oklahoma*, 286–88; "Chief Sam's Party Can't Stay in Liberia," *Clearview Patriarch*, September 12, 1914, 1.

75 "Concentration of UNIA Divisions by Regions," in Hill, *Marcus Garvey and Universal Negro Improvement Association Papers*, 7:1001–2.

76 Napoleon Davis, interview with the author, November 21, 1999, Muskogee, Oklahoma. Lucy Grayson appears opposite number 1,592 on the Creek Freedman roll of U.S. Commission to the Five Civilized Tribes, *Final Rolls of Citizens and Freedmen*.

77 Napoleon Davis interview.

78 Ibid.

CHAPTER 6

1 *Muskogee Times Democrat*, May 31, 1923, 1; N. Clay Jewett, "The Definition of Klankraft and How to Disseminate It," *Imperial Night-Hawk*, November 7, 1923, 2.

2 David Roediger has influentially argued that antebellum white industrial workers defined their class in relation to their whiteness. Roediger demonstrates how whiteness and industrial working-class consciousness were structurally related to republicanism, the notion that the right to participate as a member in the republic required (and derived from) both racial capacity and economic sovereignty. This link to republicanism has strongly influenced my thinking on the relationship between whiteness, nationalism, and class consciousness in white agrarianism. David R. Roediger, *The Wages of Whiteness: Race and the Making of the American Working Class* (London: Verso, 1991), 43–64.

3 W. E. B. Du Bois, *Black Reconstruction in America* (New York: Atheneum, 1992), 700. Via the work of David Roediger, this notion of a wage became foundational to whiteness studies, most of which center on white wage earners and especially the white, industrial working class. Roediger, *Wages of Whiteness*, 12.

4 U.S. Bureau of the Census, *Statistics for Oklahoma. Thirteenth Census of the United States, 1910* (Washington: Government Printing Office, 1913), 634–49.

5 Jim Bissett has used this same contrast between agrarian expectation and tenant reality to explain the background to the socialist movement in Oklahoma. Jim Bissett, *Agrarian Socialism in America: Marx, Jefferson, and Jesus in the Oklahoma Countryside, 1904–1920* (Norman: University of Oklahoma Press, 1999), 12–13.

6 "Territory Farmers' Union," *Muskogee Comet*, September 29, 1904, 8. The next year, farmers organized the Twin Territory Farmers' Union. *Muskogee Unionist*,

February 12, 1905, 4; "Territory Farmers' Union," *Muskogee Unionist*, March 5, 1905, 4.

7 "Farmers' Cooperative Union of America," *Muskogee Pioneer*, December 2, 1905, 5.

8 Stephen Kantrowitz, *Ben Tillman and the Reconstruction of White Supremacy* (Chapel Hill: University of North Carolina Press, 2000), 1, 110–12, 130–31.

9 *Eufaula Indian Journal*, October 19, 1906, 1. On Tillman and black disenfranchisement, see Francis Butler Simkins, *Pitchfork Ben Tillman, South Carolinian* (Columbia: University of South Carolina Press, 2002), 394. A few months after Tillman's 1906 talk in Muskogee, Tillman's good friend and fellow South Carolinian John Sharp Williams would publish an article bearing the very same title, "The Negro and the South." It is possible that the Tillman's talk was close in spirit and argument to Sharp's article, which made the argument for the necessity of disenfranchising African Americans. See Lee D. Baker, *From Savage to Negro: Anthropology and the Construction of Race, 1896–1954* (Berkeley: University of California Press, 1998), 75.

10 Danney Goble, *Progressive Oklahoma: The Making of a New Kind of State* (Norman: University of Oklahoma Press, 1980), 8, 10.

11 Bissett, *Agrarian Socialism in America*, 23–30; James R. Scales and Danney Goble, *Oklahoma Politics: A History* (Norman: University of Oklahoma Press, 1982), 16.

12 James Green, *Grass-Roots Socialism: Radical Movements in the Southwest, 1895–1943* (Baton Rouge: Louisiana State University Press, 1978), 66–72; Garin Burbank, *When Farmers Voted Red: The Gospel of Socialism in the Oklahoma Countryside* (Westport, Conn.: Greenwood, 1976), 44–48; Scales and Goble, *Oklahoma Politics*, 20–43.

13 Scales and Goble, *Oklahoma Politics*, 64.

14 Ibid., 76, Green, *Grass-Roots Socialism*, 286–93.

15 "Socialist Party State Platform," 1910, folder 40, box 12, Fred Barde Collection, OHS. In the 1914, the party platform called for a system meant to fulfill most of the goals of landownership—security in land use, transfer of wealth to the next generation—without allowing a risk of land consolidation. "The commonwealth" would own lands (preventing the growth of a landlord class), and farmers would rent them. Once rent payments equaled the value of the land, however, the farmer and "his children" would retain use and occupancy rights. Garin Burbank, "Agrarian Radicals and Their Opponents: Political Conflict in Southern Oklahoma, 1910–1924," *Journal of American History* 58 (June 1971).

16 Bissett, *Agrarian Socialism in America*, 61–69; Burbank, *When Farmers Voted Red*, 44–51; State Platform, Socialist Party of Oklahoma, folder 1, box 1, Socialist Party of Oklahoma Collection, OHS. See especially "Renters' and Farmers' Platform," 8–9.

17 Bissett, *Agrarian Socialism in America*, 61–69; John Thompson, *Closing the Frontier: Radical Response in Oklahoma, 1889–1923* (Norman: University of Oklahoma Press, 1986), 137.

18 D. Bryan to Gov. Robert L. Williams, January 17, 1916, folder 2, box 1, RG 8-C-1-2, General Correspondence 1916, Robert Lee Williams Papers, OSA.

19 R. L. Williams to Mr. Jim Wilson, August 19, 1916, folder 5, box 4, Robert Lee Williams Collection, OHS.

20 Burbank, *When Farmers Voted Red*, 108–9.

21 Bissett, *Agrarian Socialism in America*, 132–36; Thompson, *Closing the Frontier*, 130–31.

22 Sherry Warrick, "Radical Labor in Oklahoma: The Working Class Union," *Chronicles of Oklahoma* 52 (Summer 1974): 180–81.

23 Scales and Goble, *Oklahoma Politics*, 81; Warrick, "Radical Labor in Oklahoma," 183–84, 186.

24 R. E. Simpson to Robert L. Williams, March 29, 1917, folder 1, box 36, Robert Lee Williams Collection, OHS; Warrick, "Radical Labor in Oklahoma," 185; Nigel Anthony Sellars, *Oil, Wheat, and Wobblies: The Industrial Workers of the World in Oklahoma, 1905–1930* (Norman: University of Oklahoma Press, 1998), 11, 78.

25 Sellars, *Oil, Wheat, and Wobblies*, 35–56.

26 On the oil industry in Oklahoma, see Kenny A. Franks, Paul F. Lambert, and Carl N. Tyson, *Early Oklahoma Oil: A Photographic History, 1859–1936* (College Station: Texas A&M University Press, 1981).

27 Paul F. Lambert and Kenny A. Franks, eds., *Voices from the Oil Fields* (Norman: University of Oklahoma Press, 1984), 23; Sellars, *Oil, Wheat, and Wobblies*, 83.

28 Sellars, *Oil, Wheat, and Wobblies*, 57–76, 87.

29 Ibid., 63.

30 Ibid., 52.

31 In this reference and following references, I draw from "Clure Isenhouer, et al., versus United States, transcript, 1917," bound volume 1, box 37, Robert Lee Williams Collection, OHS. The circuit court decision affirming the conviction is *Isenhouer v. United States*, 256 F. 842 (8th Cir. 1919). An African American was present at a Lone Dove local meeting at Wewoka according to Elzie Markle, "Clure Isenhouer, et al., versus United States, transcript, 1917," 457. The organization admitted men and women and all races, testimony of H. P. Brennell, ibid., 701.

32 Warrick, "Radical Labor in Oklahoma," 187.

33 Ibid., 185.

34 Charles Clement Bush, "The Green Corn Rebellion" (M.A. thesis, University of Oklahoma, 1932), 9 n. 6. On WCU membership, see Scales and Goble, *Oklahoma Politics*, 81.

35 Sellars, *Oil, Wheat, and Wobblies*, 85.

36 *Harlow's Weekly*, August 15, 1917, 4; *Ada Weekly News*, "To Resist Draft Law," August 2, 1917; both quoted in Warrick, "Radical Labor in Oklahoma," 187; Green, *Grass-Roots Socialism*, 357–59.

37 Sellars, *Oil, Wheat, and Wobblies*, 90;

38 Warrick, "Radical Labor in Oklahoma," 188–89.

39 Ibid., 189–93; Bush, "Green Corn Rebellion," 60–68.

40 Jeannette Keith, "The Politics of Southern Draft Resistance, 1917–1918: Class, Race, and Conscription in the Rural South," *Journal of American History* 87 (March 2001): 1352.

41 Ibid., 1356.

42 On American Indians and the draft, see Thomas A. Britten, *American Indians in World War I: At Home and at War* (Albuquerque: University of New Mexico Press, 1997), 51–73.

43 Bush, "Green Corn Rebellion," 22, app. A.

44 John Womack Jr., "Oklahoma's Green Corn Rebellion: The Importance of Fools" (senior thesis, Harvard University, 1959), 113; Bush, "Green Corn Rebellion," 40; Virginia Carrollton Pope, "The Green Corn Rebellion: A Case in Newspaper Self-Censorship" (Ph.D. diss., Oklahoma Agricultural and Mechanical College, 1940), 6; Warrick, "Radical Labor in Oklahoma," 193. Clark's name is sometimes given as Clay.

45 Bush, "Green Corn Rebellion," 1.

46 "Clure Isenhouer, et al., versus United States."

47 Otis Hume, "From a Personal Interview with Bud Gordon, Wewoka, Oklahoma," *IPH*, 26:189–91.

48 Of course, the fact that newspapers and officials used the term "Snake" also reflects the inability of white outsiders who were hostile to the rebellion and to Indian people to conceive of Native resistance as anything but atavistic. Bush, "Green Corn Rebellion," 1; Womack, "Oklahoma's Green Corn Rebellion," 77.

49 Warrick, "Radical Labor in Oklahoma," 113, 121, 185.

50 Sellars, *Oil, Wheat, and Wobblies*, 107–10; Scott Ellsworth, *Death in a Promised Land: The Tulsa Race Riot of 1921* (Baton Rouge: Louisiana State University Press, 1982), 30.

51 Sellars, *Oil, Wheat, and Wobblies*, 108–9.

52 National Civil Liberties Bureau, "The 'Knights of Liberty' Mob and the I.W.W. Prisoners at Tulsa, Oklahoma" (New York: National Civil Liberties Bureau, 1918); Sellars, *Oil, Wheat, and Wobblies*, 108–9; Green, *Grass-Roots Socialism*, 371.

53 O. A. Hilton, "The Oklahoma Council of Defense and the First World War," *Chronicles of Oklahoma*, 20 (March 1942); Green, *Grass-Roots Socialism*, 374–80; Sellars, *Oil, Wheat, and Wobblies*, 96–97. For examples of the minimal oversight that the office of the governor exercised over county Councils of Defense, see Carl J. O'Hornett to R. L. Williams, September 18, 1917; E. H. Moore to Adjutant General, 12, September 1918; Chief Clerk to E. H. Moore, September 26, 1918; Jesse L. Day to R. L. Williams, July 15, 1918; Chief Clerk to Jesse L. Day, August 29, 1918, all in folder 3, box 3, RG 8-C-4-2, State Council of Defense, Robert L. Williams Papers, OSA.

54 Interview with Ira M. Finley, April 21, 1973, transcript, Carter Blue Clark Collection, folder 4, box 1, WHC; Charles W. Smith, "The Selling of America in Oklahoma: The First and Second Liberty Bond Drives," *Chronicles of Oklahoma* 73 (Winter 1995–96); Green, *Grass-Roots Socialism*, 375–78; John A. Simpson, "Economic Righteousness," *Congressional Record* (reprint), 77nd Cong., 1st sess., 1932, 1; Carter Blue Clark, "A History of the Ku Klux Klan in Oklahoma" (M.A. thesis, University of Oklahoma, 1976), 24.

55 David H. Bennett, *The Party of Fear: From Nativist Movements to the New Right in American History* (Chapel Hill: University of North Carolina Press, 1988), 187–90.

56 Oscar Ameringer, *If You Don't Weaken: The Autobiography of Oscar Ameringer* (Norman: University of Oklahoma Press, 1983).

57 Stephen Vaughn, *Holding Fast the Inner Lines: Democracy, Nationalism, and the Committee on Public Information* (Chapel Hill: University of North Carolina Press, 1980); John Milton Cooper, *Pivotal Decades: The United States, 1900–1920* (New York: Norton, 1990), 294–96.

58 J. R. Lamb to R. L. Williams, November 20, 1918, folder 7, box 4, Robert Lee Williams Collection, OHS.

59 James R. Grossman, "A Chance to Make Good, 1900–1929," in *To Make Our World Anew: A History of African Americans*, ed. Robin D. G. Kelly and Earl Lewis (Oxford: Oxford University Press, 2000), 400.

60 *Manual of the True Order of the White Brotherhood of the World* (n.p., n.d.) in folder 1, box 21, Robert Lee Williams Collection, OHS, 6, 8; J. R. Lamb to Governor Williams, January 8, 1918, folder 7, box 4, Robert Lee Williams Collection, OHS.

61 Thompson, *Closing the Frontier*, 167–68; James E. Shideler, *Farm Crisis, 1919–1923* (Berkeley: University of California Press, 1957), 36.

62 Angie Debo, *And Still the Waters Run: The Betrayal of the Five Civilized Tribes* (Princeton, N.J.: Princeton University Press, 1940), 303–9.

63 Dover P. Trent, "Okmulgee County: County Agent Annual Report 1923," T-881, reel 16, NA, 2.

64 George W. Vincent, "Northeast District," 1920, in "Report of the Extension Division. A & M. College, Year of 1919–1920," T-881, reel 6; "[Northeastern Oklahoma] Annual Report," 1921, T-881, both in NA.

65 C. W. Callarman, "South Central District," in W. A. Conner, "Annual Report of the Extension Division, Oklahoma Agricultural and Mechanical College, 1920–1921," T-881, reel 6, NA, 42.

66 In a limited number of cases, federal Farm Loan money was available to help farmers who had defaulted avoid foreclosure. See H. G. Howard, "Report of Work of the County Agent," T-881, reel 13, NA, 38 verso.

67 U.S. Bureau of the Census, *Fourteenth Census of the United States* (Washington: Government Printing Office, 1922), vol. 6, pt. 2:628–635; U.S. Bureau of the Census, *1925 Census of Agriculture* (Washington: Government Printing Office: 1927), 1038–46.

68 U.S. Bureau of the Census, *Fourteenth Census of the United States*, vol. 6, pt. 2:628–635; U.S. Bureau of the Census, *1925 Census of Agriculture*, 1038–46.

69 My understanding of the way that the Klan stood at the intersection of class and cultural conflict is influenced by Nancy MacLean, *Behind the Mask of Chivalry: The Making of the Second Ku Klux Klan* (Oxford: Oxford University Press, 1994).

70 Effie S. Jackson, "Interview with Major Frank Van Voorhis," *IPH*, 48:184–88. The information in this paragraph is largely drawn from Oklahoma Commission to Study the Tulsa Race Riot of 1921, "Tulsa Race Riot: A Report of the Oklahoma Commission to Study the Tulsa Race Riot of 1921," February 28, 2001, <www.okhistory.mus.ok.us/trrc/freport.pdf> (May 25, 2008). See also Ellsworth, *Death in a Promised Land*; Tim Madigan, *The Burning: Massacre, Destruction, and the Tulsa*

Race Riot of 1921 (New York: Thomas Dunne Books and St. Martin's Press, 2001); Hannibal B. Johnson, *Black Wall Street: From Riot to Renaissance in Tulsa's Historic Greenwood District* (Austin, Tex.: Eakin Press, 1998); James S. Hirsch, *Riot and Remembrance: The Tulsa Race War and Its Legacy* (Boston: Houghton Mifflin, 2002); Alfred L. Brophy, *Reconstructing the Dreamland: The Tulsa Race Riot of 1921: Race, Reparations, and Reconciliation* (Oxford: Oxford University Press, 2002).

71 Clark, "History of the Ku Klux Klan," 42. David Chalmers dates the arrival of the Klan in Oklahoma to early summer 1921. David Chalmers, *Hooded Americanism: The History of the Ku Klux Klan, 1865–1965* (Garden City, N.Y.: Doubleday, 1965), 48, cited in Laurie Jane Croft [Barr], "The Women of the Ku Klux Klan in Oklahoma" (Ph.D. diss., University of Oklahoma, 1984), 19.

72 Sheldon Neuringer, "Governor Walton's War on the Ku Klux Klan: An Episode in Oklahoma History, 1923 to 1924," *Chronicles of Oklahoma* 45 (Summer 1967): 153; Scales and Goble, *Oklahoma Politics*, 108.

73 The 1920 census counted 475,605 native white males twenty years of age and over, including those of native parentage and those of foreign or mixed parentage. U.S. Bureau of the Census, *Fourteenth Census of the United States*, 3:813.

74 Many of these towns also boasted chapters of the Women of the Ku Klux Klan, the Women's American Protestant Study Club, the Kamelia, K-DUO, and other women's groups (some independent, some affiliated with the Klan) that were supportive of the all-male Klan. Clark, "History of the Ku Klux Klan," 83–84, 153; Thompson, *Closing the Frontier*, 36; "Chartered Klans in Good Standing as of April 10, 1922," box 2, folder 22, Ku Klux Klan Women Collection, WHC; "District Meetings, Realm of Oklahoma," box 2, folder 19, Ku Klux Klan Women Collection, WHC; Women of the Ku Klux Klan, "Women of America! The Past! The Present! The Future!" folder Coalgate Ku Klux Klan Chapter, unnumbered box, entry 82–279: Arvard Hudson Collection, OHS. "Americans Gather under the Fiery Cross on the Rolling Prairies of Oklahoma," *Imperial Night-Hawk*, August 15, 1923, 4; "Peaceable Meetings Like This Are Banned in Oklahoma by Walton," *Imperial Night-Hawk*, October 10, 1923, 5; "Tulsa Klan's New $200,000 Klavern Will Accommodate 3,000 Klansmen," *Imperial Night-Hawk*, May 30, 1923, 5.

75 Interview with Leon Hirsch, April 25, 1974, transcript, folder 4, box 1, Carter Blue Clark Collection, WHC; Neuringer, "Governor Walton's War," 153.

76 Scales and Goble, *Oklahoma Politics*, 119–22; Garin Burbank, "Agrarian Radicals," 14–16.

77 *Muskogee Times Democrat*, May 31, 1923, 1; Jewett, "Definition of Klankraft," 2.

78 Clark, "History of the Ku Klux Klan," 147.

79 Ibid., 54.

80 Jewett, "Definition of Klankraft," 2.

81 Thompson, *Closing the Frontier*, 193; Clark, "History of the Ku Klux Klan," 147.

82 Jewett, "Definition of Klankraft," 2. For another expression of Klan ideology in Oklahoma, see "Food for Thought," folder 12, box 9, John C. Walton Collection, WHC.

83 Clark, "History of the Ku Klux Klan," 153.

84 Vicky Withers, "Boom Town," 4, 8–11, box 1, folder 18, collection 83.95: "Beggs, Oklahoma," OHS.

85 For accounts of the boisterous life and sometimes dangerous working-class life in the towns near the oil fields, see Lambert and Franks, *Voices from the Oil Fields*, 58–61, 150–55, 157–62.

86 Klansmen were probably not guilty of all the attacks that Oklahomans attributed to them because some non-Klansmen used the guise of the Ku Klux Klan to pursue private vendettas. *New Republic*, January 14, 1925, 198.

87 The following testimony identifies Klansmen with the given occupations: Jim Allen, garage manager, doctor; O. E. Arnold, garage manager, principal, doctor, policemen, chief of police; L. W. Franklin, schoolteacher, hotel manager; H. C. Jones, principal; John P. Rhodes testimony, September 21, 1923, folder 36, box 12, John C. Walton Collection, WHC. See also Withers, "Boom Town," 11.

88 Clark, "History of the Ku Klux Klan," 116; Green, *Grass-Roots Socialism*, 402; Sellars, *Oil, Wheat, and Wobblies*, 62.

89 Clark, "History of the Ku Klux Klan," 154.

90 Withers, "Boom Town," 11.

91 Alice Chesher [*sic*] testimony, September 22, 1923; William L. Perry testimony, September 21, 1923; Hazel Powell testimony, September 21, 1923; R. F. Crowder testimony, September 21, 1923; John P. Rhodes testimony, September 21, 1923, all in folder 36, box 12, John C. Walton Collection, WHC.

92 "Lazy Youths at Beggs Told to Go to Work," *Muskogee Oklahoma Herald*, February 7, 1922, 3.

93 O. E. Arnold testimony, September 22, 1923, folder 16, box 12, John C. Walton Collection, WHC; Clark, "History of the Ku Klux Klan," 128; Joe Rebseman testimony, September 29, 1923; W. W. Wills testimony, September 13, 1923; Andrew Bartlett testimony, September 13, 1923; L. W. Franklin testimony and L. W. Franklin (recalled) testimony, September 22, 1923; A. W. Hoddad testimony, September 13, 1923, all in folder 21, box 12, John C. Walton Collection, WHC; A. M. Marks testimony, September 14, 1923; John Snyder testimony, September 29, 1923; Jim Allen testimony, September 14, 1923; H. C. Jones testimony, September 26, 1923; Anton Snyder testimony, September 22, 1923; A. L. Stockstill testimony, September 22, 1923, all in folder 48 box 13, John C. Walton Collection, WHC.

94 In fact, Klansmen denounced minorities that were few and far between in eastern Oklahoma—Jews, Catholics, and immigrants—but not the many Native Americans who lived among them. Croft, "The Women of the Ku Klux Klan," 44, 64, 69.

95 On attacks on Indians, see, for example, Clark, "History of the Ku Klux Klan," 113; Howard A. Tucker, *History of Governor Walton's War on Ku Klux Klan, the Invisible Empire* (Oklahoma City: Southwest Publishing, 1923), 14.

96 Chas. Smith to W. F. Davis, October 3, 1923, folder 20, box 14, John C. Walton Collection, WHC; J. P. Lovell testimony, September 26, 1923, box 14, folder 20, John C. Walton Collection, WHC; O. E. Arnold testimony; W. W. Wills testimony.

97 Because authorities were more likely to investigate crimes against whites than against African Americans, it is almost certain that the proportion of white victims

is higher in documented cases than it was in the totality of cases. For examples of cases of attacks on African Americans in the Beggs area that appear to have received less attention than attacks on whites, see J. P. Lovell testimony; W. W. Wills testimony; Jim Allen testimony.

98 "Lazy Youths at Beggs Told to Go to Work."

99 O. E. Arnold testimony.

100 A. M. Marks testimony; John Snyder testimony; Jim Allen testimony; H. C. Jones testimony; Anton Snyder testimony; A. L. Stockstill testimony.

101 Neil Foley, *The White Scourge: Mexicans, Blacks, and Poor Whites in Texas Cotton Culture* (Berkeley: University of California Press, 1997), 64–91; Henry Herbert Goddard, *The Kallikak Family: A Study in the Heredity of Feeble-Mindedness* (New York: Macmillan, 1912), 12.

102 Tucker, *History of Governor Walton's War*, 7; Scales and Goble, *Oklahoma Politics*, 112–15, 119–20; Neuringer, "Governor Walton's War," 159–60.

103 G. R. Cundiff to Gov. J. C. Walton, September 24, 1923, box 17, folder 11, John C. Walton Papers, WHC.

104 S. M. Abbott, Wallace Brown, and W. H. Deshazer to J. C. Walton, September 17, 1923, folder 2, box 11, John C. Walton Collection, WHC. See also R. C. Tyre to J. C. Walton, August 25, 1923, folder 11, box 17, John C. Walton Collection, WHC.

105 Scales and Goble, *Oklahoma Politics*, 116; Burbank, "Agrarian Radicals," 15–20.

106 Burbank, "Agrarian Radicals," 18; C. M. Mills, W. H. Hicks, J. M. Massey et al. to J. C. Walton, September 17, 1923, folder 10, box 17, John C. Walton Collection, WHC.

107 Gardner Knupp to J. C. Walton, September 28, 1923, folder 1, box 11, John C. Walton Collection, WHC; Roediger, *Wages of Whiteness*, 65–66; Clark, "History of the Ku Klux Klan," 129.

108 Tyre to Walton; Knupp to Walton; Abbott, Brown, and Deshazer to Walton. The phenomenon is analogous to that Earl Lewis discovered in his study of black and white organized labor in Norfolk, Virginia. Lewis found that "although some black workers manifested a semblance of worker consciousness, that consciousness was so imbedded in the perspective of race that neither blacks nor whites saw themselves as equal partners in the same labor movement." Earl Lewis, *In Their Own Interests: Race, Class, and Power in Twentieth-Century Norfolk, Virginia* (Berkeley: University of California Press, 1991), 58, as quoted in Robin D. G. Kelley, *Race Rebels: Culture, Politics, and the Black Working Class* (New York: Free Press, 1994), 26.

109 [John C. Walton], "The Skeleton Covered by the Mask and Robe," n.d., box 9, folder 28, John C. Walton Collection, WHC, 2, 3, 6–8; [John C. Walton], "The Klan and the People," n.d., box 9, folder 28, John C. Walton Collection, WHC, 3. Walton considered that a prime example of the supremacy of the white race was the conquest of North America by Europeans over Native Americans. See Walton, "Klan and the People," 3.

110 Great Titan of the Realm of Oklahoma, "How to Operate a Model Province," folder 3, box 1, Carter Blue Clark Collection, WHC, 104.

111 The politics of the Klan battle are covered in detail in Neuringer, "Governor Walton's War," 159–175, and Scales and Goble, *Oklahoma Politics*, 122–134.

112 KKK to Prop. Manhatan Cafe [*sic*], [date illegible], 1922, folder 16, box 17, John C. Walton Collection, WHC.

EPILOGUE

1 Billy Byrd, "Ochai Tribe, an Interview with Hully Proctor . . . ," *IPH* 40:481–82; U.S. Bureau of the Census, Fifteenth Census of the United States, 1930, NA, microfilm T626, Oklahoma, McIntosh County, Hanna Township, Enumeration District 46-17, sheet 2A, line 11.

2 Earnest Gouge, *Totkv Mocvse/New Fire: Creek Folktales by Earnest Gouge*, ed. and trans. Jack B. Martin, Margaret McKane Mauldin, and Juanita McGirt (Norman: University of Oklahoma Press, 2004), xix.

3 Effie S. Jackson, "An Interview with Agnes Kelley," *IPH*, 32:102–14.

4 The bulk of this epilogue is based on an interview with Mr. Rufus ("Buddy") Cox, Oklahoma City, November 30, 1999. For descriptions of the Newtown Church, camp houses, and cemetery, see Jackson, "An Interview with Agnes Kelley"; Roosevelt Derrisaw, "Cemeteries—Creek Haynes," *IPH*, 111:143–45; Derrisaw, "Cemeteries—Creek Haynes," *IPH*, 32:150–52; Jerome M. Emmons, "Burial Ground Form New Town," *IPH*, 97:165–79.

5 Sam'l J. Haynes, D. M. Hodge, Billy G. Barnett, and J. P. Davidson to Hon. Moty Tiger, October 26, 1909, typescript copy in folder 6, portfolio 4, box 2, Grayson Family Papers, WHC; Angie Debo, *And Still the Waters Run: The Betrayal of the Five Civilized Tribes* (Princeton, N.J.: Princeton University Press, 1940), 143.

6 The *IPH* oral history collection contains a number of variant accounts of his background and that of his wife, who was a Creek woman apparently belonging to a group of Catawbas who had been adopted into the Creek Nation. Effie S. Jackson, "Haynes, Samuel J. Second Interview," *IPH*, 92:332–42; Margaret McGuire, "Interview with Mrs. Alice McCombs," *IPH*, 78:425–26; Effie S. Jackson, "Interview with D. M. Smith," *IPH*, 69:465–68.

7 "Lerblance, Elijah Hermigine," in H. F. O'Beirne and E. S. O'Beirne, *The Indian Territory: Its Chiefs, Legislators and Leading Men* (St. Louis: C. B. Woodward Co., 1892), 182–84.

8 Angie Debo, *The Road to Disappearance: A History of the Creek Indians* (Norman: University of Oklahoma Press, 1941), 339, 341.

9 Jerome M. Emmons, "Interview with Hal W. Griffin," *IPH*, 4:177–79.

10 Jackson, "Haynes, Samuel J. Second Interview," 341.

11 U.S. Bureau of the Census, Manuscript Census, 1920, Okmulgee County, Oklahoma, vol. 50, enumeration district 110, sheet 3, line 94, as it appears on NA 1920 census reel OK-22.

ARCHIVAL AND MANUSCRIPT MATERIALS

Fort Worth, Texas
   National Archives and Records Administration Center
      Records of the Bureau of Indian Affairs
      Records of the Dawes Commission
Norman, Oklahoma
   Carl Albert Center, University of Oklahoma
      Oklahoma Taxpayers League Collection, Robert Lee Williams Papers
   Western History Collections, University of Oklahoma
      Carter Blue Clark Collection
      Creek Nation Papers
      C. Guy Cutlip Collection
      Grayson Family Papers
      Isparhecher Collection
      Ku Klux Klan Collection
      Ku Klux Klan Women Collection
      Oklahoma Constitutional Convention Collection
      Oklahoma State Grange Collection
      Pleasant Porter Collection
      John A. Simpson Collection
      John C. Walton Collection
      Thomas W. Woodrow Collection
Oklahoma City, Oklahoma
   Oklahoma Historical Society, Manuscripts Division
      Fred Barde Collection
      Rufus Cox Collection
      Creek Nation Records

Alice B. Davis Collection

Grant Foreman Collection

Arvard Hudson Collection

Muskogee Newspaper Index

Frederick Severs Papers

Socialist Party of Oklahoma Collection

Robert Lee Williams Collection

Vicky Withers, "Boom Town" manuscript

Oklahoma State Archives

Lee Cruce Papers

Records of the Commissioners of Agriculture

Records of the Corporation Commission

Records of the School Lands Commission

J. B. A. Robertson Papers

Robert L. Williams Papers

Washington, D.C.

Library of Congress Manuscript Reading Room

NAACP Papers

Booker T. Washington Papers

Works Progress Administration, Federal Writers Project Papers

Washington, D.C., and College Park, Maryland

National Archives

Records of the Agricultural Adjustment Administration

Records of the Bureau of Agricultural Economics

Records of the Bureau of Indian Affairs

Records of the Extension Service

Records of the Farm Credit Administration

Records of the Farmers Home Administration

Records of the Farm Security Administration

Records of the Secretary of Agriculture

Records of the United States Department of Agriculture

INTERVIEWS

Mr. Rufus ("Buddy") Cox, November 30, 1999, Oklahoma City.

Mr. Napoleon Davis, November 21, 1999, Taft, Oklahoma.

Mr. Robert Guess, December 7, 1999, Del City, Oklahoma.

NEWSPAPERS AND MAGAZINES

Ada Weekly News

Boley Progress

Claremore Progress

Clearview Patriarch

Eufaula Indian Journal

Fort Gibson Post

Harlow's Weekly

Imperial Night-Hawk

Kingfisher Free Press

Muskogee Cimeter

Muskogee Comet

Muskogee Indian Journal

Muskogee Oklahoma Herald

Muskogee Our Brother in Red

Muskogee Phoenix
Muskogee Pioneer
Muskogee Times Democrat
Muskogee Unionist
New Republic
Okemah Independent
Oklahoma City Daily Oklahoman
Oklahoma City Oklahoma News

Oklahoma City Times
Purcell Register
South McAlester Capital
Tahlequah Cherokee Advocate
Tulsa Democrat
Vinita Indian Chieftain
Wagoner Weekly Sayings
Wewoka and Lima Courier

MICROFILM COLLECTIONS

Works Progress Administration. *Indian Pioneer History Collection*. Edited by Grant Foreman. 1937. Oklahoma City: Oklahoma Historical Society Microfilm Publications, 1978.

GOVERNMENT DOCUMENTS AND COURT DECISIONS

English v. Richardson, 224 U.S. 680 (1912).

Isenhouer v. United States, 256 F. 842 (8th Cir. 1919).

Muscogee (Creek) Nation. *Constitution of the Muscogee (Creek) Nation*. [Okmulgee, Okla.]: Muscogee (Creek) Nation, 1979.

Turner v. United States, 248 U.S. 354 (1919).

U.S. Board of Indian Commissioners. *Annual Report of the Board of Indian Commissioners for the Year 1885*. Washington: Government Printing Office, 1886.

U.S. Bureau of the Census. *Agriculture 1909 and 1910*. Vol. 5 of *Thirteenth Census of the United States*. Washington: Government Printing Office, 1913.

—————. *Extra Census Bulletin: The Five Civilized Tribes of the Indian Territory*. Washington: Government Printing Office, 1894.

—————. Fifteenth Census of the United States, 1930. Microfilm T626. National Archives, Washington, D.C.

—————. *Fourteenth Census of the United States*. 11 vols. Washington: Government Printing Office, 1922.

—————. Fourteenth Census of the United States, 1920. Microfilm T625. National Archives, Washington, D.C.

—————. *1925 Census of Agriculture*. Washington: Government Printing Office, 1927.

—————. *Statistics for Oklahoma, Thirteenth Census of the United States, 1910*. Washington: Government Printing Office, 1913.

—————. Thirteenth Census of the United States, 1910. Microfilm T624. National Archives, Washington, D.C.

—————. *Thirteenth Census of the United States Taken in the Year 1910*. 11 vols. Washington: Government Printing Office, 1913.

U.S. Commissioner of Indian Affairs. *Annual Report of the Commissioner of Indian Affairs for the Year 1842*. Washington: Government Printing Office, [1843].

—————. *Annual Report of the Commissioner of Indian Affairs to the Secretary of the Interior for the Year 1881*. Washington: Government Printing Office, 1881.

—————. *Annual Report of the Commissioner of Indian Affairs to the Secretary of the Interior for the Year 1883*. Washington: Government Printing Office, 1883.

—————. *Report of the Commissioner of Indian Affairs for the Year 1866.* Washington: Government Printing Office, 1866.

—————. *Report of the Commissioner of Indian Affairs for the Year 1887.* Washington: Government Printing Office, 1887.

—————. *Report of the Commissioner of Indian Affairs* in *Annual Report of the Secretary of the Interior, 1881.* Washington: Government Printing Office, 1881.

U.S. Commission to the Five Civilized Tribes. *The Final Rolls of Citizens and Freedmen of the Five Civilized Tribes in Indian Territory.* 2 parts. Washington: Government Printing Office, 1907.

U.S. Congress. Senate. *In the Senate of the United States. March 24, 1896.* 54th Cong., 1st sess., 1896. Washington: Government Printing Office, 1896.

—————. Committee on Indian Affairs. *Report of the Committee on Indian Affairs, United States Senate, on the Condition of the Indians in the Indian Territory, and other Reservations, etc.* 49th Cong., 1st sess. 1885–86. Washington: Government Printing Office, 1886.

—————. Committee on Territories. *Report.* 45th Cong., 3rd sess. 1879. Washington: Government Printing Office: 1879.

—————. Select Committee. *Report of the Select Committee to Investigate Matters Connected with Affairs in the Indian Territory with Hearings. November 11, 1906–January 9, 1907.* 2 vols. 59th Cong., 2nd sess. 1906–7. Washington: Government Printing Office, 1907.

U.S. Department of the Interior. *Indian Affairs, Territories.* Vol. 2 of *Reports of the Department of the Interior for the Fiscal Year Ending June 30, 1910: Administrative Reports.* Washington: Government Printing Office, 1911.

BOOKS AND PAMPHLETS

Abel, Annie Heloise. *The American Indian as Slaveholder and Secessionist.* Vol. 2 of *The Slaveholding Indians.* Cleveland: Arthur A. Clark Co., 1919.

Allen, Theodore. *The Invention of the White Race.* London: Verso, 1994.

Ameringer, Oscar. *If You Don't Weaken: The Autobiography of Oscar Ameringer.* Norman: University of Oklahoma Press, 1983.

Anderson, Benedict. *Imagined Communities: Reflections of the Origin and Spread of Nationalism.* London: Verso, 1983.

Ashton, Sharron Standifer, ed. *Indians and Intruders.* 5 vols. Norman, Okla.: Sharon Standifer Ashton, 1998–2002.

Athearn, Robert G. *In Search of Canaan: Black Migration to Kansas, 1879–80.* Lawrence: Regents Press of Kansas, 1978.

Bailey, Minnie Thomas. *Reconstruction in Indian Territory: A Story of Avarice, Discrimination, and Opportunism.* Port Washington, N.Y.: Kennikat Press, 1972.

Baker, Lee D. *From Savage to Negro: Anthropology and the Construction of Race, 1896–1954.* Berkeley: University of California Press, 1998.

Baker, T. Lindsay, and Julie P. Baker, eds. *The WPA Oklahoma Slave Narratives.* Norman: University of Oklahoma Press, 1996.

Baker, Terri M., and Connie Oliver Henshaw, eds. *Women Who Pioneered Oklahoma: Stories from the WPA Narratives.* Norman: University of Oklahoma Press, 2007.

Bartram, William. *Travels through North & South Carolina, Georgia, East & West Florida, the Cherokee Country, the Extensive Territories of the Muscogulges, or Creek Confederacy, and the Country of the Chactaws; Containing an Account of the Soil and Natural Productions of Those Regions, Together with Observations on the Manners of the Indians.* Philadelphia: James and Johnston, 1791.

Bay, Mia. *The White Image in the Black Mind: African-American Ideas about White People, 1830–1925.* New York: Oxford University Press, 2000.

Bederman, Gail. *Manliness and Civilization: A Cultural History of Gender and Race in the United States, 1880–1917.* Chicago: University of Chicago Press, 1995.

Bennett, David H. *The Party of Fear: From Nativist Movements to the New Right in American History.* Chapel Hill: University of North Carolina Press, 1988.

Bissett, Jim. *Agrarian Socialism in America: Marx, Jefferson, and Jesus in the Oklahoma Countryside, 1904–1920.* Norman: University of Oklahoma Press, 1999.

Bittle, William E., and Gilbert Geis. *The Longest Way Home: Chief Alfred C. Sam's Back-to-Africa Movement.* Detroit: Wayne State University Press, 1964.

Blum, Edward J. *Reforging the White Republic: Race, Religion, and American Nationalism, 1865–1898.* Baton Rouge: Louisiana State University Press, 2005.

Braund, Kathryn E. Holland. *Deerskins and Duffels: The Creek Indian Trade with Anglo-America, 1685–1815.* Lincoln: University of Nebraska Press, 1993.

Britten, Thomas A. *American Indians in World War I: At Home and at War.* Albuquerque: University of New Mexico Press, 1997.

Brodkin, Karen. *How Jews Became White Folks and What That Says about Race in America.* New Brunswick, N.J.: Rutgers University Press, 1998.

Brookings Institution and the Institute for Government Research. *The Problem of Indian Administration.* Baltimore: Johns Hopkins Press, 1928.

Brooks, James. *Captives and Cousins: Slavery, Kinship, and Community in the Southwest Borderlands.* Chapel Hill: University of North Carolina Press, 2002.

————, ed. *Confounding the Color Line: The Indian-Black Experience in North America.* Lincoln: University of Nebraska Press, 2002.

Brophy, Alfred L. *Reconstructing the Dreamland: The Tulsa Race Riot of 1921: Race, Reparations, and Reconciliation.* Oxford: Oxford University Press, 2002.

Brown, Richard Maxwell. *No Duty to Retreat: Violence and Values in American History and Society.* New York: Oxford University Press, 1991.

Burbank, Garin. *When Farmers Voted Red: The Gospel of Socialism in the Oklahoma Countryside, 1910–1924.* Westport, Conn.: Greenwood, 1976.

Burton, Jeffrey. *Indian Territory and the United States, 1866–1906: Courts, Government, and the Movement for Oklahoma Statehood.* Norman: University of Oklahoma Press, 1995.

Bush, Rod. *We Are Not What We Seem: Black Nationalism and Class Struggle in the American Century.* New York: New York University Press, 1999.

Campbell, J. B., ed. *Campbell's Abstract of Creek Freedman Census Cards and Index.* Muskogee: Phoenix Job Printing Co., 1915.

Carter, Kent. *The Dawes Commission and the Allotment of the Five Civilized Tribes, 1893–1914.* Orem, Utah: Ancestry.com, 1999.

Cashin, Edward J. *Lachlan McGillivray, Indian Trader: The Shaping of the Southern Colonial Frontier*. Athens: University of Georgia Press, 1992.

Chalmers, David. *Hooded Americanism: The First Century of the Ku Klux Klan, 1865–1965*. Garden City, N.Y.: Doubleday, 1965.

Champagne, Duane. *Social Order and Political Change: Constitutional Governments among the Cherokee, the Choctaw, the Chickasaw, and the Creek*. Stanford, Calif.: Stanford University Press, 1992.

Chatterjee, Partha. *The Nation and Its Fragments: Colonial and Postcolonial Histories*. Princeton, N.J.: Princeton University Press, 1993.

Clifford, James. *The Predicament of Culture: Twentieth-Century Ethnography, Literature, and Art*. Cambridge, Mass.: Harvard University Press, 1988.

Cooper, John Milton. *Pivotal Decades: The United States, 1900–1920*. New York: Norton, 1990.

Crellin, John K. *Reference Guide to Medicinal Plants*. Durham, N.C.: Duke University Press, 1989.

Crockett, Norman L. *The Black Towns*. Lawrence: Regents Press of Kansas, 1979.

Dale, Edward Everett, and Morris L. Wardell. *History of Oklahoma*. New York: Prentice Hall, 1948.

Daniel, Pete. *Breaking the Land: The Transformation of Cotton, Tobacco, and Rice Cultures since 1880*. Urbana: University of Illinois Press, 1985.

Debo, Angie. *And Still the Waters Run: The Betrayal of the Five Civilized Tribes*. Princeton, N.J.: Princeton University Press, 1940.

———. *The Rise and Fall of the Choctaw Republic*. Norman: University of Oklahoma Press, 1934.

———. *The Road to Disappearance: A History of the Creek Indians*. Norman: University of Oklahoma Press, 1941.

Deloria, Philip J. *Indians in Unexpected Places*. Lawrence: University Press of Kansas, 2004.

Deloria, Philip J., and Neal Salisbury, eds. *A Companion to American Indian History*. Malden, Mass.: Blackwell, 2002.

Denman, D. R. *Origins of Ownership: A Brief History of Land Ownership and Tenure in England from Earliest Times to the Modern Era*. London: George Allen and Unwin, 1958.

Denton, Virginia Lantz. *Booker T. Washington and the Adult Education Movement*. Gainesville: University Press of Florida, 1993.

Dippie, Brian W. *The Vanishing American: White Attitudes and U.S. Indian Policy*. Middletown, Conn.: Wesleyan University Press, 1982.

Dowd, Gregory Evans. *A Spirited Resistance: The North American Indian Struggle for Unity, 1745–1815*. Baltimore: Johns Hopkins University Press, 1992.

Drinnon, Richard. *Facing West: The Metaphysics of Indian-Hating and Empire-Building*. Norman: University of Oklahoma Press, 1997.

Duara, Prasenjit. *Rescuing History from the Nation: Questioning Narratives of Modern China*. Chicago: University of Chicago Press, 1995.

Du Bois, W. E. B. *Black Reconstruction in America*. New York: Atheneum, 1992.

Edmunds, R. David. *The Shawnee Prophet*. Lincoln: University of Nebraska Press, 1983.

————. *Tecumseh and the Quest for Indian Leadership.* Boston: Little, Brown, 1984.

Edwards, Laura F. *The People and Their Peace: Legal Culture and the Transformation of Inequality in the Post-Revolutionary South.* Chapel Hill: University of North Carolina Press, 2009.

Ellsworth, Scott. *Death in a Promised Land: The Tulsa Race Riot of 1921.* Baton Rouge: Louisiana State University Press, 1982.

Ethridge, Robbie. *Creek Country: The Creek Indians and Their World.* Chapel Hill: University of North Carolina Press, 2003.

Fields, Barbara Jeanne. *Slavery and Freedom on the Middle Ground: Maryland during the Nineteenth Century.* New Haven, Conn.: Yale University Press, 1985.

Foley, Neil. *The White Scourge: Mexicans, Blacks, and Poor Whites in Texas Cotton Culture.* Berkeley: University of California Press, 1997.

Foner, Eric. *Reconstruction: America's Unfinished Revolution, 1863–1877.* New York: Harper and Row, 1988.

Forbes, Jack D. *Africans and Native Americans: The Language of Race and the Evolution of Red-Black Peoples.* Urbana: University of Illinois Press, 1993.

Fowler, Loretta. *Shared Symbols, Contested Meanings: Gros Ventre Culture and History, 1778–1984.* Ithaca, N.Y.: Cornell University Press, 1987.

Frank, Andrew. *Creeks and Southerners: Biculturalism on the Early American Frontier.* Lincoln: University of Nebraska Press, 2005.

Franklin, Jimmie Lewis. *Journey toward Hope: A History of Blacks in Oklahoma.* Norman: University of Oklahoma Press, 1982.

Franks, Kenny A., Paul F. Lambert, and Carl N. Tyson. *Early Oklahoma Oil: A Photographic History, 1859–1936.* College Station: Texas A&M University Press, 1981.

Fredrickson, George M. *The Black Image in the White Mind: The Debate on Afro-American Character and Destiny, 1817–1914.* New York: Harper and Row, 1971.

Gallay, Alan. *The Indian Slave Trade: The Rise of the English Empire in the American South, 1670–1717.* New Haven, Conn.: Yale University Press, 2002.

Gates, Paul Wallace. *History of Public Land Law Development.* New York: Arno Press, 1979.

Gerstle, Gary. *American Crucible: Race and Nation in the Twentieth Century.* Princeton, N.J.: Princeton University Press, 2001.

Gibson, Arrell M. *Oklahoma: A History of Five Centuries.* Norman, Okla.: Harlow, 1965.

Giddings, Paula. *When and Where I Enter: The Impact of Women on Race and Sex in America.* New York: Morrow, 1984.

Goble, Danney. *Progressive Oklahoma: The Making of a New Kind of State.* Norman: University of Oklahoma Press, 1980.

Goddard, Henry Herbert. *The Kallikak Family: A Study in the Heredity of Feeble-Mindedness.* New York: Macmillan, 1912.

Goldenweiser, E. A., and Leon E. Truesdell. *Farm Tenancy in the United States.* Vol. 4 of *Census Monographs.* Washington: Government Printing Office, 1924.

Gomez, Michael A. *Exchanging Our Country Marks: The Transformation of African Identities in the Colonial and Antebellum South.* Chapel Hill: University of North Carolina Press, 1998.

Gouge, Earnest. *Totkv Mocvse/New Fire: Creek Folktales by Earnest Gouge.* Edited and translated by Jack B. Martin, Margaret McKane Mauldin, and Juanita McGirt. Norman: University of Oklahoma Press, 2004.

Grantham, Bill. *Creation Myths and Legends of the Creek Indians.* Gainesville: University Press of Florida, 2002.

Grayson, George Washington. *A Creek Warrior for the Confederacy: The Autobiography of Chief G. W. Grayson.* Edited by W. David Baird. Norman: University of Oklahoma Press, 1988.

Green, Donald, ed. *Rural Oklahoma.* Oklahoma City: Oklahoma Historical Society, 1977.

Green, James. *Grass-Roots Socialism: Radical Movements in the Southwest, 1895–1943.* Baton Rouge: Louisiana State University Press, 1978.

Green, Michael D. *The Politics of Indian Removal: Creek Government and Society in Crisis.* Lincoln: University of Nebraska Press, 1982.

Gregory, James N. *American Exodus: The Dust Bowl Migration and Okie Culture in California.* New York: Oxford University Press, 1989.

Grenier, John. *The First Way of War: American War Making on the Frontier, 1607–1814.* Cambridge: Cambridge University Press, 2005.

Hahn, Steven C. *The Invention of the Creek Nation: 1670–1763.* Lincoln: University of Nebraska Press, 2004.

Hamilton, Kenneth Marvin. *Black Towns and Profit: Promotion and Development in the Trans-Appalachian West, 1877–1915.* Urbana: University of Illinois Press, 1991.

Haney Lopez, Ian F. *White by Law: The Legal Construction of Race.* New York: New York University Press, 1996.

Harmon, Alexandra. *Indians in the Making: Ethnic Relations and Indian Identities around Puget Sound.* Berkeley: University of California Press, 1998.

Harring, Sidney L. *Crow Dog's Case: American Indian Sovereignty, Tribal Law, and the United States.* Cambridge: Cambridge University Press, 1994.

Harris, Marvin. *Patterns of Race in the Americas.* New York: Walker, 1964.

Hastain, E. *Hastain's Township Plats of the Creek Nation.* Muskogee: Model Printing Co., 1910.

Hawkins, Benjamin. *The Collected Works of Benjamin Hawkins, 1796–1810.* Edited by H. Thomas Foster. Tuscaloosa: University of Alabama Press, 2003.

——————. *Letters, Journals, and Writings of Benjamin Hawkins.* Edited by C. L. Grant. Savannah, Ga.: Beehive Press, 1980.

Hendrix, Janey B. *Redbird Smith and the Nighthawk Keetoowahs.* Park Hill, Okla.: Cross-Cultural Education Center, 1983.

Hertzberg, Hazel W. *The Search for an American Indian Identity: Modern Pan-Indian Movements.* Syracuse, N.Y.: Syracuse University Press, 1971.

Higham, John. *Strangers in the Land: Patterns of American Nativism, 1860–1925.* New Brunswick, N.J.: Rutgers University Press, 1955.

Hill, Robert A., ed. *The Marcus Garvey and Universal Negro Improvement Association Papers.* 10 vols. Berkeley: University of California Press, 1983–2006.

Hirsch, James S. *Riot and Remembrance: The Tulsa Race War and Its Legacy.* Boston: Houghton Mifflin, 2002.

Hitchcock, Ethan Allen. *A Traveler in Indian Territory: The Journal of Ethan Allen Hitch-

cock, *Late Major-General in the United States Army.* Edited by Grant Foreman. Cedar
Rapids, Iowa: Torch Press, 1930.

Hobsbawm, Eric, and Terence Ranger, eds. *The Invention of Tradition.* Cambridge: Cambridge University Press, 1983.

Holm, Tom. *The Great Confusion in Indian Affairs: Native Americans and Whites in the Progressive Era.* Austin: University of Texas Press, 2005.

Horsman, Reginald. *Race and Manifest Destiny: The Origins of American Racial Anglo-Saxonism.* Cambridge, Mass.: Harvard University Press, 1981.

Hosmer, Brian. *American Indians in the Marketplace: Persistence and Innovation among the Menominees and Metlakatlans, 1870–1920.* Lawrence: University Press of Kansas, 1999.

Hoxie, Frederick E. *A Final Promise: The Campaign to Assimilate the Indians, 1880–1920.* Lincoln: University of Nebraska Press, 1984.

Hurt, R. Douglas. *Indian Agriculture in America: Prehistory to the Present.* Lawrence: University Press of Kansas, 1987.

Ignatiev, Noel. *How the Irish Became White.* New York: Routledge, 1995.

Jacobson, Matthew Frye. *Barbarian Virtues: The United States Encounters Foreign Peoples at Home and Abroad, 1876–1917.* New York: Hill and Wang, 2001.

————. *Whiteness of a Different Color: European Immigrants and the Alchemy of Race.* Cambridge, Mass.: Harvard University Press, 1999.

James, Winston. *Holding Aloft the Banner of Ethiopia: Caribbean Radicalism in Early Twentieth-Century America.* London: Verso, 1998.

Jaynes, Gerald. *Branches without Roots: Genesis of the Black Working Class in the American South, 1862–1882.* New York: Oxford University Press, 1986.

Johnson, Hannibal B. *Black Wall Street: From Riot to Renaissance in Tulsa's Historic Greenwood District.* Austin, Tex.: Eakin Press, 1998.

Jones, Jacqueline. *Labor of Love, Labor of Sorrow: Black Women, Work, and the Family from Slavery to the Present.* New York: Basic Books, 1985.

Jordan, Winthrop D. *White over Black: American Attitudes toward the Negro, 1550–1812.* Chapel Hill: University of North Carolina Press, 1968.

Joseph, Miranda. *Against the Romance of Community.* Minneapolis: University of Minnesota Press, 2002.

Kantrowitz, Stephen. *Ben Tillman and the Reconstruction of White Supremacy.* Chapel Hill: University of North Carolina Press, 2000.

Kappler, Charles J., ed. *Indian Treaties. 1778–1883.* Vol 2 of *Indian Affairs. Laws and Treaties.* New York: Interland, 1972.

Kasinitz, Philip. *Caribbean New York: Black Immigrants and the Politics of Race.* Ithaca, N.Y.: Cornell University Press, 1992.

Kauanui, J. Kēhaulani. *Hawaiian Blood: Colonialism and the Politics of Sovereignty and Indigeneity.* Durham, N.C.: Duke University Press, 2008.

Kelley, Robin D. G. *Race Rebels: Culture, Politics, and the Black Working Class.* New York: Free Press, 1994.

Kelley, Robin D. G., and Earl Lewis, eds. *To Make Our World Anew: A History of African Americans.* New York: Oxford University Press, 2000.

Kersh, Rogan. *Dreams of a More Perfect Union.* Ithaca, N.Y.: Cornell University Press, 2001.

Kevles, Daniel J. *In the Name of Eugenics: Genetics and the Uses of Human Heredity.* New York: Knopf, 1985.

Krech, Shepard. *The Ecological Indian: Myth and History.* New York: Norton, 1999.

Krueckeberg, Donald A. "Who Rents America? Owners, Tenants, and Taxes." Working Paper no. 32. Land Tenure Center, Madison, Wisconsin, 1999.

Lambert, Paul F., and Kenny A. Franks, eds. *Voices from the Oil Fields.* Norman: University of Oklahoma Press, 1984.

La Vere, David. *Contrary Neighbors: Southern Plains and Removed Indians in Indian Territory.* Norman: University of Oklahoma Press, 2000.

Lawson, John, and Frances Latham Harriss. *Lawson's History of North Carolina, Containing the Exact Description and Natural History of That Country. Together with the Present State Thereof and a Journal of a Thousand Miles Traveled through Several Nations of Indians, Giving a Particular Account of Their Customs, Manners, Etc., Etc.* 1714. Richmond, Va.: Garrett and Massie, 1951.

Lemelle, Sidney J., and Robin D. G. Kelley, eds. *Imagining Home: Class, Culture, and Nationalism in the African Diaspora.* London: Verso, 1994.

Lewis, David Levering. *W. E. B. Du Bois: Biography of a Race, 1868–1919.* New York: Henry Holt, 1993.

Lewis, Earl. *In Their Own Interests: Race, Class, and Power in Twentieth-Century Norfolk, Virginia.* Berkeley: University of California Press, 1991.

Littlefield, Daniel F. *Africans and Creeks: From the Colonial Period to the Civil War.* Westport, Conn.: Greenwood, 1979.

———. *Africans and Seminoles: From Removal to Emancipation.* Westport, Conn.: Greenwood, 1977.

———. *Alex Posey: Creek Poet, Journalist, and Humorist.* Lincoln: University of Nebraska Press, 1992.

———. *The Cherokee Freedmen: From Emancipation to American Citizenship.* Westport, Conn.: Greenwood, 1978.

———. *The Chickasaw Freedmen: A People without a Country.* Westport, Conn.: Greenwood, 1980.

MacLean, Nancy. *Behind the Mask of Chivalry: The Making of the Second Ku Klux Klan.* New York: Oxford University Press, 1994.

Madigan, Tim. *The Burning: Massacre, Destruction, and the Tulsa Race Riot of 1921.* New York: Thomas Dunne Books and St. Martin's Press, 2001.

Marshall, T. H. *Citizenship and Social Class and Other Essays.* Cambridge: Cambridge University Press, 1950.

Martin, Jack B., and Margaret McKane Mauldin. *A Dictionary of Creek/Muskogee: With Notes on the Florida and Oklahoma Seminole Dialects of Creek.* Lincoln: University of Nebraska Press, 2000.

Martin, Joel W. *Sacred Revolt: The Muskogees' Struggle for a New World.* Boston: Beacon Press, 1991.

Mather, Frank Lincoln, ed. *Who's Who of the Colored Race.* Vol. 1. 1915. Detroit: Gale Research Co., 1976.

May, Katja. *African Americans and Native Americans in the Creek and Cherokee Nations,*
    1830s to 1920s: Collision and Collusion. New York: Garland, 1996.

McLoughlin, William G. *After the Trail of Tears: The Cherokees' Struggle for Sovereignty,*
    1839–1880. Chapel Hill: University of North Carolina Press, 1993.

McMillen, Neil R. *Dark Journey: Black Mississippians in the Age of Jim Crow.* Urbana:
    University of Illinois Press, 1990.

McNickle, D'Arcy. *Native American Tribalism: Indian Survivals and Renewals.* New York:
    Oxford University Press, 1973.

Mehta, Uday Singh. *Liberalism and Empire: A Study in Nineteenth-Century British Liberal*
    Thought. Chicago: University of Chicago Press, 1999.

Meredith, Howard. *Agrarian Socialism in Oklahoma.* Norman: University of Oklahoma,
    1970.

Meyer, Melissa L. *The White Earth Tragedy: Ethnicity and Dispossession at a Minnesota*
    Anishinaabe Reservation, 1889–1920. Lincoln: University of Nebraska Press, 1994.

Miles, Tiya. *Ties That Bind: The Story of an Afro-Cherokee Family in Slavery and Freedom.*
    Berkeley: University of California Press, 2005.

Miles, Tiya, and Sharon Patricia Holland, eds. *Crossing Waters, Crossing Worlds: The Afri-*
    can Diaspora in Indian Country. Durham, N.C.: Duke University Press, 2006.

Miller, Floyd J. *The Search for a Black Nationality: Black Emigration and Colonization,*
    1787–1863. Urbana: University of Illinois Press, 1975.

Mills, Lawrence. *The Lands of the Five Civilized Tribes: A Treatise upon the Law Applicable*
    to the Lands of the Five Civilized Tribes in Oklahoma. St. Louis: F. H. Thomas Law
    Book Co., 1919.

Minges, Patrick N. *Slavery in the Cherokee Nation: The Keetoowah Society and the Defining*
    of a People, 1855–1867. London: Routledge, 2003.

Mitchell, Thomas W. "From Reconstruction to Deconstruction." Research Paper
    no. 132. Land Tenure Center, Madison, Wisconsin, 1999.

Montoya, María E. *Translating Property: The Maxwell Land Grant and the Conflict over*
    Land in the American West, 1840–1900. Lawrence: University Press of Kansas, 2005.

Morgan, Anne Hodges, and H. Wayne Morgan, eds. *Oklahoma: New Views of the Forty-*
    sixth State. Norman: University of Oklahoma Press, 1982.

Morgan, Edmund Sears. *American Slavery, American Freedom: The Ordeal of Colonial*
    Virginia. New York: Norton, 1975.

Morgan, Francesca. *Women and Patriotism in Jim Crow America.* Chapel Hill: University
    of North Carolina Press, 2005.

Morris, John W., Charles R. Goins, and Edwin C. McReynolds. *Historical Atlas of Okla-*
    homa. 3rd ed. Norman: University of Oklahoma Press, 1986.

Morris, Michael P. *The Bringing of Wonder: Trade and the Indians of the Southeast, 1700–*
    1783. Westport, Conn.: Greenwood, 1999.

Mulroy, Kevin. *Freedom on the Border: The Seminole Maroons in Florida, the Indian Terri-*
    tory, Coahuila, and Texas. Lubbock: Texas Tech University Press, 1993.

Nash, Gary B., and Weiss, Richard, eds. *The Great Fear: Race in the Mind of America.*
    New York: Holt, Rinehart and Winston, 1970.

National Civil Liberties Bureau. "The 'Knights of Liberty' Mob and the I.W.W. Pris-
    oners at Tulsa, Oklahoma." New York: National Civil Liberties Bureau, 1918.

Naylor, Celia. *African Cherokees in Indian Country.* Chapel Hill: University of North Carolina Press, 2008.

O'Beirne, H. F., and E. S. O'Beirne. *The Indian Territory: Its Chiefs, Legislators and Leading Men.* St. Louis: C. B. Woodward Co., 1892.

O'Leary, Cecilia Elizabeth. *To Die For: The Paradox of American Patriotism.* Princeton, N.J.: Princeton University Press, 1999.

Omi, Michael, and Howard Winant. *Racial Formation in the United States: From the 1960s to the 1990s.* New York: Routledge, 1994.

Otis, D. S. *The Dawes Act and the Allotment of Indian Lands.* Norman: University of Oklahoma Press, 1973.

Oubre, Claude F. *Forty Acres and a Mule: The Freedmen's Bureau and Black Landownership.* Baton Rouge: Louisiana State University Press, 1978.

Painter, Nell Irvin. *Exodusters: Black Migration to Kansas after Reconstruction.* New York: Knopf, 1977.

—————. *Standing at Armageddon: The United States, 1877–1919.* New York: Norton, 1987.

Parker, Linda S. *Native American Estate: The Struggle over Indian and Hawaiian Lands.* Honolulu: University of Hawaii Press, 1996.

Patterson, Orlando. *Slavery and Social Death: A Comparative Study.* Cambridge, Mass.: Harvard University Press, 1982.

Perdue, Theda. *Cherokee Women: Gender and Culture Change. 1700–1835.* Lincoln: University of Nebraska Press, 1998.

Perryman, L. C., ed. *Constitution and Laws of the Muskogee Nation.* 1890. Wilmington, Del.: Scholarly Resources, 1975.

Pfister, Joel. *Individuality Incorporated: Indians and the Multicultural Modern.* Durham, N.C.: Duke University Press, 2004.

Pickus, Noah. *True Faith and Allegiance: Immigration and American Civic Nationalism.* Princeton, N.J.: Princeton University Press, 2005.

Piker, Joshua Aaron. *Okfuskee: A Creek Indian Town in Colonial America.* Cambridge, Mass.: Harvard University Press, 2004.

Porter, Kenneth Wiggins. *The Black Seminoles: History of a Freedom-Seeking People.* Gainesville: University Press of Florida, 1996.

Posey, Alexander Lawrence. *The Fus Fixico Letters: A Creek Humorist in Early Oklahoma.* Edited by Daniel F. Littlefield Jr. and Carol A. Petty Hunter. Norman, Okla.: Red River Books, 2002.

Prucha, Francis Paul, ed. *Americanizing the American Indians: Writings by the "Friends of the Indian," 1880–1900.* Cambridge, Mass.: Harvard University Press, 1973.

—————, ed. *Atlas of American Indian Affairs.* Lincoln: University of Nebraska Press, 1990.

—————. *The Great Father: The United States Government and the American Indians.* 2 vols. Lincoln: University of Nebraska Press, 1984.

Pukui, Mary Kawena. *'Ōlelo No'eau: Hawaiian Proverbs and Poetical Sayings.* Honolulu: Bishop Museum Press, 1983).

Redkey, Edwin S. *Black Exodus: Black Nationalist and Back-to-Africa Movements, 1890–1910.* New Haven, Conn.: Yale University Press, 1969.

Rister, Carl Coke. *Land Hunger: David L. Payne and the Oklahoma Boomers*. Norman: University of Oklahoma Press, 1942.

Roediger, David R. *The Wages of Whiteness: Race and the Making of the American Working Class*. London: Verso, 1991.

Rosen, Ellen. *Peasant Socialism in America? The Socialist Party in Oklahoma before the First World War*. New York: City University of New York, 1975.

Royce, Edward. *The Origins of Southern Sharecropping*. Philadelphia: Temple University Press, 1993.

Satz, Ronald N. *American Indian Policy in the Jacksonian Era*. Lincoln: University of Nebraska Press, 1974.

Saunt, Claudio. *Black, White, and Indian: Race and the Unmaking of an American Family*. New York: Oxford University Press, 2005.

————. *A New Order of Things: Property, Power, and the Transformation of the Creek Indians. 1733–1816*. Cambridge: Cambridge University Press, 1999.

Scales, James R., and Danney Goble. *Oklahoma Politics: A History*. Norman: University of Oklahoma Press, 1982.

Schultz, Jack M. *The Seminole Baptist Churches of Oklahoma: Maintaining a Traditional Community*. Norman: University of Oklahoma Press, 1999.

Sellars, Nigel Anthony. *Oil, Wheat, and Wobblies: The Industrial Workers of the World in Oklahoma, 1905–1930*. Norman: University of Oklahoma Press, 1998.

Semple, W. F. *Oklahoma Indian Land Titles, Annotated*. St. Louis: Thomas Law Book Co., 1952.

Shideler, James H. *Farm Crisis, 1919–1923*. Berkeley: University of California Press, 1957.

Simkins, Francis Butler. *Pitchfork Ben Tillman, South Carolinian*. Columbia: University of South Carolina Press, 2002.

Spillman, Lyn. *Nation and Commemoration: Creating National Identities in the United States and Australia*. Cambridge: Cambridge University Press, 1997.

Spoehr, Alexander. *Changing Kinship Systems: A Study in the Acculturation of the Creeks, Cherokee, and Choctaw*. Field Museum of Natural History Publication 583. Anthropological series, vol. 33, no. 4. Chicago: Field Museum, 1947.

Stein, Judith. *The World of Marcus Garvey: Race and Class in Modern Society*. Baton Rouge: Louisiana State University Press, 1986.

Steinbeck, John. *The Grapes of Wrath*. 1939. New York: Viking, 1986.

Stuckey, Sterling. *Slave Culture: Nationalist Theory and the Foundations of Black America*. New York: Oxford University Press, 1987.

Swanton, John Reed. *Creek Religion and Medicine*. Lincoln: University of Nebraska Press, 2000.

————. *Social Organization and Social Usages of the Indians of the Creek Confederacy*. Bureau of American Ethnography Annual Report, vol. 42. Washington: Government Printing Office, 1928.

Takaki, Ronald T. *Iron Cages: Race and Culture in Nineteenth-Century America*. New York: Knopf, 1979.

Taylor, Graham D. *The New Deal and American Indian Tribalism: The Administration of the Indian Reorganization Act, 1935–45*. Lincoln: University of Nebraska Press, 1980.

Taylor, Quintard. *In Search of the Racial Frontier: African Americans in the American West, 1528–1990*. New York: Norton, 1998.

Teall, Kaye M., ed. *Black History in Oklahoma: A Resource Book*. Oklahoma City: Oklahoma City Public Schools, 1971.

Thompson, John. *Closing the Frontier: Radical Response in Oklahoma, 1889–1923*. Norman: University of Oklahoma Press, 1986.

Thorne, Tanis C. *The World's Richest Indian: The Scandal over Jackson Barnett's Oil Fortune*. Oxford: Oxford University Press, 2003.

Todorov, Tzvetan. *The Conquest of America: The Question of the Other*. New York: Harper and Row, 1984.

Tolson, Arthur L. *The Black Oklahomans: A History, 1541–1972*. New Orleans: Edwards Printing Co., 1972.

Tucker, Howard A. *History of Governor Walton's War on Ku Klux Klan, the Invisible Empire*. Oklahoma City: Southwest Publishing, 1923.

Vaughn, Stephen. *Holding Fast the Inner Lines: Democracy, Nationalism, and the Committee on Public Information*. Chapel Hill: University of North Carolina Press, 1980.

Vizenor, Gerald. *Fugitive Poses: Native American Indian Scenes of Absence and Presence*. Lincoln: University of Nebraska Press, 1998.

Waldstreicher, David. *In the Midst of Perpetual Fetes: The Making of American Nationalism, 1776–1820*. Chapel Hill: Omohundro Institute of Early American History and Culture/University of North Carolina Press, 1997.

Warde, Mary Jane. *George Washington Grayson and the Creek Nation, 1843–1920*. Norman: University of Oklahoma Press, 1999.

Washington, Booker T. *The Negro in Business*. Coshocton, Ohio: Hertel, Jenkins and Co., 1907.

Watkins-Owens, Irma. *Blood Relations: Caribbean Immigrants and the Harlem Community, 1900–1930*. Bloomington: Indiana University Press, 1996.

Weaver, Jace, Craig S. Womack, and Robert Allen Warrior. *American Indian Literary Nationalism*. Albuquerque: University of New Mexico Press, 2006.

Webb, Walter Prescott, ed. *The Handbook of Texas*. Austin: Texas State Historical Association, 1952.

Weisiger, Marsha. *Land of Plenty: Oklahomans in the Cotton Fields of Arizona, 1933–1942*. Norman: University of Oklahoma Press, 1995.

White, Richard. *The Roots of Dependency: Subsistence, Environment, and Social Change among the Choctaws, Pawnees, and Navajos*. Lincoln: University of Nebraska Press, 1983.

Wickett, Murray. *Contested Territory: Whites, Native Americans, and African Americans in Oklahoma, 1865–1907*. Baton Rouge: Louisiana State University Press, 2000.

Wilder, Laura Ingalls. *Little House on the Prairie*. 1935. New York: Harper and Row, 1971.

Wilkins, David E. *American Indian Politics and the American Political System*. Lanham, Md.: Rowman and Littlefield, 2002.

Williamson, Joel. *The Crucible of Race: Black-White Relations in the American South since Emancipation*. New York: Oxford University Press, 1984.

Wintz, Cary D., ed. *African American Political Thought, 1890–1930: Washington, Du Bois, Garvey, and Randolph*. Armonk, N.Y.: Sharpe, 1996.

Wise, Donald A. *Broken Arrow: City of Roses and Pure Water*. Chicago: Arcadia, 2002.

Womack, Craig S. *Red on Red: Native American Literary Separatism*. Minneapolis: University of Minnesota Press, 1999.

Woodward, Thomas Simpson. *Woodward's Reminiscences of the Creek, or Muscogee Indians: Contained in Letters to Friends in Georgia and Alabama*. Mobile, Ala.: Southern University Press, 1965.

Worster, Donald. *Dust Bowl: The Southern Plains in the 1930s*. New York: Oxford University Press, 1979.

Wright, J. Leitch. *Creeks and Seminoles: The Destruction and Regeneration of the Muscogulge People*. Lincoln: University of Nebraska Press, 1986.

Zellar, Gary. *African Creeks: Estelvste and the Creek Nation*. Norman: University of Oklahoma Press, 2007.

ESSAYS

Bartram, William. "Observations on the Creek and Cherokee Indians." 1789. In *William Bartram on the Southeastern Indians*, edited by Gregory A. Waselkov and Kathryn E. Holland Braund, 139–91. Lincoln: University of Nebraska Press, 1995.

Deutsch, Sarah. "Being American in Boley, Oklahoma." In *Beyond Black and White: Race, Ethnicity, and Gender in the U.S. South and Southwest*, edited by Stephanie Cole and Alison M. Parker, 97–122. College Station: Texas A&M University Press, 2004.

Donaldson, Laura E. "The Breasts of Columbus: A Political Anatomy of Postcolonialism and Feminist Religious Discourse." In *Postcolonialism, Feminism, and Religious Discourse*, edited by Laura E. Donaldson and Kwok Pui-lan, 41–61. New York: Routledge, 2002.

Ethridge, Robbie. "Raiding the Remains: Indian Slave Traders and the Collapse of the Southeastern Chiefdoms." In *Light on the Path: The Anthropology and History of the Southeastern Indians*, edited by Robbie Ethridge and Thomas J. Pluckhahn, 207–18. Tuscaloosa: University of Alabama Press, 2006.

Fields, Barbara J. "Ideology and Race in America." In *Region, Race, and Reconstruction: Essays in Honor of C. Vann Woodward*, edited by J. Morgan Kousser and James M. McPherson, 143–77. New York: Oxford University Press, 1982.

Franklin, Jimmie L. "Black Oklahomans: An Essay on the Quest for Freedom." In *Alternative Oklahoma: Contrarian Views of the Sooner State*, edited by Davis D. Joyce, 36–52. Norman: University of Oklahoma Press, 2007.

Grossman, James R. "A Chance to Make Good, 1900–1929." In *To Make Our World Anew: A History of African Americans*, edited by Robin D. G. Kelley and Earl Lewis, 345–408. Oxford: Oxford University Press, 2000.

Habermas, Jürgen. "On the Past and Future of Sovereignty and Citizenship." In *The European Nation-State: Its Achievements and Its Limits*, edited by Gopal Balakrishnan, 281–94. London: Verso in association with New Left Review, 1996.

Harmon, Alexandra. "Wanted: More Histories of Indian Identity." In *A Companion to American Indian History*, edited by Philip J. Deloria and Neal Salisbury. Malden, Mass.: Blackwell, 2002.

Hoffman, Abraham. "The Black Panther and the Thlocco Case." In *Twin Territories*

Times: The Way It Was in Old Oklahoma, edited by Edward A. Shaw, 123–34. Oklahoma City: Indian Territory Posse of Oklahoma Westerners, 1982.

Kidwell, Clara Sue. "Native American Systems of Knowledge." In *A Companion to American Indian History*, edited by Philip J. Deloria and Neal Salisbury, 87–102. Malden, Mass.: Blackwell, 2002.

Krauthamer, Barbara. "In Their 'Native Country': Freedpeople's Understandings of Culture and Citizenship in the Choctaw and Chickasaw Nations." In *Crossing Waters, Crossing Worlds: The African Diaspora in Indian Country*, edited by Tiya Miles and Sharon Patricia Holland, 100–120. Durham, N.C.: Duke University Press, 2006.

———. "A Particular Kind of Freedom: Black Women, Slavery, Kinship, and Freedom in the American Southeast." In *Women and Slavery*, edited by Gwyn Campbell, Suzanne Miers, and Joseph C. Miller, 2:100–127. Athens: Ohio University Press, 2008.

Marx, Karl. "Capital, Vol. 1." In *The Marx-Engels Reader*, edited by Robert C. Tucker, 294–438. New York: Norton, 1978.

McAuliffie, Dennis, Jr. "Little House on the Diminished Osage Prairie." In *A Broken Flute: The Native Experience in Books for Children*, edited by Doris Seale and Beverly Slapin, 49–52. Berkeley, Calif.: Oyate, 2006.

Naylor-Ojurongbe, Celia. "'Born and Raised among These People, I Don't Want to Know Any Other': Slaves' Acculturation in Nineteenth-Century Indian Territory." In *Confounding the Color Line: The Indian-Black Experience in North America*, edited by James Brooks, 161–92. Lincoln: University of Nebraska Press, 2002.

Opler, Morris Edward. "The Creek 'Town' and the Problem of Creek Indian Reorganization." In *Human Problems in Technological Change, a Casebook*, edited by Edward Holland Spicer, 165–80. New York: Russell Sage Foundation, 1952.

Vorenberg, Michael. "Reconstruction as a Constitutional Crisis." In *Reconstructions: New Perspectives on the Postbellum United States*, edited by Thomas J. Brown, 141–71. Oxford: Oxford University Press, 2006.

Washington, Booker T. "The Negro in the New Southwest" (December 30, 1905). Reprinted in *The Booker T. Washington Papers*, edited by Louis R. Harlan and Raymond W. Smock, 8:472–73. Urbana: University of Illinois Press, 1979.

Williamson, Joel. "Black Self-Assertion before and after Emancipation." In *Key Issues in the Afro-American Experience*, edited by Nathan I. Huggins, Martin Kilson, and Daniel M. Fox, 213–39. New York: Harcourt Brace Jovanovich, 1971.

Womack, Craig S. "The Integrity of American Indian Claims (or, How I Learned to Stop Worrying and Love My Hybridity)." In *American Indian Literary Nationalism*, edited by Jace Weaver, Craig S. Womack, and Robert Allen Warrior, 91–177. Albuquerque: University of New Mexico Press, 2006.

ARTICLES

Beeth, Howard. "A Black Elite Agenda in the Urban South: The Call for Political Change and Racial Economic Solidarity in Houston during the 1920s." *Essays in Economic and Business History* 10 (1992): 41–55.

Bolster, Mel H. "The Smoked Meat Rebellion: Early Oklahoma and Creek Unrest." *Chronicles of Oklahoma* 31 (Spring 1953): 37–55.

Braund, Kathryn E. Holland. "Guardians of Tradition and Handmaidens to Change: Women's Roles in Creek Economic and Social Life during the Eighteenth Century." *American Indian Quarterly* 14 (Summer 1990): 239–58.

Burbank, Garin. "Agrarian Radicals and Their Opponents: Political Conflict in Southern Oklahoma, 1910–1924." *Journal of American History* 58 (June 1971): 5–23.

Davis, Mace. "Chitto Harjo." *Chronicles of Oklahoma* 13 (June 1935): 139–45

Doran, Michael F. "Population Statistics of Nineteenth Century Indian Territory." *Chronicles of Oklahoma* 53 (Winter 1975): 492–515.

Fite, Gilbert C. "Oklahoma's Reconstruction League: An Experiment in Farmer-Labor Politics." *Journal of Southern History* 13 (November 1947): 535–55.

Freeman, Charles R. "The Battle of Honey Springs." *Chronicles of Oklahoma* 13 (June 1935): 154–68.

Graebner, Norman Arthur. "Pioneer Indian Agriculture in Oklahoma." *Chronicles of Oklahoma* 23 (Autumn 1945): 232–48.

Grinde, Donald A., Jr., and Quintard Taylor. "Red vs Black: Conflict and Accommodation in the Post Civil War Indian Territory, 1865–1907." *American Indian Quarterly* 8 (Summer 1984): 220–21.

Hagan, William T. "Full Blood, Mixed Blood, Generic, and Ersatz: The Problem of Indian Identity." *Arizona and the West* 27 (Winter 1985): 309–26.

———. "Private Property, the Indian's Door to Civilization." *Ethnohistory* 3 (Spring 1956): 126–37.

———. "Tribalism Rejuvenated: The Native American since the Era of Termination." *Western Historical Quarterly* 12 (January 1981): 5–16.

Harmon, Alexandra. "American Indians and Land Monopolies in the Gilded Age." *Journal of American History* 90 (June 2003): 106–33.

———. "Tribal Enrollment Councils: Lessons on Law and Indian Identity." *Western Historical Quarterly* 32 (Summer 2001): 175–200.

———. "When Is an Indian Not an Indian? The 'Friends of the Indian' and the Problems of Indian Identity." *Journal of Ethnic Studies* 18 (Summer 1990): 95–123.

Harring, Sidney L. "Crazy Snake and the Creek Struggle for Sovereignty: The Native American Legal Culture and American Law." *American Journal of Legal History* 34 (October 1990): 365–80.

Harris, Cheryl I. "Whiteness as Property." *Harvard Law Review* 106 (June 1993): 1707–91.

Hickman, Christine B. "The Devil and the One Drop Rule: Racial Categories, African Americans, and the U.S. Census." *Michigan Law Review* 95 (March 1997): 1161–1265.

Hilton, O. A. "The Oklahoma Council of Defense and the First World War." *Chronicles of Oklahoma* 20 (March 1942): 18–24.

Irwin, Lee. "Freedom, Law, and Prophecy: A Brief History of Native American Religious Resistance." *American Indian Quarterly* 21 (Winter 1997): 35–55.

Itagaki, Lynn M. "Transgressing Race and Community in Chester Himes's 'If He Hollers Let Him Go.'" *African American Review* 37 (Spring 2003): 65–80.

Jewett, N. Clay. "The Definition of Klankraft and How to Disseminate It." *Imperial Night-Hawk*, November 7, 1923, 2.

Keith, Jeannette. "The Politics of Southern Draft Resistance, 1917–1918: Class, Race, and Conscription in the Rural South." *Journal of American History* 87 (March 2001): 1335–61.

Littlefield, Daniel F., and Lonnie E. Underhill. "The Crazy Snake Uprising of 1909: A Red, Black or White Affair?" *Arizona and the West* 20 (Winter 1978): 307–24.

Marable, Manning. "The Politics of Black Land Tenure, 1877–1915." *Agricultural History* 53 (January 1979): 142–52.

Meredith, Howard. "Oscar Ameringer and the Concept of Agrarian Socialism." *Chronicles of Oklahoma* 45 (Winter 1967): 77–83.

Meserve, John B. "Chief Isparhecher." *Chronicles of Oklahoma* 10 (March 1932): 52–76.

———. "Chief Samuel Checote, with Sketches of Chiefs Locher Harjo and Ward Coachman." *Chronicles of Oklahoma* 16 (December 1938): 401–9.

———. "The Perrymans." *Chronicles of Oklahoma* 15 (June 1937): 166–84.

Morton, Ohland. "Reconstruction in the Creek Nation." *Chronicles of Oklahoma* 9 (June 1931): 171–79.

Neuringer, Sheldon. "Governor Walton's War on the Ku Klux Klan: An Episode in Oklahoma History, 1923 to 1924." *Chronicles of Oklahoma* 45 (Summer 1967): 153–79.

Nolen, Curtis L. "The Okmulgee Constitution: A Step towards Indian Self-Determination." *Chronicles of Oklahoma* 58 (Fall 1980): 264–81.

Pasour, E. C., Jr. "The Capitalization of Real Property Taxes Levied on Farm Real Estate." *American Journal of Agricultural Economics* 57 (November 1975): 539–48.

Robinson, Ella M. "The Daugherty Ranch, Creek Nation." *Chronicles of Oklahoma* 38 (Spring 1960): 75–77.

Saunt, Claudio. "Telling Stories: The Political Uses of Myth and History in the Cherokee and Creek Nations." *Journal of American History* 93 (December 2006): 673–97.

Shoemaker, Nancy. "How Indians Got to Be Red." *American Historical Review* 102 (June 1997): 625–44.

Simpson, John A. "Economic Righteousness." *Congressional Record* (reprint), 77th Cong., sess. 1, 1932, 1.

Smith, Charles W. "The Selling of America in Oklahoma: The First and Second Liberty Bond Drives." *Chronicles of Oklahoma* 73 (Winter 1995–96): 438–53.

Snipp, C. Matthew. "Who Are American Indians? Some Observations about the Perils and Pitfalls of Data for Race and Ethnicity." *Population and Policy Review* 5 (January 1986): 237–52.

Spoehr, Alexander. "Oklahoma Seminole Towns." *Chronicles of Oklahoma* 14 (December 1941): 376–80.

Turner, C. W. "Events among the Muskogees during Sixty Years." *Chronicles of Oklahoma* 10 (March 1932): 21–34.

Vaughan, Alden T. "From White Man to Redskin: Changing Anglo-American Perceptions of the American Indian." *American Historical Review* 87 (October 1982): 917–53.

Warrick, Sherry. "Radical Labor in Oklahoma: The Working Class Union." *Chronicles of Oklahoma* 52 (Summer 1974): 180–95.

Wickham, John A. "September 11 and America's War on Terrorism: A New Manifest Destiny?" *American Indian Quarterly* 26 (Winter 2002): 116–44.

DISSERTATIONS, THESES, AND PAPERS

Bateman, Rebecca Belle. "'We're Still Here': History, Kinship, and Group Identity among the Seminole Freedmen of Oklahoma." Ph.D. diss., Johns Hopkins University, 1991.

Bell, Amelia Rector. "Creek Ritual: The Path to Peace." Ph.D. diss., University of Chicago, 1984.

Bush, Charles Clement. "The Green Corn Rebellion." M.A. thesis, University of Oklahoma, 1932.

Chang, David A. Y. O. "'The Land Owners Are Ruining the Land': Race, Class, and the Politics of Soil Depletion in Oklahoma, 1907–1940." Paper presented at Social Science History Association Annual Meeting, Fort Worth, Texas, November 14, 1999.

Clark, Carter Blue. "A History of the Ku Klux Klan in Oklahoma." Ph.D. diss., University of Oklahoma, 1976.

Croft, Laurie Jane [Barr]. "The Women of the Ku Klux Klan in Oklahoma." M.A. thesis, University of Oklahoma, 1984.

Goodwin, Ralph William. "Pleasant Porter, Tribal Statesman." M.A. thesis, University of Oklahoma, 1953.

Graham, Donald Ralph. "Red, White and Black: An Interpretation of Ethnic and Racial Attitudes of Agrarian Radicals in Texas and Oklahoma, 1880–1920." M.A. thesis, University of Saskatchewan, 1973.

McIntosh, Kenneth Waldo. "Chitto Harjo, the Crazy Snakes and the Birth of Indian Political Activism in the Twentieth Century." Ph.D. diss., Texas Christian University, 1993.

Pope, Virginia Carrollton. "The Green Corn Rebellion: A Case in Newspaper Self-Censorship." Ph.D. diss., Oklahoma Agricultural and Mechanical College, 1940.

Robbins, Lester Eugene. "The Persistence of Traditional Religious Practices among Creek Indians." Ph.D. diss., Southern Methodist University, 1976.

Rosen, Ellen I. "Peasant Socialism in America? The Socialist Party in Oklahoma before the First World War." Ph.D. diss., City University of New York, 1976.

Sameth, Sigmund. "Creek Negroes: A Study in Race Relations." M.A. thesis, University of Oklahoma, 1940.

Womack, John, Jr. "Oklahoma's Green Corn Rebellion: The Importance of Fools." Senior thesis, Harvard University, 1959.

Wortham, John M. "The Economic Ideologies of Booker T. Washington and W. E. B. Du Bois: 1895–1915." Ph.D. diss., Boston University, 1997.

WEBSITES

Cherokee Nation Cultural Resources Center. "Redbird Smith Story." <http://www.thepeoplespaths.net/Cherokee/RedbirdSmithStory.htm>. June 30, 2008.

"1869 Dunn Roll, Creek Freedmen, Index Re-Se." <http://freepages.genealogy.rootsweb.com/~texlance/dunnroll/dunnname17.htm>. May 25, 2008.

"1870 Loyal Creek Abstract." <http://freepages.genealogy.rootsweb.com/~texlance/loyalcreek/index.htm#index>. July 20, 2008.

Murray, Thomas, ed. *Selected Works of Charles Gibson.* Digital Library, American Native

Press Archives, University of Arkansas at Little Rock. <www.anpa.ualr.edu>. July 20, 2008.

Oklahoma Commission to Study the Tulsa Race Riot of 1921. "Tulsa Race Riot: A Report of the Oklahoma Commission to Study the Tulsa Race Riot of 1921." February 28, 2001. <www.ok-history.mus.ok.us/trrc/freport.pdf>. May 25, 2008.

University of Virginia, Geospatial and Statistical Data Center. "Historical Census Browser." <http://fisher.lib.virginia.edu/collections/stats/histcensus/index.html>. July 20, 2008.

Index

Note: All places are located in Indian Territory or Oklahoma unless otherwise indicated.

Abbott, S. M., 201, 202
Adams, T. J., 83, 95, 96
African Americans: black Creeks' relationship to, 90, 142–43, 149–52, 158–59, 161–64, 169–71, 173, 174; Booker T. Washington counsels accommodationism by, 156, 158; class differences among, 150–51; Creek citizenship, 56–57, 64, 90, 95, 223 (n. 9), 229 (n. 30); draft resistance efforts, 186–88; in east-central Oklahoma, 2–4; efforts to achieve autonomy, 154, 165; Ku Klux Klan violence against, 199, 254 (n. 97); labor unionism and, 184–85; landlessness, 109, 120–21, 173; landownership, 4, 121, 132, 134–36, 161–62, 165–67; landownership and manhood, 156–58; landownership as freedom and empowerment, 7; migrations, 3, 152–54; nationhood conceptions of, 6, 9–11; political involvement, 141, 155, 178, 181; population statistics, 153 (ill.); racial self-construction, 8, 90; settle in Creek Nation, 152–58; as tenant farmers, 130,

131–32, 158, 165, 166, 173, 187; U.S. citizenship, 11, 33–34, 40, 111, 160–61; use of term, 13; voting rights and disenfranchisement of, 93, 160, 161, 163–65, 170, 173, 180, 188, 245 (n. 39), 248 (n. 9); W. E. B. Du Bois counsels activism by, 150, 155, 163, 177; in white racial imaginary, 158; women, 157, 158, 215 (n. 6); in World War I, 191. *See also* Blackness; Black towns; Creeks: black; "Negro"; Slavery/slaves
African descent, people of: calls for racial unity, 91–92; Creek citizenship in antebellum period, 33–34; Dawes Commission categorization of, 94, 95, 120, 232 (n. 74); enslavement by Creeks, 22–25; ethnic diversity of, 10, 45, 150–51; exclusion by Creek racial nationalism, 44; incorporation into Creek society, 21–22; landownership, 150–51; in Redstick War, 37; scholarship on Indians of, 10; in Snake movement, 142; terms used for, 13. *See also* Creeks: black

Afro-American Independent Suffragist League, 160

Afro-Caribbean immigrants, 10

Agrarianism, 192; African American ideas of, 112, 157; of Boomers, 77; insurgent, 175, 183, 194; Jeffersonian and republican, 77; landowning yeoman as central figure of, 112; politics of, 178; racialized, 77; socialism and, 180–82; white, 112, 129–30, 132, 134, 176–78, 180, 188, 200–202, 247 (n. 2); working-class, 184

Agricultural extension agents, 132, 193; African American, 165–67

Agricultural Workers Organization, 183, 184

Agriculture: capitalist, 120, 176; Creek practices, 17–18, 20–21, 28–29, 48–49, 145, 218 (n. 5); crisis in, 192–94; in eastern Oklahoma, 4, 6. *See also* Farmers/farming

Akim Trading Company, 169–70, 171

Aklin, Lida Davis, 48, 49

Alabama: allotment in, 25–26, 36; Creek farming in, 17–18, 20, 28; Creek land cessions of, 25

Allen, Jim, 253 (n. 87)

Allotment(s), 74, 75–76, 212; in Alabama, 25–26, 36; alienation of, 117–18, 134, 210; Creek resistance to, 59–60, 80–82, 84–91, 96–103, 115, 140, 188, 230 (n. 37); dissatisfaction of landless whites with, 109–10, 203; goals of, 143–48; homestead portions, 89, 116, 117, 118, 121, 135; laws regarding, 110–17, 134, 137; leasing, 117, 120–21, 123, 125, 127, 132, 134, 145–48; politics of, 75–76, 83–84, 101, 103–4; pressure to accept, 76, 78, 79–80, 81, 83, 88, 178; process of, 90–93, 123–29; as racial policy, 79–81, 83–84, 93–96, 105, 123, 141; removal of restrictions, 117–21, 123, 124, 135–36, 161–63, 173, 236 (n. 35); restrictions on, 89, 109–14, 125, 128–31, 133–34, 161, 187, 238 (n. 67),

244 (n. 29); sale of, 109–10, 112–16, 119–21, 123–29, 136–37, 192–93, 209, 235 (n. 22), 236 (n. 35); selecting, 144, 231 (n. 60); surplus portions, 89, 117, 118, 121, 235 (n. 30); taxation of, 89, 115, 116, 117, 118, 133, 135–37. *See also* Enrollment of Creeks by Dawes Commission

American Federation of Labor, 184

American Indians. *See* Indians

Americanism, 23, 176, 189–92. *See also* White Americans

American Slavery, American Freedom (Morgan), 7

Ameringer, Oscar, 190

Anti–Jim Crow League, 160

Arkansas Colored Town, 55, 65

Arkansas District/Arkansas River valley, 26, 29, 45, 152. *See also* Lower Creek towns

Arnold, O. E., 200, 253 (n. 87)

Autonomy: African American, 154, 165; black Creek, 40; Creek, 7, 112, 128, 145–48; defending, 12, 53, 54–57; of towns, 32, 34, 90

Back-to-Africa movement, 165, 167–73

Bankers/banks, 2, 114, 116, 117, 162; lending policies, 134–37, 193; racial discrimination by, 132, 135, 194; tax evasion by, 136; Working Class Union seeks usury prosecutions of, 183. *See also* Mortgages

Banks, Eldee, 30

Banks, Phoebe, 29–30, 37

Barnett, Jackson, 144

Barnett, Ketch, 222 (n. 7)

Barnett, Scipio, 222 (n. 7)

Bartram, William, 217 (n. 2)

Battle of Honey Springs (1863), 37, 38

Battle of Horseshoe Bend (1814), 37–38

Bay, Mia: *The White Image in the Black Mind*, 8

Beggs: Klan activity in, 197–201, 254 (n. 97)

Belonging (social): ideas about, 6, 32–33, 76

Biological determinism, 114

Bissett, Jim, 181, 247 (n. 4)

Black Creek–Conservative Creek alliance, 40–44, 101, 223 (n. 14); allotment's effects on, 82, 87; Civil War and, 64–69; landownership issues, 61, 62, 158; opponents, 95; political power, 93, 98, 103; Snake movement and, 141, 142; weakening of, 83

Black Creeks. *See* Creeks: black

Black Image in the White Mind, The (Frederickson), 7–8

Blackness: Creek concept of, 22–23, 92; legal creation of, 161; marked by ability to sell allotment lands, 120–21; as mark of slavery, 22–23. *See also* African Americans

Black towns, 90, 93, 96, 155, 158–59, 173; political involvement, 11, 55–57, 64–67, 82, 139

Blood: politics of, 212; terminology of, 13, 95

Blood quantum, 94–95, 103, 119–20; use of term, 13

Boarding schools, 66, 228 (n. 12)

Boley, 158, 159, 162, 244 (n. 29)

Boll weevil infestation, 170

Bookertee, 156, 173

Boomers, 76–78, 81, 129, 183, 192

Bradley, C. M., 115

Brant, Billie, 97, 233 (n. 91), 241 (n. 100)

Brasfield, Perry and Tilda, 77

Brotherhood of Timber Workers, 183

Brown, B. F., 166, 202

Brown, Jack, 222 (n. 7)

Brown, Wallace, 201

Bruner, Joe, 99

Bruner, Lewis, 58

Bruner, Parah, 88, 91, 92

Bryan, William Jennings, 180

Bullett, Edward. *See* Emarthla, Hotulke

Bullwer, Henry and Winey, 126

Burnett, Jackson, 146

Bushyhead, Dennis, 74

Busk. *See* Green Corn *poskita*

Cade, Moses and Clarissa, 168

Callahan, Sam, 166

Canadian Colored Town, 55, 65, 87–88

Canadian District/Canadian River valley, 26, 29, 48, 152, 187. *See also* Upper Creek towns

Capital: land as, 6, 7

Capitalism: agricultural, 120, 176; class and, 6, 177; classical liberal theory and, 78, 112; culture of, 112, 114; public policy and the making of, 12; racial fixity and the making of, 12, 110, 119, 120, 121; white agrarianism and, 176; whiteness and, 112, 177

Carruth, E. H., 35

Carter, Kent, 232 (n. 74)

Cattle. *See* Ranches/ranching

Census Bureau: racial categories, 130–31, 211, 212

Champagne, Duane, 47

Checote, Samuel, 35–36, 56, 65, 66, 67, 206

Checote faction, 57, 67. *See also* Southern Creeks

Cherokees: allotment's effects on, 3, 84, 102; black, 154; children, 207 (ill.); former slaves, 65; Keetoowahs, 140; political and spiritual movements, 140; removal of, 27; U.S. citizenship, 160; and U.S. Civil War, 35. *See also* Four Mothers Nation

Chesser, Norman, 198–99

Chickasaws: allotment's effects on, 3, 84, 102; black, 154; former slaves, 65; political and spiritual movements, 140; removal of, 27; U.S. citizenship, 160. *See also* Four Mothers Nation

Childers, Ellis B., 231 (n. 47)

Children, 159; agricultural role, 17; allotments for, 14, 144, 192–93; Cherokee, 207 (ill.); inheritance, 139; of intermarriage, 21, 22; racial status, 94, 211

Choctaws: allotment's effects on, 3, 84, 102; black, 154; former slaves, 65; political and spiritual movements, 140; removal of, 27; U.S. citizenship, 160. *See also* Four Mothers Nation

Choska Bottoms region, 45, 47, 62

Christianity/Christians, 45, 47, 208

Churches, Creek, 45, 64, 139, 161. *See also* Newtown Creek Methodist Church grounds

Citizenship

—Creek, 13, 90, 225 (n. 45); for black settlers, 57, 64, 95, 160–61, 223 (n. 9), 229 (n. 30); Civil War's effects on, 35–38, 41–43; equal rights for, 68, 115–16, 229 (n. 27); for former slaves, 33, 42, 43, 55; land tenure and, 38, 39–40, 83–84, 95–96, 159; race and, 31–34, 36, 83–84, 102–4

—U.S.: for African Americans, 11, 40; for American Indians, 79, 118; Creek refusal of, 98–99; poststatehood, 160–61

Citizenship law of 1859 (Creek), 33–34

Civil War: Creek experience of, 35–38, 41; Creek Nation alliance with Confederacy, 35–37, 39, 41, 42, 43, 44. *See also* Northern Creeks; Southern Creeks

Clans, Creek: governance by, 19, 148; matrilineal nature, 21–22; membership in, 32, 139–40. *See also* Creeks: kinship loyalties

Clark, Carter Blue, 198

Clark, Clifford, 186

Class/classes: allotment's effects on, 89; Anglo-American expectations of, 124–25; Civil War allegiances and, 35; economic, 200–201; Ku Klux Klan views on, 197, 198, 199–202; land and, 10–11, 111, 162–63, 175; politics of, 67–68, 176, 177, 183–85, 201–4; race and, 173, 174, 184, 188, 202; race and land in relation to, 137, 176–77, 182; race and nation in relation to, 6, 7–11, 67, 68, 212, 247 (n. 2). *See also* Interracial

alliances: class-related; White people: middle-class; Working class; Working Class Union

Class conflict, 176, 177, 195, 200, 203; white supremacy and, 195

Class consciousness: Ku Klux Klan efforts to suppress, 201; and race in Canadian River valley, 187; republicanism and race in relation to, 247 (n. 2); and socialism, 184; in white agrarianism, 176; and Working Class Union, 187

Clothing, 45, 52–54

Coal mining: boom in, 184. *See also* Mining

Coker family, 233 (n. 91)

Colonialism, American: allotment as policy of, 75, 76, 78, 83; Creeks' struggles against, 41, 69; effects on slavery, 23; land laws influenced by, 115; as prerogative of whiteness, 81

"Colored Creeks": legal definition of, 161; use of term, 222 (nn. 3, 4). *See also* Creeks: black

Communal lands, Creek, 18–20, 210; defense of, 40, 67, 68, 84, 85–87, 97–101, 103–4, 115; dependence on, 54–55, 62; enclosure of, 57–61, 68, 82, 87; renting, 248 (n. 15); white opposition to, 78–79. *See also* Allotment(s); Town fields, Creek

Conservative Creeks. *See* Creeks: conservative

Conservative towns, 62, 65, 82

Constitutions: Creek Nation, 13, 56, 64, 225 (n. 45); Oklahoma, 160–61, 164–65, 167, 182, 245 (n. 39)

Cook, Zachariah, 63

Co-operative Negro Farmers Industrial State Fair, 166–67

Cotchoche, 65

Cotton: prices for, 147, 170, 182, 192, 193; raising of, 3, 18, 145

Council, J. R., 166

Councils of Defense, 190, 191

County governments, 134, 139–40, 141; taxation by, 36–37

Coweta, 63

Cox, Dorothy Kailey, 209, 210

Cox, Porter, 208–9, 211, 212

Cox, Rufus, 209, 210

Cox, Rufus "Buddy," 206–12

Cox, Stella Haynes, 208–9, 210, 211

Crazy Snake. *See* Harjo, Chitto

Credit, 134–37, 183. *See also* Bankers/banks; Mortgages

Creek Citizens' Realty Bank and Trust Company, 162

Creek Council House (Okmulgee), 104–5

Creek Nation, 6, 8, 9, 10–11; African American settlers in, 152, 156, 210, 212; after allotment, 239 (n. 89); allotment's effects on, 109–12, 141; composite nature of, 40, 62, 64, 69, 91, 96; as confederacy, 21, 55, 91, 222 (n. 4); defense of, 84, 85, 87, 97–101, 115, 140; factionalism in, 35–38, 40–44, 55, 56–57, 64–67, 91; formation of, 23–25, 34, 62–64, 217 (n. 4), 219 (n. 25); heterogeneity of, 22, 43–45, 47–48, 54–55, 67, 91, 210–12; landownership in, 4, 6, 91; map, 46; as polity, 7, 13, 40–41, 89, 140; population figures, 221 (n. 3); post–Civil War, 42, 44–45, 47–48; poststatehood, 137–41; racial constructions of, 34, 76, 82–83, 96, 104–5, 141; sovereignty, 7, 9, 24–25, 27, 36, 40, 42–43, 53, 62–63, 69, 82, 89, 97–99, 104, 140, 168; use of term, 13. *See also* National Council, Creek

Creeks, 2–4; Dawes Commission categorization of, 95, 110; draft resistance efforts, 188; economic and political autonomy, 7, 12, 53, 54–57, 112, 128, 145–48; intermarriage, 21–22, 43, 94; kinship loyalties, 21–22, 64, 92, 140, 144; literary traditions, 9; oral tradition, 62–64, 69, 87–88; political and spiritual movements, 141; poor, 35, 60;

population statistics, 230 (n. 39); post-statehood, 111–12, 137–41; racial constructions of, 10–11, 20, 22–23, 33, 104, 141–42; removal of, 17, 25–27, 29, 88, 102; resistance to Indian Affairs agents, 123, 128–29; U.S. citizenship for, 160. *See also* Allotment(s): Creek resistance to; Citizenship: Creek; Four Mothers Nation; Land: Creek system of; Landownership: Creek concept of; Slavery/slaves: Creek ownership of

—black, 45, 51–52 (ill.); allotment and, 84, 87–88, 91, 118–19; Back-to-Africa movement, 168; black settlers' relationship to, 161, 169, 173; Creek citizenship, 33–34, 39–40, 43, 95; Dawes Commission categorization of, 94; efforts to suppress or exclude from Creek Nation, 43, 62, 65, 103; electoral power in Creek Nation, 56–57; in Green Peach War, 66–67; in Indian Territory, 98, 154; landlessness, 173; land tenure rights of after Civil War, 39, 43, 57, 67; political action of, 67, 93, 139, 141; population statistics, 221 (n. 3); race and political action in allotment period, 101; ranching's effects on, 60; in Redstick War, 24–25; sale of allotment lands, 117–18, 120, 126, 130; small-scale farming by, 40, 49, 57; in Snake movement, 101, 141–42; solidarity with African Americans, 142–43, 149–52; taxation of allotment lands, 136; trading by, 52; use of term, 13, 222 (nn. 3, 4); white perceptions of as incapable, 113–14. *See also* Black towns; "Colored Creeks"

—conservative: allotment's effects on, 80; defense of Creek Nation, 96; landownership ideas, 75; ranching's effects on, 60; use of term, 13, 222 (n. 4); views on race and citizenship, 229 (n. 30). *See also* Black Creek–Conservative Creek alliance; Isparhecher; Northern Creeks

Emarthla, Hotulke, 26, 85, 205

Emigrationism, 150, 154, 165, 167–73, 246 (n. 67)

English, Bessie Brown, 137

Enrollment of Creeks by Dawes Commission, 90, 93–96, 212, 233 (n. 81); Creek resistance to, 96–101

Equality: conceptions of, 6, 78; individual equality in liberalism, 115, 120

Erosion, 3, 133, 135, 147

Este-vpuekv (slave): use of term, 30. *See also* Slavery/slaves

Ethnicity, 67, 210–12

Ethridge, Robbie, 24

Eufaula, 48

Eugenics, 200

Exclusion: ideas about, 6, 33, 43, 62, 64–65, 103

Exodusters (African American settlers in Kansas), 154

Farmers/farming: African American, 90, 135, 154, 165–67; Creek, 3, 7, 27–31, 48, 57, 208; in eastern Oklahoma, 4; labor unionism and, 183–84, 185; leasing, 243 (n. 14); 1920s depression, 3; non-white, 194; opposition to Ku Klux Klan, 198, 201–2; white, 90, 192, 204. *See also* Agriculture; Sharecroppers; Small-scale farmers/farming; Tenant farmers; Yeoman farmers

Farmers Union, 178, 182, 201

Farm-Labor Union, 201

Federal government, 9, 13, 27, 114, 120; Creek land cessions to, 19, 25–27; taxation by, 135–36

Fisher, Samuel, 58

Fisher, William, 58

Five Tribes ("Five Civilized Tribes"), 3, 35, 84, 88, 92. *See also* Cherokees; Chickasaws; Choctaws; Creeks; Seminoles

Five Tribes Act of 1906, 118

Florida: white settlement in, 21

Foley, Neil, 200, 214 (n. 5)

Four Mothers Nation, 140, 142, 143, 240 (n. 94); on race, 102–3

Franklin, L. W., 253 (n. 87)

Frederickson, George: *The Black Image in the White Mind*, 7–8

Freedmen, 210; allotments for, 235 (n. 30); black settlers' relationship with, 158–59, 161–63, 170, 171; citizenship for, 33–34; Dawes Commission categorization of, 94, 95, 118, 120, 232 (n. 74); examples of, 173–74; population statistics, 221 (n. 3); sale of allotments, 121, 123, 132, 155–56, 161–63; in Snake movement, 101; taxation of, 135; use of term, 82, 222 (n. 4); white perceptions of, 113, 222 (n. 3). *See also* Creeks: black

Freedom, ideas about: in Snake movement, 97–98; tied to landownership for African Americans, 7; tied to slavery for white Americans, 7; whiteness as mark of, 22–23

"Full-blood" Creeks. *See* Creeks: "full-blood"

Gardens: Creek women's, 20, 21, 28–29, 31, 145. *See also* Women: agricultural role of Creek

Garvey, Marcus, 150, 165, 172

Gender: allotment as means of enforcing Anglo-American norms, 75, 125; Anglo-American norms, 124–25, 127; Boomer's white agrarianism and, 77–79; among late nineteenth-century Creeks, 48; liberalism and, 78; ties to race, nationalism, and private landownership, 81, 177–78; white supremacy and, 195. *See also* Manhood; Women

General Allotment Act of 1887. *See* Dawes General Allotment Act of 1887

Gentry, W. E., 208

Georgia: Creek land cessions of, 25; white settlement in, 21

Goddard, Henry, 200

statistics, 152; protections for, 119; racial constructions, 6–9; taxation of, 135; as tenant farmers, 122 (ill.), 130, 187; tribalism, 8–9; use of term, 13, 82; white perceptions of, 113, 114, 125, 126–29. *See also* Cherokees; Chickasaws; Choctaws; Creeks; Seminoles

Indian Territory, 3–4, 26–31; African American migration to, 152–59; allotments in, 79–81; Civil War in, 35–38, 41; Creek removal to, 20; map, 4, 27; migration to, 2, 7, 21, 56–60, 64, 76–78, 81–82, 90, 92, 95; population statistics, 29, 76, 152–54, 237 (n. 56); white agrarianism in, 178. *See also* Oklahoma

Industrial Workers of the World (IWW), 183, 184, 185, 189, 190

Inequality: ideas about, 6, 78, 116; of races in law and making of land market, 120

Ingalls, Laura, 73, 74

Interest rates, 135, 183

Intermarriage: between black settlers and black Creeks, 159, 174; Civil War allegiances based on, 35; between Indians and whites, 21–22, 43, 77–78, 90, 161; between Indians of different tribal nations, 94

Inter-National Afro-American League, 92

Interpreters, Creek, 21, 35, 42, 223 (n. 10)

Interracial alliances, 103, 142–43; Civil War, 37; class-related, 176, 180–88, 189, 201, 203; Green Peach War, 67; Ku Klux Klan opposition to, 200–201; repression of, 189–92. *See also* Black Creek–Conservative Creek alliance

Intertribal activities, 92, 99, 102, 139, 140–41, 148, 240 (n. 94)

Irwin, Lee, 240 (n. 94)

Isenhour v. United States, 249 (n. 31)

Island, Harry, 42, 222 (n. 7), 223 (n. 10)

Isparhecher: allotment and, 80, 85, 87; Civil War and, 63, 64, 66, 68; in Green Peach War, 66–67; Snake movement

and, 98, 99; statements on race and black Creeks, 82–83, 96, 101, 229 (n. 30), 231 (n. 47); statements on racial equality, 44, 103–4, 229 (nn. 27, 30)

Jackson, Andrew, 24, 25, 180

Jackson, Effie S., 225 (n. 55)

Jacobs, Harry, 142

Jefferson, Thomas, 180

Jeffersonianism, 77, 116, 133. *See also* Agrarianism; Yeoman farmers

Jewett, N. Clay, 175, 197

Jim Crow laws, 170, 187, 210; blacks' efforts to defeat, 150–52, 160, 161. *See also* Segregation

Johnson, J. Coody, 113–14, 139, 160, 166, 167, 171

Johnson, Sallie, 205

Jones, H. C., 253 (n. 87)

Jumper, John, 35

Kansas: African American migration to, 154

Kasihta, 63

Katy rail line. *See* Missouri, Kansas and Texas rail line

Kauanui, J. Kēhaulani, 115

Keith, Jeannette, 186

Kelley, Agnes, 205, 206

Kidd, Meredith, 85

Knights of Liberty, 189–90

Knupp, Gardner, 201–2

Krauthamer, Barbara, 65

Ku Klux Klan, 175, 176, 192, 212, 253 (n. 86); class views, 197, 198, 199–202; moral vision of, 196–201; 1920s, 196–97, 202, 252 (n. 71); opposition to, 201–3; Reconstruction-era, 202; version of whiteness, 194–204; violence by, 195–201; white religious and ethnic minorities denounced by, 253 (n. 94); women of, 252 (n. 74)

Labor: Creek laws regarding, 77; ideologies of, 184; owning product of, 31–34,

39–40; racializing, 22–23, 174. *See also* Property; Working class

Lamb, J. R., 191, 192

Land: citizenship related to, 95, 159; class and, 10–11, 111, 162–63, 175; conflicts over, 40, 158–59, 175; Creek system of, 6–7, 22–23, 54–55, 62, 87, 91; economic power of, 1–2; market in, 110, 114–16, 120, 125–26, 134, 147, 236 (n. 35); nationhood and, 38, 87, 89; politics of, 53, 59–60, 102, 149–50, 182, 185; prices for, 193, 198; and race and class, 137, 176–77, 182; and race and nation, 1–3, 6–7, 75, 81, 83–84, 91, 105, 150, 206; racializing, 1–2, 115, 133, 159, 174; tax-forfeit, 137, 235 (n. 22); transfers of, 20, 121, 161–63, 235 (n. 22). *See also* Communal lands, Creek

Land cessions, Creek, 19, 25–27

Landlessness, 109–10, 123, 129–32; black, 120–21, 173; Creek, 210; racializing, 214 (n. 5); white, 177, 180, 189, 192. *See also* Sharecroppers; Tenant farmers

Landlords, 110, 111, 203; conflicts with tenant farmers, 176; Creek, 68, 129–30, 145; income for, 147; lending practices, 135, 183; political involvement, 180; tax evasion, 136. *See also* Tenant farmers

Landownership, 2–3, 134–37, 175; African American, 10–11, 130, 132, 149–52, 154–59, 161–63, 165–67; concentrations of, 79–81, 133, 135, 137; Creek concept of, 6–7, 18–20, 31, 73–74, 75, 144; goals of, 248 (n. 15); Indian, 132–34; in Indian Territory, 27–31; non-white, 194; political power of, 149–52, 167, 171–72, 178, 181, 212; private, 78–79; and race and class, 137, 176–77, 182; and race and nation, 150, 206; racially transformative power of idea of, 112; slavery's influence on, 38; voting rights and, 163–65; white American concept of, 20, 31, 74, 77–78, 134, 177,

203. *See also* Communal lands, Creek; Titles, land

Land policy: as racializing policy, 110–11, 112–21, 123, 134

Land tenure systems

—American fee-simple, 20, 91–92, 177; landlords and tenants under, 109–10, 129; as tool to transform allottees, 125; whites entitled to impose on others, 75

—Creek, 91; bustles as symbol of, 52–54; citizenship related to, 39–40, 43; community and, 62, 79–80; controversies over, 59–61; defense of, 82, 85–87, 93, 97–101, 115; as defining factor in Creek identity, 87; ownership of improvements in, 31, 43; prestatehood, 110; race and, 54–57; sale of improvements in, 73; slavery and, 32; white criticisms of, 74, 77–78

Langston (black town), 158, 159

Languages, Creek Nation, 45, 47

Laws

—Creek: citizenship, 33–34; labor-related, 77; land-related, 43, 73–74, 110; race and property linked in, 32; ranching, 68

—U.S.: allotment, 110–17, 134, 137; regarding Indians, 27; land-related, 31, 112–21, 123, 147–48, 231 (n. 47); racializing, 117–19, 136–37, 174. *See also* Supreme Court rulings

Lee, R. C., 171

Lerblance, Elijah Hermigine, 208, 255 (n. 6)

Leupp, Francis, 115

Lewis, Earl, 254 (n. 108)

Lewis, Jackson, 64

Lewis, John and Kendle, 29

Liberalism (classical), 78, 112, 120, 221 (n. 56)

Lighthorsemen, 64–65, 66, 144

Literacy requirements for voting. *See* African Americans: voting rights and disenfranchisement of

Little River area, 187–88

Livestock raising, 49, 52, 53, 54. *See also* Ranches/ranching

Łiwahali, 63

Long family allotments, 144, 145 (ill.)

Lower Creek towns: Confederacy supported by, 37, 39; councils in, 34; map, 19; in Redstick War, 24–25; relocation to Indian Territory, 26; slavery in, 23, 29

Loyal Creeks. *See* Northern Creeks

Loyal Party, 66, 67

Luker, William, 77

Lynchings, 170, 191

MacLean, Nancy, 195

Manhood: landownership in African American politics and, 156–58; white agrarianism and, 74, 77–78, 81–82, 177, 178; whiteness and, 81. *See also* Men: agricultural role of Creek

Marriage patterns, Creek, 139–40. *See also* Intermarriage

Marshall, Ben, 29, 37

Marshall, John, 27

Marshall, Lafayette, 29

Marxism: land as means of production in, 181. *See also* Socialism/Socialist Party

Matrilineal society, Creek, 94, 218 (n. 9); agriculture in, 20, 28; citizenship through, 33; clan membership in, 21–22, 139

Matthews, Leonard, 200

May, Katja, 229 (n. 30)

McGillivray, Alexander, 22

McIntosh, Daniel N., 42, 43

McIntosh, Jackson and Hagar, 39

McIntosh, John, 222 (n. 7)

McIntosh, Nellie, 39, 40

McIntosh, Roley, 29, 39, 58

McIntosh, Scott, 66

McIntosh, Siegel, 34

McIntosh, Thomas, 127

McIntosh, Una, 58

McIntosh, William: execution of, 88

McIntosh faction, 26. *See also* Lower Creek towns; Southern Creeks

McKennon, Archibald, 79, 85

Medicine and ritual practices, Creek, 26, 45, 47, 63, 139–40, 240 (n. 90)

Men: agricultural role of Creek, 17, 29, 217 (n. 2)

Meyer, Melissa, 128

Micco, Lahtah, 97–98

Miccos (town leaders), 23, 25–26, 30; use of term, 98

Middleton, D. H., 59

Midwifery, 47

Miles, Tiya, 65

Militias, 24, 190

Miller, W. T., 77

Mineral rights, 184; leasing, 146, 147, 148

Mining, 176, 183, 184, 188

Missouri, Kansas and Texas ("Katy") rail line, 57, 58, 60, 90

"Mixed-blood" Creeks. *See* Creeks: "mixed-blood"

Modernity: Indian form of, 53

Moore, E. R., 167

Morey, Caledonia Perryman, 47, 224 (n. 25)

Morgan, Edmund: *American Slavery, American Freedom*, 7

Mortgages, 124, 127, 133–36, 146, 155, 161–63, 193

Mott, M. L., 113, 114

Munson, H. H. "Rube," 184

Murff, Joe, 170

Music, Creek, 47

Muskogee (town), 90, 121, 152

Muskogee Comet (African American newspaper), 162

Muskogee Confederacy, 21, 55; towns of, 67. *See also* Creek Nation; Creek towns

Nation/nationhood: citizenship and, 103; Creek ideas of, 6, 9, 10–11, 34, 40–41, 62–65, 67–69, 141; definition of, 8; land and, 38, 87, 89; race and, 10–11, 13, 92–93, 103, 176; race and class in,

6, 7–11, 67, 68, 212, 247 (n. 2); race
and land in, 1–3, 6–7, 75, 81, 83–84, 91,
105, 150, 206
National Association for the Advancement of Colored People (NAACP), 164
National Council, Creek, 217 (n. 4); allotment's effects on, 86, 88, 90, 136–37,
148, 239 (n. 89); black members of,
93; Confederacy supported by, 36–37;
formation of, 23–24, 26, 32, 34, 55–56;
land governance, 43, 61; poststatehood
status of, 89, 137–39. *See also* Creek
Nation
Nationalism: African American, 10–11,
171; American, 6–9, 75, 77, 190;
Indian, 9; influence on Civil War
allegiances, 36; racial, 40–41, 44, 57,
62, 64, 78, 101, 168, 173, 180, 247
(n. 2); white, 189–92
National Party, 82
National state: Creek building of, 18–20,
23–25; definition of, 8
Native Americans. *See* Indians
Naylor, Celia, 45
"Negro": Dawes Commission categoriza-
tion, 94; Oklahoma constitutional defi-
nition, 161; use of term, 126, 174, 211.
See also African Americans; Creeks:
black; States Negroes
Negro Business League, 167
Negro Protective Association, 164, 167
Negro Suffrage League, 164, 167
Nelson, Levi, 166
Newspapers, African American, 155 (ill.),
162
Newtown Creek Methodist Church
grounds, 206, 208, 209, 210
Ninnywageechee, 23
Noble, Annie, 58
Nokosi, Judge, 63
Nonblack Creeks. *See* Creeks: nonblack
North Canadian River valley, 62
Northern Creeks, 41, 55, 56, 57
North Fork Colored Town, 55, 65
Northwest Ordinance of 1787, 26–27

Ochese Nation: British treaty with Creeks
as, 219 (n. 25)
Odom, Sarah Aklin, 35, 52, 53
Office of Indian Affairs, 123–24, 129, 137,
138, 146. *See also* Indian Affairs agents
Oil lands: discovery of, 183–84, 192,
197–98; income from, 209; leasing,
146–47, 148
Oil production, 176, 193
Oil workers, 176, 184, 189; Ku Klux Klan
violence against, 198–99
Okchiye, 26, 85, 205
Okfuskee, 49
Okfuskee Negro County Fair, 166–67
Oklahoma: Black Belt, 152–54; history
of, 1–4; landownership in, 4, 6; land
tenure system, 109–11, 129; popu-
lation statistics, 153 (ill.), 214 (n. 3),
252 (n. 73); postallotment, 203–4;
segregation in, 132, 160–61, 170, 173;
territorial map, 4. *See also* East-central
Oklahoma; Indian Territory; Statehood,
Oklahoma
Oklahoma Land Run of 1889, 2, 3, 78,
154
Okmulgee, 104–5, 208
Old Tallassee plantation, 22
One-drop rule, 94–95, 119–20
Opothleyahola, 29, 37, 140, 205–6
Oral tradition, Creek, 62–64, 69, 87–88

Pan-Africanism, 9–10, 169, 172
Pan-Indianism, 9, 240 (n. 94)
Parkinson, Jim, 88
Pastures on Creek lands, 40, 57–61, 68,
82, 87
Patriarchs of America, 246 (n. 67)
Patriotism, racialized, 190–91
Patterson, Orlando, 30
Peck, Carrie, 143
People's (Populist) Party, 178
Perryman, Cornelius, 113, 114
Perryman, Ellen, 143
Perryman, George, 58, 59
Perryman, Joseph, 67

Racial uplift theory, 154–56, 158, 163, 165–67, 171, 173

Radicalism, 177, 184, 204; repression of, 189–92

Railroad-building: interference with, 103. *See also* Missouri, Kansas and Texas rail line

Ranches/ranching: Creek, 44, 57–61, 68, 85, 208; by settlers, 90

Redstick War (1813), 19, 24–25, 34, 37–38

Reformers, white, 81–82, 112, 113, 114

Religion. *See* Christianity/Christians; Four Mothers Nation; Green Corn *poskita*; Medicine and ritual practices, Creek

Removal Act of 1830, 25–26

Rentie, I. A., 92

Rentie, Morris, 66, 91

Republicanism, 77, 247 (n. 2)

Republican Party, 164, 178

Rich people–poor people conflicts, 176, 195, 200, 203. *See also* Wealth

Roasting Ear Rebellion. *See* Green Corn Rebellion

Robbins, Lester, 240 (n. 90)

Robertson, Alice, 113, 114

Roediger, David R., 202, 247 (nn. 2, 3)

Roosevelt, Theodore, 160, 191

Rowland, Dick, 195

Sam, Chief Alfred Charles, 167, 169–70, 171, 246 (n. 67)

Samuels, C. G., 170

Sands. *See* Harjo, Oktarharsars

Sands faction, 65, 223 (n. 14). *See also* Northern Creeks

Sango, A. G. W., 160, 244 (n. 25)

Saunt, Claudio, 43, 60, 217 (n. 4), 220 (n. 42)

Segregation: Booker T. Washington on, 156; in Creek Nation, 55, 64–65, 186; in Oklahoma, 132, 160–61, 170, 173, 191–92. *See also* Jim Crow laws

Self-determination, African American, 10, 150, 154, 156, 173; landownership and, 165–67, 172

Sellars, Nigel Anthony, 184

Seminoles, 3, 98; African Americans among, 154; Creek border with, 27; draft resistance efforts, 188; intermarriage with Creeks, 94; in Redstick War, 24; removal of, 27; Union supported by, 35, 37; U.S. citizenship, 160

Seminole Nation, 123, 152

Senate hearings (Tulsa, 1906), 102, 112–16, 118, 133, 231 (n. 47)

Settlement/settlers. *See* African Americans; Boomers; Indian Territory: migration to; White settlers

Severs, Frederick: dry goods store, 52; ranch, 59

Sharecroppers, 3, 40, 130, 174

Shoemaker, Nancy, 8

Simmons, Jake, 88, 91

Slavery/slaves: of African Americans, 7, 10, 21; Anglo-American concepts of, 21, 23, 32, 202; blackness as mark of, 22–23; chattel, 18, 22–25, 30, 31–34; conflicts over, 24–25; Creek ownership of, 18–20, 21, 27–34, 91, 210, 218 (n. 9), 222 (n. 4); emancipated, 33, 35, 37, 39–40, 42–43, 45, 55, 143, 222 (n. 3); nonchattel captive, 218 (n. 9); property ownership by restricted, 34, 38; statistics on, 29, 220 (n. 42). *See also* Black towns; Freedmen

Sleeper, D. S., 116

Small-scale farmers/farming, 40, 48–55; allotment's effects on, 86, 145; cotton prices, 192; political involvement, 44, 82, 180–81; ranching's effects on, 57–58, 60–61, 68–69; relationship to land, 62; taxation of, 136

Smith, C. R., 133

Smith, Charles, 199

Smith, Cora, 41

Smith, Isaac and Hannah, 49

Smith, Louisa B., 127

Snake movement, 97–101, 111–12, 128, 140, 186, 188, 241 (n. 99), 250 (n. 48); and people of African descent, 101,

American Order of the White Brotherhood of the World

White people: class conflicts among, 189, 194–95, 203, 212; crimes against, 253 (n. 97); disenfranchisement of, 182; draft resistance efforts, 186–88; Ku Klux Klan violence against, 198–201; landownership by, 150; meaning of race and nation to, 6; middle-class, 176, 196, 198, 200–201, 203

White settlers, 90; allotment's effects on, 76–78, 81–82, 117–18, 121, 132; citizenship for, 160–61; intermarriage with Creek citizens, 21–22, 43, 77–78, 90, 161; landlessness, 109, 129, 134; landownership, 2–3, 7, 154; population statistics, 152; ranching by, 58–59; as tenant farmers, 130, 132–34

White supremacy, 151, 254 (n. 109); agrarianism and, 180, 201; interwar period, 191–92; land-related, 119, 181, 192; maintenance of, 164, 175; threats to, 191, 203; violence associated with, 195–97. *See also* Ku Klux Klan

Wickham, John A., 240 (n. 94)

Wilkins, David, 9

Williams, John Sharp, 248 (n. 9)

Williams, Robert Lee, 116, 129, 130, 160, 164, 182

Wise, Donald A., 225 (n. 55)

Womack, Craig, 9, 55, 63, 64

Women: African American, 157, 158, 215 (n. 6); agricultural role of Creek, 17, 20, 28–29, 31, 48, 49, 145

Women of Ku Klux Klan, 252 (n. 74)

Working class: antebellum white, 202; effects of literacy tests on white, 182; interracial action by, 176, 183–85, 188; Ku Klux Klan violence against white, 198–201; labor unionism and, 187; political involvement, 190; racial perspectives of black and white, 254 (n. 108); white, 201–2, 204, 247 (nn. 2, 3)

Working Class Union (WCU), 182–87, 189, 190, 201, 203

World War I, 185; repression during, 189–92; resistance to, 185–87

Wright, J. Leitch, 67

Wvcenv: use of term, 159, 174

Yahola, Napoleon, 63

Yargee, John, 91

Yeoman farmers: black aspirations toward, 152–58; defense of, 180; failure of, 130, 145, 146, 148, 178, 189, 203; racial connotations of, 165; turning allottees into, 125, 134, 143; white ideal of, 112, 116, 119, 129, 134, 150, 177, 192

Young Men's Democratic Club, 164

CPSIA information can be obtained
at www.ICGtesting.com
Printed in the USA
LVOW12s0852150817
545081LV00004B/216/P